THE WOMEN'S GREAT LAKES READER

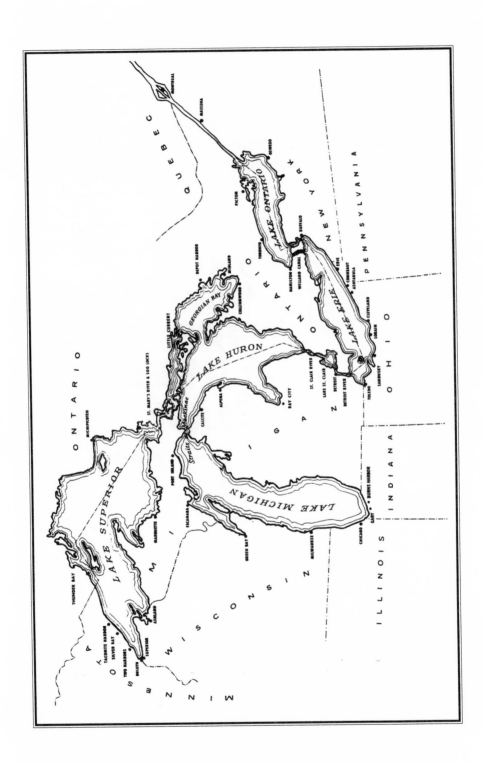

THE WOMEN'S GREAT LAKES READER

Edited by
Victoria Brehm

HOLY COW! PRESS · DULUTH MINNESOTA · 1998

Copyright ©1998 by Holy Cow! Press
Introduction and chapter notes ©1998 by Victoria Brehm. Cover Painting, *Land and Lake: North Shore*, oil on linen, by Ann Jenkins

Library of Congress Cataloging-in-Publication Data
The women's Great Lakes reader / edited by Victoria Brehm.
404 p.   cm.   ill.
Includes bibliographical references.
ISBN 0-930100-79-4 (paper edition)
1. Women pioneers—Great Lakes Region—Biography. 2. Women pioneers—Great Lakes Region—Social life and customs. 3. Indian women—Great Lakes Region—Biography. 4. Indian women—Great Lakes Region—Social life and customs. 5. Frontier and pioneer life—Great Lakes Region. 6. Great Lakes Region—Biography. I. Brehm, Victoria, 1947-.
F551.W66 1998   97-42415
977' . 03—dc21   CIP

This project is supported, in part, by grants from The St. Paul Companies, the Beverly J. and John A. Rollwagen Fund of the Minneapolis Foundation, Elmer L. Anderson, and the Arrowhead Regional Arts Council through an appropriation from the Minnesota State Legislature, and by generous individuals.

Holy Cow! Press books are distributed to the trade by Consortium Book Sales and Distribution, 1045 Westgate Drive, Saint Paul, Minnesota 55114. Our books are also available through all major library distributors and jobbers, and through most small press distributors, including Bookpeople and Small Press Distribution. For personal orders or other information, please write to:

HOLY COW! PRESS
Post Office Box 3170
Mount Royal Station
Duluth, Minnesota 55803

To my mother
Helen Campbell Brehm

Contents

Women Travellers on the Lakes

Women's Work

Women's Lives, Women's Lakes

FROM "PALMISTRY FOR BLIND MARINERS"
(1981)
Judith Minty

The North Woods
>Summer passes too quickly.
>Winter brings pain. The past
>dries like strawflowers.
>We must change camp before withering
>begins. In this Indian summer
>the sun lowers its flame
>over the lake, ignites
>on the flint stone of the Chippewa fathers.
>
>Our canoe is ready, stripped bark
>from birch trees. We will travel light,
>eat berries and roots
>along the way, leave footprints in sand.
>Deer will drink from our hands
>and the hoot of owls will guide us.
>But I warn you, there will be
>wailing and a beating of breasts.
>
>Dip your paddle as you pass the bear,
>asleep at the foot of her dune,
>who mourns cubs, lost
>in the crossing from Wisconsin.
>Forget love rites and matings
>and children. Bury them
>deep under Mercury's mound.
>This lake and mothers are cruel.
>
>Hold close to the calm
>of fingers, pass gulls who curse
>from their rookery.
>Let fog cling like webs
>to your face, your hair. Glide
>into whispers of vapor.
>Grope for land if you wish. Go ashore
>if you are tired of seafaring.

For my part, I know this hand
and cannot turn in again.
If you must, follow me. I am going
past the islands out
into the lake. There is a place
I have heard of where you can sink
deep into the center of dreams, where waves
will rock you in sleep, where everything
is as you wished it to be.

JUDITH MINTY (1937-) is the author of nine books of poetry, including *Lake Songs and Other Fears* (1974), which won the United States Award from the International Poetry Forum. She has also been honored with the Atherton Award from Breadloaf, fellowships to Yaddo, and awards from PEN. *"Palmistry For Blind Mariners"* is from her book *In the Presence of Mothers*.

The Women's Great Lakes Reader

INTRODUCTION

Courtesy Michigan City Lighthouse Museum

HARRIET COLFAX was thirty-seven when she became keeper of the Michigan City, Indiana, lighthouse in 1861, and she would have long been considered an old maid, dependant on relatives to supplement whatever meager wages she could earn giving music lessons to the daughters of her neighbors or working at her brother's newspaper as a compositor setting type. But Colfax happened to live outside Chicago when the Great Lakes were still a frontier—what had been the Old Northwest Territories—and there were more opportunities for unmarried women there than in New York State where she had been born. Because Chicago was the center of a boom economy fueled by lakes' shipping, railroads, the development of the prairies, and northern mining, labor was scarce. Seizing her chance to be independent and, rare for the time, earn the same salary as a man, Colfax applied for the position of lightkeeper. This tiny, delicate music teacher with curling hair and firm features immediately faced vocal opposition to her appointment because a number of men believed her petite stature would make her unfit for the physical rigors she would face. Fortunately, her cousin was Schuyler Colfax, a Congressman who would become Vice President for Ulysses S. Grant, and because civil service exams were far in the future, she was given the position to tend the light at Indiana's only port on the Great Lakes.

Like many during the nineteenth century, she had come west with her family in 1851 to try for a better life. Chicago was one of the fastest-growing cities in the US, and many who wanted to succeed left friends and family to try to make their fortunes. Her brother, Richard Colfax, had founded a newspaper, the *Michigan City Transcript,* but sold it because of failing health. When he moved to a better climate, Harriet, described as "unlucky in love" (whatever the truth may have been), decided to stay in what was then called "the West." While the opportunity to become a lightkeeper may have begun as a lark, she quickly realized the position would free her from genteel poverty and the condescending charity of relatives. The men who opposed her appointment, like the government officials who later tried to have her dismissed along with other women keepers on the lakes, should have noted her firm features, rather than her delicate stature.

What did she think that first day when she dropped her valise on the floor of the lighthouse which was built on an isolated stretch of beach a few miles from the nearest town? Did she feel free? Or was she scared she would fail? Her light stood where the river cut through the dunes, its channel marked by twin piers that reached into Lake Michigan. Until her friend, Ann Hartwell, came to live with her, she would be alone. Even after she formed this relationship that would last the rest of her life, Colfax would still be alone every night of the next four decades while she tended the light. She would see sunsets and moon rises and rainbows and eclipses and Northern Lights and Lake Michigan in its fury tearing apart the breakwaters that protected the harbor entrance. In the early years she heated pails of lard oil on the wood-fired range in the kitchen of the lighthouse and carried them down the breakwater to light the east pierhead light which was also in her care. Sometimes the waves smashing against the stones broke over her head and nearly carried her into the lake. If the weather was too cold and her trip too long, the lard oil congealed before she got to the lamp and she had to make the dangerous journey again, reheating the oil, traversing the pier back and forth. In later years, when the pierhead light was moved inexplicably to the west pier, she had to row a scow across the river to reach the pier, then walk down it to light the beacon—in a skirt that swept the ground and several petticoats and a coat to keep her warm. Although after numerous petitions she eventually received an elevated walkway to keep her from the fury of the waves, storms tore the walkway to matchsticks nearly every year and she was left, once again, to pick her way across the ice between the waves to do her job.

That she did that job for forty-three years without one black mark against her record seems amazing, but it is no less so than the changes she observed from her tower during the years she religiously polished lenses and lit lamps and recorded the weather and the notable marine happenings in her log. From her sometimes storm-battered vantage point she saw the maritime world of the Great Lakes evolve from an easy-going, exciting frontier of high-masted, fast-running schooners bound down for Buffalo with their white wings spread wide to catch the wind to an industrialized, technologically-advanced merchant marine of steamships that could carry six schooners on their decks and still have room for cargo. The gregarious, independent masters of wooden ships gave way to uniformed, professional captains sailing iron and steel ships on a rigorous schedule for a corporation, and the Lighthouse Service she had promised to uphold and obey was changed by civil service exams and uniforms (with pants that she refused wear) and little tolerance for women. But Harriet Colfax endured, sometimes against nearly insurmountable odds, to persevere until she finally retired in 1904. She was eighty. Ann Hartwell had died shortly before and, troubled with heart problems, Harriet Colfax died on April 16, 1905. All Michigan City mourned.

She left behind a collection of lighthouse logs that are among the most interesting of any in the United States since, especially in the early years, she used them as a diary as well as a log. In so doing, she left a record of what it meant to be a woman lightkeeper on the frontier as it became the industrialized heartland of the United States. What she recorded as well were the changes that affected women as the Great Lakes become civilized and industrialized, and women's roles, correspondingly, became restricted.

On the frontier gender roles were fluid. Without enough hands to do the work, women were often allowed—and needed—to do jobs that otherwise would have been the provenance of men. When Colfax took command of her light, men held more difficult jobs than tending a lighthouse: they had to break the prairie to make farms, work in the new industries and businesses in Chicago, Detroit, Cleveland, and Toronto, and fight the American Civil War. A lighthouse keeper didn't earn a large salary—Colfax received $350 her first year—and men could earn more elsewhere. As the century progressed, however, economics changed and women keepers came under increasing pressure to resign and give their lights to men. During the 1870s one of the worst depressions in the history of the United States occurred, and men desperate for secure work saw a lightkeeper's job as a plum position. That Colfax managed to keep her light despite the maneuverings to oust her is testament to her intelligence and political acumen, but the emotional cost is recorded in her logs, portions of which are reprinted in the section "Women's Work." Many of her fellow women keepers were less protected and lost their lights. Eventually the U. S. Treasury Department, which administered lighthouses, appears to have resigned itself to the fact of Harriet E. Colfax as a treasured public institution who would retire when she chose.

In some ways, Colfax's life epitomizes the situation of women in the world of the Great Lakes in the nineteenth century where the opening of the frontier had allowed them access to respected positions that paid well. A number of women fur traders, notably Madame LaFramboise on Mackinac Island, made fortunes by virtue of their experience, mixed blood connections, and business skills. Women cooks on lakes' ships were sometimes in great demand and could command high salaries. (At other periods, as the newspaper clippings in "The Fickle Fortunes of Female Cooks" demonstrate, they were vilified by the wives and sweethearts left on shore and could not be hired.) Because the geography of the Great Lakes and their connecting rivers had fostered the early development of maritime transportation, women writers from the cosmopolitan East and Europe could explore remote wilderness outposts without insurmountable difficulties and then return home to write travel narratives, one of the most saleable genres of the time. Additionally, after the US Civil War a vogue developed for what is called "local color" fiction, stories about curious characters in remote places, particularly west of the Alleghenies. Several women who later developed lucrative careers as novelists, such as Constance Fenimore Woolson, got their start publishing short stories set on the lakes in intellectual Eastern magazines like *Harper's*. Without the conjunction of mass literacy to support magazine publishing, Eastern readers' desire for imaginative escapes from the urban problems caused by unrestrained immigration and the Industrial Revolution, and the accessibility of the Great Lakes frontier, these women writers would have found their opportunities for publication often limited to religious topics and sentimental domestic fiction that revolved around romantic plots. For women who had to work, as many did at some point in their lives, the frontier could be an auspicious place.

For a minority, however, the Great Lakes meant pain and unhappiness. The image of the frustrated settler's wife living miserably in her barren log cabin has come down to us from women's journals, letters, and fiction. Women travellers noted the unhappily-transplanted wives they encountered, women who had been torn from all they knew and loved to follow their husbands west. Because much of the lakes' region was settled before land grant acts, pioneers purchased their land from developers or were given it as a reward for military service. Many came from comfortable situations. Unless they were formerly farmers, their wives had been trained to be genteel ladies fulfilling their domestic and social responsibilities in small towns. For these women, moving to a frontier meant a rude change of expectations and often an overwhelming amount of hard physical labor with little help. While women who were European immigrants or had come from poorer, lower class families in the East welcomed the opportunity to begin new lives with great economic opportunity, no matter how demanding, others who had grown up with expectations of middle-class comfort were miserable. There are few unhappy frontier wives in this collection, however, and that is because even after a decade of collecting women's writings about their experiences on the Great Lakes, I have not found many letters, diaries, journals, or fiction that focus on the negative. Women's writings about the overland journey to far western frontiers may be different, but on the lakes women more often appeared to be mistresses of their fates and have continued to be so. But the pain of those who were not happy, however keenly felt, pales beside the genocide experienced by the North American Indian women they replaced.

Native peoples had lived near the lakes for ten thousand years until Europeans came in the seventeenth century seeking the Northwest Passage to the Orient and found furs. The fur trade originally proved beneficial for both cultures, but the coming of missionaries who privileged patriarchal control rather than the traditionally egalitarian relationships between the sexes, and later the decline of fur bearers, significantly undermined Native women's positions in their societies. Eventually their life-ways, religions, and cultures were nearly destroyed, and epidemics decimated the population. Some became "daughters of the country," married by white fur traders for their profitable family and tribal connections. Too often, when these traders moved on or became successful, Native wives and their mixed-blood children were abandoned. Yet these interracial families also made the Great Lakes a unique middle ground, a fluid, accepting frontier society that sometimes developed into a wealthy, proud, multi-ethnic culture at places like Mackinac Island.

But the end of the fur trade and the increasingly rapid pace of white settlement that required Natives to relinquish their ancestral lands and livelihoods led, by the end of the nineteenth century, to the disparagement of Native cultures, particularly by missionaries. Their well-meaning but condescending efforts to acculturate Natives in white values and require them to speak English are a subtext in several of the narratives reprinted here. Schooled to see Natives, who had experienced more than a century of economic and cultural crisis, as a degraded race without potential except as laborers, farmers, and craftsmen, observations by writers such as Soaphy Anderson and Emma Baylis are made across the gulf of ethnic and philosophical distance that had developed between the races and would not be bridged until the 1960s.

Perhaps the most difficult development for women of all races on the lakes was the coming of industrialization and the social changes that accompanied it. The opportunities that allowed Anna Jameson to explore the frontier, that made it possible for Harriet Colfax to become a lightkeeper, diminished after the 1860s when the Great Lakes became a center of industrial capitalism and technological innovation without par on the continent. As families came to depend on work outside the home for sustenance, women often became confined to the domestic sphere and their social contributions were restricted to religious and charity work. The professionalized merchant marine of the late nineteenth and early twentieth century became closed to them except for very low-paying jobs as porters and maids on passenger ships. Positions as lightkeepers or assistant keepers for their husbands were likewise denied them. Educated women could still teach school and write; those less lucky worked as clerks or maids or labored in factories in cities for poverty wages. As the frontier era passed, cultural restrictions of class and gender familiar from more settled regions were reimposed and the distinction between "ladies" who did not work outside the home and "women" who did became more pronounced. It is during this time, in the late nineteenth-century on the lakes, that women became responsible for the success or failure of their husbands and children. Because they were prohibited from doing meaningful work outside the home, their task was limited to elevating culture and society by doing volunteer work and by creating a domestic space that nurtured the next generation and made it possible for their husbands to succeed. Those whose husbands died or became incapacitated survived as best they could: going out as daily help, taking in laundry or boarders, working as porters or maids on passenger ships while relatives raised their children. The brief "New Woman" movement of the late nineteenth and early twentieth century that encouraged women to develop careers in business and the professions was quelched by the anti-feminist rhetoric of the 1920s and the diminished economic opportunities of 1930s.

The restrictions of domesticity can be difficult to overcome without models, however, and Great Lakes women writers who rejected ethnic and racial prejudices have often appropriated the example of Native women and Native cultures as mentors. In both the earliest document reprinted here, Ann Powell's journal of her trip to Detroit in 1789, and the most recent, Ann Linnea's description of her kayak circumnavigation of Lake Superior in *Deep Water Passage* (1995), the respect for and influence of Native cultures is clear. This may be because relations between whites and Natives in the lakes' region were more long-standing and amicable than those experienced by settlers to the far West where there were fewer shared economic endeavors and settlement took place much more quickly, in decades rather than centuries, and a strong multi-ethnic culture of French, Indians, English, and immigrant Americans was less likely to develop. It may also be because many Indian tribes were never removed since much of the land around the northern part of the lakes is unsuitable for farming. There have always been North American Indian lands near the lakes and Natives worked side-by-side with whites in the shipping and lumbering industries. The major reason, however, is that many white women, early and late, were forced to acknowledge that Indian women had more freedom and more respect than they. North American Indian women owned the property they created such as their lodges, they controlled the maple sugaring and ricing lands, they had the power of voting on important community decisions, and they could divorce their husbands and retain custody of their children, power white women did not achieve until the twentieth century. Native women's independent self-sufficiency was a strong example and it is not surprising that they have proved endlessly fascinating to white women writers.

Another compelling attraction for women writers has been the landscape of the lakes themselves, which even after their shores were settled, mined, lumbered, industrialized, and developed have resisted most efforts to control them. This collection begins with two texts, a poem by Judith Minty that describes her longing desire to escape the confines of shore-bound domesticity into the world of water where "everything is as you wished it to be," and Sylvia Kelley's short story "Ozymandias," which insists the Great Lakes are still a true wilderness that will never be tamed. Between these two poles, one of desire and the other of sober recognition, fall the various responses of women writers to the landscape they could not ignore. For some writers represented here, the wilderness world of the lakes and their ability to prove themselves in it functioned as a replacement for the worlds of professionalism that became closed to them. For others, the hardships of making lives and homes for themselves and their families in difficult conditions became an achievement of which they could be proud. The lakes, still untamed and always genderless, have allowed women opportunities to make journeys and to take risks that they otherwise might not have had and their satisfaction with their achievements is obvious.

Some readers may object to a collection that is devoted exclusively to writings by women, especially when many of them are virtually unknown and have written only the one text that is reprinted here. Others will insist that women pioneers in the interior of the lakes' region were less sanguine about their experiences. Certainly that may be true, and a collection that balances men's and women's narratives on the lakes and from the interior is called for. But I wished to offer a Great Lakes Reader that recovered different viewpoints from Walter Havinghurst's excellent *Great Lakes Reader* (1966) which included sixty-five writers of whom only seven were women and none, to my knowledge, was Indian. Havighurst's book portrays a Great Lakes region that was the fair field of opportunity for male explorers and venture capitalists who conquered nature and lived dramatically interesting lives doing so. To them, Natives were a curious culture that was quickly replaced by settlement and then industrialization, which continued to progress until, with the opening of the St. Lawrence Seaway, the world of the lakes stretched to the ocean. This is a Great Man theory of history that concentrates on the extractive possibilities of the landscape developed by capitalistic endeavor and technological superiority, and it's only part of the story. Accompanying those men as wives, cooks, lighthouse keepers, sailors, and explorers in their own right were women, and their narratives concentrate less on what they did to the lakes or could take from them to make a profit, and more on what their experiences on lakes did for them. And that was to confirm their strengths and abilities outside their expected domestic and social realms in a maritime landscape.

This collection is also offered as an alternative model for rethinking our role on the Great Lakes. If we are to preserve the lakes for later generations to enjoy and to learn from, we must begin learning from our history on them, and we cannot do that unless we know all that history, not just the stories of nationalistic conquest and development, which is often what society expects men to write. Women have been luckier in this regard; since they were not confined by cultural expectations to be leaders or explorers or successful businessmen wresting progress from place, they could write more freely. The result is narratives that are often provocative and unexpectedly undomestic, a record of individual lives and astutely observed detail that offers a counterpoint to the usual story of nation-building known as history. No one in this collection founds a city, or begins an industrial empire, or survives repeated storms on the Great Lakes to carry the cargoes that built two nations. Instead, these are the records of what women did while white men conquered that part of the continent we call the Great Lakes, and they tell us less about mastering a landscape and more about adjusting to it, a lesson we may find necessary for the late twentieth century.

But the writings in *The Women's Great Lakes Reader* still do tell the entire story. Most of the writers collected here were white, middle or upper class, educated, and either wrote for a living or were fortunate to have leisure in which to compose. For example, there are no narratives by African-American women since their role on the lakes is difficult to discover. Because the Northwest Ordinance forbade slave trading in 1787 and several states and Canada outlawed it, there are provocative hints in the historical record that many freed or escaped slaves made their way to the Great Lakes frontier and worked in maritime occupations. In the late 1700s African-Americans were running shipping operations on the western shoreline of Michigan in which women no doubt played a part. In the nineteenth century several African-American Detroiters purchased ships, but were required to list white men as the de facto owners. If African-American women worked in the lakes trades as cooks or porters, and there is no reason to think they did not, the records—always spotty for lower-paid crew members, particularly women—are silent.

These lacunae reflect the reality of a history of discrimination not only in employment, but also in what is recorded and preserved. Much as historians like to believe we are objective, we seldom are. Our cultural expectations determine what we decide is important to keep for posterity. Because women did not actively participate in the great events of nation building, they were seldom interviewed or encouraged to write. We have a detailed, if prejudicial, record of North American Indian lives in the Great Lakes region only because the Jesuit missionaries were required to send reports of their observations back to France. Later, in the nineteenth century, Henry Rowe Schoolcraft was appointed an Indian agent, married a mixed-blood woman, became fascinated by Native culture and, with Jane Johnston Schoolcraft's help, initiated Great Lakes ethnology. Twentieth-century historians became interested in the numerous shipwrecks on the what is one of the world's most wreck-strewn coasts and, as they recovered shipwreck history, also unintentionally discovered the working-class world of those who sailed the ships as well. Women, who were usually the lowest-paid members of the crew, were seldom recorded in ships' logs and so have generally been ignored, as have the experiences of working-class people of color. In addition, since most historians were not female, working-class minorities and many workers were, the unexamined assumptions of gender, race, and class influenced what experiences were preserved.

One well-known, academically-celebrated travel narrative is a case in point. When the New England feminist and Transcendentalist Margaret Fuller wrote about her travels in *Summer on the Lakes in 1843*, she mentions briefly two women chambermaids on her ship: "I was the only lady, and attended in the cabin by a Dutch girl and an Indian woman. They both spoke English fluently, and entertained me much by accounts of their different experiences."[1] Fuller notes that the Indian woman had divorced her husband because he mistreated her and was supporting herself and her child by working as a chambermaid. But Fuller's choice of terms is revealing: she was a *lady*; those who waited upon her were a *girl* and a *woman*. Fuller was poor, but she was white, educated, upper middle class, and assumed automatically a superior stance. Other than a brief paragraph noting the Indian woman would not have had such freedom to divorce "in civilized life," Fuller does not record any other experiences related by her, nor does Fuller make more than a condescending reference to her hostess on Mackinac Island—who appears to have been Madame La Framboise. Fuller wrote *Summer on the Lakes* to make money, but she also wrote to showcase the sometimes difficult lives of middle and upper-class women on the frontier. Women who were not "ladies" and who had survived independently, such as her chambermaid, merited only brief notice because they did not fit into her project of reforming middle-class women's education beyond the finishing school model then common that prepared women only to do embroidery and speak French. Blinded by her prejudices, Fuller could not see that the answer to women's dangerous dependence on others stood in front of her, holding out a towel.

In fairness to Fuller and other recorders, what is preserved is also influenced by what readers want to read. Few Americans before the mid-twentieth century were interested in "how the other half lived" on the lakes and so

---

[1] Margaret Fuller, *Summer on the Lakes in 1843*, (1844. Reprint. Urbana: University of Illinois Press, 1991), 146.

scant documentation exists. Working class women, no matter what their race, had little opportunity for education, and may also have had home and child care responsibilities in addition to outside work. They would have found few hours in which to write and, too often, fewer readers interested in what they had to say. To give these women voices they could not claim for themselves, I have included news accounts and interviews of nineteenth and twentieth-century working women on the lakes and have used fiction when no other documents were available. This compromise is not as revealing as their autobiographies would be—women's experiences on lakes ships made the newspapers only when something dramatic happened so readers lose the sense of the everyday reality of their lives—but it is the best available record. The result of mixing these different genres of autobiography, essay, traveller's observations, ethnology, fiction, news reports, and poetry gives this book the appearance of an old patchwork quilt made of scraps of lives and experiences, but combining pieces to make a pattern has long been women's art.

And what is the pattern made by the lives of the women represented here? At the end of *Deep Water Passage*, Ann Linnea's kayaking narrative, she realizes that her experiences surviving the cold, stormy world of Lake Superior have changed her so profoundly she can never again accept the thoughtless domesticity and perfectionism that had governed her life before. A number of other writers collected in *The Women's Great Lakes Reader* came to the similar conclusions. Like Harriet Colfax, they may have begun their journeys with fear and trepidation, but they emerged stronger, braver, more competent, and confident.

If the history revealed by these women's accounts does not conform to 1970s and 1980s feminist theories of women's writing as necessarily being "woman centered" or domestic, if it does not uniformly portray women on the US and Canadian Great Lakes' frontiers as victims of men who dragged them west to suffer insanity in rude shacks in the bush, perhaps it is time, as Nina Baym suggests, for a reassessment of what women wrote about how they lived. In a speech on Mackinac Island, made not far from where Madame LaFramboise ran a fur-trading empire that even John Jacob Astor, try as he might, could not undermine, Baym said "We must revise the theory that there is one particular kind of 'women's writing' that always and everywhere distinguishes the feminine."[2] Women's writing is not always centered in the home, or the church, or even the community. It may be personal or regional, but it may also be political and national. Instead, the writings by women about their lives and the places they lived are always individual. Scholars, trained to look for patterns that conform to theories and to argue

---

[2] Speech delivered at the convention, "Constance Fenimore Woolson's Nineteenth Century," Grand Hotel, Mackinac Island, Michigan, October 5, 1996.

their theses accordingly, often say more about themselves than their subjects. Women's writings about the lakes are, as I hope this collection demonstrates, a record of individuals encountering a wild and still untamed landscape with its evolving challenges during three centuries and responding bravely and intelligently to those challenges. While the writers reprinted here encountered the Great Lakes as women, they encountered it primarily as workers, helpmates, travellers, explorers—each with her particular story to tell which refuses to be subsumed into any easily-diminished theoretical category. Storms on the Great Lakes, which the marine insurer Lloyds of London ranks as some of the most devastating and destructive on the continent, do not distinguish the gender of the person manning the tiller of the boat or keeping the lighthouse.

This too, is the history of the Great Lakes.

OZYMANDIAS
(1997)
Sylvia Kelley

THIRTY YEARS AGO we walked, balancing on one foot before the next, along the top edge of the second breakwater, arms out for balance and looking down at the brackish water caught between the boards we walked on and the ragged outer breakwater, knowing if we fell there were pits where the water was over our heads and sharp metal spikes thrusting out from the green-bearded pilings to scrape or skewer us in our falling. We walked it anyway, once a day or more, going from one of our cottages to the other, laughing, looking down at the collection of floating cellophane, butterfly wings, sticks, cigarette filters, decayed hunks of fish that had become merely heads trailing spinal columns and deflated rubbery skin, unidentifiable torn pieces of bright plastic, sometimes a can or bottle, always watching for something of value to wash within reach. When the waves were big after a storm they banged against the outer breakwater with a noise like gunshots, sending gouts of spray into the air even sometimes as far back as we were, drenching us, and we laughed even harder: there was no danger that could touch us.

The neighbors all said Mr. Jarecki was crazy, trying to stop the lake with his money, like he thought he had all that wealth he must be god. You don't stop the Big Lake, they said; it'll do what it wants to do. And it looked that way: the three breakwaters went in, one against his bank, shoring it up where the bathhouse was starting to lean a little over the edge and Mrs. J. had already lost some of her plantings—actually, the gardener's plantings—the second one fifty yards out from that, the one we walked on, with a double row of two-by-fours strapped together with other two-by-fours and big rusting bolts and every so often pilings big around as phone poles to hold it all steady, and then fifty yards out from that the big, heavy-duty one sunk into the lake itself where the water was over our heads, and the dock, jutting only a few yards beyond the outer one, but much higher up, above even the tallest waves it seemed, and ten days after it was completed the lake destroyed that dock.

It was the Fourth of July, I remember, and all my friends were gone visiting relatives, so I was missing our usual fireworks on the beach. A storm came up, stalking in from the west across the lake, first turning the water deep green and then purple and poisonous blue and then enormous black thunderheads came tumbling in behind the wind that slammed the windows and blew the beach chairs across the yard so fast we had to run to get everything in. Then I stood outside to watch it as it moved over the water, the slanted edge of the oncoming rain flattening the surface of the waves and the wind behind it whipping them to whitecaps again. The gulls cried out and wheeled up away from the shore, back into the woods, so you knew it was going to be fierce and I went inside just as the first raindrops hit.

When it came it wasn't the worst storm we'd ever had; the saplings in the back yard bent first in one direction, then, lashing their branches almost to the ground, limber as dancers, bent just as far in the other direction. Pieces of torn leaf and tiny sticks ticked against the window panes and we sprang the usual leaks Mother had to put towels down for. It was beautiful but not particularly powerful as lake storms go.

That's why I had no idea when I heard those noises like shots from the beach; I thought it was fireworks. The storm had walked on past, muttering toward town maybe ten minutes before and the waves continued to build, getting more and more violent, the way we loved them for swimming, when it would be all you could do to stand in one spot, the water foaming and tearing at you, pounding you and making you feel if you stood up to it you were a part of it as wild as the lake itself, you were in some sense immortal for those moments, and nothing could touch you. I was wishing my friends were there for those waves because Mother would never let me go in alone, when I heard the cracking noises. Outside on the deck, I leaned out as far as I could to look down the beach toward their cottages and didn't even notice at first the dock doing its crazy dance. The water had built into great rolling combers which swept in from the northwest and slammed against the far breakwater, which was bending in toward shore in a gentle curve, two huge pilings snapped somewhere beneath the surface but still attached at the top and dragging on the waves, pulling the entire center of the breakwater back in an arc. But that was a silent struggle of the wood and the water; the noise I heard came from the dock itself on the water. The flooring, complete with that little lift-up seat where you could store life preservers and tackle for fishing, had been torn loose from the sides and hung now in one long section reaching out from the second breakwater where it was still attached to the end pilings and flopping on the surface of the waves with giant whiplike snappings, at every snap hitting the water below it a thunderous crack. I watched it for hours and I have to give Mr. Jarecki credit: it lasted a whole lot longer than I thought it would before the boards began peeling off one or two at a time and rolling into shore like slim dark surfboards riding the waves. The next day his dock was scattered along half a mile of beach, but my friends were back by then and there was lots more interesting stuff that had washed up than those boards. We didn't even wonder what Dad was talking about when he looked down at the destruction from our deck and smiled and said, "Ozymandias, Kings of Kings."

Sometimes when the water is rough in August, that brilliant thick green it gets, with long strings of whitecaps and cloud shadows moving across the surface purple as bruises, we go in and swim until we're giddy. When you finally stop fighting the waves and let them wash you back to shore, your legs are almost too rubbery to carry you up the stairs. At night, lying in bed listening to the surf, your blood continues to surge from side to side within you like that of a sailor on his ship, and you feel again that reassurance.

More than a hundred years ago the ship set out with 180 passengers and a load of apples. It was October, when storms can come up suddenly on the lake, and a big one hit them just at dusk. The ship was sighted, having trouble but on course; then it disappeared.

For three days the water churned white as chalk, and then the apples and bodies rolled up, tumbling playfully over and over in the surf for miles along the shore. The backboard of the ship's piano washed up, with a note wrapped in oilskin tucked inside. It read: *We're breaking up. Pray for us.*

Today the hull is buried in the sand beneath the water out front, with only its sides and the stump of the mast visible, coated with dark seaweed and lurking under the surface like ominous arms reaching to pull you down. If you walk on the sand between the sides you can feel the deck give springily beneath your feet. Sometimes when you poke down into the sand with the end of a stick or a paddle bubbles will stream up through the water, suddenly released after a hundred years.

My brother saved a boy from drowning in the wreck when we were little and the water around it was deeper. We always thought having it there was lucky, except when you accidentally got washed against it, forgetting where it was under the waves. Then sometimes you got so scared you had to get out of the water and sit on the beach in a big towel until the chill went away. Just for a few minutes you thought about mortality, about things reaching up unexpectedly from the depths; the tenuousness.

Today as we walked on the beach the ends of Mr. Jarecki's dock pilings poked up one at a time through the waves like a family of otters peeking at us as we passed. One long section of corrugated metal attached to two pilings waved a thick green skirt of moss at us. The water around it is knee-deep this year and the second breakwater doesn't even show above the sand. We take the canoe down the beach on calm days to dig along the shore where there are no cottages for more of those nice bricks from the fallen bath house. We're making a brick walkway next to our new deck.

Sylvia Kelly (1938-) grew up in Grand Rapids, Michigan, and still returns each summer to the family cottage on Lake Michigan. A public school teacher who also volunteers as a creative writing instructor in migrant labor camps, prisons, and senior citizen centers, she has won several awards for her fiction in New York.

Anishnaabeg
The First People of the Lakes

Indian Mother and Daughter, Mackinac Island, (c. 1900)
Francis Benjamin Johnston (1864-1952)

Courtesy Library of Congress. One of the first great women photographers, Johnston became known in the 1890s as America's "Court Photographer" for her portraits of residents of the White House and Official Washington. She was also a documentary photographer who recorded Hampton and Tuskegee Institutes, the Carlyle Indian School, mining operations on the Mesabi Range, and women factory workers.

GREAT LAKES INDIAN LITERATURES

THE FIRST WOMEN on the Great Lakes were not settlers' wives or travellers, but Anishnaabe-kweg or "First Women." Indian women. Although they belonged to different tribes and spoke many languages, their life-ways were similar. Powerful in their cultures, sometimes leaders, they were equal partners with men in their marriages and controlled much property, including the maple sugar groves the bands tapped in spring and the ricing groves they harvested in fall. Women were responsible for any agriculture their tribes practiced. They wove the mats or stripped the bark which covered the lodges, thus they owned them too. They decided how the game the men captured would be distributed. If their husbands were cruel or improvident, they could divorce and retain custody of their children, rights white women did not achieve until the twentieth century. American Indian women's meekness and docility, their manner of never looking anyone directly in the eye—which was considered highly rude—confused many EuroAmerican observers who often saw them as degraded beasts of burden. Nothing is less accurate.

Women were also most often the bearers of culture, and in a pre-literate society, culture was transmitted by stories, either myths (auwaetchigum) which conveyed important cultural information and could be told only in winter when the creatures discussed were underground and could not hear and be offended, or tales (daebaudjimowin), chronicles of personal experience which often illustrated exemplary personal behaviors and could be told any time of year. Many storytellers were older women who expected nothing in return for their wisdom except a comfortable place in the lodge and small presents.

When North American Indian cultures were transformed, first by the fur trade and then the industrialization of the Great Lakes basin, the roles of women were profoundly affected. White missionaries attempted to undermine their power by destroying traditional belief, sometimes so they could manipulate the tribes for economic gain. Native subsistence economies gave way under pressure of the fur trade to a system where fur bearers were exploited for financial gain, and successful hunters took more wives to process more pelts, subjugating women to a capitalistic economy in which their labor was exchanged for goods and credit, rather than directly meeting the needs of their families. The late fur trade was essentially a factory system where Indian women did piece work, little different from the young girls and children who worked in the first factories in the United States, the New England textile mills. When the fur trade collapsed in the nineteenth century and hunting was no longer possible on circumscribed reservations, women often became the economic mainstay of their families. They had traditionally practiced agriculture and made baskets; these then became the only source of ready cash for many families. Mrs. Johnston of Sault Ste. Marie, who figures in Anna Jameson's travel narrative reprinted in the "Women Travellers" section, assumed just such a role.

Mrs. Johnston was the mother-in-law of one of the first ethnographers of the United States, Henry Rowe Schoolcraft, who was able to collect his myths and tales of the Great Lakes because of his wife, Jane Johnston Schoolcraft, and her mother. Without the community of Native women into which he married, Schoolcraft's work would have been far less impressive, since most of the narratives he collected were transcribed by his wife from stories her mother told. Later ethnologists are equally indebted to Native women who were willing to share their cultures.

Those cultures are difficult for most Westernized readers to comprehend because nature is visible and tangible, as well as invisible and immaterial, and all elements of it are capable of metamorphosis. All parts of the North American Indian world, whether rocks, or trees, or stars, or animals, can be animate. Formerly, when young persons reached puberty, their task was to blacken their faces with charcoal, refuse food, and retreat into the forest to fast in vision quests. During this time, the faster took only water and waited for the spirits, or manidog, to appear. The manido that appeared became that person's guardian spirit for the rest of life, to be propitiated and called upon in times of need. Some spirits were and are more powerful than others, for example the thunderers, the spirits of the air which were once the manidog of the young men who would become warriors. The underwater spirits of the great snakes or Missipeshu, a great horned lynx, gave knowledge of medicines and controlled food supplies, but could also be evil and teach vegetable poisoning or the methods for killing an enemy many miles away. Only the bravest and strongest accepted the visitations of the underwater manidog, since acceptance might mean the faster would become a sorcerer, condemned to live alone and feared by all.

In the Great Lakes region, where North American Indian cultures persisted long after white settlement, the interactions between European and North American women and Indian women were frequently described in the fiction and travel narratives white women wrote. These writers were fascinated with Indian culture, and often more sympathetic than men to the problems Indians faced as their life-ways were changed irrevocably. Astute white women writers also noticed that Indian women had more freedom and power than they, and they were sometimes envious. The most prescient observers, such as Anna Jameson, reveled in the acceptance and affection they received from Indian "mothers," and returned to their lives empowered by contact with a culture which did not denigrate women of achievement and talent as did their own.

Nearly all the women who have written about the Great Lakes, early and recent, have been affected by the cultures and the examples of North American Indian women. That they recognized Indian women as sisters is not feminist rhetoric, for most writers were not feminists, but an acknowledgment of all women's changing roles in a place where, after the 1860s, control of their lives and families was increasingly usurped by an economic system that did not value women. Many recognized that Indian women were subjected to the same system, and they respected Indian women for whatever lessons of survival they could teach. Nineteenth-century women caught in the constraints of Victorian proscriptions for women's dress and behavior often envied Native women's freedom of movement and personal relationships. Twentieth-century women seek in Native cultures a harmony and respect for nature they believe to be lacking in their own. When the last fiction writer represented in this *Reader*, Joan Skelton, sends her character into Lake Superior to die, she has her invoke the manido of Missipeshu—that most powerful and sometimes malevolent of Indian spirits—as if he could give her the strength she needs to meet her death bravely, a death caused by the condescending attitude of modern medicine toward women. In her moment of greatest crisis when her own culture has failed her, she reaches back to another—North American Indian culture—to empower her.

That empowerment comes not from money or machines, but from stories, and those collected here testify to the continuing power of storytelling in Native cultures. North American Indian stories can now be written down, they can be sent on the Internet, or recorded on video, although nothing can replace the role of communal storytelling in the traditional way where the audience participates with the teller and each gesture is replete with meaning. Reading a traditional tale is like listening to a recording of a particularly lively concert: half the experience is missing. In addition, readers accustomed to westernized conventions of narrative that follow a familiar pattern of introduction, development, and conclusion neatly organized in paragraphs with topic sentences and examples will be enlightened by the often understated, discursive method of traditional American Indian narratives. Native stories make their points subtly to allow the listener to contribute to meaning; they seldom insist or eliminate possible interpretations. In so doing, they reflect an accepting, communal culture that believes in the equality and intelligence of all creatures.

Purists may object to the inclusion of stories about Indians written by non-Indians, such as the chapter from *The Loon Feather* by Iola Fuller, but I wished to demonstrate not only the influence Native cultures exerted on the white writers, but equally important, how different narrative methods shape meaning. Fuller's detailed realistic descriptions leave little to her readers' imaginations; we are not required to share in making meaning. "The Underwater Lion," however, a typical traditional American Indian tale, may confuse some readers because of its brevity and their unfamiliarity with supplying the imaginative and cultural details that give greater depth. Yet both stories are essentially alike, for both describe brave young women who, when confronted by very fearful things, act courageously and triumph. What happens, however, to Native literature when its creators are acculturated and use Western forms? Readers many enjoy thinking about how writers such as Pauline Johnson and Susan Power incorporate North American Indian themes and concerns in their work.

THE UNDERWATER LION
A CHIPPEWA TALE

ALMOST ALL NORTH American Indian tribes believed in a water monster, usually a great horned snake. The Ojibwa and Chippewa also believed in Missipeshu (Micipijiu), the underwater lynx or lion, who was probably inspired by the panthers native to the Great Lakes region who were sometimes seen swimming. As a creature of myth, Missipeshu is one of the most powerful, and not always positive, manidog in the Native universe. Only those who had dreamed of Thunderers, the spirits of the air, commonly young men who would become warriors, would be empowered to survive his attacks. But in this story, a young woman who has dreamed of thunderers is able to triumph over Missipeshu and enrich her family because of her courage.

Folklorists classify creatures like Missipeshu as "demon lovers," bestial creatures who try to become the mates or husbands of human women. Folktales with this theme are told the world over, but interestingly, the endings differ according to the cultures doing the telling. In societies where relations between the sexes are egalitarian, women are usually able to resist being pulled down into the underworld to be mated to the monster. In patriarchial societies, women do not fare as well. "The Underwater Lion," a tale frequently collected by ethnologists in the lakes' region, reflects the confidence of North American Native women. Although in this tale they disobey a community sanction, they are equal to the task of extricating themselves from danger, and their success is a symbol of the power they wielded in their cultures.

⋯⊱━◉◼━⊰⋯

THERE WAS A big lake; Indians lived on both sides of it. There was a big island of mud in the center, and if anyone wanted to go to the other village across the lake, they would have to paddle around the edge of the lake. If they tried to go straight across, something would happen to them. A bad manido lived there in the island.

One day there was a medicine dance across the lake, and people started around the lake in their canoes. Two women started later, after the others had gone. There were sisters-in-law. One of them was rather foolish. She was steering in the stern and headed straight across. The other warned her not to do it, but in vain. The first girl had a little cedar paddle with her. She never left it out of her sight—always took it along, even when she went out gathering wood. She held it but did not use it for paddling. As they got to the middle, they crossed the mud, and in the center of the mud was a hole of clear water. The water was swirling around the hole, and as they started to cross it, a lion came out of the middle and switched his tail across the boat, trying to turn it over. The girl picked up her little paddle and hit the lion's tail with it, saying, "Thunder is striking you." The paddle cut off the lion's tail, and the end dropped into the boat. When they picked it up, it was a solid piece of copper about two inches thick. They watched the lion running away through the mud, and the steerer laughed hard. She said, "I scared him. He won't bother us again." When they got across, the girl gave the piece of copper to her father, and he got rich through having it. The copper had certain powers. People would give her father a blanket just for a tiny piece of that copper. They would take that bit for luck in hunting and fishing, and some just kept it to bring good luck.

Collected by Robert Ritzenthaler at Court Oreilles in 1942
Narrator: Pete Martin

Missipeshu

PROFILE:
JANE JOHNSTON SCHOOLCRAFT
1800-1842

Courtesy Bentley Historical Library

HER INDIAN NAME was Bamewawagezhikaquay, "Woman of Stars Rushing Through Sky," one of eight children of John Johnston, the fur-trading son of a wealthy Scots-Irish landowner in Ireland, and Ozhaguscodaywayquay, "Woman of the Green Valley," the youngest daughter of the powerful Chippewa chief at La Pointe, Waub Ojeeg. That chief had had his suspicions about marriages between fur traders and native women, or "daughters of the country," which were usually prompted by the potentially lucrative connections the women would bring to their trader husbands. Too often these marriages were for convenience only and ended when the fur trade moved on. Eventually Johnston convinced Waub Ojeeg of his sincere intentions, renamed his bride Susan, and for a number of years made a great deal of money in the trade, enabling him to educate his children at private schools in Canada. But the War of 1812 demolished his fortunes, and he was never able to recover. Even so, when Henry Rowe Schoolcraft, the newly-appointed Indian Agent at Sault Ste Marie, asked to marry his daughter, Jane, Johnston managed to settle her with a large dowry.

Jane was her father's favorite child and had often accompanied him on business trips to Detroit, Montreal, and Quebec. She had received further schooling in Ireland, and Schoolcraft found her well-read, intelligent, and witty. She was also attractive and highly sentimental in the best genteel tradition, qualities which, with her dowry, would have appealed to Schoolcraft, isolated as he was on the frontier. Most important, Jane was eager to help him with his studies of Indian cultures by translating the stories her mother told that had been passed down from Waub Ojeeg who was known as the greatest storyteller of his tribe.

During the long winters at the Sault the Schoolcrafts began a small literary magazine, *The Literary Voyager or Muzzeniegun* (printed document or book), to circulate information about the tribes living near the Sault to interested students of Indian cultures in Detroit and the Eastern cities. In it were published the stories Jane told or transcribed, usually under the pseudonym of "Leelinau," one of the words Schoolcraft coined to sound like an Indian name. In 1839 Schoolcraft published the first formal collection of tales, *Algic Researches*, which inspired Longfellow to write "Hiawatha." Later ethnologists have faulted the Schoolcrafts for rewriting the stories in a complex, Westernized prose style and for censoring most sexual and scatological elements, but they knew what their readers expected and would accept.

Unfortunately, Jane lacked the robust health of her mother and her pregnancies were always difficult. After their beloved first son died in 1827, her health never recovered and she described herself as a "nervous invalid . . . drag[ging] out a wretched miserable existence—" She eventually became addicted to laudanum, a nineteenth-century form of opium routinely prescribed for women, and despite the family's move to the East to restore her health, died in 1842. Their children did not fare well, perhaps because Schoolcraft, following nineteenth-century prejudice, believed that persons of mixed-blood lacked "*foresight* and *firmness*—two traits that man *cannot* spare and excell in the sterner duties of human life. . . ."

Jane Johnston Schoolcraft, like many other mixed-blood or Indian women who married white men, may have been irrevocably caught between two different cultures all her life. Her mother, Ozhaguscodaywayquay, never assimilated to white ways, never learned to speak English, and indeed her retention of Indian life-ways of gardening and basket-making supported her family after Johnston lost his fortune. Jane would have been raised in a typically loving and indulgent Indian household. Marriage to Schoolcraft, a man his biographer describes as cold, unfeeling, and ever nervous about his social standing and the failure of his remaining son to conform to white standards, may have contributed to her unhappiness.

Mishosha, or the Magician and His Daugthers
A Chippewa Tale or Legend

Bamewawagezhikaquay
Jane Johnston Schoolcraft

"MISHOSHA" is not a myth, which conveys important cultural information such as the origin of a clan totem, but was meant for entertainment during long winter evenings in the lodge. Set on Grand Island in Lake Superior, there are repeated trials of magic, and the story is discursive, as Ojibwa stories often are. But lodge stories were also meant for edification. "Mishosha" teaches proper behavior when one is angry, it suggests that bravery and aggressiveness against a foe will be rewarded, it reinforces the proper way to accomplish rituals and spells, and it describes how some personal guiding spirits, or manidog, are more powerful than others. Most importantly, it describes how an abandoned child of thoughtless parents can overcome adversity. This theme, that of the "forsaken brother," is one of the most common in Great Lakes Indian literatures, perhaps because of the wars and resulting population shifts that plagued the region for centuries.

->==)O==<-

IN AN EARLY AGE of the world, when there were fewer inhabitants in the earth than there now are, there lived an Indian, who had a wife and two children, in a remote situation. Buried in the solitude of the forest, it was not often that he saw any one out of the circle of his own family. Such a situation seemed favorable for his pursuits; and his life passed on in uninterrupted happiness, till he discovered a wanton disposition in his wife.

This woman secretly cherished a passion for a young man whom she accidentally met in the woods, and she lost no opportunity of courting his approaches. She even planned the death of her husband who, she justly concluded, would put her to death should he discover her infidelity. But this design was frustrated by the alertness of the husband, who having cause to suspect her, determined to watch narrowly to ascertain the truth before he should come to a determination how to act. He followed her silently one day at a distance, and hid himself behind a tree. He soon beheld a tall, handsome man approach his wife and lead her away.

He was now convinced of her crime, and thought of killing her the moment she returned. In the meantime he went home and pondered on his situation. At last he came to the determination of leaving her forever, thinking that her own conscience would in the end punish her sufficiently, and relying on her maternal feelings to take care of the two boys, whom he determined to leave behind.

When the wife returned she was disappointed in not finding her husband, having concerted a plan to dispatch him. When she saw that day after day passed and he did not return, she at last guessed the true cause of his absence. She then returned to her paramour, leaving the two helpless boys behind, telling them that she was going a short distance and would return, but determined never to see them more.

The children thus abandoned soon made way with the food that was left in the lodge and were compelled to quit it in search of more. The eldest boy possessed much intrepidity, as well as great tenderness for his little brother, frequently carrying him when he became weary, and gathering all the wild fruit he saw. Thus they went deeper into the forest, soon losing all traces of their former habitation, till they were completely lost in the labyrinths of the wilderness.

The elder boy fortunately had a knife with which he made a bow and arrows, and was thus enabled to kill a few birds for himself and brother. In this way they lived some time, still pressing on they knew not whither. At last they saw an opening through the woods and were shortly after delighted to find themselves on the borders of a broad lake. Here the elder boy busied himself in picking the seed pods of the wild rose. In the meanwhile the younger amused himself by shooting some arrows into the sand, one of which happened to fall into the lake. The elder brother, not willing to lose his time in making another, waded into the water to reach it. Just as he was about to grasp the arrow, a canoe passed by him with the rapidity of lightning. An old man, sitting in the center, seized the affrighted youth and placed him in the canoe. In vain the boy addressed him. "My grandfather" (a term of respect for old people) "pray take my little brother also. Alone, I cannot go with you; he will starve if I leave him." The old magician (for such was his real character) laughed at him. Then giving his canoe a slap and commanding it to go, it glided through the water with inconceivable swiftness. In a few minutes they reached the habitation of Mishosha, standing on an island in the center of the lake. Here he lived with his two daughters, the terror of all the surrounding country.

Leading the young man up to the lodge, "Here my eldest daughter," said he, "I have brought a young man who shall become your husband." The youth saw surprise depicted in the countenance of the daughter, but she made no reply, seeming thereby to acquiesce in the commands of her father.

In the evening he overheard the daughters in conversation. "There again!" said the elder daughter, "our father has brought another victim, under the pretence of giving me a husband. When will his enmity to the human race cease; or when shall we be spared witnessing such scenes of vice and wickedness, as we are daily compelled to behold."

When the old magician was asleep, the youth told the elder daughter how he had been carried off and compelled to leave his helpless brother on the shore. She told him to get up and take her father's canoe, and using the charm he had observed, it would carry him quickly to his brother. That he could carry him food, prepare a lodge for him, and return by morning. He did in everything as he had been directed, and after providing for the subsistence of his brother, told him that in a short time he should come for him. Then returning to the enchanted island, he resumed his place in the lodge before the magician awoke. Once during the night Mishosha awoke, and not seeing his son-in-law, asked his eldest daughter what had become of him. She replied that he had merely stepped out and would be back soon. This satisfied him. In the morning, finding the young man in the lodge, his suspicions were completely lulled. "I see, my daughter, you have told me the truth."

As soon as the sun rose, Mishosha thus addressed the young man. "Come, my son, I have a mind to gather gulls' eggs. I am acquainted with an island where there are great quantities; and I wish your aid in gathering them." The young man saw no reasonable excuse, and getting into the canoe, the magician gave it a slap, and bidding it go, in an instant they were at the island. They found the shore covered with gulls' eggs, and the island surrounded with birds of this kind. "Go, my son," said the old man, "and gather them, while I remain in the canoe." But the young man was no sooner ashore than Mishosha pushed his canoe a little from land and exclaimed: "Listen ye gulls! You have long expected something from me. I now give you an offering. Fly down and devour him." Then striking his canoe, left the young man to his fate.

The birds immediately came in clouds around their victim, darkening all the air with their numbers. But the youth, seizing the first that came near him and drawing his knife, cut off its head, and immediately skinning the bird, hung the feathers as a trophy on his breast. "Thus," he exclaimed, "will I treat every one of you who approaches me. Forbear, therefore, and listen to my words. It is not for you to eat human food. You have been given by the Great Spirit as food for man. Neither is it in the power of that old magician to do you any good. Take me on your backs and carry me to his lodge, and you shall see that I am not ungrateful."

The gulls obeyed, collecting in a cloud for him to rest upon, and quickly flew to the lodge, where they arrived before the magician. The daughters were surprised at his return, but Mishosha conducted as if nothing extraordinary had taken place.

On the following day he again addressed the youth. "Come, my son," said he, "I will take you to an island covered with the most beautiful pebbles, looking like silver. I wish you to assist me in gathering some of them. They will make handsome ornaments, and are possessed of great virtues." Entering the canoe, the magician made use of his charm, and they were carried in a few moments to a solitary bay in an island where there was a smooth sandy beach. The young man went ashore as usual. "A little further, a little further," cried the old man, "upon that rock you will get some finer ones." Then pushing his canoe from land, "Come thou great king of fishes," cried he, "you have long expected an offering from me. Come, and eat the stranger I have put ashore on your island." So saying, he commanded his canoe to return, and was soon out of sight. Immediately a monstrous fish shoved his long snout from the water, moving partially on the beach, and opening wide his jaws to receive his victim.

"When," exclaimed the young man, drawing his knife and placing himself in a threatening attitude, "when did you ever taste human food? Have a care of yourself. You were given by the Great Spirit to man, and if you or any of your tribes taste human flesh, you will fall sick and die. Listen not to the words of that wicked old man, but carry me back to his island, in return for which I shall present you a piece of red cloth." The fish complied, raising his back out of water to allow the young man to get on. Then taking his way through the lake, landed his charge safely at the island before the return of the magician.

The daughters were still more surprised to see him thus escaped a second time from the arts of their father. But the old man maintained his taciturnity. He could not, however, help saying to himself, "What manner of boy is this who ever escapes from my power? His spirit shall not however save him. I will entrap him tomorrow. Ha! ha! ha!"

Next day the magician addressed the young man as follows: "Come, my son," said he, "you must go with me to procure some young eagles. I wish to tame them. I have discovered an island where they are in great abundance." When they had reached the island, Mishosha led him inland until they came to the foot of a tall pine upon which the nests were. "Now, my son," said he, "climb up this tree and bring down the birds." The young man obeyed. When he had with great difficulty got near the nest, "Now," exclaimed the magician, addressing the tree, "stretch yourself up and be very tall." The tree rose up at the command. "Listen, ye eagles," continued the old man, "you have long expected a gift from me. I now present you this boy, who has had the presumption to molest your young. Stretch forth your claws and seize him." So saying he left the young man to his fate, and returned.

But the intrepid youth, drawing his knife and cutting off the head of the first eagle that menaced him, raised his voice and exclaimed, "Thus will I deal with all who come near me. What right have you, ye ravenous birds, who were made to feed on beasts, to eat human flesh? Is it because that cowardly old canoe-man has bid you do so? He is an old woman. He can neither do you good nor harm. See, I have already slain one of your number. Respect my bravery, and carry me back that I may show you how I shall treat you."

The eagles, pleased with his spirit, assented, and clustering thick around him formed a seat with their backs and flew toward the enchanted island. As they crossed the water they passed over the magician, lying half asleep in his canoe.

The return of the young man was hailed with joy by the daughters, who now plainly saw that he was under the guidance of a strong spirit. But the ire of the old man was excited, although he kept his temper under subjection. He taxed his wits for some new mode of ridding himself of the youth who had so successfully baffled his skill. He next invited him to go a-hunting.

Taking his canoe, they proceeded to an island and built a lodge to shelter themselves during the night. In the meanwhile the magician caused a deep fall of snow with a storm of wind and severe cold. According to custom, the young man pulled off his moccasins and leggings and hung them before the fire to dry. After he had gone to sleep the magician, watching his opportunity, got up, and taking one moccasin and one legging, threw them into the fire. He then went to sleep. In the morning, stretching himself as he arose and uttering an exclamation of surprise, "My son," said he, "what has become of your moccasin and legging? I believe this is the moon in which fire attracts, and I fear they have been drawn in." The young man suspected the true cause of his loss, and rightly attributed it to a design of the magician to freeze him to death on the march. But he maintained the strictest silence, and drawing his conaus over his head thus communed with himself: "I have full faith in the Manito who has preserved me thus far, I do not fear that he will forsake me in this cruel emergency. Great is his power, and I invoke it now that he may enable me to prevail over this wicked enemy of mankind."

He then drew on the remaining moccasin and legging, and taking a dead coal from the fireplace, invoked his spirit to give it efficacy, and blackened his foot and leg as far as the lost garment usually reached. He then got up and announced himself ready for the march. In vain Mishosha led him through snows and over morasses, hoping to see the lad sink at every moment. But in this he was disappointed, and for the first time they returned home together.

Taking courage from this success, the young man now determined to try his own power, having previously consulted with the daughters. They all agreed that the life the old man led was detestable, and that whoever would rid the world of him would entitle himself to the thanks of the human race.

On the following day the young man thus addressed his hoary captor.

"My grandfather, I have often gone with you on perilous excursions and never murmured. I must now request that you will accompany me. I wish to visit my little brother and to bring him home with me." They accordingly went on a visit to the mainland and found the little lad in the spot where he had been left. After taking him into the canoe, the young man again addressed the magician: "My grandfather, will you go and cut me a few of those red willows on the bank. I wish to prepare some smoking mixture." "Certainly, my son," replied the old man, "what you wish is not very hard. Ha, ha, ha! do you think me too old to get up there?" No sooner was Mishosha ashore than the young man, placing himself in the proper position struck the canoe with his hand, and pronouncing the charm, N'CHIMAUN POLL, the canoe immediately flew through the water on its return to the island. It was evening when the two brothers arrived and carried the canoe ashore. But the elder daughter informed the young man that unless he sat up and watched the canoe and kept his hand upon it, such was the power of their father, it would slip off and return to him. Panigwun watched faithfully till near the dawn of day, when he could no longer resist the drowsiness which oppressed him and fell into a short doze. In the meantime the canoe slipped off and sought its master, who soon returned in high glee. "Ha, ha, ha! my son," said he; "you thought to play me a trick. It was very clever. But you see I am too old for you."

A short time after, the young again addressed the magician. "My grandfather, I wish to try my skill in hunting. It is said there is plenty of game on an island not far off, and I have to request that you will take me there in your canoe." They accordingly went to the island and spent the day in hunting. Night coming on, they put up a temporary lodge. When the magician had sunk into a profound sleep the young man got up, and taking one of Mishosha's leggings and moccasins from the place where they hung, threw them into the fire, thus retaliating the artifice before played upon himself. He had discovered that the foot and leg were the only vulnerable parts on the magician's body. Having committed these articles to the fire, he besought his Manito that he would raise a great storm of snow, wind, and hail, and then laid himself down beside the old man. Consternation was depicted on the countenance of the latter when he awoke in the morning and found his moccasin and legging missing. "I believe, my grandfather," said the young man, "that this is the moon in which fire attracts, and I fear your foot and leg garments have been drawn in." Then rising and bidding the old man follow him, he began the morning's hunt, frequently turning to see how Mishosha kept up. He saw him faltering at every step and almost benumbed with cold, but encouraged him to follow saying, we shall soon get through and reach the shore; although he took pains at the same time to lead him in roundabout ways, so as to let the frost take complete effect. At length the old man reached the brink of the island where the woods are succeeded by a border of smooth sand. But he could go no farther; his legs became stiff and refused motion, and he found himself fixed to the spot. But he still kept stretching out his arms and swinging his body to and fro. Every moment he found the numbness creeping higher. He felt his legs growing downward like roots, the feathers of his head turned to leaves, and in a few seconds he stood a tall and stiff sycamore, leaning toward the water.

Panigwun leaped into the canoe, and pronounced the charm, was soon transported to the island, where he related his victory to the daughters. They applauded the deed, agreed to put on mortal shapes, become wives to the two young men, and for ever quit the enchanted island. And passing immediately over to the main land, they lived lives of happiness and peace.

MOOWIS, THE INDIAN COQUETTE

Leelinau

Jane Johnston Schoolcraft

"MOOWIS" is of a different order than "Mishosha" and this humorous plot teaches proper courting behavior for young women. The woman who spurns her lover is behaving badly, since her handsome beau would have never paid court to her if she had not encouraged him. She has led him to believe she will accept him, thus he comes to the family tent at night, and as the custom, lifts the side and crawls in beside her. If they were still together in the morning when the family awoke, a marriage would then be planned. This time, however, the coquette has evidently changed her mind, and in so doing, caused great embarrassment to her suitor, a loss of face he is not about to forgive. Schoolcraft described the name "Moowis," derived from the Ojibwa noun "mo," meaning filth or excrement, as being one of the most derogative and offensive possible. He did not publish the story until after his wife's death, and he appears to have changed little from her transcription.

--◄━●●━►--

THERE WAS A village full of Indians, and a noted belle or muhmuhdawgoqua was living there. A noted beau or muhdawgoninnie was there also. He and another young man went to court this young woman, and laid down beside her, when she scratched the face of the handsome beau. He went home and would not rise till the family prepared to depart, and he would not then arise. They then left him, as he felt ashamed to be seen even by his own relations. It was winter and the young man, his rival, who was his cousin, tried all he could to persuade him to go with the family, for it was now winter, but to no purpose, till the whole village had decamped and had gone away. He then rose and gathered all the bits of clothing and ornaments of beads and other things that had been left. He then made a coat and leggings of the same, nicely trimmed with the beads, and the suit was fine and complete. After making a pair of moccasins, nicely trimmed, he also made a bow and arrows. He then collected the dirt of the village and filled the garments he had made, so as to appear as a man, and put the bow and arrows in its hands, and it came to life. He then desired the dirt image to follow him to the camp of those who had left him, who thinking him dead by this time, were surprised to see him. One of the neighbors took in the dirt-man and entertained him. The belle saw them come and immediately fell in love with him. The family that took him in made a large fire to warm him, as it was winter. The image said to one of the children, "sit between me and the fire, it is too hot," and the child did so, but all smelt the dirt. Some said, "some one has trod on and brought in dirt." The master of the family said to the child sitting in front of the guest, "get away from before our guest, you keep the heat from him." The boy answered saying, "he told me to sit between him and the fire." In the meantime, the belle wished the stranger would visit her. The image went to his master and they went out to different lodges, the image going as directed to the belle's. Towards morning, the image said to the young woman (as he had succeeded) "I must now go away," but she said, "I will go with you." He said, "it is too far." She answered, "it is not so far but that I can go with you." He first went to the lodge where he was entertained and then to his master and told him of all that had happened, and that he was going off with her. The young man thought it a pity she had treated him so, and how sadly she would be punished. They went off, she following behind. He left her a great way behind, but she continued to follow him. When the sun rose high, she found one of his mittens and picked it up, but to her astonishment, found it full of dirt. She, however, took it and wiped it, and going on further, she found the other mitten in the same condition. She thought, "fie!! why does he do so," thinking he dirtied in them. She kept finding different articles of his dress on the way all day in the same condition. He kept ahead of her till towards evening when the snow was like water, having melted by the heat of the day. No signs of her husband appearing, after having collected all the cloths that held him together, she began to cry, not knowing where to go as their track was lost on account of the snow's melting. She kept crying Moowis has led me astray, and she kept singing and crying Moowis nin ge won e win ig, ne won i win ig.

MY LOVE HAS DEPARTED

(c. 1907)

Mrs. Mary English

Mangodugwin	A loon
Nindinendum	I thought it was
Wigwenawin	But it was
Ninimuce	My love's
Eniwawasa boyezud	Splashing oar.
Bawiting	To Sault Ste. Marie
Ginamadja	He has departed
Ninimuce	My love
Animadja	Has gone on before me
Kawininawa	Never again
Nindawabamasi	Can I see him

Frances Densmore, the ethomusicologist, collected this song from Mary English in northern Minnesota in the first decade of the twentieth century. Densmore's note accompanying this song reads: "The singer of this song is a sister of William Warren, the historian of the Chippewa. Her family lived on Madeline Island when she was a child, and this song came from there. It is a strange experience to talk with one who remembers when there were only one or two boats on Lake Superior, and who stood on the present site of Duluth when it was peopled only by a few Indians. On one occasion Mr. Warren and his sister, with a party of Chippewa, camped where Duluth now stands. As they were taking their departure Mr. Warren stood beside his canoe on the shore, stretched out his hand over the water, and said, 'Some day this lake will be a highway of water where hundreds of boats will come and go,' then he pointed to the little group of tipis and said, 'My brothers, you and I will never see it, but some day a great city will stand there.' The Indians pointed significantly to their foreheads. Their brother had been too long in the hot sun, and even his sister entered the canoe with a heavy heart."

FROM The Loon Feather
(1940)
Iola Fuller

IOLA FULLER MCCOY (1906-1993) was a Phi Beta Kappa graduate of the University of Michigan whose first novel, *The Loon Feather*, won the University's prestigious Avery Hopwood Award. *The Loon Feather* is the story of Oneta, the daughter of Tecumseh, a great warrior who attempted to organize the scattered Great Lakes tribes to fight the movement of white settlers into the region in the early 1800s. After Tecumseh was killed, Oneta's mother married a French fur trader, Pierre Debans, on Mackinac Island where the new family lived in the Indian settlement. When Oneta's mother died, Pierre brought his mother from Montreal and Oneta's life changed abruptly. The family cabin was abandoned for a French house in town, and she was subsequently sent to Montreal to be educated. The selections included here describe Oneta's feelings as she begins her life in the convent and then when she returns to the island, years later. She eventually marries the young doctor she first met on the ship that returns her to her beloved Mackinac.

Oneta's experiences of being caught between cultures were not uncommon in the Great Lakes region during the fur trade era in the eighteenth and nineteenth centuries. There was much intermarriage between white men and Indian women, and the children of those unions, particularly if the man was wealthy, were frequently sent to private schools in eastern Canada and the United States to be educated after a childhood learning Indian customs. Because Jane Johnston Schoolcraft left no record of her feelings when her father took her away to be educated, we can only surmise what she felt. Like Oneta, that may have been abandonment and trauma, the same later generations of Indian children would experience when forced into government boarding schools in the twentieth century. *The Loon Feather* is interesting not only for its portrayal of Oneta's dilemma, however, but also for its detailed descriptions of the world of the fur trade on the Great Lakes which began in the 1600s and lasted until the mid-nineteenth century.

⇥⊕⇤

Part Three, Chapter One

Early one morning, in a birch canoe swiftly paddled by four Hurons that knew the St. Lawrence like the inside of their own medicine bags, Pierre and

I passed the last of the close-set fences of the ribbon farms stretching back from the river toward the Laurentian hills, and approached Quebec. From many leagues down the river we had seen glistening roofs high on a towering rock—the reflections of bright sunshine on the spires and towers of the upper town. Down to our ears had come the sounds of many bells as the city was called to prayers. I paid no attention to the cluster of buildings along the river below, for I knew I was to go up there among the spires. We came to the wharf among other canoes with paddles, rafts, and heavy-oared craft, and a few boats with flying sails. Still looking up, I saw that around the edge of the rocky height, enclosing those gleaming towers, was a solid wall of stone and wood, with breaks in it only where black cannons poked their muzzles through, or a heavy gate was set in it below a tower.

Pierre and I left the wharf and made our way through a winding street between the irregular old tenements of the lower town and started the ascent of the hill, climbing a narrow pathway broken now and then by steep stairs where the rise was especially abrupt. Mountain Street, Pierre called it, and he followed its zigzag course to the top with the sureness of one whose foot had been often upon it.

At the top, we stood for a moment on the parapet before the arched gate. Wondering whether, once inside that fortress town, I could see flowing water, I leaned over in silent farewell to the sparkling curve of the St. Lawrence, stretching out far below like a sky-tinted highway. I knew it was the outlet for all the great lakes and connecting rivers over which we had traveled eastward from the berry moon to the beginning of the moon of falling leaves, and I thought some of that very water might once have caressed the far-away pebbled shore of Mackinac before our cabin and Marthe's. "Long ago," said Pierre softly, just behind me, "someone called it 'beautiful as the Seine, rapid as the Rhone, and deep as the sea.'" The words meant nothing to me, but somehow in that moment of gazing on the blue water together, I felt closer to Pierre than I had since my mother's death, the approach that ever comes to two souls gazing on the same object with affection.

And then the feeling was gone, and confusion came as Pierre drew me through the broad gate into one of the narrow, irregular streets of the upper town. It rambled here and there like the trail of an aimlessly browsing deer, but it had been a long time, I thought, since any deer had found a path for his foot on this uneven summit. The close-set houses of gray stone or wood, with their tall, steep roofs and tiny dormer windows, had a look of great age about them, and the narrow shops were fronted with crumbling pillars of brick around their doors of time-stained wood. The sidewalks bordering the dirt roadway were of boards laid end to end, with grass growing through where they had rotted away. Tall posts with lamps on top seemed to have grown through the walk in the same fashion.

The spires I had seen from below were on high stone buildings scattered everywhere among the broad roofs of the houses. Pierre pointed them out reverently one after the other, his voice rich with the joy of recognizing old acquaintances—the chateau, the cathedral, the Jesuit college, churches, schools and convents. Twice, as we neared the wall again, he pointed out the rutted dirt roads of St. Louis and St. John passing out through city gates toward near-by, straggling towns.

The bells were still ringing as we walked, and the sounds of chants poured from convent windows—two sounds I hear in memory whenever I think of Quebec. I noticed that Pierre had not pointed out the convent where I was to be left, but I asked no questions, tremulously glad to put off the moment of parting. Each winding street seemed much like the others to me, but each brought new pleasure to Pierre's face with every turn. He pointed out the house where he had lived, the shops of the cobbler who had made his shoes and the tailor who had made his suits, and the great house of the rich man his father had worked for. Once we came out on an open square filled with little tables roofed from the sun and heaped up with vegetables and fruits. Saturday was market day, Pierre told me. Among the tables were French habitants like those I had seen at Detroit, with lively eyes and sunburned skin, long coats of dark gray with hoods to be pulled over their heads when it rained, and drawn in at the waist by a worsted sash of red, orange, or green, and heavily trimmed with beads. Since the day was fair, the hood hung down the back, and on each head a bonnet rouge sat above a long queue of black hair.

As some of the chants came to an end, black-robed men and women began to fill the street, bringing the odor of incense as they passed us. A clamor arose in the market-place as little crowds gathered around the tables to examine the produce. Pierre looked at his big gold watch.

"Come." He turned away from the market-place and set out purposefully on a street marked "St. Anne's" that led toward the end of town far back on the heights, where we turned on Des Jardins Street. In silence Pierre walked along past the houses until he came to a high picket fence enclosing a stretch of rising ground at the top of which I saw, high-perched, a long, plain building of brick and stone.

"This is the convent of the Ursuline nuns," said Pierre. He opened a little gate and we went through and ascended the path to the low arched doorway. The heavy door grated on its hinges, and an old man with a short beard, whom I came to know later as the porter, faced us in the opening.

"I am Pierre Debans. I should like to speak to the Superior."

The porter nodded, and motioned for us to follow him. Pierre took off his high beaver hat and we went inside. The old man led us through a dim corridor into a small room with walls and ceiling darkened by smoke. He pointed to a bench where we could sit and wait.

Trying to hide the choked feeling those plain walls gave me, avoiding the pity and something like regret I saw rising in Pierre's eyes, I stared at the floor sparsely covered by braided rugs of black and gray. On the largest one, just across the room from me, sat a chair before a grille in the wall separating the little parlor from another enclosure beyond. As I looked, a woman in billowing black robes and a white coif about her face entered that enclosure. Pierre rose, and as the nun seated herself close to the grille-work, he took the chair on our side of it, and they began to talk through the opening. I watched the sunlight from a high window play on the blue cloth of Pierre's shoulders, the smooth brown waves of his hair, and throw shadows of the grille on the nun's white coif and tranquil face framed in the fullness of her black dress and veil. I heard their voices dully, while I tried to repress the panic, the desire to run out of this place where there was so little light, to force my way out of all the doors between me and the air, to find a place where there were no walls, no corridors and heavy doors, where only a swaying blanket hung between me and the friendly woods.

I heard the nun tell Pierre that he need not pay for my necessities, since it was for the teaching of Indian girls that Mere Marie had long ago brought her band of nuns to begin the convent in the new world. I heard Pierre's voice saying that this was a special case, that he was responsible for me and would pay whatever the parents of the French girls did. After that, I understood dimly that Pierre was trying to reassure himself that he was doing right to leave me there.

"I hope she will not be unhappy here. My mother thought it was the best place to have her taught."

"Madame votre mére was right. All the efforts of the Ursuline order are devoted to the teaching of young girls in Christian doctrine and the conduct suited to their sex. We care for their bodies and nurture their souls, like true and loving mothers." The nun sounded as if she were reciting.

"I do not doubt that," said Pierre. "It is well known how the Ursulines have given their whole soul and effort to the work here for nearly two hundred years. But you may need much patience at first with Oneta. She has never known anything about regularity and formal training." He sent a worried look to where I sat motionless on the bench.

The nun smiled, but the change brought no softness to a face firm of character and clear of purpose. "Put your mind at ease, sir. She will soon be contented here. We teach by the value of good example, and our discipline is mild. Now," she went on, business-like, "we require that girls be at least six years old and know their alphabets when we take them. This girl is well above the age—"

"I am sorry to say that she can neither write nor read French," said Pierre, "but she speaks it well, and she is very quick. She has a truthful, dependable character."

The nun looked at me thoughtfully. "I think we can admit her. It will not be long before she makes up the lack. Our instruction will fit her case very well, for it is all individual or in very small groups. She can progress as fast as she wants to. I shall ask Sister Celeste to devote all her time to your ward until she can take her place with the others."

She rose and looked at me. Mildly severe, as one at all times intent on the duty of the moment, she spoke. "Come, Oneta." She pointed toward a little door in the corner of the room.

Pierre crossed the room and took my hand, and I stood up.

"You will like it here when you are used to it." A question hovered about his words.

I could find nothing to say. The nun, complacent and heavy, had opened the door. She stood waiting beyond it, and Pierre let my hand slip from his, as if I had already been removed beyond his control.

I do not remember that I said good-by, or turned to watch him go. I went through the door and the nun closed it. The lock snapped into place behind me with a sound of finality. I followed those gently swaying black skirts into a long hallway, cold, bare, excessively clean, but full of the odor of stale incense. Around a turn, we met a procession of nuns, chanting and walking two by two. Seemingly all alike in their full black robes, they looked like an army against me. I pressed close to the wall as they passed. I know now that their chants were in Latin, but then the sounds only alarmed me as one more unfamiliar thing, and I believe there is nothing that makes one feel more alone than hearing words from human lips fall strange upon the ear. I felt like one lost in a bewildering land with no blazed trail to guide him.

The nun I had been following did not pause or turn around, even though she must have known that I had stopped and had to run to catch up. Up a flight of stairs we went, and then another, and down a hollow-sounding corridor. Around a dark corner at the end, the nun opened a door, and we were in a large room with two long rows of beds stretching across toward high windows at the far end.

"This is the dormitory. The other girls are at breakfast," said the nun gently. "I shall let you rest here alone for a time. In a half-hour, a tray of food will be brought up to you. A little later, Sister Celeste will come, and give you a short reading lesson, and begin your instruction in prayers. Tomorrow you will begin with the regular order of the day."

I was obedient because there was nothing else to be. When she had gone, I lay on the white spread of the iron cot, looking at the walls so determinedly closing me in, and thought of how far I had come from the lodge-days. I felt like a plant uprooted and thrown to lie on strange ground, withering and feeling its roots parched by wind and sun, not knowing whether there is strength enough in them to reach down into cool earth again. Pierre had seemed dismayed at the bareness, but it was not that which depressed me. It was the lack of color. I thought how strangely uniform were the black and white of the nuns' garb, the gray of the stone and the braided rugs. Strange to my eyes, used to the hues of green trees and blue water, of purple and yellow and red flowers on hillsides and river banks, bright palpitating colors repeated in the bright wool coats and sashes of the voyageur, and the embroidery on the garments of braves and women, animated and vivid to match the life that went with them.

The nun had left the door open, and I could hear matin-chants faintly from a chapel. The words came softly through the resonant halls, ". . . from anger and hatred and every evil will, O Lord, deliver us . . . lift our minds . . . we beseech Thee . . . deliver our souls. . . grant eternal rest. . . ." The sound echoed on, down the corridor as if it would leave no space unfilled, and then all was still, as if all life had ceased. But at least I had no fear of silence. It was natural to my people, who knew better than others what wondrous things took place in it. No shouts or beat of drums announced the opening of a bud to full bloom, a blade of grass pushing through the earth, or the morning return of the sun. A little flicker of light passed over the window nearest me, as some branch outside moved in the wind. The sun is in his place, I thought, and tried to hold fast to the tiny comfort. The sun will come up tomorrow. At last I closed my eyes and slept like a tired voyageur.

Beginning the order of the day the nun had spoken of, I was amazed that every moment from rising at 5:30 to bed at 8:00 was parceled out for a definite purpose. There is no chance that I will ever forget that order, forced gently but relentlessly upon me for twelve years. Toilette and morning prayers were followed by mass and then breakfast. At the sound of a bell, we marched two by two in silence to class, curtseying to the nuns who opened the doors. In the classroom, gray and bare except for a religious picture in front, and benches and tables scattered about the uneven floor, we curtseyed again to the class mistress, and took our places, kneeling at our benches for morning prayer, with one of the older girls leading. Then we rose, curtseyed to the mistress and sat upon the bench. Every morning we had reading lessons, and I had mine alone with the aged, thin Sister Celeste, while most of the others recited together. Now and again a nun would appear in the doorway, and a small group of girls would rise, curtsey, and go out two by two after her to another room for writing lessons, to return an hour later and resume reading, while another group went out.

After dinner, we were allowed to walk in the grounds, or play battledore and shuttlecock or bowls, but if the weather was bad we stayed indoors and played chess. When time was up, we went to our places, knelt and recited the Litany of the Blessed Virgin. Catechism came next, followed by our second lesson in reading, with groups leaving for arithmetic as they had for writing in the morning. At the end of the day we had a quarter hour for examen of conscience, and another nun instructed us in the catechism. Then supper, recreation, prayers and bed.

All was senseless and confused at first. To me a prayer meant a dance of invocation, of petition for rain, for game, or for a good crop of corn. I could see that here I was asked to substitute other symbols for the ones I knew, and, guided by the gentle teachings and repressions of Sister Celeste, I put up with the inconvenience in the same way I accepted shoes instead of moccasins. The fussing about the right way to make the sign of the cross, the insistence on exact wordage in catechism answers, seemed to me childish, but any idea of revolting was repressed—not from fear, but with a dread of the special attention the unruly girls received. I wanted to be let alone as much as I could be, to wait out my time. I do not believe the nuns felt I was a very difficult girl to teach. In childhood I had been taught that inattention to a speaker was unpardonable, and they took my politeness for interest.

Slowly I made friends with the other girls, mostly French with a few Iroquois and Hurons among them, and here and there a French girl who had borrowed something from a half-Iroquois grandmother—a special straightness of the hair, a way of keeping her feelings to herself, a way of not looking straight at you to offend. Since they were not of my tribe, I felt little more akin to the other Indian girls there than to the French, but they had at least prepared the way so no special curiosity was directed at me.

When I began to learn English, I started writing in a composition book the unusual happenings of each day. If the dullness and coldness around me failed to give me words to put down, I tried reviving memories of my childhood, and set down here and there a legend. Only once did I tell one of these stories to the others. It happened when I was eighteen, after I had been at the convent six years. Whenever our morning and afternoon lessons were done, we always took up some handwork and sat quietly over it at our benches. That particular day was so fair that the nun took us out of doors and we sat under a tree in the convent court, our hands variously busy with knitting, mending, embroidery on muslin or silk, or making of flowers in cloth and wire. As we worked the nun read aloud an instructive story, but in the midst of it, another nun came and called her away inside, and we were left with one of the older girls in charge. It chanced to be Annette, special friend of mine, a solid girl with copper lights in her hair.

"We shall tell stories," she said. "It is your turn, Oneta."

Instead of repeating some story that had been read to us, as we usually did, I began one of Marthe's.

"Long ago a woman of my tribe fell in love with the morning star. She sat in adoration whenever he shone in the sky. All her people told her how foolish she was, for the star was distant and could never be approached. But in secret she went on loving him.

"One day when she went to the river for water, she saw a handsome young man on its banks. 'I am the morning star,' he told her. 'I have come to take you to my home in the sky.' She trembled, for she knew this must be a god, but he took her by the hand, and they rose to the sky-country, to his great and shining lodge, and they dwelt there in content and happiness."

I paused to break off a thread in my sewing, and Annette leaned forward. "Is that all? Did she never want to go home?"

"Yes. She became at last sad and homesick, and returned to earth like a falling star."

"Was she happy then?" asked another of the girls.

"No. Happiness never came back again. As much as she might stretch her arms to the eastern sky, morning star could not take her back. She was forever shut out of the sky-country."

Tears came to my eyes, and I wiped them away, ashamed because I did not know why they were there, and I bent low over my sewing. The others fell to talking of the legend, and then of men—the men they would like to marry. They chattered like a tree-full of birds making plans for a long flight, as they variously praised a good habitant farmer, a trader, a government official.

"You have not told us what kind of man you would like to marry, Oneta," said Annette at last.

Strangely stirred, I lifted my eyes and told of the prophecy at my birth.

"A chief or a medicine man it must be," said one of the Iroquois girls when I had finished. "Only such men are greater than a warrior."

⊷⊱◉⊰⊶

Chapter Two

Detroit in 1830, seen from the water, was a little settlement clustering about a fort high on the river bank, with pigs wandering about its unpaved streets among people on foot and in wagons and carriages. Above the noise of a general bustle came the shouts of chimney-sweeps and itinerant locksmiths calling their trades, and the bells of ragmen's carts. . . .

The *North Star* fired a small cannon to give notice of its arrival. Ropes made it fast at the busy wharf, and the gangplank was put down. As over a bridge to an unknown world, settlers' families began to flow across it, huddling together, the mothers carrying the smallest children and moving on toward a new life with a courage that could not quite cover the dread in their eyes. Leaving them, I made my way through the piles of freight already being unloaded, picking my footing around barrels and bags, plows, pigs, and crates of chickens. . . . There was a schooner at anchor, and passengers were going aboard. I wondered if by any chance it were sailing north. Inquiring, I was told by a deck hand that I was just in luck. The *Andrew Jackson* was loading for Mackinac.

Within an hour all the passengers were aboard and we had left the wharf. Once beyond the town, the captain used all his skill to keep us off the St. Clair Flats that often caught and held vessels for days before they could be pulled loose. Across the smooth, broad basin of Lake St. Clair we sailed, and through the swift water above, until the lake of the Hurons came from the farthest horizon to meet us. As one clings to the shelter of a wall instead of venturing alone into great space, the schooner sailed up the lake close to the forest rising from the western shore. No storms came to delay us, and at last, on the fourth night, the captain told us that the next morning would find us close to Mackinac.

Perhaps sitting on deck so late that last night, peering ahead and hoping for the sight of familiar land, made me sleep later in the morning than usual. The sun was well up when I awoke, and the other women sharing the cabin had dressed and gone out. By the time I had on my white cotton stockings and my shoes, I knew something was wrong with the ship. Its motion had stopped, as if we were resting like a canoe on glassy water. And yet we were not in a harbor, for there was no noise of embarking, no sound of feet, of the captain shouting orders and the crew springing to obey. I put on my gray dress and my bonnet and went out on deck.

Passengers and crew stood at the rail, looking off, but not as if they were seeing anything in particular. The captain stood at the bow. His usual energetic motion suspended, he leaned against a rope, one foot curled behind him. With him stood a young man I had noticed since the first day out of Detroit. Well-dressed in gray, with a tall gray hat, he had an immaculate look, while most of the men had grown careless in the many days on board. He was a little taller than the captain as they stood there, and he had an arrow-like straightness I had always taken for granted as a child, but had not often seen among white men. With it he had no stiffness like the dignity of Pierre. This young man was lithe and active.

His hair was brown, like Pierre's, but with reddish lights in it in the sun. I had decided that he was handsome, but it was not so much in perfection of features as in a sort of aliveness in his face. He had not shown the bored, idle curiosity of the rest of the passengers at the sights along the way. Whenever something new had appeared on the shore line—a group of lodges, a tree being felled, a brush row burning, a canoe being launched for night fishing with a pine torch in the bow—this young man had hung over the rail with eager interest.

I had wondered a little about him, because he did not seem to belong in any of the regular classes of passengers. He showed only a slight interest in the talk about western lands. Though it was plain that he was well educated, he was not a priest, not a teacher. None of the passengers had been able to find out much about him. I had heard him turn aside their prying questions, seeming to find an amusement in doing it that I was sure covered the same reluctance I felt about satisfying the merely curious.

I hesitated a moment as I saw him there, and then went on to speak to the captain. "What is wrong, please?" My low voice seemed to shake the silence like the beat of a drum.

The captain paused in the act of pulling out his pipe from the side pocket of his blue pea-jacket. "A calm, just a calm," he said mildly, but he sent an impatient glance aloft and began jamming tobacco vengefully into his pipe.

"Can't something be done?"

The captain turned a gray-whiskered face to me. "Nothing but wait, Miss. The sailor hasn't been discovered yet that can do anything about a calm but wait."

I looked out over the water. "Oh—! That's Bois Blanc! Then Mackinac is not far—"

"Nope, not far. But might just as well be a hundred miles unless we get some wind."

"We are degraded, then," I said.

"That's voyageur talk. You from up here?"

"Yes. Mackinac is my home. I haven't been there for twelve years."

"Well, it's too bad you have to wait like this, right on its doorstep. There's something tricky about the winds here between these big lakes. I've been held up as much as a day and a half without a speck of wind. If it wasn't for that mist you could almost see your island."

Something I hadn't thought about for years came into my mind. "Have you offered tobacco to the spirits of the water?"

Some of the near-by passengers laughed, and the captain heard them and scowled. "Have I what?" he asked kindly.

Quite a knot of passengers, having nothing else to do, gathered around. The captain looked up at them from under the greasy rim of his cap.

"It's one of the beliefs I was brought up on," I said simply.

"The French have a belief like that, too," said the young man. His words were eager and yet so polite that they did not seem an intrusion, but he at once bowed and said, "I beg your pardon. Captain, may I have the honor—?"

The captain, caressing his pipe in his hand, introduced us. "Miss, er— Debans, isn't it?—Mr. Martin Reynolds."

The young man bowed again, and beneath his small brown mustache a quick smile came to his lips. "Miss Debans," he said. "Please excuse my joining your conversation so abruptly. I heard about the French custom when I was at Detroit. I had to wait there three days. I wasn't as lucky as you."

So he had noticed me leaving the steamboat and coming on board the schooner.

"I spent a lot of time along Jefferson Street and the docks," he went on. "Picked up some fascinating things there. One of them was that precaution of the French voyageurs—throwing offerings in the water for la vieille—the old woman of the water, who could let them go safely, or turn up all sorts of danger."

"Well, now, I tell ye, I never pass up any chance," said the captain, taking in the attentive passengers out of one corner of his eye. "Might as well be on the safe side." He pulled a huge twist of tobacco from his pocket and tossed it over the rail. The young man smiled at me, as if we shared something the others couldn't understand.

The three of us fell silent. I looked at the heavily wooded Bois Blanc, with no sign of life upon its shaggy shores. Since it had always been full of marshy land and was heavily infested with mosquitoes, no one lived there, and it was not the season for woodchoppers. It was too late for Mackinac people who did their cutting during the winter when wood could be hauled on the ice, and it was not yet time for choppers to be getting wood to make the lyed corn for voyageur rations. As early as this, it was possible not a single boat had returned from the winter's trading. Everything was still, even the clouds hanging motionless above silent dark forests that looked like a double fringe along the rim of the smooth water, reaching as far down into it as they reached toward the sky.

From the shore a single crow arose into the still air and flew toward Round Island beyond. The young man ended our silence.

"A calm doesn't keep him from going where he wants to," he said lightly, his eyes following the deliberation of the bird's flight.

"No," I said. "Did you know that the crow was once as white as snow?"

"No, really?" The young man smiled. "What happened to him?"

"He was caught in a hollow tree with a fire beneath and smoked until he was black."

"Why?"

"Punishment for mischief," I said.

As I spoke I was watching a large birch canoe, one of the thirty-five-foot canot du nord, pushing away from the beach at Bois Blanc where voyageurs from the north often stopped and scraped off their whiskers and put on their best clothes before going on to Mackinac. The men, taking in our situation, looked toward the ship and waved.

"Get out your paddles!" one of them shouted derisively.

"You know what they're sayin'?" asked the captain.

I repeated it in English. The captain grinned, half amused, half annoyed.

More laughing and scornful shouts came toward us, from men glorying in pushing their craft along by the strength of their arms, glad to see a new-fangled usurper of their waters lying helpless. The better to taunt, they swerved from their straight course and came closer to the ship.

How glad I was to see buckskin-fringed arms dipping paddle blades in those waters again! I could count nine men in bright headbands or caps of red wool, gay neckerchiefs, fringes on their arms, and a breadth of striped shirt where their buckskin jackets hung open in front. They were just like men of their occupation had always been, broad in shoulder, stronger in arms than in legs, light in weight, thinner now than they would be after a summer on Mackinac, and with long hair they had let grow as a protection against mosquitoes.

The captain waved a nonchalant salute to them, and I raised my arm in greeting. They were coming nearer, so I could hear them talking among themselves.

"Wonder who the girl is? She looks ver-ree happy," said one of them.

And then in the center of the canoe a voyageur got up so suddenly that the rest let loose a flow of curses. "Sacré diable! Want to spill the whole winter's catch in the water?"

The one who had jumped up paid no attention.

"Oneta! It's Oneta!"

I looked at the gold rings in his ears, and his buckskin coat heavy with beading.

"Don't you know me?" He pulled off the red handkerchief knotted about his head and waved it at me.

"Don't you remember me?" A shock of black curls fell over his forehead.

"Jacques!" I cried.

"Yes, it is Jacques." He laughed, and his white teeth shone in the sunlight. "Coming in from my fifth year in the woods." He said it proudly, paying no attention to the burst of laughter from the other men.

"Oh, Jacques, I'm so glad to see you. I'm so anxious to get to the island—"

He snapped his fingers with sudden thought, and turned to the steersman, a tall, heavy-built man with a crow's feather gleaming black against his red cap—the brigade leader. I could hear Jacques talking to him in a low voice. "Her mother married M'sieu Debans of the fur company, you remember."

The leader finally nodded, and Jacques turned back to me. "Want to ride in with us?"

"Oh, Jacques, could I?"

"Of a certainty. One moment."

Some of the others grumbled a bit. Before getting out at Bois Blanc, they had sat motionless for hours to avoid breaking the bark seams of the canoe. And now here was Jacques leaping up, and then inviting a passenger to jump in from above.

"Never mind," said the steersman. "We are so close we can bail if we crack now." He seemed to be looking for something near his feet.

"You won't need the big sponge," said Jacques. "She was brought up in a canoe." The others looked more closely at my face under the round brim of my bonnet. "An Indian!" I heard them say in wonder.

They lifted their paddles and shot the canoe to the side of the schooner.

"Sure," said the captain. "You go along, Miss. You'll be puttin' your feet under a good dinner-table on Mackinac while we huddle here and wait. I'll bring in your baggage safe and sound when the wind blows up."

Swiftly he uncoiled a rope ladder and lowered it to the canoe. Jacques seized the end, and while the other voyageurs steadied the canoe, I swung down easily, hand over hand—that being easier than using the rungs of the ladder, with my hampering long skirt.

"Well," drawled the captain. "That's darned good, for a girl. Where did you learn to go down a rope like that?"

Jacques answered for me. "On grapevines in the woods."

Then I remembered Mr. Reynolds and realized what he must be thinking. Young gentlemen didn't approve of undignified actions in young ladies. I knew how distressed Pierre would have been if he had seen me. For years at the convent I had been drilled in ladylike behavior. This sudden leap into a boatful of voyageurs was anything but that. Almost against my will I raised my head to see the young man's face.

I found myself looking full into his blue eyes as he leaned over the rail, and what I saw in them was pure admiration and a spirit of fun, as if he were taking part with me in a fascinating adventure.

Jacques had noticed his interest. "Very sorry we can't take any more of you," he said.

The young man laughed. "I'll see you later. I'm going to Mackinac, too. I'm to be the new surgeon at the fort."

The men, occupied in balancing the canoe, sent quick glances upward. They would have plenty to do with the fort doctor before the summer was over, what with one fight and another they were sure to get into.

"Eh bien, glad you're going to be on Mackinac," said Jacques. "It's a great place."

"I can see it is," the young man laughed, looking down at the canoe.

We were pulling away from the schooner's side, and, mindful of not disturbing the balance, I crouched down among the bearskin-covered packs of fur in the center. The steersman took his place in the stern, grasping a paddle longer than the others. Jacques was back in his place, and all the fringed arms were dipping and rising together.

I settled myself among the bundles. A corner of the bearskin over one pack of beaver had slipped away, and I stroked the fur, soft, brown, and with the silky sheen I remembered. My fingertips lingered on its smoothness in sheer delight in its beauty and in being back where such things were a part of life.

I turned to Jacques, as I heard his voice joining in the boat song the men immediately struck up. It was one they used for rapid paddling, for they were near their destination.

> "Derrier' chez nous, y a-t-un etang
> En roulant ma boule
> Trois beaux canadrs s'en vont baignant
> En roulant ma boule
> Rouli, roulant, ma boule roulant,
> En roulant ma boule roulant
> En roulant ma boule,"

they sang and Jacques's voice was as deep as the rest. Even yet I found it hard to believe that he was one of these men. He was still short and stocky, with a face full of expression. At that moment it was of joy, like the faces of all the other men as they swayed, dipping and lifting their paddles—anticipation of the summer they would have on Mackinac, the joy of being at the end of their winter's work, the thought of having money in their pockets, and being where it would buy pleasure. Long-bladed hunting knives shone at their hips, catching reflections of the sun faster and faster as the boat song grew livelier, and the paddles kept up with the rhythm. Gently swaying in the lift of the canoe with each stroke of the paddles, I felt I was in a fur-lined cradle.

"How far have you come today?" I asked Jacques in the first pause of the song.

"Trois pipes," he said. "A short journey."

Three pipes—that was about twelve miles, I remembered. It had been a long time since I had heard distance measured by the intervals of stopping for a five-minute smoke.

"Where did you spend the winter, Jacques? What outfit is this?"

"Tahquamenon River."

"Now, Jacques, your song," said one of the men, and they all laughed. I didn't know why, for it was usual for each man to have his special song in which he led, giving the verse alone, to be repeated in chorus.

"J'aimerai toujours," Jacques began with a full voice, and the men laughed again. "Suppose she's still there?" one of them asked. Jacques went on with the song without answering, and the rest joined in.

"Jacques is in good voice today," jested one when they had finished.

"Yes," agreed another, "he drives everyone else off key."

Jacques paid no attention, as one who knows such aspersions are untrue.

"We wouldn't put up with him at all," commented another, "except for the way he can spot a honey-tree or a turtle to flavor our lyed corn and tallow."

"And who is it that can pull fish from a stream where none of the rest of you can find even a minnow?" demanded Jacques. They laughed.

They pulled up even with Round Island, and passed it. Suddenly the leader called out, "There messieurs, is ze gem of ze lakes."

I sat up, eager for my first glimpse of Mackinac. A little breeze had come up, and was lifting the fog that lay over the island, showing it rising steeply from the water to a height greater even than I remembered. The dense and fleecy mist drifted away, and I saw the white cliffs and green foliage. Other canoes were close around us, the rest of the brigade coming up, but I had no eyes for them. At the same time, near the western point we heard the sound of a musket, and after a pause for reloading, it was fired again.

"Baptiste!" I said.

"Yes, he's seen us," laughed Jacques. "He's announced the first boats that way ever since he's lived on the island."

The men dipped their paddles still faster. I kept my eyes on the village, looking for changes.

"Oh, Jacques—a church, two churches!" I exclaimed at the sight of two white spires pointing upward against the heights, with nearly the width of the village between them, contending with each other and with the flagpole at the fort for one's attention; but all three of them were as nothing as we drew nearer and the huge fur warehouse rose higher and higher before us, casting its shadow over half the settlement.

A RED GIRL'S REASONING

(1893)

Tekahionwake

E. Pauline Johnson

A STAGE PERFORMER, a poet, and a writer, Emily Pauline Johnson was born on the Six Nations Reserve near Brantford, Ontario, in 1861. Her father and grandfather were Mohawk leaders; her mother was English. Johnson adopted her grandfather's name, Tekahionwake, when she began her stage career in 1892 and toured for fifteen years, becoming one of the most popular performers in Canada as she presented dramatic recitations of her poetry and skits about Indian life. When entertaining paled, she turned to writing short stories for boys and women's magazines, continuing her work even after being diagnosed with the inoperable breast cancer that would kill her in 1913. "A Red Girl's Reasoning" was her first published short story and portrays not only the pain experienced by mixed-blood women in white culture, but their strength as well. The "half-breed" was a popular character in late nineteenth-century fiction, but most authors who wrote about mixed-blood persons took pains to be more sentimental or charming than Johnson. Although popular and successful, she had also experienced being marginalized first-hand, and her bitter irony at the hypocrisy of white culture does not spare her readers' feelings.

⋯⊷⊜⊶⋯

"BE PRETTY GOOD to her, Charlie, my boy, or she'll balk sure as shooting."

That was what old Jimmy Robinson said to his brand new son-in-law, while they waited for the bride to reappear.

"Oh! you bet, there's no danger of much else. I'll be good to her, help me Heaven," replied Charlie McDonald, brightly.

"Yes, of course you will," answered the old man, "but don't you forget, there's a good big bit of her mother in her, and," closing his left eye significantly, "you don't understand these Indians as I do."

"But I'm just as fond of them, Mr. Robinson," Charlie said assertively, "and I get on with them too, now, don't I?"

"Yes, pretty well for a town boy; but when you have lived forty years among these people, as I have done; when you have had your wife as long as

I have had mine—for there's no getting over it, Christine's disposition is as native as her mother's, every bit—and perhaps when you've owned for eighteen years a daughter as dutiful, as loving, as fearless, and, alas! as obstinate as that little piece you are stealing away from me to-day—I tell you, youngster, you'll know more than you know now. It is kindness for kindness, bullet for bullet, blood for blood. Remember, what you are, she will be," and the old Hudson Bay trader scrutinized Charlie McDonald's face like a detective.

It was a happy, fair face, good to look at, with a certain ripple of dimples somewhere about the mouth, and eyes that laughed out the very sunniness of their owner's soul. There was not a severe nor yet a weak line anywhere. He was a well meaning young fellow, happily dispositioned, and a great favorite with the tribe at Robinson's Post, whither he had gone in the service of the Department of Agriculture, to assist the local agent through the tedium of a long census-taking.

As a boy he had the Indian relic-hunting craze, as a youth he had studied Indian archaeology and folk-lore, as a man he consummated his predilections for Indianology by loving, winning and marrying the quiet little daughter of the English trader, who himself had married a native woman some twenty years ago. The country was all backwoods, and the Post miles and miles from even the semblance of civilization, and the lonely young Englishman's heart had gone out to the girl who, apart from speaking a very few words of English, was utterly uncivilized and uncultured, but had withal that marvellously innate refinement so universally possessed by the higher tribes of North American Indians.

Like all her race, observant, intuitive, having a horror of ridicule, consequently quick at acquirement and teachable in mental and social habits, she had developed from absolute pagan indifference into a sweet, elderly Christian woman, whose broken English, quiet manner, and still handsome copper-colored face were the joy of old Robinson's declining years.

He had given their daughter Christine all the advantages of his own learning—which, if truthfully told, was not universal; but the girl had a fair common education, and the native adaptability to progress.

She belonged to neither and still to both types of the cultured Indian. The solemn, silent, almost heavy manner of the one so commingled with the gesticulating Frenchiness and vivacity of the other, that one unfamiliar with native Canadian life would find it difficult to determine her nationality.

She looked very pretty to Charles McDonald's loving eyes, as she reappeared in the doorway, holding her mother's hand and saying some happy words of farewell. Personally she looked much the same as her sisters, all Canada through, who are the offspring of red and white parentage—olive-complexioned, grey-eyed, black-haired, with figure slight and delicate, and the wistful, unfathomable expression in her whole face that turns one so heart-sick as they glance at the young Indians of today—it is the forerunner too frequently of "the white man's disease," consumption—but McDonald was pathetically in love, and thought her the most beautiful woman he had ever seen in his life.

There had not been much of a wedding ceremony. The priest had cantered through the service in Latin, pronounced the benediction in English, and congratulated the "happy couple" in Indian, as a compliment to the assembled tribe in the little amateur structure that did service at the post as a sanctuary.

But the knot was tied as firmly and indissolubly as if all Charlie McDonald's swell city friends had crushed themselves up against the chancel to congratulate him, and in his heart he was deeply thankful to escape the flower-pelting, white gloves, rice-throwing, and ponderous stupidity of a breakfast, and indeed all the regulation gimcracks of the usual marriage celebrations, and it was with a hand trembling with absolute happiness that he assisted his little Indian wife into the old muddy buckboard that, hitched to an underbred-looking pony, was to convey them over the first stages of their journey. Then came more adieus, some handclasping, old Jimmy Robinson looking very serious just at the last, Mrs. Jimmy, stout, stolid, betraying nothing of visible emotion, and then the pony, roughshod and shaggy, trudged on, while mutual handwaves were kept up until the old Hudson's Bay Post dropped out of sight, and the buckboard with its lightsome load of hearts, deliriously happy, jogged on over the uneven trail.

She was "all the rage" that winter at the provincial capital. The men called her a "deuced fine little woman." The ladies said she was "just the sweetest wildflower." Whereas she was really but an ordinary, pale, dark girl who spoke slowly and with a strong accent, who danced fairly well, sang acceptably, and never stirred outside the door without her husband.

Charlie was proud of her; he was proud that she had "taken" so well among his friends, proud that she bore herself so complacently in the drawingrooms of the wives of pompous Government officials, but doubly proud of her almost abject devotion to him. If ever human being was worshipped that being was Charlie McDonald; it could scarcely have been otherwise, for the almost godlike strength of his passion for that little wife of his would have mastered and melted a far more invincible citadel than an already affectionate woman's heart.

Favorites socially, McDonald and his wife went everywhere. In fashionable circles she was "new"—a potent charm to acquire popularity, and the little velvet-clad figure was always the centre of interest among all the women in the room. She always dressed in velvet. No woman in Canada, has she but the faintest dash of native blood in her veins, but loves velvets and silks. As beef to the Englishman, wine to the Frenchman, fads to the Yankee, so are velvet and silk to the Indian girl be she wild as prairie grass, be she on the borders of civilization, or, having stepped within its boundary, mounted the steps of culture even under its superficial heights.

"Such a dolling little appil blossom," said the wife of a local M.P., who brushed up her etiquette and English once a year at Ottawa. "Does she always laugh so sweetly, and gobble you up with those great big grey eyes of hers, when you are togetheah at home, Mr. McDonald? If so, I should think youah pooah brothah would feel himself terribly de trop."

He laughed lightly. "Yes, Mrs. Stuart, there are not two of Christie; she is the same at home and abroad, and as for Joe, he doesn't mind us a bit; he's no end fond of her."

"I'm very glad he is. I always fancied he did not care for her, d'you know."

If ever a blunt woman existed it was Mrs. Stuart. She really meant nothing, but her remark bothered Charlie. He was fond of his brother, and jealous for Christie's popularity. So that night when he and Joe were having a pipe he said:

"I've never asked you yet what you thought of her, Joe." A brief pause, then Joe spoke. "I'm glad she loves you."

"Why?"

"Because that girl has but two possibilities regarding humanity—love or hate."

"Humph! Does she love or hate you?"

"Ask her."

"You talk bosh. If she hated you, you'd get out. If she loved you I'd make you get out."

Joe McDonald whistled a little, then laughed.

"Now that we are on the subject, I might as well ask—honestly, old man, wouldn't you and Christie prefer keeping house alone to having me always around?"

"Nonsense, sheer nonsense. Why, thunder, man, Christie's no end fond of you, and as for me—you surely don't want assurances from me?"

"No, but I often think a young couple—"

"Young couple be blowed ! After a while when they want you and your old surveying chains, and spindle-legged tripod telescope kickshaws, farther west, I venture to say the little woman will cry her eyes out—won't you, Christie?"

This last in a higher tone, as through clouds of tobacco smoke he caught sight of his wife passing the doorway.

She entered. "Oh, no, I would not cry; never do cry, but I would be heart-sore to lose you, Joe, and apart from that"—a little wickedly — "you may come in handy for an exchange some day, as Charlie does always say when he hoards up duplicate relics."

"Are Charlie and I duplicates?"

"Well—not exactly"—her head a little to one side, and eyeing them both merrily, while she slipped softly on to the arm of her husband's chair— "but, in the event of Charlie's failing me"—everyone laughed then. The "some day" that she spoke of was nearer than they thought. It came about in this wise.

There was a dance at the Lieutenant-Governor's, and the world and his wife were there. The nobs were in great feather that night, particularly the women, who flaunted about in new gowns and much splendor. Christie McDonald had a new gown also, but wore it with the utmost unconcern, and if she heard any of the flattering remarks made about her she at least appeared to disregard them.

"I never dreamed you could wear blue so splendidly," said Captain Logan, as they sat out a dance together.

"Indeed she can, though," interposed Mrs. Stuart, halting in one of her gracious sweeps down the room with her husband's private secretary.

"Don't shout so, captain. I can hear every sentence you uttah—of course Mrs. McDonald can wear blue—she has a morning gown of cadet blue that she is a picture in."

"You are both very kind," said Christie. "I like blue; it is the color of all the Hudson's Bay posts, and the factor's residence is always decorated in blue."

"Is it really? How interesting—do tell us some more of your old home, Mrs. McDonald; you so seldom speak of your life at the post, and we fellows so often wish to hear of it all," said Logan eagerly.

"Why do you not ask me of it, then?"

"Well—er, I'm sure I don't know; I'm fully interested in the Ind—in your people—your mother's people, I mean, but it always seems so personal, I suppose; and—a—a—"

"Perhaps you are, like all other white people, afraid to mention my nationality to me."

The captain winced, and Mrs. Stuart laughed uneasily. Joe McDonald was not far off, and he was listening, and chuckling, and saying to himself, "That's you, Christie, lay 'em out; it won't hurt 'em to know how they appear once in a while."

"Well, Captain Logan," she was saying, "what is it you would like to hear—of my people, or my parents, or myself?"

"All, all, my dear," cried Mrs. Stuart clamorously. "I'll speak for him—tell us of yourself and your mother—your father is delightful, I am sure but then he is only an ordinary Englishman, not half as interesting as a foreigner, or—or, perhaps I should say, a native."

Christie laughed. "Yes," she said, "my father often teases my mother now about how very native she was when he married her; then, how could she have been otherwise? She did not know a word of English, and there was not another English-speaking person besides my father and his two companions within sixty miles."

"Two companions, eh? one a Catholic priest and the other a wine merchant, I suppose, and with your father in the Hudson's Bay, they were good representatives of the pioneers in the New World," remarked Logan, waggishly.

"Oh, no, they were all Hudson's Bay men. There were no rumsellers and no missionaries in that part of the country then."

Mrs. Stuart looked puzzled. *"No missionaries?"* she repeated with an odd intonation.

Christie's insight was quick. There was a peculiar expression of interrogation in the eyes of her listeners, and the girl's blood leapt angrily up into her temples as she said hurriedly, "I know what you mean; I know what you are thinking. You are wondering how my parents were married—"

"Well—er, my dear, it seems peculiar—if there was no priest, and no magistrate, why—a—" Mrs. Stuart paused awkwardly.

"The marriage was performed by Indian rites," said Christie.

"Oh, do tell me about it; is the ceremony very interesting and quaint— are your chieftains anything like Buddhist priests?" It was Logan who spoke.

"Why, no," said the girl in amazement at that gentleman's ignorance. "There is no ceremony at all, save a feast. The two people just agree to live only with and for each other, and the man takes his wife to his home, just as you do. There is no ritual to bind them; they need none; an Indian's word was his law in those days, you know."

Mrs. Stuart stepped backwards. "Ah!" was all she said. Logan removed his eye-glass and stared blankly at Christie. "And did McDonald marry you in this singular fashion?" he questioned.

"Oh, no, we were married by Father O'Leary. Why do you ask?"

"Because if he had, I'd have blown his brains out to-morrow."

Mrs. Stuart's partner, who had hitherto been silent, coughed and began to twirl his cuff stud nervously, but nobody took any notice of him. Christie had risen, slowly, ominously—risen, with the dignity and pride of an empress.

"Captain Logan," she said, "what do you dare to say to me? What do you dare to mean? Do you presume to think it would not have been lawful for Charlie to marry me according to my people's rites? Do you for one instant dare to question that my parents were not as legally—"

"Don't, dear, don't," interrupted Mrs. Stuart hurriedly; "it is bad enough now, goodness knows; don't make—" Then she broke off blindly. Christie's eyes glared at the mumbling woman, at her uneasy partner, at the horrified captain. Then they rested on the McDonald brothers, who stood within ear-shot, Joe's face scarlet, her husband's white as ashes, with something in his eyes she had never seen before. It was Joe who saved the situation. Stepping quickly across towards his sister-in-law, he offered her his arm, saying, "The next dance is ours, I think, Christie."

Then Logan pulled himself together, and attempted to carry Mrs. Stuart off for the waltz, but for once in her life that lady had lost her head. "It is shocking!" she said, "outrageously shocking! I wonder if they told Mr. McDonald before he married her!" Then looking hurriedly round, she too saw the young husband's face and knew that they had not.

"Humph! deuced nice kettle of fish—poor old Charlie has always thought so much of honorable birth."

Logan thought he spoke in an undertone, but "poor old Charlie" heard him. He followed his wife and brother across the room. "Joe," he said, "will you see that a trap is called?" Then to Christie, "Joe will see that you get home all right." He wheeled on his heel then and left the ball-room.

Joe *did* see.

He tucked a poor, shivering, pallid little woman into a cab, and wound her bare throat up in the scarlet velvet cloak that was hanging uselessly over her arm. She crouched down beside him, saying, "I am so cold, Joe; I am so cold," but she did not seem to know enough to wrap herself up. Joe felt all through this long drive that nothing this side of Heaven would be so good as to die, and he was glad when the poor little voice at his elbow said, "What is he so angry at, Joe?"

"I don't know exactly, dear," he said gently, "but I think it was what you said about this Indian marriage."

"But why should I not have said it? Is there anything wrong about it?" she asked pitifully.

"Nothing, that I can see—there was no other way; but Charlie is very angry, and you must be brave and forgiving with him, Christie, dear."

"But I did never see him like that before, did you?"

"Once."

"When?"

"Oh, at college, one day, a boy tore his prayerbook in half, and threw it into the grate, just to be mean, you know. Our mother had given it to him at his confirmation."

"And did he look so?"

"About, but it all blew over in a day—Charlie's tempers are short and brisk. Just don't take any notice of him; run off to bed, and he'll have forgotten it by the morning."

They reached home at last. Christie said goodnight quietly, going directly to her room. Joe went to his room also, filled a pipe and smoked for an hour. Across the passage he could hear her slippered feet pacing up and down, up and down the length of her apartment. There was something panther-like in those restless footfalls, a meaning velvetyness that made him shiver, and again he wished he were dead—or elsewhere.

After a time the hall door opened, and someone came upstairs, along the passage, and to the little woman's room. As he entered, she turned and faced him.

"Christie," he said harshly, "do you know what you have done?"

"Yes," taking a step nearer him, her whole soul springing up into her eyes, "I have angered you, Charlie, and—"

"Angered me? You have disgraced me; and, moreover, you have disgraced yourself and both your parents."

"Disgraced?"

"Yes, disgraced; you have literally declared to the whole city that your father and mother were never married, and that you are the child of—what shall we call it—love? certainly not legality."

Across the hallway sat Joe McDonald, his blood freezing; but it leapt into every vein like fire at the awful anguish in the little voice that cried simply, "Oh! Charlie!"

"How could you do it, how could you do it, Christie, without shame either for yourself or for me, let alone your parents?"

The voice was like an angry demon's—not a trace was there in it of the yellow-haired, blue-eyed, laughing-lipped boy who had driven away so gaily to the dance five hours before.

"Shame? Why should I be ashamed of the rites of my people any more than you should be ashamed of the customs of yours—of a marriage more sacred and holy than half of your white man's mockeries?"

It was the voice of another nature in the girl—the love and the pleading were dead in it.

"Do you mean to tell me, Charlie—you who have studied my race and their laws for years—do you mean to tell me that, because there was no priest and no magistrate, my mother was not married? Do you mean to say that all my forefathers, for hundreds of years back, have been illegally born? If so, you blacken my ancestry beyond—beyond—beyond all reason."

"No, Christie, I would not be so brutal as that; but your father and mother live in more civilized times. Father O'Leary has been at the post for nearly twenty years. Why was not your father straight enough to have the ceremony performed when he did get the chance?"

The girl turned upon him with the face of a fury. "Do you suppose," she almost hissed, "that my mother would be married according to your white rites after she had been five years a wife, and I had been born in the meantime? *No*, a thousand times I say, *no*. When the priest came with his notions of Christianizing, and talked to them of re-marriage by the Church, my mother arose and said, "Never—never—I have never had but this one husband; he has had none but me for wife, and to have you re-marry us would be to say as much to the whole world as that we had never been married before. You go away; I do not ask that *your* people be re-married; talk not so to me. I *am* married, and you or the Church cannot do or undo it."

"Your father was a fool not to insist upon the law, and so was the priest."

"Law? *My* people have *no* priest, and my nation cringes not to law. Our priest is purity, and our law is honor. Priest? Was there a *priest* at the most holy marriage known to humanity—that stainless marriage whose offspring is the God you white men told my pagan mother of?"

"Christie—you are *worse* than blasphemous; such a profane remark shows how little you understand the sanctity of the Christian faith—"

"I know what I *do* understand; it is that you are hating me because I told some of the beautiful customs of my people to Mrs. Stuart and those men."

"Pooh! who cares for them? It is not them; the trouble is they won't keep their mouths shut. Logan's a cad and will toss the whole tale about at the club before tomorrow night; and as for the Stuart woman, I'd like to know how I'm going to take you to Ottawa for presentation and the opening, while she is blabbing the whole miserable scandal in every drawing-room, and I'll be pointed out as a romantic fool, and you—as worse; I *can't* understand why your father didn't tell me before we were married; I at least might have warned you to never mention it." Something of recklessness rang up through his voice, just as the panther-likeness crept up from her footsteps and couched itself in hers. She spoke in tones quiet, soft, deadly.

"Before we were married! Oh! Charlie, would it have—made—any—difference?"

"God knows," he said, throwing himself into a chair, his blonde hair rumpled and wet. It was the only boyish thing about him now.

She walked towards him, then halted in the centre of the room. "Charlie McDonald," she said, and it was as if a stone had spoken, "look up." He raised his head, startled by her tone. There was a threat in her eyes that, had his rage been less courageous, his pride less bitterly wounded, would have cowed him.

"There was no such time as that before our marriage, for *we are not married now*. Stop," she said, outstretching her palms against him as he sprang to his feet, "I tell you we are not married. Why should I recognize the rites of your nation when you do not acknowledge the rites of mine? According to your own words, my parents should have gone through your church ceremony as well as through an Indian contract; according to my words, we should go through an Indian contract as well as through a church marriage.

If their union is illegal, so is ours. If you think my father is living in dishonor with my mother, my people will think I am living in dishonor with you. How do I know when another nation will come and conquer you as you white men conquered us? And they will have another marriage rite to perform, and they will tell us another truth, that you are not my husband, that you are but disgracing and dishonoring me, that you are keeping me here, not as your wife, but as your—your *squaw*."

The terrible word had never passed her lips before, and the blood stained her face to her very temples. She snatched off her wedding ring and tossed it across the room, saying scornfully, "That thing is as empty to me as the Indian rites to you."

He caught her by the wrists; his small white teeth were locked tightly, his blue eyes blazed into hers.

"Christine, do you dare to doubt my honor towards you? *You*, whom I should have died for; do you dare to think I have kept you here, not as my wife, but—"

"Oh, God! You are hurting me; you are breaking my arm," she gasped.

The door was flung open, and Joe McDonald's sinewy hands clinched like vices on his brother's shoulders.

"Charlie, you're mad, mad as the devil. Let go of her this minute."

The girl staggered backwards as the iron fingers loosed her wrists. "Oh, Joe," she cried, "I am not his wife, and he says I am born—nameless."

"Here," said Joe, shoving his brother towards the door. "Go downstairs till you can collect your senses. If ever a being acted like an infernal fool, you're the man."

The young husband looked from one to the other, dazed by his wife's insult, abandoned to a fit of ridiculously childish temper. Blind as he was with passion, he remembered long afterwards seeing them standing there, his brother's face darkened with a scowl of anger—his wife, clad in the mockery of her ball dress, her scarlet velvet cloak half covering her bare brown neck and arms, her eyes like flames of fire, her face like a piece of sculptured greystone.

Without a word he flung himself furiously from the room, and immediately afterwards they heard the heavy hall door bang behind him.

"Can I do anything for you, Christie?" asked her brother-in-law calmly.

"No, thank you—unless—I think I would like a drink of water, please."

He brought her up a goblet filled with wine; her hand did not even tremble as she took it. As for Joe, a demon arose in his soul as he noticed she kept her wrists covered.

"Do you think he will come back?" she said.

"Oh, yes, of course; he'll be all right in the morning. Now go to bed like a good little girl, and—and, I say, Christie, you can call me if you want anything; I'll be right here, you know."

"Thank you, Joe; you are kind—and good."

He returned then to his apartment. His pipe was out, but he picked up a newspaper instead, threw himself into an armchair, and in a halfhour was in the land of dreams.

When Charlie came home in the morning, after a six-mile walk into the country and back again, his foolish anger was dead and buried. Logan's "Poor old Charlie" did not ring so distinctly in his ears. Mrs. Stuart's horrified expression had faded considerably from his recollection. He thought only of that surprisingly tall, dark girl, whose eyes looked like coals, whose voice pierced him like a flint-tipped arrow. Ah, well, they would never quarrel again like that, he told himself. She loved him so, and would forgive him after he had talked quietly to her, and told her what an ass he was. She was simple-minded and awfully ignorant to pitch those old Indian laws at him in her fury, but he could not blame her; oh, no, he could not for one moment blame her. He had been terribly severe and unreasonable, and the horrid McDonald temper had got the better of him; and he loved her so. Oh! he loved her so! She would surely feel that, and forgive him, and— He went straight to his wife's room. The blue velvet evening dress lay on the chair into which he had thrown himself when he doomed his life's happiness by those two words, "God knows." A bunch of dead daffodils and her slippers were on the floor, everything—but Christie.

He went to his brother's bedroom door.

"Joe," he called, rapping nervously thereon; "Joe, wake up; where's Christie, d'you know?"

"Good Lord, no," gasped that youth, springing out of his armchair and opening the door. As he did so a note fell from off the handle. Charlie's face blanched to his very hair while Joe read aloud, his voice weakening at every word:

"*Dear old Joe* —I went into your room at daylight to get that picture of the Post on your bookshelves. I hope you do not mind, but I kissed your hair while you slept; it was so curly, and yellow, and soft, just like his. Good-bye, Joe.

"*Christie*"

And when Joe looked into his brother's face and saw the anguish settle in those laughing blue eyes, the despair that drove the dimples away from that almost girlish mouth; when he realized that this boy was but four-and-twenty years old, and that all his future was perhaps darkened and shadowed forever, a great, deep sorrow arose in his heart, and he forgot all things, all but the agony that rang up through the voice of the fair, handsome lad as he staggered forward, crying, "Oh! Joe what shall I do—what shall I do?"

It was months and months before he found her, but during all that time he had never known a hopeless moment; discouraged he often was, but despondent, never. The sunniness of his ever boyish heart radiated with a warmth that would have flooded a much deeper gloom than that which settled within his eager young life. Suffer? ah! yes, he suffered, not with locked teeth and stony stoicism, not with the masterful self-command, the reserve, the conquered bitterness of the stillwater sort of nature, that is supposed to run to such depths. He tried to be bright, and his sweet old boyish self. He would laugh sometimes in a pitiful, pathetic fashion. He took to petting dogs, looking into their large, solemn eyes with his wistful, questioning blue ones; he would kiss them, as women sometimes do, and call them "dear old fellow," in tones that had tears; and once in the course of his travels, while at a little way-station, he discovered a huge St. Bernard imprisoned by some mischance in an empty freight car; the animal was nearly dead from starvation, and it seemed to salve his own sick heart to rescue back the dog's life. Nobody claimed the big starving creature, the train hands knew nothing of its owner, and gladly handed it over to its deliverer. "Hudson," he called it, and afterwards when Joe McDonald would relate the story of his brother's life he invariably terminated it with, "And I really believe that big lumbering brute saved him." From what, he was never known to say.

But all things end, and he heard of her at last. She had never returned to the Post, as he at first thought she would, but had gone to the little town of B——, in Ontario, where she was making her living at embroidery and plain sewing.

The September sun had set redly when at last he reached the outskirts of the town, opened up the wicket gate, and walked up the weedy, unkept path leading to the cottage where she lodged.

Even through the twilight, he could see her there, leaning on the rail of the veranda—oddly enough she had about her shoulders the scarlet velvet cloak she wore when he had flung himself so madly from the room that night.

The moment the lad saw her his heart swelled with a sudden heat, burning moisture leapt into his eyes, and clogged his long, boyish lashes. He bounded up the steps— "Christie," he said, and the word scorched his lips like audible flame.

She turned to him, and for a second stood magnetized by his passionately wistful face; her peculiar greyish eyes seemed to drink the very life of his unquenchable love, though the tears that suddenly sprang into his seemed to absorb every pulse in his body through those hungry, pleading eyes of his that had, oh! so often, been blinded by her kisses when once her whole world lay in their blue depths.

"You will come back to me, Christie, my wife? My wife, you will let me love you again?"

She gave a singular little gasp, and shook her head. "Don't, oh! don't," he cried piteously. "You will come to me, dear? it is all such a bitter mistake—I did not understand. Oh! Christie, I did not understand, and you'll forgive me, and love me again, won't you—won't you?"

"No," said the girl with quick, indrawn breath.

He dashed the back of his hand across his wet eyelids. His lips were growing numb, and he bungled over the monosyllable "Why?"

"I do not like you," she answered quietly.

"God! Oh! God, what is there left?"

She did not appear to hear the heart-break in his voice; she stood like one wrapped in sombre thought; no blaze, no tear, nothing in her eyes; no hardness, no tenderness about her mouth. The wind was blowing her cloak aside, and the only visible human life in her whole body was once when he spoke the muscles of her brown arm seemed to contract

"But, darling, you are mine—mine—we are husband and wife! Oh, heaven, you must love me, you must come to me again."

"You cannot make me come," said the icy voice, "neither church, nor law, nor even"—and the voice softened— "nor even love can make a slave of a red girl."

"Heaven forbid it," he faltered. "No, Christie, I will never claim you without your love. What reunion would that be? But, oh, Christie, you are lying to me, you are lying to yourself, you are lying to heaven."

She did not move. If only he could touch her he felt as sure of her yielding as he felt sure there was a hereafter. The memory of times when he had but to lay his hand on her hair to call a most passionate response from her filled his heart with a torture that choked all words before they reached his lips; at the thought of those days he forgot she was unapproachable, forgot how forbidding were her eyes, how stony her lips. Flinging himself forward, his knee on the chair at her side, his face pressed hardly in the folds of the cloak on her shoulder, he clasped his arms about her with a boyish petu-lance, saying, "Christie, Christie, my little girl wife, I love you, I love you, and you are killing me."

She quivered from head to foot as his fair, wavy hair brushed her neck, his despairing face sank lower until his cheek, hot as fire, rested on the cool, olive flesh of her arm. A warm moisture oozed up through her skin, and as he felt its glow he looked up. Her teeth, white and cold, were locked over her under lip, and her eyes were as grey stones.

Not murderers alone know the agony of a death sentence.

"Is it all useless? all useless, dear?" he said, with lips starving for hers.

"All useless," she repeated. "I have no love for you now. You forfeited me and my heart months ago, when you said *those two words*."

His arms fell away from her wearily, he arose mechanically, he placed his little grey checked cap on the back of his yellow curls, the old-time laughter was dead in the blue eyes that now looked scared and haunted, the boyish-ness and the dimples crept away forever from the lips that quivered like a child's; he turned from her, but she had looked once into his face as the Law Giver must have looked at the land of Canaan outspread at his feet. She watched him go down the long path and through the picket gate, she watched the big yellowish dog that had waited for him lumber up to its feet—stretch—then follow him. She was conscious of but two things, the vengeful lie in her soul, and a little space on her arm that his wet lashes had brushed.

It was hours afterwards when he reached his room. He had said nothing, done nothing—what use were words or deeds? Old Jimmy Robinson was right; she had "balked" sure enough.

What a bare, hotelish room it was! He tossed off his coat and sat for ten minutes looking blankly at the sputtering gas jet. Then his whole life, deso-late as a desert, loomed up before him with appalling distinctness. Throwing himself on the floor beside his bed, with clasped hands and arms outstretched on the white counterpane, he sobbed. "Oh! God, dear God, I thought you loved me; I thought you'd let me have her again, but you must be tired of me, tired of loving me, too. I've nothing left now, nothing! It doesn't seem that I even have you to-night."

He lifted his face then, for his dog, big and clumsy and yellow, was lick-ing at his sleeve.

LAKE OF DREAMS

(1997)

Susan Power

A MEMBER OF the Standing Rock Souix tribe, Susan Power's (1961-) first novel, *The Grass Dancer* (1994), won the 1995 PEN/Hemingway Award for first fiction. In this autobiographical essay about growing up in Chicago, Power expresses well the relationship of mingled love and respect for the waters of the Great Lakes that many know. Describing herself as a "small, anonymous fish," her memoir traces how she became baptized in, and finally a part of, the waters she loves.

⋯⊨⊕⊜⊨⋯

MY MOTHER USED to say that by the time I was an old woman, Lake Michigan would be the size of a silver dollar. She pinched her index finger with her thumb to show me the pitiful dimensions. "People will gather around the tiny lake, what's left of it, and cluck over a spoonful of water," she told me.

I learned to squint at the 1967 shoreline until I had carved away the structures and roads built on landfill and could imagine the lake and its city as my mother found them in 1942 when she arrived in Chicago. I say "the lake and its city" rather than "the city and its lake" because my mother taught me another secret: The city of Chicago belongs to Lake Michigan.

But which of my mother's pronouncements to believe? That Chicago would swallow the Midwestern sea, smother it in concrete? Or that the lake wielded enough strength to outpolitick even Mayor Richard J. Daley?

Mayor Daley Sr. is gone now, but the lake remains, alternately tranquil and riled, changing colors like a mood ring. I guess we know who won.

When my mother watches the water from her lakeside apartment building, she still sucks in her breath. "You have to respect the power of that lake," she tells me. And I do now. I do.

I was 15 years old when I learned that the lake did not love me or hate me but could claim me, nevertheless. I was showing off for a boy, my best friend, Tommy, who lived in the same building. He usually accompanied me when I went for a swim, but on this particular day he decided the water was too choppy. I always preferred the lake when it was agitated because its temperature warmed, transforming it into a kind of Jacuzzi.

Tommy is right, I thought, once I saw the looming swells that had looked so unimpressive from the 12th floor. Waves crashed against the breakwater wall and the metal ladder that led into the lake, like the entrance to the deep end of a swimming pool.

I shouldn't do this, I told myself, but I noticed Tommy watching me from his first-floor window. "I'm not afraid," I said to him under my breath. "I bet you think that I'll chicken out just because I'm a girl."

It had been a hot summer of dares, and sense was clearly wanting. I took a deep breath and leapt off the wall into the churning water. How could I possibly get out? I hadn't thought that far ahead. When I bobbed to the surface, I was instantly slapped in the face and smashed under again and again, until I began gasping for air. *I'm going to die now,* I realized, and my heart filled with sorrow for my mother, who had already lost a husband and would now lose a daughter. I fought the waves, the sound of breakers swelling in my ears, unnaturally loud, like the noise of Judgment Day. *Here we go,* I thought. Then I became unusually calm. I took a quick gulp of air, plunged to the bottom of the lake where the water was a little quieter, and swam to the beach next door until I reached shallow waters. I burst to the surface then, my lungs burning, and it took me nearly five minutes to walk 15 feet to shore, continually knocked off balance by the waves that sucked at my legs. Tommy was no longer watching me, bored by my private games, unaware of the danger. I didn't tell my mother what had happened until hours later. I was angry at myself for being so careless with my life, but I was never for a moment angry at the lake. I didn't come to fear it, either, though it is a mighty force that drops 923 feet in its deepest heart. I understood that it struck indifferently; I was neither target nor friend. My life was my own affair, to lose or to save. Once I stopped struggling with the great lake, I flowed through it, and was expelled from its hectic mouth.

My mother still calls Fort Yates, North Dakota, home, despite the fact that she has lived in Chicago for nearly 55 years. She has taken me to visit the Standing Rock Sioux Reservation, where she was raised, and although a good portion of it was flooded during the construction of the Oahe Dam, she can point to significant hills and buttes and creeks. The landscape there endures, outlives its inhabitants. But I am a child of the city, where landmarks are human-made, impermanent. My attachments to place are attachments to people, my love for a particular area only as strong as my local relationships. I have lived in several cities and will live in several more. I visit the country with curiosity and trepidation, clearly a foreigner, and envy my mother's connection to a dusty town, the peace she finds on the prairie. It is a kind of religion, her devotion to Proposal Hill and the Missouri River, a sacred bond that I can only half-understand. If I try to see the world through my mother's eyes, find the point where my own flesh falls to earth, I realize my home is Lake Michigan, the source of so many lessons.

As a teenager I loved to swim in the dark, to dive beneath the surface where the water was as black as the sky. The lake seemed limitless and so was I, an arm, a leg, a wrist, a face, indistinguishable from the wooden boards of a sunken dock, from the sand I squeezed between my toes. I always left reluctantly, loath to become a body again and feel more acutely the oppressive pull of gravity.

It was my father who taught me to swim, with his usual patience. First he helped me float, his hands beneath my back and legs, his torso shading me from the sun. Next he taught me to flutter-kick, and I tried to make as much noise as possible. I dog-paddled in circles, but my father swam in a straight line perpendicular to shore, as if he were trying to leave this land forever, just as he had left New York State after a lifetime spent within its borders, easily, without regret. His swim was always the longest, the farthest. Mom and I would watch him as we lounged on our beach towels, nervous that a boat might clip him. It was a relief to see him turn around and coast in our direction.

"Here he comes," Mom would breathe. "He's coming back now."

My father also showed me how to skip a stone across the water. He could make a flat rock jump like a tiny, leaping frog, sometimes five or six hops before it sank to the bottom. It was the only time I could imagine this distinguished, silver-haired gentleman as a boy, and I laughed at him affectionately because the difference in our years collapsed.

My mother collects stones in her backyard—a rough, rocky beach in South Shore. She looks for rocks drilled with holes, not pits or mere scratches, but tiny punctures worn clear through.

"I can't leave until I find at least one," she tells me.

"Why?" I ask.

"There are powerful spirits in these stones, trying to tunnel their way out."

What I do not ask is why she selects them, these obviously unquiet souls, why she places them in a candy dish or a basket worn soft as flannel. What good can it do them? What good can it do her to unleash such restless forces on the quiet of her rooms?

I finger my mother's collection when I'm home for a visit and sometimes even press a smooth specimen against my cheek. The stones are mute and passive in my hand. At first I think it must be a failing on my part: I cannot hear what my mother hears. Then I decide that the spirits caught in these stones have already escaped. I imagine them returning to the lake, to the waves that pushed them onto the beach and washed their pebble flesh, because it is such a comfort to return to water.

And then I remember my own weightless immersion, how my body becomes a fluid spirit when I pull myself underwater, where breath stops. And I remember gliding along the lake's sandy bottom as a child, awed by the orderly pattern of its dunes. Lake Michigan is cold, reliably cold, but occasionally I passed through pockets of tepid water that always came as a surprise. I am reminded of cold spots reputedly found in haunted houses, and I wonder: Are these warm areas evidence of my lost souls?

A young man drowned in these waters behind my mother's building some years ago. Mom was sitting in a lawn chair, visiting with another tenant on the terrace. They sat together facing the lake so they could watch it, though it was calm that day, uninteresting. A young man stroked into view, swimming parallel to the shore, and headed north. He was close enough for them to read his features; he was 15 feet away from the shallows, where he could have stood with his head above water. He called out and asked in a calm voice how far south he was. The 7300 block, they told him. He moved on. A marathon swimmer, the women decided. But eventually my mother and her friend scanned the horizon and were unable to see his bobbing head and strong arms. They alerted the doorman, who called the police. The young man was found near the spot where he'd made his cordial inquiry.

"Why didn't he cry for help? Why didn't he signal his distress?" my mother asked the response unit.

"This happens all the time with men," she was told. "They aren't taught to cry for help."

So he is there too, the swimmer, a warm presence in cold water or a spirit in a stone.

I have gone swimming in other places—a chlorinated pool in Hollywood, the warm waters of the Caribbean, the Heart River in North Dakota—only to be disappointed and emerge unrefreshed. I am too used to Lake Michigan and its eccentricities. I must have cold, fresh water. I must have the stinking corpses of silver alewives floating on the surface as an occasional nasty surprise, always discovered dead, never alive. I must have sailboats on the horizon and steel mills on the southern shore, golf balls (shot from the local course) clustered around submerged pilings and breakwater boulders heavy as tombs lining the beach. I must have sullen lifeguards who whistle at anyone bold enough to stand in three feet of water, and the periodic arguments between wind and water that produce tearing waves and lake-spattered windows.

When I was little, maybe 7 or 8, my parents and I went swimming in a storm. The weather was mild when we set out, but the squall arrived quickly, without warning, as often happens in the Midwest. We swam anyway, keeping an eye on the lightning not yet arrived from the north. There was no one to stop us since we were dipping into deep water between beaches, in an unpatrolled area. The water was warmer than usual, the same temperature as the air, and when the rain wet the sky, I leapt up and down in the growing waves, unable to feel the difference between air and water, lake and rain. The three of us played together that time; even my father remained near shore rather than striking east to swim past the white buoys. We were joined in this favorite element, splashing and ducking. I waved my arms over my head. My father pretended to be a great whale, heavy in the surf, now and then spouting streams of water from his mouth. He chased me. My mother laughed.

Dad died in 1973 when I was 11, before my mother and I moved to the apartment on the lake. We always thought it such a shame he didn't get to make that move with us. He would have enjoyed finding Lake Michigan in his backyard.

We buried him in Albany, New York, because that is where he was raised. My mother was born in North Dakota, and I was born between them, in Chicago. There is a good chance we shall not all rest together, our stories playing out in different lands. But I imagine that if a rendezvous is possible—and my mother insists it is—we will find one another in this great lake, this small sea that rocks like a cradle. We are strong swimmers in our separate ways, my mother like a turtle, my father like a seal. And me? I am a small anonymous fish, unspectacular but content.

Women Pioneers on the Frontier

WOMEN PIONEERS ON THE FRONTIER

NATIVE PEOPLES DIDN'T call the Great Lakes region a frontier, nor did they see it as a wilderness. To them, it was home. It provided all their needs and gave them comfortable lives without great hardship. Some of the white settlers who replaced them knew only hardship for many years as they struggled to turn lands the Indians had used for hunting, gathering, and subsistence agriculture into intensively-cultivated farms. In their hopes for a better life than the scarce lands and worn-out soils they had turned from in New England or Europe could provide, the pioneers abandoned everything. In return for freedom and the chance to succeed, they began from the beginning, without roads, towns, churches, or sometimes even equipment with which to build them. Caroline Kirkland's *A New Home, Who'll Follow* (1839) and Susanna Moodie's *Roughing It In The Bush* (1852), descriptions of their families' lives on the Great Lakes frontier, are classic narratives of immigration to rough cabins from comfortable homes in the East and England. Like most frontier women, Kirkland and Moodie met challenges with the best wry humor they could muster, although some women they describe were less strong.

But for every transplanted wife who languished in misery, many others reveled in the freedom and excitement they found at the end of long and difficult journeys. They made do with what they had, even when everything they owned had fallen in the lake or a river, and concentrated on what they could see and learn from those they met, either other whites or the Indians. The cultural expectations that may have felt confining to them no longer operated, and if they liked being out-of-doors or traveling or the excitement of new experiences, the frontier provided plenty. For women like Juliette Kinzie and Ann Powell, travelling with family to remote outposts was a wonderful lark, no matter how difficult conditions became. For others like Soaphy Anderson, whose memoir about being part of the first white settlement on Manitoulin Island in northern Lake Huron describes appalling hardships, what remains in memory is the strength of the women in their party.

Much has been written by feminist historians about the deprived and miserable lives of women on the frontier, but they have told only half the story. For just as many others, the rewards far outweighed the disadvantages. Even when, as in Emma Baylis's diary of her missionary work on the North Shore of Lake Huron, homesickness and fear spill out on the pages at the end of the day, sadness never lasts long. Baylis returned each summer to her mission for years, convinced that the work she was doing mattered more than any temporary discomfort. Although few white women ever became as comfortable and skilled in the environment as Native women, they learned from those women what they could and improvised the rest.

Perhaps the most accurate assessment of women's lives on the frontier is that their reactions to what they found were individual. Even if they did not choose to move, if they followed husbands or brothers or family, how they adapted depended largely on their attitudes. Although some writers collected here may have seen the past through rose-colored memories, they still describe the same difficulties as women who were unhappy. Nearly everyone was wet and cold at some point, and many had to travel in leaky, storm-tossed ships or stay in miserable lodgings. The feminist focus on displaced, ill-adapted, pining women may owe as much to twentieth-century class and gender politics as it does to reality, for the reality, as the selections here suggest, was seldom one-dimensional.

What emerges from these narratives is a group of women who faced great challenges and wasted little time in regret. They, like many others, saw not only what was missing on the frontier but, equally important, what new opportunities this wild place gave them to learn, to experience freedom, to achieve. A quiet satisfaction echoes through their words.

JOURNAL OF A TOUR TO NIAGARA
AND DETROIT IN 1789
Ann Powell

THE WRITER OF the following journal was the daughter of a British Loyalist merchant who fled to England during the Revolutionary War. She returned to Canada to accompany her brother William Dummer Powell to Detroit when he was appointed the first judge of common pleas there in 1789. William Powell eventually became the first Chief Justice of Upper Canada (Ontario), and Ann Powell married Issac Winslow Clarke, another refugee Boston Loyalist merchant, whose family firm had owned the tea American patriots threw in Boston Harbor in 1773. She died in childbirth at Montreal in 1792, and copies of the irreverent journal of her trip were preserved by friends. Her writing gives us a picture of the lakes when they were largely wilderness, seen by a young woman of independent opinions and a good deal of spunk who described what must have been a physically difficult and dangerous trip as "the pleasantest vagabond life you can imagine." She notes as she goes the typical pattern of frontier settlement of the time, when families often moved more than once, increasing their holdings each time. Clarke is remarkably free from the prejudices against Indians of her era, and while observing treaty negotiations with none other than Red Jacket, she recognized that the power of Indian women was worth noting.

-◦=◦◦=◦-

WHEN I TALKED of keeping a journal from Montreal to Detroit I was not aware of the difficulties attending the journey. I expected it would be tedious, and thought writing would be a very pleasant employment, and so it might have proved, had it been practicable, but the opportunities for writing were so few that I found it would be impossible to keep a journal with any degree of regularity so I left it wholly alone and trusted to my memory (which never deserved such a compliment) for recalling whatever was worth communicating.

We left Montreal on the 11th of May 1785, with large party of our friends, who paid us the compliment of seeing us to the first stage, where we took a farewell dinner and the party, except Mr. Clarke, left us. It was a melancholy parting scene—I was the person least interested in it, and partook of it more from sympathy than any real sorrow that I felt. All whom I was much attached to were going with me, but on these occasions crying is catching and I took the infection. I felt melancholy for though I had no particular friendships, I had passed some months very pleasantly with the people of Montreal and received many civilities. I felt a general regret at bidding these good people "Good-bye." Mr. Clarke stole off in the morning before we were aware, but an honest German whom my brother had discharged followed us to Lochine, and caused me a tear at parting, though I cannot exactly say from what motive it flowed. With his eyes full of tears he came into the room, and kissed all the children round, then wiping away his tears, he attempted to thank his master for past kindness, but the poor fellow's voice failed, he caught my brother's hand with emotion, and held it to his lips, then cast a look at my sister. I suppose he saw encouragement in our faces, for he took our extended hands, and dropt a tear on each, then with blessings which I am convinced flowed from his heart, bid us Adieu!

We now went to our boats, one was fitted up with an awning to protect us from the weather and held the family and bedding. It was well filled, eighteen persons in all, so you may suppose we had not much room. As it happened, it was of no consequence, it was cold on the water and we were glad to sit close. This mode of travelling is very tedious; we are obliged to keep along shore and go on very slowly.

The first night we slept at the house of a "Habitan" who turned out with his family to give his best room, where we spread our beds and slept in peace. I entertained myself with looking at the Canadian family who were eating their supper, saying their prayers, and conversing at the same time. The next day we reached a part of the river where the boats were obliged to be unloaded and taken through a Lock, the rapids being too strong to pass; these rapids were the first of any consequence that I had seen. Perhaps you do not know what I mean by a rapid—it is when the water runs with swiftness over large rocks, every one of which forms a cascade and the river here is all a bed of rocks.—There is no describing the grandeur of the water when thrown into this kind of agitation—the sea, after a tempest, is smooth to it.

We breakfasted with the man who keeps the Lock and then dispatched Mr. Smith with a message to Mr. Denie who lives at the distance of a few miles and with whom we had promised to dine. I believe I have not mentioned Mr. Smith before, as he is to be our fellow traveller I will now tell you who he is.—Mr. Smith was a clerk of my brother's, a sensible, well disposed young man who lost his parents early, and was cheated of his little fortune by his guardian. When my brother gave up business he had no further occasion for a clerk and Mr. Smith saw himself without friends or protection; he therefore preferred following the fortunes of his only friend, to being left at Montreal, and readily embraced the offer of making one of our party to Detroit.

As soon as Mr. Denie heard of our arrival, a calash was dispatched for the ladies, a saddle horse for Mr. Powell and a wagon for the children and servants. Mrs. Powell was unwilling to place the little girls out of her sight, so we each took one in our laps, but went only a little way before the carriage broke down, but fortunately, none of us were hurt. My brother had rode on and we were in a good deal of perplexity what to do. I proposed getting into the wagon but my sister would trust neither herself or the infant in it. There was no alternative but walking, and letting the servant carry the baby, till the man could go home for another calash. The sun was hot, and the road dusty. One carriage for me was as good as another, so up I mounted and a very pleasant ride I had with a fine view of the country. Mrs. Powell was heartily tired before the Calash met her. The hospitable welcome and good dinner we received at Mr. Denie's set all right. In the evening we went on ten miles further to a public house.—We then determined not to stop at another inn if we could possibly meet with other accommodations. My brother had travelled the road before, and knew the people, and the distance from house to house. This part of the country has been settled since the Peace, and it was granted to the troops raised in America during the war. We went from a Colonel to a Captain, and from a Captain to a Major. They have most of them built good houses and with the assistance of their half-pay live very comfortably.

We spent one night at the house of a Captain Duncan whose wife I had heard often mentioned by my sister and whose story I had commiserated before I had seen her. She is now only nineteen, and has been five years married to a man who is old, disagreeable, and vicious. But he was supposed to be rich and her friends absolutely forced her to marry him. She is one of the prettiest young women I ever saw in my life, both in person and manners. I never heard of such a series of cruelties being practiced on any poor creature in my life, both before and after her marriage. The dislike she felt towards him is now a fixed aversion, which can never change as it is founded on principle! After the sacrifice was made her friends had the mortification to find themselves deceived in his circumstances; so far from being rich, he was deeply in debt, and had nothing to live upon but his half-pay, and his new lands which were then in a state of nature. There, however, he brought her and there she lived in a hut, without society and almost without the necessaries of life, till he built a house which he has begun on so large a scale that it never will be finished.

My sister had been strongly attached to Mrs. Duncan, when she was quite a child, and very much beloved by her. I felt much interested by this sweet young woman, and should feel great pleasure in hearing her tyrant was dead; the only means by which she can be released.

At that moment I thought with pleasure on a circumstance that has often mortified me, the slightness of my constitution, which will never leave me to struggle with any great misfortune. A good flow of spirits buoys me up above the common vexations of life, few people I believe bear them with more temper, but an evil too great for the strength of my mind would send me to the grave.

The night following that we passed at Captain Duncan's we reached the house of an old servant of Mrs. Powell's; the children were delighted to see her and I was well pleased to view a new scene of domestic life. Nancy, it seems, had married a disbanded soldier, who had a small lot of land where they immediately went to live, and cultivated it with so much care that in a few years they were offered in exchange for it a farm, twice its value, to which they had just removed and were obliged to live sometime in a temporary log house, which consisted only of one room, in which was a very neat bed where a lovely babe of three months old lay crowing and laughing by itself. A large loom was on one side, on the other all the necessary utensils of a family, everything perfectly clean.

Nancy went to the door and brought in two more fine children, and presented them to her mistress. We asked her if she was happy—she replied "perfectly so." She worked hard, but it was for herself and children; her husband took care of the farm, and she of the family. At their leisure hours she wove cloth and he mended shoes for their neighbors, for which they were well paid and every year expected to do better.

Small as this place was, we chose to stay all night, so while Mrs. Powell was giving orders for arranging the beds, my brother and I walked out to enjoy a very fine evening. The banks of the river were very high and woody, the moon shone bright through the trees. Some Indians were on the river taking fish with harpoons, a mode of fishing I had never seen before. They made large fires in their canoes, which attract the fish to the surface of the water, when they can see by the fire to strike them. The number of fires moving on the water had a pretty and singular effect. When we returned to the house we found the whole floor covered with beds. The man and woman of the house with their children had retired to their own room and left us to manage as we pleased. A blanket was hung before my mattress which I drew aside to see how the rest were accommodated. My brother and sister, myself, five children and two maid servants made up the group, a blazing fire (not in the chimney, for there was none, but on one side of the room which was opened at the top to let the smoke out and gave us a fine current of air) showed every object distinctly. I was in a humour to be easily diverted and found a thousand things to laugh at. It struck me that we were like a party of strolling players. At night we always drest a dinner for the next day. When we were disposed to eat it, the cloth was laid in the boat, and our table served up with as much decency as could be expected, if we could be contented with cold provisions. Not so our sailors, they went on shore and boiled their pots and smoked their pipes. One day we happened to anchor at a small Island where the men themselves had some difficulty in climbing the banks which were very steep. I finished my dinner before the rest of the party, and felt an inclination to walk. I took one of the maids and made one of the men help us up; we strolled to the other side of the Island and when we turned around I saw the whole of the ground covered with fire. The wind blew fresh, and the dried leaves had spread it from where the people were cooking. We had no alternative, so were obliged to make the best of our way back. I believe we took very few steps, for neither of us had our shoes burnt through. The weather was so fine that we ventured to sleep out and I liked it so much that I regretted that we had ever gone into a house.

It is the pleasantest vagabond life you can imagine. We stopt before sun-set when a large fire was instantly made and tea and chocolate were prepared. While we were taking it, the men erected a tent, the sails of the boat served for the top and blankets were fastened to the sides. In a few minutes they had made a place large enough to spred all our beds, where we slept with as much comfort as I ever did in any chamber in my life. It was our own fault if we did not choose a fine situation to encamp. You can scarcely conceive a more beautiful scene than was one night exhibited. The men had piled up boughs of trees for a fire before our tent, till they made a noble bonfire. In the course of the evening it spread more than half a mile, the ground was covered with dry leaves, which burnt like so many lamps, with the fire running up the bushes and trees. The whole formed the most beautiful illumination you can form an idea of.

The children were in ecstacies, running about like so many savages, and our sailors were encamped near enough for us to hear them singing and laughing. We had before we left Montreal heard of his majesty's recovery,— so if you please, you can set this all down as rejoicings on that account, though I doubt whether it once occurred to our minds, yet we are a very loyal People.

On the tenth day we reached Kingston; it is a small town and stands in a beautiful bay at the foot of Lake Ontario. The moment we reached the wharf a number of the people came down to welcome us. A gentleman, in his hurry to hand out the ladies, brushed one of the children into the lake; he was immediately taken out but that did not save his mother a severe fright. We went to the house of a Mr. Forsyth, a young bachelor, who very politely begged we would consider it as our own. Here we staid three days and then sailed with a fair wind for Niagara. At Kingston we were overtaken by two officers of the Artillery, one going to Niagara, the other to Detroit. Mr. Meredith we had been introduced to at Montreal. Mr. Suckling was a stranger. They both expressed themselves pleased with joining our party, and preferred accepting an offer my brother made them to cross the Lake in a vessel appointed for him, to waiting for another where they would be much less crowded.

My brother had also given a passage to another young man, and Captain Harrow, a gentleman who commanded ship on Lake Erie. We were fifteen where there were only four berths. When the beds were put down at night every one remained in the spot he had first taken, for there was no moving without general consent. One night after we had lain down and begun to be composed Mrs. Powell saw one of the maids standing where she had been making the children's beds and asked her why she staid there. The poor girl who speaks indifferent English, answered "I am quazed, ma'am." Sure enough she was wedged in beyond the power of moving without assistance. I heard a great laugh among the gentlemen who were divided from us by a blanket partition. I suppose they were "quazed" too! Lake Ontario is two hundred miles over; we were four days crossing it. We were certainly a very good humored set of people, for no one complained or seemed rejoiced when we arrived at Niagara.

The fort is by no means pleasantly situated; it is built close upon the lake which gains upon its foundations so fast that in a few years they must be overflowed. There, however, we passed some days very agreeably at the house of a Mr. Hamilton, a sensible, worthy and agreeable man. Mrs. Hamilton is an amiable sweet little woman. I regretted very much she did not live at Detroit instead of Niagara. We received the most polite attentions from Colonel Hunter, the commanding officer, and all his officers. Lord Edward Fitzgerald had been some months at Niagara before us, and was making excursions among the Indians, of whose society he seems particularly fond. Joseph Brant, a celebrated Indian chief lives in that neighborhood. Lord Edward had spent some days at his house and seemed charmed with his visit. Brant returned to Niagara with his lordship. He was the first and indeed the only savage I ever dined at table with. As the party was large he was at too great a distance from me to hear him converse and I was by no means pleased by his looks.

These people pay great deference to rank—with them it is only obtained by merit.—They attended Lord Edward from the house of one chief to another, and entertained him with dancing, which is the greatest compliment they can pay. Short as our stay was at Niagara, we made so many acquaintances we were sorry to leave them. Several gentlemen offered to escort us to Fort Erie, which made the journey very cheerful. Mr. Hamilton, Mr. Meredith of the Engineers,—Mr. Robinson of the 50th Regiment,—Mr. Humphries with Captain Harrow,—Mr. Smith and my brother went in the boat with us to the landing which is eight miles from the Fort. There the river becomes impassable and all the luggage was drawn up a steep hill in a cradle—a machine I never saw before.

We walked up the hill and were conducted to a good garden, with an Arbour in it, where we found a cloth laid for dinner, which was provided for us by the officers of the post. After dinner we were to get to Fort Schlofser, seven miles, by any means we could—two calashes were procured, in one of them my brother drove my sister, and Mr. Hamilton, me, in the other. Mr. Meredith got a horse and the rest of the gentlemen made use of their feet.—The road was good, the weather charming and our ride would have been delightful only the horses were so bad that they could scarcely crawl. I never breathe freely when a horse seems tired; I always feel as if I were committing a crime in driving it. Mr. H—who is very humane, gave up the point of whipping the poor devil out of respect to Captain Watson, to whom the horse had once belonged, a circumstance which increased my compassion, for of all men living, Watson was the most compassionate and in the condition the animal was, would as soon have attempted to carry as to drive him. It was not to be borne, so we took one of the horses from the cart the children and servants were in and made the best of the way after the party.—

The afternoon was wearing away and this was the only opportunity we should have of seeing the Falls. All our party collected half a mile above the Falls, and walked down to them. I was in raptures all the way. The Falls I had heard of forever, but no one had mentioned the Rapids! For half a mile the river comes, foaming down immense rocks, some of them forming cascades 30 or 40 feet high! The banks are covered with woods, as are a number of Islands, some of them very high out of the water.

One in the centre of the river runs out into a point, and seems to divide the Falls which would otherwise be quite across the river into the form of a crescent. I believe no mind can form an idea of the immensity of the body of water, or the rapidity with which it hurries down. The height is 189 feet, and long before it reaches the bottom, it loses all appearance of a liquid.—The spray rises like light summer clouds and when the rays of the sun are reflected through it they form innumerable rainbows, but the sun was not in a situation to show this effect when we were there. One thing I could find nobody to explain to me, which is, the stillness of the water at the bottom of the Falls—it is as smooth as a lake for half a mile, deep and narrow, the banks very high and steep with trees hanging over them. I was never before sensible of the power of scenery, nor did I suppose the eye could carry to the mind such strange emotions of pleasure, wonder, and solemnity. For a time every other impression was erased from my memory! Had I been left to myself I am convinced I should not have thought of moving whilst there was light to distinguish objects. With reluctance I at length attended to the proposal of going, determining in my own mind that when I returned I would be mistress of my own time, and stay a day or two at least.

As Fort Schlofser was only at the distance of a pleasant walk, we all chose to go on foot. We were received by Mr. Foster of the 60th Regt.—one of the most elegant young men I ever saw. Here we were extremely well accommodated, and much pleased with the house and garden. I never saw a situation where retirement wore so many charms.

The next day we went in a batteau to Fort Erie—when we arrived there we found the commanding officer, Mr. Boyd was gone in a party with Lord Edward and Mr. Brisbane to the other side of the river where the Indians were holding a council. The gentlemen all returned in the evening, and seemed so much pleased with their entertainment, that when they proposed our going over with them the next day we very readily agreed to it. I thought it a peculiar piece of good fortune having an opportunity of seeing a number of the most respectable of these people collected together. We reached the spot where the council began and as we passed along, saw several of their chiefs at their toilets.—They sat upon the ground with the most profound gravity dressing themselves before a small looking-glass, for they are very exact in fixing on their ornaments, and not a little whimsical. I am told that one of these fellows will be an hour or two painting his face, and when any one else would think him sufficiently horrible, some new conceit will strike him and he will rub all off and begin again.

The women dress with more simplicity than the men, at least all that I have seen, but at this meeting there were not many of the fair sex—some old squaws who sat in council, and a few young ones to dress their provisions; for these great men, as well as those of our world, like a good dinner, after spending their lungs for the good of their country. Some women we saw employed in taking fish in a basket; a gentleman of our party took the basket from one of them and tried to catch the fish as she did, but failing they laughed at his want of dexterity.

One young squaw sat in a tent weaving a sort of worsted garter inter-mixed with beads. I suppose she was a lady of distinction, for her ears were bored in different places with ear-rings in them all. She would not speak English but seemed to understand what was said to her. A gentleman intro-duced Mrs. Powell and me to her, as white squaws, begging she would go on with her work as we wished to see how it was done. She complied immedi-ately with great dignity, taking no more notice of us than if we were posts. A proof of her good breeding! We then went up a steep bank to a very beautiful spot—the tall trees were in full leaf and the ground covered with wild flowers.

We were seated on a log in the centre where we could see all that passed.—Upwards of 200 chiefs were assembled and seated in proper order. They were the delegates of six nations—each tribe formed a circle under the shade of a tree, their faces towards each other; they never changed their places but sat or lay on the grass as they liked. The speaker of each tribe stood with his back against a tree, the old women walked one by one with great solemnity and seated themselves behind the men,—they were wholly covered with their blankets and sought not by the effect of ornaments to attract or fright the other sex, for I cannot tell whether the men mean to make themselves charming or horrible by the pains they take with their persons. On seeing this respectable band of matrons I was struck with the different opinions of mankind.

In England, when a man grows infirm and his talents are obscured by age, the wits decide upon his character by calling him an old woman. On the banks of Lake Erie, a woman becomes respectable as she grows old, and I suppose the greatest compliment you can pay a young hero is that he is as wise as an old woman, a good trait of savage understanding—These ladies preserve a modest silence in the debates (I fear they are not like women of other countries) but nothing is determined without their advice and approbation. I was very much struck with the figures of these Indians as they approached us. They are remarkably tall and finely made and walk with a grace and dignity you can have no idea of. I declare our beaux looked quite insignificant by them. One man called to my mind some of Homer's finest heroes. One of the gentlemen told me that he was a chief of great distinction and spoke English and if I pleased he should be introduced to me. I had some curiosity to see how a chief of the Six Nations would pay his compliments but little did I expect the elegance with which he addressed me. The Prince of Wales does not bow with more grace than Captain David. He spoke English with propriety and returned all the compliments that were paid him with ease and politeness.

As he was not only the handsomest but the best drest man I saw, I will endeavor to describe him. His person is tall and fine as it is possible to conceive—his features handsome and regular, with a countenance of much softness—his complexion not disagreeably dark, and I really believe he washes his face, for it appeared perfectly clean without paint; his hair was all shaved off except a little on the top of his head to fasten his ornaments to—his head and ears painted a glowing red. Round his head was fastened a fillet of highly polished silver, from the left temple hung two straps of black velvet covered with silver beads and brooches. On the top of his head was fixed a Foxtail feather which bowed to the wind, as did a black one in each ear—a pair of immense ear-rings which hung below his shoulders completed his head-dress which I assure you was not unbecoming, though I must confess somewhat fantastical. His dress was a shirt of colored calico, the neck and shoulders covered so thick with silver brooches as to have the appearance of a net—his sleeves much like those the ladies wore when I left England, fastened about the arm with a broad bracelet of highly polished silver, and engraved with the arms of England. Four smaller bracelets of the same kind about his wrists and arms, around his waist was a large scarf of a very dark coloured stuff lined with scarlet, which hung to his feet. One part he generally drew over his left arm which had a very graceful effect when he moved. His legs were covered with blue cloth made to fit neatly, with an ornamental garter bound below the knee. I know not what kind of a being your imagination will represent to you but I sincerely declare to you that altogether Captain David made the finest appearance I ever saw in my life!

Do not suppose they were all dressed with the same taste,—their clothes are not cut by the same pattern, like the beaux of England—every Indian is dressed according to his own fancy, and you see no two alike, even their faces are differently painted,—some of them wear their hair in a strange manner—others shave it entirely off. One old man diverted me extremely; he was dressed in a scarlet coat, richly embroidered, that must have been made at least half a century, with waistcoat of the same, that reached halfway down his thighs—no shirt or breeches, but blue cloth stockings. As he strutted about more than the rest, I concluded that he was particularly pleased with his dress and with himself! They told us that he was a chief of distinction.

We only staid to hear two speeches—they spoke with great gravity and no action—frequently making long pauses for hum of applause. Lord Edward, Mr. Brisbane and Mr. Meredith remained with them all night and were entertained with dancing.

We were detained some days at Niagara by a contrary wind. On the 4th of June as we were drinking the King's health, like good loyal subjects, the wind changed and we were hurried on board. We were better accommodated than when we crossed Lake Ontario, for the weather was so fine that the gentlemen all slept on deck. Lake Erie is 280 miles over—we were five days on our passage. The river Detroit divided Lake Erie from Lake St. Clair, which is again separated by a small river from Lake Huron. The head of Lake Erie and the entrance into the river Detroit is uncommonly beautiful. Whilst we were sailing up the river, a perverse storm of rain and thunder drove us all into the cabin and gave us a thorough wetting. After it was over we went on shore; the fort lies about half way up the river which is 18 miles in length. In drawing the line between the British and American possessions, this fort was left within their lines, a new town is now to be built on the other side of the river, where the Courts are held and where my brother must of course reside. As soon as our vessel anchored several ladies and gentlemen came on board. They had agreed upon a house for us till my brother could meet with one that would suit him, so we found ourselves at home immediately. We were several weeks at the Fort, which gave us an opportunity of making a little acquaintance with the inhabitants. The ladies visited us in full dress, though the weather was boiling hot. What do you think of walking about when the Thermometer is above 90 degrees? It was as high as 95 the morning we returned our visits. Mrs. Powell and myself spent the most of our time in our chambers. We found all the people civil and obliging. In point of society we could not expect much, as it depends entirely on the military. An agreeable regiment makes the place gay. The 55th which we found on our arrival there was a corps that would improve almost any society; the loss of it has made the place extremely dull and sets the other regiment in a disadvantageous light which it cannot bear.

While we staid at the Fort several parties were made for us, a very agreeable one by the 65th to an island a little way up the river. Our party was divided into five boats, one held the music, and in each of the others were two ladies and as many gentlemen as it would hold. Lord Edward and his friend arrived just time enough to join us—they went round the Lake by land to see some Indian settlements and were highly pleased with their jaunt.

Lord Edward speaks in raptures of the Indian hospitality—he told me one instance of it which would reflect honour on the most polished society.

By some means or other the gentlemen lost their provisions, and were entirely without bread, in a place where they could get none. Some Indians travelling with them had one loaf which they offered his Lordship, but he would not accept it—the Indians gave him to understand that they were used to do without, and therefore it was less inconvenient to them. They still refused and the Indians then disappeared and left the loaf of bread in the road the travellers must pass and the Indians were seen no more.

Our party on the Island proved very pleasant which those kind of parties seldom do; the day was fine, the country cheerful and the band delightful. We walked some time in the shady part of the Island and then were led to a bower where the table was spread for dinner. Everything here is on a grand scale—do not suppose we dined in an English arbour! This was made of forest trees, that grew in a circle, and it was closed by filling up the spaces with small trees, and bushes, which being fresh cut, you could not see where they were put and the bower was the whole height of the trees through closed quite at the top.—The band was placed without and played whilst we were at dinner. We were hurried home in the evening by the appearance of a thunder storm—it was the most beautiful I ever remember to have seen. The clouds were collected about the setting sun, and the forked lightning, darting in a thousand different directions from it. You can form no idea from anything you have seen of what the lightning is in this country.—These lakes, I believe, are the nurseries of thunder storms! What you see are only stragglers who lose their strength before they reach you. I had the pleasure of being on the water in one of them, and being completely wet, my clothes were so heavy when I got out of the boat that I could scarcely walk. We were a very large party, going on what is called a party of pleasure; most of the ladies were as wet as myself—we could get no dry clothes, and were obliged to dry our own, the best way we could. A pretty set of figures we were when we met to dance, which upon these occasions is customary. Before dinner I had resolved not to dance, for the day was very warm, the party large and the room small. I was prevailed upon to alter my mind by their assuring me that exercise would prevent my feeling any ill effects from my wetting, and I found it so. Some good ought to come from it, for I doubt whether the people in the Black Hole in Calcutta suffered more, only ours was voluntary, and there was not.

The disasters of the day were not over yet; the evening was fine, but the ground was wet so that calashes were ordered to take us to our boats. A Mrs. Murphy and myself were seated in one; as the distance was small we intended a servant should lead the horse, but the gallantry of the gentlemen would not suffer that. Captain Blacker of the 65th seated himself at our feet, with his legs on the shafts to drive. Mr. Spriet of the Artillery got up behind the carriage—they were laughing and asking me what I would give to be seen going into London in that way? Before I could answer, we heard a loud crash and I recollect no more till I was on my feet in the road. I then saw Mrs. Murphy on the ground, and on the other side of the calash, and Mr. Blacker endeavoring to disengage his feet from the shafts which were broken entirely off and separated from the carriage. I shall never forget the horror expressed in his countenance. He was not hurt himself, but fully expected all our bones were broken. Poor Mr. Spriet had fallen with his head in the seat we were thrown from and was badly stunned by the blow. When we found no mischief done, we all laughed heartily, which added to the fright, threw Mrs. Murphy into hysterics, and discomposed us all again. By the time she recovered I found I was bruised and had broken a tooth —however, I had no right to complain; we were highly fortunate to be no more hurt. I hope never to be pressed into the same kind of party again, voluntarily I am sure I shall never make one.

Passing by a house as we went down the river we heard a most horrid scream of distress within it, which continued without intermission, till we were out of hearing. Some of the gentlemen told us it was an insane man who had been so for six years. He had continued constantly to walk up and down on one particular plank in the floor with his hands clasped together crying "O mon Dieu." He went to bed at night and sat down at table with his family, but never spoke any other words, returning to his walk immediately. I think the universe would not tempt me to live with this poor creature, or within hearing of his cries.

FROM REMINISCENCES OF EARLY DAYS
ON MACKINAC ISLAND
(c.1890)

Elizabeth Thérèse Baird

BORN IN PRAIRIE du Chien, Wisconsin Territory in 1810, the great-great granddaughter of Kewinaquot or "Returning Cloud," an Ottawa chief, Elizabeth Thérèse Baird grew up on Mackinac Island where her father, Henry Fisher, a fur trader for the American Fur Company, was stationed. At fourteen she married Henry Baird, who became the first professional attorney to practice in Wisconsin. She acted as an interpreter for his French clients and made her home the center of early Green Bay society. In her *Reminiscences* she writes of life on the Island when French and Indian cultures were still strong, when marriages between women of Indian descent, such as herself, and English or Americans or French were relatively common, and the roles of women on the frontier were not circumscribed by the Victorian notions of femininity that would restrict women later in the century. Her grandmother ran a fur trading company after her husband became incapacitated, as did another strong woman who influenced her. Her aunt, Madame LaFramboise, took over her husband's business after he was shot by an Indian while saying his evening prayers at their fur-trading camp near the Grand River in central Michigan. (Baird's memoir of her aunt is reprinted in "Women's Work.")

When Baird wrote her memoirs shortly before her death in 1890, cultural attitudes toward mixed marriages had changed considerably and prejudice against American Indians was stronger than it had been when the Old

Northwest was the frontier. At first glance, her narrative appears to be a charming tale of maple sugar making, visiting the Kinzies in Chicago, and seasonal rituals on the Island, but Baird is careful to note that Mackinac society was "aristocratic" and that many members of that society were mixed blood. She details who married whom of which race and invariably notes how beautiful the part-Indian women were, particularly Josette Laframboise who married Captain Benjamin K. Pierce, commandant of Fort Mackinac in 1816, and the brother of US President Franklin Pierce. When Laframboise was referred to in the memoirs of an officer's wife as a "half-breed girl," Baird is quick to point out that Josette was "a highly educated and cultivated woman," and that her mother and aunt attended the wedding in full Indian costume.

The marriages Baird describes, however, occur only between mixed-race women and white men, never the reverse, since that would overturn a long-standing American prohibition against associating white women with the wilderness represented by Indian men. Such marriages would also mean acceptance of Indian culture without trying to civilize it, which would then interfere with white claims to Indian land. Thus Baird and her narrative illustrate how successful the Jesuits and fur traders had been at "civilizing" the Indians; she and her family were completely acculturated, and considered it an act of status to marry a white man. *Reminiscences* is an interesting cultural document not only because it portrays a vanished way of life on the frontier, but also because Baird attempts to demonstrate that the mixed blood society of the Island she had known was better educated and more cosmopolitan than most of her readers, rendering their prejudices absurd.

Baird does not always focus on the politics of social relations, and she often writes with great good humor. The section reprinted here describes a lighthearted trip from Green Bay after her marriage at age fourteen to visit her mother on the Island and bear her first child. No where in the annals of lakes voyaging is there another a trip quite like this one. Summer sailors who frequent Egg Harbor on the Door Peninsula will smile to learn how it received its name.

By Bateau to Mackinac

IN 1824, A BRIDE of but fourteen years, I went with my husband to live in Green Bay, and thenceforth my lot was cast with the new and growing Territory west of Lake Michigan. On the 23d of June, 1825, we entered upon a return trip to Mackinac, by a Mackinac boat or bateau, the details of which may prove of interest.

Our route lay along the eastern coast of Green Bay and the northern shore of Lake Michigan. My husband was going to the island to attend court, and I to visit my relatives. Judge Doty had gone there by schooner, some time before. We took passage on one of a fleet of six boats laden with furs, belonging to the American Fur Company, and in charge of my brother-in-law, Joseph Rolette, of Prairie du Chien. Having attended a wedding ceremony in the afternoon, it was so late when we reached the boats, in waiting by the river-side, that at first it seemed hardly worth while to start that day. Yet the men were all in their places, which was always the experience in the days when there was no whistle or bell to call them to duty, and it was prudent to start when they were secured; otherwise, the grog shops might entice them away.

In each of the boats there were seven men, six to row and a steersman, all being Frenchmen. There was, in addition, in each boat, a clerk of the American Fur Company, to act as commander, or bourgeois. The furnishing of these boats, each thirty feet long, was quite complete. The cargo being furs, a snug-fitting tarpaulin was fastened down and over the sides, to protect the pelts from the rain. This cargo was placed in the center of the boat. A most important feature of the cargo was the mess basket, one of the great comforts of the past days, and a perfect affair of its kind. It was well filled with everything that could be procured to satisfy both hunger and thirst, such as boiled ham, tongue, roast chickens, bread, butter, hard or sea biscuit, crackers, cheese (when that luxury could be procured), tea, coffee, and chocolate, pickles, etc., and abundance of eggs. Then there were wines, cordials, and brandy. All this the mess baskets held; yet in addition, we depended upon securing fresh game and fish on the way. Rolette was a generous provider, sending to St. Louis for all that this part of the world could not supply. The mess basket on this occasion seemed to have an extra supply of eggs. It seemed strange that such faithful workers as the men were, should have been fed so poorly. They had nothing but salt pork, lyed corn, and bread or biscuit. This was the general food of workmen in the fur trade. It was the custom, when a man wished to enter the employ of any one, to put the manner of living in the indenture. Our boat carried two tents, and had a cot bed and camp stool for my use.

The party in our boat consisted of Rolette (the head man), John Kinzie, my husband, and myself. One of the other boats was in the charge of Edward Ploudre, another in charge of Jean Baptist Mairand; Monsieur Eustubise was in charge of the fourth boat. I have forgotten the names of the bourgeois of the two remaining craft.

Starting so late in the day, we were only enabled to get as far as the Red Banks, before it was time to stop and camp for the night. As I stepped from the boat, I saw that my tent was almost ready for me, so quickly did these men arrange matters for the encampment.

Next morning dawned most gloriously, and we started off in our boats, after breakfast, in fine spirits, cheered and enlivened by the merry song of the boatmen, who always start with a song. The day was charming, there was no wind, and the men rowed as if it were a pleasure. This was indeed a delightful way to travel; keeping always within easy reach of shore, in case of a sudden squall or violent wind.

The camping hour is always hailed with gladness by the men, strange as it may seem, as it came at the close of a hard day's work. It seemed always to be another pleasure of the voyage, and was an agreeable change to passengers as well as men. The men would pitch the tent with rapidity, in front of it quickly kindle a fire, and then immediately prepare the meal, which was greatly enjoyed. Then, all being refreshed, came the time for sports, merriment, and fun of all kinds.

As we rowed away from the Red Banks on that most charming June morning, many were the amusements that followed each other. The boats would sometimes come near enough to allow an interchange of conversation, jest, and play. This began that morning, by the throwing of hard tack at each other. This, however, did not last long, the prospect of needing the biscuits, later, serving to save them. Our boat had at first shared in the contest, but on my account they soon desisted. Shortly after the war of the biscuits ceased, we began to see eggs flying in the air, and a very pretty sight they made too. The men entered fully into the fun, although the oarsmen did not dare slack their oars. They gave vent, however to their enjoyment by a cri di joie, fairly quivering with excitement. It was about as animated a contest as any these men had ever witnessed or expected to. Not to spoil the fun, I crawled under the tarpaulin, where I was comparatively safe, although an occasional egg would strike me on the head. Rolette—an irritable old man—tried his best to stop the battle, but the fun was too fierce to be readily given up, and on a pretence of not hearing their commander's order they kept on with the fight.

At the second pipe or rest, we left the boat for a ramble, as a beautiful beach made walking a delight. Although not dinner-time, Rolette ordered an early meal, so that we might take another walk. He directed the men, after their meal, to start on with the boats, telling them where to encamp. Pointing to a bit of land that projected into the bay, which did not seem very far away, he said, "You may encamp just past that point. We will walk; be sure and have supper ready." Barrette, Rolette's serving-man, remained with us. Rolette never went unattended, as he was a very helpless person.

We sat awhile when we had dined, then started off on our walk. The fleet of boats presented a handsome appearance, disappearing and reappearing with the inequalities of the shore. We had not walked far when we came to a bluff which extended into the bay, and which was perfectly perpendicular. There was no path around it, none over it, and the water at its base was deep. What was I to do? Good Barrette immediately said he could carry me; and he did so. How I pitied him. The distance around the bluff was several yards. When we had doubled the promontory and got upon dry land, we stopped to rest. Starting off again we soon came to a small stream, narrow but deep. It had not been observed by the men in the boats, owing to the rushes. Now, what was to be done? The crew were out of sight, hidden by the point of land at first mentioned, and consequently were out of hearing. But the same faithful servant again undertook the task of carrying me, although the water was now quite deep—too deep for my husband to be of any assistance to me, as he was a short man. Mr. Kinzie, being taller, walked beside us and held my feet out of the water. The gentlemen were up to the armpits in the stream, which fortunately was narrow.

We soon after met some of the other gentlemen of our party coming to meet us, and were not long in reaching the encampment, which looked very inviting. The tents were pitched, my cot all ready for a good rest, a bright fire at a little distance, and supper ready.

But in the mean time a storm was brewing, another egg storm! As we arrived at the camp, we all noticed the strange appearance which Edward Ploudre presented. He had on white duck pantaloons and a frock coat, and had both pockets filled with eggs, which he had provided for a second battle and fancied his coat would conceal. But the keen eyes of both Mr. Kinzie and Mr. Baird were too much for him, as was their fleetness, for they immediately set in pursuit of him, and when they caught him slapped his pockets until the eggs were broken and the contents ran in a stream down his pantaloons and white stockings, and into his low shoes. The men laughed until exhausted. Then there was another call for more eggs, and another fight ensued, which only ceased for want of ammunition. Never did any one ever enter with greater zest into any sport than did the gentlemen on this occasion. However, at last quiet was restored and we found ourselves with good appetites for supper, and soon after retired to refreshing sleep. The next morning the field of battle presented a strange appearance, strewn as it was with egg-shells, and many were the regrets expressed that the ammunition was exhausted.

Before leaving the shore, speeches befitting the occasion were made by most of the gentlemen, and the place was formally christened "Egg Harbor," the name it has ever since borne.

Occasionally, as we coasted along the east shore of Green Bay, we would, when it presented an inviting appearance, take other walks along the bank. The men always took pains to secure a handsome spot for the pipe or rest. The tent was scarcely ever pitched for dinner except in wet weather.

As I do not remember distances from point to point, I will not attempt to give each day's travel. The names of some of the islands have been changed since our trip in 1825; and many more that in that day had no names, have since been christened. Then we knew by names, only Washington Island, the Beavers,—Big and Little,—Chambers, Manitou, Fox, Pottawattamie or Rock Island, formerly known as Isle de Pou, or Louse Island. Many were the beautiful spots we passed. Never were we obliged to dine or encamp on the east shore at any spot not attractive.

One night we encamped at a place called Petit Detroit, which is not far from Death's Door. It is a small island, formed like a half-moon, the inner portion being a most beautiful harbor, with a high bank; and beyond this rise higher hills. The whole island was then a perfect garden of wild roses. Never have I at one time seen so many flowers of any kind, as I then saw. The charms of the place so attracted us that we made an early landing. The men had to clear a spot to pitch the tent, and in finishing their work they very thoughtfully decorated my tent with roses.

Here again, and indeed it was so each evening, the young men began to frolic. There were no more eggs for that kind of warfare, yet there seemed to be many articles to do battle with. As soon as supper was over, all the gentlemen of the party, except Rolette, went off for a walk over the hills. They were in the finest of spirits and so were the crew—the whole island seemed to respond to their glee. The boatmen, keeping to themselves, went off to the other side of the island. Soon we heard their laughter, and well we knew there was fun somewhere. In a little while we saw the gentlemen run towards the encampment and, laughing, go to each other's tents and, catching up anything they could lay their hands on, into the lake they tossed it. Each possessed a small feather bed, that with the bedding was rolled up in an Indian mat. Soon we saw these beds sailing off, and these were followed by coats, hats, etc. Mr. Kinzie was so engaged in the "pitch battle" that he did not see his own bed start. The others secured theirs while yet in reach. The beds usually fell in the water lengthwise, but Mr. Kinzie's went in on one end, which made it sail well. When at last he discovered his bed, outward bound, it was several yards from shore. He plunged into the water and had to swim, as the water was quite deep, before he reached it.

The boats are never unloaded, from the time they leave port until they reach their destination. This fleet of boats was originally loaded at Prairie du Chien, and then unloaded at the portage between the Wisconsin and Fox rivers, where the men carried first the packs of furs on their backs, then returned for the boats, and reloading them would run down to the Big Chute, now Appleton. Here the boats again had to be unloaded, and the furs portaged around by the men. The boats, however, made the journey down the swift water, which was called "jumping the rapids," and was an interesting sight if one had nerve enough to look on. The unloading was repeated at

Grand Kaukauna; but at Rapides Croche and at Rapides des Peres, now DePere, the loads would be carried through, all of the men walking in the water to guide the boats and their valuable loads. Our boats, it will be seen, were loaded for the last time at Kaukauna, not to be unloaded until they reached Mackinac.

We will return now to our last camping place at that charming island and harbor. After the gentlemen had played to their hearts' content, they retired to their moist beds. One would have thought they might all have taken cold, but not one word of complaint did I hear from any of them.

We now traveled slowly, waiting for a day which would show signs of being fine throughout, that we might make in safety "La Grande Traverse"— to cross the lake from the east shore to the west, or north. The crossing started from Rock Island. There were some scattered islands on the route, where shelter was sought in case of a storm or high wind. On the day we attempted the crossing, there was a slight east wind, strong enough to warrant the sails being hoisted. The wind at last dying away they were taken down, and it was with difficulty we reached our destined port. These boats carry but one sail—a square one. The mast is attached to the side of the boat, and when wanted is hoisted to its place and the sail put up. When in the middle of the lake, a strange sight it was to see the boats arranged in a regular line, near each other, while the men took a rest. (The men never smoked except when ashore.) The boats floated gently on, carried by the current, and always guided by the steersman. The motion was a delightful one. We made a successful crossing, and the men were rewarded by a supper from our mess baskets, and a little extra grog. I have forgotten to mention that the crew each morning and evening received a gill of whiskey.

On our arrival at the other shore, we were no longer able to secure as fine camping grounds as those of the preceding days. As the gentlemen no longer could find a good play-ground, they devoted themselves to their books.

We were six days in making the journey from Green Bay to Mackinac, being wind-bound for twenty-four hours in a very dreary camping ground. I never have seen men so restless as were those of our party. They behaved like children; nothing pleased them. As for Rolette, he growled and scolded at the weather through the whole time we waited. The crew took the wisest course. They spread their blankets down and went to sleep, thus passing the greater portion of the time.

The following day was not all that could be desired; but as we were nearing our destination, we were willing to endure some discomfort for the sake of hastening on our way. We set sail, catching a little breeze that helped us along. While yet the whole crew were watching the signs of the weather, a sudden squall took us unawares and somewhat disturbed us. The sails were flapping, as the direction of the wind had changed. The boats were pitching, and Rolette, much frightened, was giving orders, which if followed would have swamped the boat. His final order was, "John! John! Take down that mast! Saw it off with the ax!" In his fright he did not notice that each man was trying his best to take down the mast in each boat, so much did these imperil the craft.

All this time we were quite near shore. When peace was restored, John Kinzie (Chicago's first settler) came up to Rolette with a very sad and peni-tent-looking face, and said: "I am very sorry I disobeyed your orders, and I hope you will forgive me." Rolette looked him squarely in the face, and re-plied: "John, you rascal, how did you disobey me?" "In taking down that mast, sir, I did not *saw it off with the ax.*"

The day following the squall, we arrived at Pointe a la Barbe—the point where one shaves. It is said this Point is so named from the fact that all voyageurs stopped there to shave and make themselves presentable upon their arrival at the "grand emporium of the West." We went on shore, giving our crew an opportunity to shave for the first time since we left Green Bay. Each man looked very well in his striped cotton shirt, blue pantaloons, red sash around the waist, and red handkerchief around the neck. Caps of all sorts they wore, but no hats. They purchased high hats when they reached Mackinac. Everybody then wore the hat since called the "stove-pipe."

The rest of the fleet stopped at the American Fur Company's landing, but our boat landed me opposite the residence of my grandparents. My hap-piness I cannot describe: it was soon turned to sadness, as before reaching the house I learned of my grandfather's serious illness. I had received but two letters from home in the past six months, and knowing I was to arrive in June, they had refrained from writing the painful news.

After court adjourned, my husband returned to Green Bay to attend to the house he was having built for us, and came back in August to Mackinac. We then returned to Green Bay, reaching there on October 28th, 1825. We went by schooner, bringing with us a little daughter of six weeks, baptized by the name of Eliza Ann: but named by our Indian relatives, Waubunoqua, "Early Morn."

My dear mother accompanied us back, to see me safely home, although she had to return in the same vessel on account of my grandfather's alarming illness. His death occurred three weeks after our departure from the dear old island.

FROM WAU-BUN: THE EARLY DAY IN THE NORTHWEST
(1856)

State Historical Society of Wisconsin

Juliette MaGill Kinzie

JULIETTE MAGILL, born in Connecticut in 1806, was a well-educated, carefully brought up New England girl who fell in love not with the local minister or the town attorney as her parents would no doubt have preferred, but with a wilderness adventurer who was the sub-Indian agent at Fort Winnebago in Wisconsin, then the wilderness. Since her childhood, she had been fascinated by the stories of the West that her uncle, Alexander Wolcott, Indian agent at Chicago, had told her. When he visited the East with his brother-in-law John Kinzie Jr. (son of the egg-tossing John in the previous narrative), Juliette MaGill met a young man quite different from those she had known. Kinzie had grown up on the frontier, spoke several Indian languages, and offered Juliette a life of adventure on a frontier only recently claimed from the British. Since Kinzie's stepfather had been removed as cashier of a bank and her parents were separated, marriage and a new life in the West where Kinzie was Indian Agent were a seductive escape. They travelled to Fort Winnebago where the only other white woman was the wife of the commandant.

Wau-Bun chronicles her travels in the wilderness with great good humor and a passion for experience, no matter what hardships that involved. In this she was like many pioneer women who relished the opportunity to live an adventurous life away from the settled communities of the East. Kinzie began her writing career by composing a pamphlet about the experiences of her husband's family during the massacre at Chicago in 1812. She then expanded the account to include her own experiences on the frontier during her marriage. There is some scholarly debate about the accuracy of her account of the Chicago massacre, which she heard second-hand, but her own narrative is delightful, filled with her love of excitement and the great sympathy she had for the Indians she knew. The chapter reprinted here is the first in the book and chronicles a typical voyage up the lakes in the days of small steamers. The trip was not without its hardships, but Kinzie notes that they were lucky not to have to take a schooner. Given her account, the reader may feel Kinzie is an optimist indeed.

The Kinzies became permanent residents of Chicago in 1834 where Mrs. Kinzie became a powerful social arbiter of frontier culture and a hostess for distinguished visitors until she died in 1870. Her granddaughter, Juliette Gorden Low, founded the Girl Scouts of America.

⤛━◉━⤜

DEPARTURE FROM DETROIT

IT WAS ON A DARK, rainy evening in the month of September, 1830, that we went on board the steamer *Henry Clay,* to take passage for Green Bay. All our friends in Detroit had congratulated us upon our good fortune in being spared the voyage in one of the little schooners which at this time afforded the ordinary means of communication with the few and distant settlements on Lakes Huron and Michigan.

Each one had some experience to relate of his own or of his friends' mischances in these precarious journeys—long detentions on the St. Clair flats—furious head-winds off Thunder Bay, or interminable calms at Mackinac or the Manitous. That which most enhanced our sense of peculiar good luck was the true story of one of our relatives having left Detroit in the month of June and reached Chicago in the September following, having been actually three months in performing what is sometimes accomplished by even a sailvessel in four days.

But the certainty of encountering similar misadventures would have weighed little with me. I was now to visit, nay, more, to become a resident of that land which had, for long years, been to me a region of romance. Since the time when, as a child, my highest delight had been in the letters of a dear relative [Alexander Wolcott], describing to me his home and mode of life in the "Indian country," and still later, in his felicitous narration of a tour with General Cass, in 1820, to the sources of the Mississippi—nay, even earlier, in the days when I stood at my teacher's knee, and spelled out the long word Mich-i-li-mack-i-nac, that distant land, with its vast lakes, its boundless prairies, and it mighty forests, had possessed a wonderful charm for my imagination. Now I was to see it!—it was to be my home!

Our ride to the quay, through the dark by-ways, in a cart, the only vehicle which at that day could navigate the muddy, unpaved streets of Detroit, was a theme for much merriment, and not less so, our descent of the narrow, perpendicular stairway by which we reached the little apartment called the Ladies' Cabin. We were highly delighted with the accommodations, which, by comparison, seemed the very climax of comfort and convenience; more especially as the occupants of the cabin consisted, beside myself, of but a lady and two little girls.

Nothing could exceed the pleasantness of our trip for the first twenty-four hours. There were some officers, old friends, among the passengers. We had plenty of books. The gentlemen read aloud occasionally, admired the solitary magnificence of the scenery around us, the primeval woods, or the vast expanse of water unenlivened by a single sail, and then betook themselves to their cigar, or their game of euchre, to while away the hours.

For a time the passage over Thunder Bay was delightful, but, alas! it was not destined, in our favor, to belie its name. A storm came on, fast and furious—what was worse, it was of long duration. The pitching and rolling of the little boat, the closeness, and even the sea-sickness, we bore as became us. They were what we had expected, and were prepared for. But a new feature of discomfort appeared, which almost upset our philosophy.

The rain, which fell in torrents, soon made its way through every seam and pore of deck or moulding. Down the stairway, through the joints and crevices, it came, saturating first the carpet, then the bedding, until, finally, we were completely driven, "by stress of weather," into the Gentlemen's Cabin. Way was made for us very gallantly, and every provision resorted to for our comfort, and we were congratulating ourselves on having found a haven in our distress, when, lo! the seams above opened, and down upon our devoted heads poured such a flood that even umbrellas were an insufficient protection. There was nothing left for the ladies and children but to betake ourselves to the berths, which in this apartment, fortunately remained dry;

and here we continued ensconced the livelong day. Our dinner was served up to us on our pillows. The gentlemen chose the driest spots, raised their umbrellas, and sat under them, telling amusing anecdotes, and saying funny things to cheer us until the rain ceased, and at nine o'clock in the evening we were gladdened by the intelligence that we had reached the pier at Mackinac.

We were received with the most affectionate cordiality by Mr. and Mrs. Robert Stuart, at whose hospitable mansion we had been for some days expected.[1]

The repose and comfort of an asylum like this, can be best appreciated by those who have reached it after a tossing and drenching such as ours had been. A bright, warm fire, and countenances beaming with kindest interest, dispelled all sensations of fatigue or annoyance.

After a season of pleasant conversation, the servants were assembled, the chapter of God's word was solemnly read, the hymn chanted, the prayer of praise and thanksgiving offered, and we were conducted to our place of repose.

---

[1] Robert Stuart was the American Fur Company's agent at Mackinac. He had been young Kinzie's employer while he was in Mackinac several years before this time.

THE JOURNEY OF THE FIRST WHITE SETTLEMENT ACROSS THE GEORGIAN BAY

(1923)

Soaphy Anderson

ONE OF SEVEN children of Thomas Gummersall Anderson, a famous fur trader and Indian Agent on the Great Lakes, Soaphy Anderson grew up on the frontier. She was probably born on Drummond Island, and spent eight years of her childhood on Manitoulin with her family. In the following narrative Soaphy Anderson describes how the first white settlement came to Manitoulin Island, the largest fresh-water island in the world, which lies between Georgian Bay and Lake Huron. After the War of 1812, the British retained the Island and many of the Indian tribes who had been loyal to them during the conflict settled there. The government of Canada then sent military families and missionaries to begin the process of acculturating the Native peoples. For some inexplicable reason, perhaps because of governmental bureaucracy, her party was forced to begin the trip in late fall, a nearly suicidal endeavor. What is striking about Miss Anderson's recounting is the unemotional tone with which she calmly details the difficulties and the losses the little party experienced. The account of an American settler to Michigan by Mary Per Lee, which follows this, is quite different, but that may be the effect of the medium and the age of the writers. Anderson appears to have written for a historical society long after the events she describes having seen as a child. Lee wrote shortly after she was uprooted from her friends and family. Moreover, as a mother she was responsible for her children in a way the young Anderson would not have understood. Grisly as are the events Anderson sometimes depicts, she also gives a portrait of the extraordinary strength of her mother who, in the midst of deplorable living conditions and want, learned Gaelic so she could read the Bible to the workers who had accompanied them and spoke nothing else.

⋅→⊨●⊜⊨←⋅

IN THE AUTUMN of 1838 my father, the late Captain T. G. Anderson, who was an officer in the Indian Department, was ordered to an entirely new field of labor, and late as it was, our home at Coldwater was broken up and arrangements made for a long and dangerous journey by water to Manitoulin

Island, a distance of some two hundred miles. A large bateau was engaged and on the eighth of October, Captain Anderson, with the officers employed by the Indian Department, their wives, children and servants, besides mechanics, employed to teach the Indians different trades, embarked from Coldwater. The bateau was heavily laden with necessary provisions for a long, cold journey. Tents, beds and bedding, besides its precious freight of thirty-four souls, i.e. the missionary, the Rev. C. C. Brough; afterwards Archdeacon of London, Ontario, Mrs. Brough, four children and two servants, Dr. Paul Darling and his wife, well known in Orillia in later years, one infant six weeks old, a nurse, the schoolmaster, Mr. Bailey, Mrs. Bailey, and three children, the Captain, his wife, four children, two young friends and one servant, the oarsmen, a pet cat and a dog. The days were short and very cold, the lake rough and freezing on the oars as the men raised them every fresh stroke.

The females of the party were not such as are usually found in those out-of-the-way places but were highly educated, refined and delicate, heretofore shielded from every storm. From there being so many women and children on board, it was necessary to encamp early in the afternoons in order to get well under canvas before nightfall, and on account of the number of children to dress and feed; beds, etc., to unpack; tents to strike and boat to be loaded, the mornings were spent, ere we were enabled to proceed on our way. Some days we had only two or three hours in which to travel, for instance, if we arrived at a good camping ground, it was advisable to go ashore for the night, as daylight might fail before reaching another.

The nights soon became very cold and the ice had to be cut away in the morning in order to get the bateau from her moorings. One day we were lost in the channels and our supplies were well nigh exhausted. After a consultation and some "hard toda" (ship biscuit), the Captain and some of the men went ashore to look about and hearing a crow cawing fancied it was tame. My father said to one of the men— "Follow that crow and it will take you to an Indian camp." He did as directed, and strange to say, the crow would fly a short distance then stop, as if waiting for the men, then off again, till at last, they arrived at a lodge. The poor Indians gave of such as they had, and came to pilot us through the maze of islands.

Our *Evangeline* had no deck or shelter of any kind; all were exposed to the fury of the biting winds, snow and rain, and the freezing spray which frequently dashed over the edge of the boat. It is a marvel how any escaped death. After three weeks of terrible suffering we at last came in sight of the "Establishment," so called, but alas! for us, one of the three houses was in flames, and by the time we reached the landing place, was reduced to a heap of ashes.

Notwithstanding this great misfortune, all hearts were raised in gratitude to that kind Providence which had brought us through so many dangers to our journey's end and all who were able set to work with a will to
make the very best of so trying a situation. My father, who never seemed to
be at a loss, soon had all comfortably housed for that night, and glad we
were to lay our numbed and weary bodies down on the floor of our log
house, with roaring fires in the chimneys, luxuries we had not enjoyed for
three weeks. Long and anxiously our father and mother talked ere closing
their eyes in sleep, arranging how best to accommodate four families in a
small house, originally intended for only one. Downstairs there were three
small rooms and two very narrow passages besides a kitchen with a large
chimney and oven. Upstairs was all in one room, not even lathed overhead.
The spans between the logs of the walls had been filled in with mud. Two of
the rooms below were given to the Broughs, the Baileys occupying the other,
all parties making use of the kitchen. A sail was stretched across the room
upstairs for a partition, the smaller portion was occupied by the doctor and
family, while we made use of the larger part. Our beds were spread on the
floor at night and we lay huddled together, father, mother, children and servants, all on a level, like a flock of sheep. In the morning beds were rolled up
into as small a space as possible to admit of our moving about, and served
for seats.

We were frequently awakened in the night by the loud cracking of our
log walls, caused by the intense frost. The ice, too, in the bay could crack
with a roar like a canon, dying away in the distance like thunder.

The men, who accompanied us, made their beds on the kitchen floor
with buffalo robes and blankets, and those workmen who were already at
work on the Island occupied the building which had been erected for a school
house for the Indians.

The day after our arrival, hearing a loud sobbing in the room below, I
put my eyes to a convenient knothole in the floor and peeped down in order,
if possible, to discover the cause and I saw the lifeless body of little Benny
Bailey, lying upon the table. The poor child, only about six or eight months
old, had died from a severe cold, the effects of unavoidable exposure. This
was my first sight of death. Here was trouble indeed. Where could the body
be laid while the grave was being prepared? My father soon hung a blanket
across a corner of one of the small passages, nailed up a few boards and upon
them laid the beautiful remains of our much-loved playmate, and there it lay
for many days, owing to the severe frost and lack of proper implements with
which to dig the tiny grave. At last all was ready. A small coffin had been
made of rough boards and with many tears we followed the dear babe to his
last resting place, a lonely little grave on the bleak hillside.

The schooner with our winter supplies on board was obliged to return to her winter quarters (though in sight of the island), on account of the ice, in consequence of which we were on short rations. There was a small supply of government stores, such as salt pork, tallow and pease, but no flour or butter. We had a little flour remaining after our journey and our good mother managed to make "salt rising bread," very sweet and nice when properly made. We children were limited to half a slice of bread a day. After the pork had been boiled, the fat which rose to the surface of the water when cooling was skimmed off and when clarified was used as butter and was far more palatable than some very high priced butter of the present day. The Indians brought us partridge, ducks, rabbits and sometimes venison.

The gentlemen soon learned the Indian mode of spearing fish in winter, through a hole in the ice. The elders alone indulged in tea, no milk, of course, but plenty of maple sugar, and though we had any quantity of the best of wood and kept a roaring fire in the chimney, our cups would freeze to the tables as we sat at meals. We were fortunate in having plenty of potatoes, grown the previous summer and stored in a root house. Such potatoes as I have never seen elsewhere—pink eyes, kidney potatoes, Sachris fingus: that latter were always roasted in the ashes.

About six weeks after our arrival, Dr. Darling's baby died from the cold and its little body lay for many days awaiting burial. (Mrs. Darling was my mother's sister.) During our eight years' residence at Manitoulin there were only three deaths amongst the white people. The two infants above mentioned and another beautiful child, Dr. Darling's only son, Basil, who died in his mother's arms without one moment's illness, of heart disease.

Soon the Indians came about us, seeking instruction, and the first two who desired to be baptized were an old man and his squaw. There were called Adam and Eve, and were lawfully married at the same time. Two of their sons, grown men were also baptized. One of them was called Abel.

The larger of the two rooms occupied by the missionary and his family served as a church, school, and council room during our first winter. Mr. and Mrs. Bailey gathered the children of our party in their room on Sunday afternoons, teaching the church catechism, collects, etc., and there I first heard and, with others, learned to sing that grand old hymn "O God of Bethel," so appropriate to our lonely isolation. Years and years have rolled on since then but the first words of that hymn send me back to that little room, and in fancy, I hear again sweet voices, long since hushed in death, and see dear faces long since mouldering in the dust.

My dear mother invited all who would to assemble in our kitchen on Sunday afternoons while she read aloud from the Bible, then a tract or two or a few chapters of Bunyan's *Pilgrim's Progress* and talked earnestly to men and women of those things which concerned their everlasting welfare. She had a supply of French and Gaelic as well as English tracts. French she could speak, read, or write as fluently as English. Many of the workmen were "hielanders" and mother got them to teach her to read Gaelic and she even mastered it sufficiently to read to them who were unable to do so for themselves. No earthly record was every kept of the good done by this devout and faithful follower of Christ, other than that kept in the hearts and minds of those who were so fortunate as to come under her influence.

Some years since, while visiting friends in Toronto, and old servant of my mother, hearing where I was, came to see me. We talked of our dear ones long gone and of old times with many tears. On leaving she took both my hands in hers, saying "An noo, Miss Soaphy, hae y ony tract or book, a bit o' onything upon which you're mither's han' has rested. Wull ye gie it a bit o't to me? I hae heard mony a Godly mon preach, an' hae talket' wi mony a Godly mon or woman, but I hae yet tae see the mon fit to tie your mither's shoes."

Good, faithful old Effie.

During the winter many Indians came great distances, bringing their sick to the doctor or to obtain religious instruction. Often a dozen or more would come down round our kitchen fire, utterly regardless of the inconvenience they caused, smoking and drying their wet moccasins and blanket sacks, besides the filth they left for their kind friends to clear away after them. Those of the Indians who were baptized were generally given Scripture names. We had three Peters in the sick list at one time; Peter Bank had spine disease; Peter Legs was paralyzed, and Peter Throat suffered from bronchitis. One poor old woman had a broken jaw and Dr. Darling, who dearly loved a joke, nicknamed her "Old Mother Mouth," and Mother Mouth she was called to the end of the chapter.

On one occasion, Mr. Brough traded dogs with an old squaw, his reverence wanting a good sleigh dog. The trade seemed quite satisfactory for a few days when back came the old woman with her dog who was in a very bad mind and pitched in the "English Black Coat" in no measured terms, gaining for herself the name of "Old Mother Spit-Fire."

During the sugar season, we frequently visited the camps and stuffed ourselves with fresh maple sugar. When boiled to a certain thickness and poured on the snow to cool, it is called Ginn sugar and, if not too highly flavored with fish, is most delicious.

In spite of all we could do to enliven the monotony, time passed very slowly. At last the long, dreary winter drew to a close. With what rapture we beheld the blue waters as the ice began to break up and was carried by the soft south wind out of the bay into the open lake. As soon as possible, after navigation was safe, a bateau was sent from Penetanguishene (the then nearest point of civilization) to our relief, though they rather expected to find a lot of skeletons. With what delight we hailed the boat as she rounded the point at the head of the bay. What warm hand clasps and heartfelt thanks went up to God, for our safety can better be imagined than I can find words to describe.

A soon as possible in the spring, building operations commenced. Log houses were erected for the missionary, doctor, and school master, as well as for the mechanics and Indians. A large workshop was built for carpenters and coopers, also a blacksmith shop, where the young Indians could learn the different trades from skilled workmen, employed by the government for that purpose. There was also a shoemaker and later on a tailor. We soon had sheep, cows, and oxen sent up on board a schooner chartered by [the] Government and we began to find ourselves not quite so much out of the world after all. Sheep did well on the stony land, and the wool was of good quality. A woman, skilled in the art of carding and spinning, was engaged to teach the Indians. They were quick to learn and delighted at being able to knit their own socks and stockings, which they did during the long winter evenings. As many as fourteen or fifteen boys would be seated round the table, knitting and chatting, sometimes singing hymns.

The Broughs and Baileys only remained for a year or two and their places were filled by the Rev. F. A. O'Meara from the Sault and Mr. John Buckill as school-master. Mr. O'Meara and his clever young wife, a Miss Dallas, whom he just brought from her home in Orillia, were fully imbued with the true missionary spirit, entering heart and soul into the work before them and were untiring in their efforts to instruct the poor heathen; the good "Black Coat" walking long distances on snow shoes, or with his dogs and sleigh, would hunt up the wanderers, scattered about in their miserable encampments, telling them the good news of salvation, persuading them to come to Establishment and live in houses prepared for them and be clothed and fed and taught to live like the white people. Many gladly came and were, after due instruction, baptized. Others preferred to live and die in the old ways of their forefathers.

It was during his residence at Manitoulin that Mr. O'Meara perfected his justly celebrated translation of the *Book of Common Prayer* into the Ojibway tongue, for which services the Government gave him a pension for life.

Until the number of inhabitants and converts warranted the building of a church, service was held in the upper flat of the store house, and the lamented Bishop Strachan visited Manitoulin on his first Confirmation tour of the Island. When the services were held in that room many Indians and a few of the whites were confirmed. The white china bowl which served as a

"Font" is now one of my most valued relics.

In 1842 or 1843 a church was erected and is, I think I may confidently affirm, still in good repair, as not long since my friend Miss O'Meara and myself were asked to contribute our "mite" towards repairing the church, the foundations of which our fathers had laid.

In the autumn of 1840 Captain Anderson received orders to proceed to Kingston, the then seat of Government, with as little delay as possible to attend to some important business. It being late to venture by canoe, he waited till the ice was safe for travelling, meanwhile making preparations for his long trip. He made a large toboggan, having a frame of ash, braced all round, the back much higher than the sides. Deer skins were stretched upon this frame, having the hair inside, so that with a blanket and some robes, he would be quite comfortable. The toboggan was drawn by light, good dogs in very gay trapping, their collars and back straps were covered with scarlet cloth; curved wires were fastened to stand erect above the back straps, upon which were strung several small bells, making a very stylish turn-out.

The Captain started off on the twelfth of November, having two or three Indians with him, carrying necessary provisions for the journey, there being no inns or houses of any kind on the way, and when night came they made a shelter of boughs for themselves and the dogs, laid down on boughs and covered themselves with robes and blankets and oftentimes were almost covered with snow. The day after their departure it commenced to snow and kept it up for thirteen days and nights. Of course, there was great anxiety as to the fate of the travellers and it was midwinter ere any news of them reached home. They did not return until the end of May. The confidential business entrusted to my father necessitated his walking upon snow-shoes (there being no other way) from a point near Kingston, out to all the small lakes back of Peterborough wherever there was an Indian encampment, coming out at length near Renna, where he found the person he was in search of.

Our family remained at Manitoulin till 1845 when my father gained promotion and was removed to Toronto, Captain George Ironsides taking his place. Dr. Darling remained till his death, which took place in 1849. Mr. and Mrs. O'Meara remained for, I think, twenty years, working faithfully for the good of the poor Indians and were the instruments in God's hands of bringing many from heathen darkness and ignorance to the knowledge of the true God.

After serving in the Department for forty years, in different parts of the country, Captain Anderson, on account of his great age and infirmities petitioned for a retired allowance, which was granted and he settled in Port Hope. Here, too, after a short time came the Rev. Dr. O'Meara and his family, having been appointed Rector of St. John's Church there. Strange that the friends who worked so happily together amongst the Indians should have drifted into the same harbor, and how they enjoyed talking of old times and their work on Manitoulin.

Dr. and Mrs. O'Meara, the "Old Captain" (as he was lovingly called) have long since "Entered into the rest which remaineth for the people of God." Their children are scattered far apart, but all looking forward to be reunited when "The day breaks and the shadows flee away."

TO MICHIGAN BY WATER—1844

Mary Per Lee

WHEN JULIETTE KINZIE went into the wilderness she knew there would be a substantial dwelling waiting for her. Sarah Christian, whose narrative of life in a mining camp on Isle Royale follows, knew she, too, would have a reasonably comfortable resting place when she disembarked. Kinzie and Christian were not homesteaders, however, but the wives of government and mining officials. Many women who ventured into the wilderness were not so lucky. There were no soldiers or miners to help with their baggage; their homes would have to be built, the land cleared, and a new life made. Caroline Kirkland described just how difficult this could be in *A New Home— Who'll Follow* in 1839, and although the book was an instantaneous best-seller, most women were still not prepared for what they might have to endure. Lee's letter reflects the sobering recognition of the hardships most pioneer women experienced when they first saw the frontier. They and their families had emigrated, sailing to their destinations on the lakes because the over-land route was impassable, to take advantage of the opportunities in the West. Land was cheap and fertile, a living could be made without doing factory work for twelve hours a day, and there would be a better life for their children. But realizing their goals would take years of backbreakingly hard work. The story of their adjustments was often written home in letters just like this one. Although the twenty-eight-year-old Lee tries to be optimistic for her readers back in Chenango County, New York, about her life on a government land grant near Grand Rapids, Michigan, her homesickness, frustration, and fear permeate nearly every line.

⊷⊶⊙⊝⊷⊶

July 14 (1844)
To all my dear friends in Chenango:
    After a residence of three weeks in Michigan I will endeavor to inform you of our adventures since we left home. It seems an age to me since we started for Canastota with heavy hearts, all but Etty who could not think why Ma cried. We left Canastota Thursday at one o'clock and I was already

more than homesick. Our boat [on the Erie Canal] was a whitened sepulchre, very fair without but furnished miserably within, our cabin was not larger than mother's bedroom and crowded to suffocation with passengers. Never did any poor creature feel as I did when I found myself placed there for one week. I could not eat, for swallowing was out of the question. There was a lump in my throat as big as an egg, so when the darksome night came on I sat me down and cried to the tune of "Home Sweet Home" sung by a little Schenectadian of the name of Vroman. We passed Syracuse at eleven o'clock in the night. Consequently I saw none of our friends but was engaged in pacifying the children to their new habitation: filthy bed without sheets and lying heads and points on their upper shift, Etty called it, and liked the novelty of the situation much better than poor little Mio who like her mother cried from very home sickness.

One side of our cabin was entirely occupied by a Mrs. Hitchcock from West Troy who believed in "first come, first served." She had her trunk, large armed rocking chair and cradle which just took one side of the cabin and if anyone ventured to set foot upon her premises they were informed by a pair of gray eyes that they had no business there. We arrived at Rochester Saturday evening just at dusk. Rochester is decidedly the queen of the Western cities, the canal through it is more splendid than I could have imagined a canal. We arrived at Buffalo Monday between one and two o'clock without accident and took passage on the *Constitution* for Chicago at seven. Here our fare was materially better. Instead of poor bread, filthy meat, and stinking butter and tea and coffee without milk, we had everything that could be desired in the way of fish, flesh, and fowl, and early vegetables. Radishes, cucumbers, and green peas were taken on board at Cleveland, and we also got early cherries there, the black hearts.

As soon as our boat got under motion, the ladies hurried to their berths; every one on board save myself and every child save my children was sick. Mrs. Carpenter was confined to her berth with her child until the second day. Mio and Etty would get very sleepy from the motion of the boat, but exhibited no signs of vomiting. Jennie was very sick when we left Cleveland, the lake was rather rough there, but as the wind fell in the afternoon the ladies regained their feet and their appetites.

We arrived in Detroit Wednesday morn, five o'clock, and passed two hours there. Here we left Mrs. Hitchcock, armed chair, cradle, and crying baby. She fed her baby, three months old, rice pudding, raw apple, and cherries—you may imagine we did not want for music. On Wednesday evening we entered Lake Huron, after which we made but few landings, except for wood, and saw little but Indian villages and one or two military stations. We stopped a few minutes at Mackinaw and many of our passengers ran up to catch a view of the fort, which has quite an imposing appearance from the Lake. The Indians came on board with their curiosities for sale, but they value them so highly that it would require quite a little fortune to purchase many of them. Our captain took on board some of their trout, which well cooked would be as delightful as anything of the fish kind ever eaten, but we had it boiled, and a wishy-washy gravy poured over it. I wished very much that father could have one of them, and had there been a Magnetic Telegraph for fish transportation I should have sent in quite a cargo of Mackinaw trout. We had also some white bass which were delightful.

On Thursday we entered the broad waters of Lake Michigan and a beautiful lake it is. The lake is dark blue, or rather more of a green than an invisible green. We drank lake water after we entered Lake Huron until we reached Chicago, and very excellent water it is if you stop thinking, and as perfectly transparent as any water I ever saw. We landed at Milwaukee, Racine, and Southport in the night and arrived at Chicago on Saturday morn and happy as I thought I should be to set foot on terra-firma, I would rather it would have been any other place in the world than Chicago. For although evidently a place of business, it is the dirtiest hole that my eyes ever rested upon. Here we were escorted to another "whitened sepulchre" where we were doomed to wait until Monday afternoon, for favorable winds, for we had to take a schooner. During our stay in Chicago it rained almost incessantly, and such depths of mud, mud, mud you never dreamed of.

Teams came in from the country with four yoke of cattle wading up to their bodies in mud the consistency of hasty pudding and glad was I to leave this filthy hole for a lumber schooner. Cellars are quite out of the question in Chicago—their houses are carried upon blocks or stilts and under them pools of stagnant water. Still the inhabitants persist in calling it a very healthy place—it is entirely surrounded by a prairie or marsh and nothing green in the way of tree, shrub, or grass greets the eye. Nothing but mud, and that as black as ink. I pray you all to shun Chicago and the Lake Street House of Chicago.

We left Chicago at one o'clock in the rain as we had entered it. Our schooner, the St. Joseph, was very much after the same sort as our canal fare except that we had sheets and pillow cases on our beds. The sailors were all foreigners. Tuesday about two o'clock the Lake was covered with a dense fog, so that we could not see a rod from the vessel, the consequence was that we were soon upon a sandbar, with the prospect of remaining two or three days as they frequently do, but as evening came and the fog cleared away we found ourselves only a few rods from the mouth [of the] Grand River, much to our joy. Our ballast [of stone] was thrown overboard and [we] were, by the excellent management of our captain soon afloat and at five o'clock landed at Grand Haven, as the settlement at the mouth of the river is called. Here are two public houses and the one where we stopped, an excellent one and entirely new, three stores and a steam saw mill, but everything so wild and new as to startle, but rather pleasant than otherwise. Here we saw the Potawatami tribe of Indians, with their chief and his son. Many of them were handsomely drest in the finest of broadcloth, embroidered as usual with beads and porcupine quills of various colours. The old chief had a plate of silver on his breast, as large as a good sized breakfast plate with the figure of a wolf engraved upon it. There was a great deal of silver about their persons, some dangle the plate tied to their hair between their shoulders, others had their coat capes ornamented with pieces as large as a dollar sewed closely together on the edge. The chief's son has a natural talent for music and played for us upon an instrument constructed by himself, a tune of his own composition. To me there was little music in it. We were obliged to wait at Grand Haven one day, as there is but one steamboat upon the river this summer, which runs up one day and back the next. It was not until Thursday morn at nine o'clock that [we] were floating up the Grand River. Etty was taken sick soon after we went on board, and the fever increased through the day. We arrived here about five in the afternoon, and found Mag with a baby more than two months old, of premature birth and a little bit of a thing it is, though it seems healthy but very troublesome. Etty seemed better in the morning but the fever soon came on again, and before evening we became alarmed and sent to Gran[d]ville for a physician. She had a dreadful cough, her fever was not broken until the seventh day, during which time she, of course, lived upon medicine and drink and when the fever left her her flesh was gone and she gained very slowly, until within the last week or ten days she gained her appetite and begins to smile again.

We were extremely homesick and disconsolate when we first came, and disposed to look upon the dark side of the picture and would rather not at present express our opinion of Michigan. Our prospects have been extremely gloomy with Etty's sickness, which was very depressing. We had to leave our goods out of door and I very much fear many of them are ruined by mildew, as they were exposed to rain for days after we got here. Abram has no barn or other place to store them and it was not until the rain was over and Etty better that we could get lumber to build a shelter for them. Here we cannot unpack, for there is scarcely house room for our bodies, and the probability is that many of our goods will be injured, after paying the enormous freight from Chenango to Grand Rapids.

I find that I have so nearly filled this last page that it must be enclosed in a wrapper and I will endeavor to fill the sheet. I have not visited the Rapids, nor do I expect to soon, for such roads nobody but wolves or wolverines ever travelled, over stumps and almost over trees. When I go up I shall take the steam-boat at my own farm....

Remember us to all our friends,   *[Signed] Mary and family*

We have also those delightful musquitoes of which you have heard and read, to fight from morning to night and vice versa. You cannot conceive anything so horribly annoying as are these insects here, thousands and tens of thousands drawing your very heart's blood. And to see my poor dear baby's face swelled to resemble a monster and screaming to tear it with her hands, and my little sick and almost insensible Etty being devoured by them, and Mio's face nobody would ever have known that had known her before, and to hear them fret and moan from morning to night was too discouraging for new comers, and we heartily wished ourselves anywhere but here, but we are getting inured to musquitoes somewhat, and our prospects otherwise are brightening. William has seen the farm and is very well pleased with it and is getting lumber to build a house. Carpenter's family are at the Rapids and are at present well. He has been sick. Baker is also at the Rapids. Otis Lyon was here a week ago. When I write again I hope we shall all be in better spirits and able to tell you something of our place. -------is talking everything and is an extremely pretty child. Mag and Abe join us in Love to All.

Mary
I shall write again soon.

FROM A NARRATIVE OF LIFE ON ISLE ROYALE DURING THE YEARS OF 1874 AND 1875

Sarah Barr Christian

PRIVATELY PUBLISHED IN 1932 as *Winter on Isle Royale*, Sarah Christian's reminiscence is one of several books written by those who lived on the Island before it became a national park. Christian, whose birth and death dates are unknown, wrote when she was an elderly widow, living then in the fashionable Kenwood area of Minneapolis. L. Lewellyn Christian may have been a second husband, since there was no employee named Christian at the Isle Royale mines when she lived there. Indeed, she never actually mentions her husband's name in her narrative, perhaps because she had remarried, and the payroll records are inconclusive; she may have been Mrs. White when she lived on the Island. Her book was, as she noted in a letter, "a very simple story—only written as memory dictated—and meant only for the eyes of my children, grandchildren, and great-grandchildren. . . . My first and doubtless my only attempt at writing."

Despite her polite disclaimers, she created a charming narrative, filled with good humor despite the necessity of travelling in unseaworthy boats, fire, and the dangers of winter. But Christian was also somewhat protected by her position as the wife of the mine superintendent of the Island Mine and because she was moving to a reasonably settled place. She mentions that she has few woman companions, but she neglects to note that there were a number of miner's wives also living on the island. They would not have been in her social circle, however. There was a vast gulf between the mine captain's wife who lived in a frame house and had her piano, and the wives of the miners or the woman running the boarding house, who at one point left what can only have been her own onerous duties to help Christian with her housework. This is not suggest Christian was spoiled—her account makes clear how much work she did—but by virtue of her husband's position she was spared the terrible drudgery many women on the frontier experienced. Her "mothers" came to stay with her, she was sometimes able to have a maid if one could be found. She was freer to take hikes and host parties and enjoy entertainments with the other educated and professional people at the mining location. That she does not notice those who were not of her class reflects the reality of life on the frontier, where social class and caste did not always disappear, but sometimes were intensified, as Elizabeth Baird took care to point out in "Reminiscences of Early Days on Mackinac Island."

Christian's account is interesting because she relates her experiences as a very young wife with a small child coping with the responsibilities of making a "respectable" home on a island in Lake Superior which could be marooned for months at a stretch, yet which could also be unexpectedly visited by mining company officials who were her husband's superiors and whom she would be expected to entertain appropriately. "Do your best for a guest," she tells us she learned, "but *never* apologize." And she doesn't.

⊷⊷◉⊶⊷

ABOUT OCTOBER TWELFTH of 1874 I left Duluth to take passage on the steamer *Metropolis*, the last passenger boat leaving that port for Buffalo. I had with me my little daughter Ruth, eleven weeks old, her mother but nineteen years; also a maid servant, who spoke very broken English.

I found we were to be the only passengers and the only women on the boat, not even a cabin maid, because no passengers were expected so late in the season. The boat was filled with freight, even the cabin was so full that it was almost impossible to walk through; a corner had to be cleared where we could sit and have our meals such as they were.

I was disturbed by only one thing—the fear that we might not quickly reach Hancock, Michigan, where I expected to meet my husband who was to come over with the tug from Isle Royale. The trip from Duluth to Hancock should have taken, under favorable conditions, about twenty hours, and, allowing for all sorts of delays, not more than thirty. However, I did not know when we started that the boat had been officially pronounced unseaworthy and was making its last trip. It was to be dry docked at Buffalo and eventually destroyed. The captain, as he told me after piloting us safely to our destination, knew it only too well, and moved with such caution that we went into every port and lingered indefinitely, hoping for better weather before he again ventured forth. He confided in me, what I am sure was the truth, that with two women and a baby aboard, he took less chances than he would otherwise have done. I know we were really a heavy burden on his mind; but if he is still living, he may, even after all these years, feel the gratitude I hold in memory of the kindness and respect shown to me on that dreary trip. Even when we did venture forth it was to plow through a forbidding and tremendous lot of water.

Blessed is youth, for I was far more concerned at the delay, and my fear was more that we might not reach the Island (because winter threatened to shut it off from the mainland) than fear for our safety, although not entirely at ease about the danger.

We were five days and as many nights in reaching Hancock, instead of the scheduled 24 hours; and a dreary, cold, rainy morning it was when we finally tied up at the dock. Much colder at that most northern point in upper Michigan on Lake Superior than I had ever known.

No husband and no tug awaited me, nor did a human being come onto the boat to welcome or explain. I sat two hours in the cabin, wondering what I should do; and realizing that when the unloading and the reloading of copper ingots was finished I would have to vacate, or be carried on to Buffalo! That couldn't be! But I was so young and inexperienced in travel I was more anxious than was necessary. I had a horrible feeling that if I stirred from that spot I might never be found. Yet sitting on the dock, with a bitter cold rain pouring down, just didn't appeal to me!

However, things are never so bad they cannot be worse, and, just before the loading was completed, my husband's sister appeared. We had never met before and no doubt the curiosity and nervousness of each for the other was mutual. I accepted her arrival as a drowning man would a straw, but she was much more support than a mere straw; knew why no husband was on hand and just what she was to do with us. The tug and husband had been—and gone! After waiting two days! My husband was obliged to return to the Island.

As I had to wait two days more for a boat coming from Buffalo my sister-in-law took us to her home. Her husband, Frank White, was superintendent of the Osceola mine—a near neighbor of the great Calumet and Hecla—where we were a year later to make our home for fourteen years. A narrow gauge railroad ten miles in length connected Hancock and the mines. Many, many trips later on did I take over that little road.

At the end of two long days the boat, by name *The Winslow*, commanded by Captain Wilkins, arrived; and back we went to Hancock and boarded the boat. There I met, also for the first time, my mother-in-law, who had kindly agreed to come on to keep us company on the Island. I had met plenty of new relatives, for there were eight in the White family, but as yet husband was a minus quantity. When all was loaded onto the steamer and it nosed out toward Lake Superior I took hope. It was forty miles across and the harbor we were bound for was, and still is, called Siskiwit Bay. It is on the south side of the Island, about eight or ten miles east of Washington Harbor, which is at the extreme western end of the Island.

It was dark, cold, and a drizzling rain was falling; but weather made no difference to me, I was so happy I had reached that Island before winter had shut me out entirely. The mine was two and a half miles inland. A road of sorts had been cut through the tall pine trees. It was my first acquaintance with them; and though perhaps they might seem dark and forbidding to some, I loved them from the first moment, and a pine forest thrills me to this day and takes me back so many years. In memory I live often in the midst of their beauty and grandeur.

We stepped from the dock into a comfortable open "Democrat Wagon" drawn by a fine span of black horses, rain gently falling on us. We jolted, tipped in and over the ruts, but little did it matter—we were victorious! We had beaten winter and reached the Island first.

• • •

The house was a story and a half frame house. It had, along with the boarding house, the distinction of being the only frame house on the mine, though I had rather hoped for a log house. On the first floor were front and rear parlors. We lived in the era of "parlors," now "living rooms." The back parlor served as a bedroom. A huge baseburner stood in the front room. In addition to these rooms were a dining room, a good sized kitchen, and off the dining room a bedroom, which provided a comfortable and quiet retreat for our mother. Upstairs there were three bedrooms; in every room a stove.

• • •

One more boat fought its way in after the one which brought me to the Island. It came several days later loaded with our last supplies. And had it failed us we should have been in dire need of food later in the season, for we saw no other boat until well into the following May. On this last boat was a great quantity of food in addition to that already delivered, and, to our surprise and delight, a quantity of quarters of fresh beef. It was very stormy coming over and that storm did one good deed for us, though rather hard on the Captain and his crew. But that beef, because of the high waves that washed over the deck where the beef lay, and because of the intense cold, was entirely coated with ice and hermetically sealed. They were removed very carefully, so that the ice would not be broken, and hung in a cold shed. They kept in perfect condition and might have lasted a good part of the winter, but the temptation for fresh meat was very great and it is possible that subconsciously each one of us feared we might not get our share, for the miners had the same chance at it that we had. It was good as long as it lasted.

• • •

We had a little building used for school weekdays and for worship on Sundays, and for the midweek prayer meeting. The minister was Methodist, as were all of the Cornish people I have ever known. They were very sincere Christian people. The men had most glorious voices, untrained to be sure, but I do feel all the more wonderful for that very reason. They often, in later years, sang carols for me, and their deep, full tones, of such beautiful harmony, carried one's soul up and up to a better realization of what the true meaning of Christmas Day should be to us.

I write, with considerable embarrassment, that I was the makeshift organist for the church and Sunday school services. But there was the little organ and not a single other person who could play it. My feeling has always been, do the best you can in any emergency if there is no one else near at hand who can do it better. So I did my very poor best. However, I trust the congregation did not suffer as much as I did.

Two or three times that winter we put on some harmless little stunts for the entertainment of our employees of the mine. All that I can say in praise of the effort is that "the house was packed." Our doctor, always boyish and full of fun, was the "funny man" of the troupe. He enjoyed his stunts; and one night he got off one that nearly cost him his meal ticket, for he came up against the wrath of woman, and he heard from me "after the ball was over!" So young and foolish was I! He was a chastened soul for a few hours, fearing the worst about his chances for food.

The stunt was this; and it was very funny, or so it seems to me at this date. There was a quartette, he being one of the number, and it was a funny song. All unknown to the other three the doctor had slipped off his coat and substituted for it a long white nightshirt. He trailed in last, and imagine my consternation as I sat at the organ ready to play the accompaniment. I felt a personal responsibility for this entertainment and I was doubtful as to how the audience would take it. Nor was this all. When the song ended this incorrigible man began turning handsprings across the stage, disappearing finally, much to my relief, but not much to my feelings. But the audience was kind and I rather suspect more entertained by this than by some of the other parts of the program.

• • •

The winter was terribly cold, the coldest, "they said" in eleven years, and for us fortunately so, because we were enabled to send and receive mail several times during the winter. Owing to the intense cold Pigeon River was frozen over solidly and the men could come over onto the mainland. Two French Canadians, with their dog teams, came to our Location and took the mail through the woods over a narrow trail to the other side of the Island. There they detoured to a distance of about two hundred miles north of Duluth, having crossed Pigeon River frozen over for the first time in eleven years. Then on down to Duluth and from there [the mail was] sent by rail to Chicago. The mail was all sent to Chicago, sorted and sent to its various destinations. Mine, for instance, at least the most important part, meant for a town in Minnesota, and other mail intended for Houghton or Hancock, just across the big lake, forty miles away, all had to go to Chicago. It took about seven or eight weeks to get letters to our friends and the answers back. My mother and I wrote each other twice a week, regardless of the possibility that the letters might never reach us. But when the mail did come there were many letters giving all the items of interest that had transpired at home; and I think no letters were lost in transit. Of course, we did not have many deliveries, only about four, I think. Oh, the joy when our postmen arrived! Later in the season when the ice melted somewhat in the streams, they brought us in wonderful strings of brook trout, and on their last trip Lake Superior white fish. Much appreciated after our months of having only salt meats and a limited variety of canned fish.

Another happy break in the monotony of our winter was the Christmas box packed by my mother and sent by express to Duluth and put on the same boat I was on in October. I put that box away in a closet and did not open it until Christmas morning. Though I do admit I often looked at it with mingled emotions. What a wonderful box it was! And no one knew better than Mother how to fill it, for she and Father always had done so much to make Christmas Day a happy one for their children. The snow was of tremendous depth. I thought I had seen snow and cold in Minnesota, but never such as we had that winter. The snow was seven feet deep on the level, and what drifts! Even so we did not get the full force of the lake winds, because we were inland, with dense forest all around us for protection.

• • •

We had a big three-seated "bob" sleigh, drawn by our two fine horses, and we often drove to the dock and sometimes during the winter months on the ice but near the shore. On April 29th—mark the date—one of our number had a birthday. I had invited our circle, including Mr. and Mrs. Opie, to have supper in celebration of the day. But some one of the adventurous souls suggested a sleigh ride first, and thinking it would be to the dock and back, a distance of five miles the round trip, we were ready for the fun. We were nine in all, three on a seat. After arriving at the dock our driver, the birthday guest of honor, started across the ice, and in spite of the protests of the two women, and the milder protests of two or three of the men, on we went, four miles straight out onto the ice of that great and terrible Lake Superior. Inasmuch as the first day of May, when we were supposed to pick May flowers, was only one day off, it seemed, to say the least, a little risky. I thought of my little daughter and my far from young mother-in-law at the house, and all of our men out on the lake, and it seemed too much to bear. It was so awful; for there was the great danger of airholes and wide cracks in the ice. I, fortunately, was speechless from fright, so kept perfectly quiet and did no "back seat driving." After four miles our Captain Hoatson showed his quiet authority and said, "We have gone far enough; turn back." And we did, returning safely. It was but fifteen days later that the first boat came in. Thus it was well we did not prolong our sleigh ride that night.

. . .

That summer I was without any help, although we made every effort to get someone from Hancock or Houghton. Even my mother tried to find someone to come with her, but all the women seemed to feel they would be leaving the world forever and would not venture forth, although we offered what was then a fabulous price. But I managed fairly well without a maid. My baby gave me no trouble, as my two mothers looked after her welfare and my two little sisters were only too happy to entertain her.

Every return of the tug, or appearance of a steamer, brought guests. I never knew whether one or ten. This made matters a little more complicated, but I took the safe course and got ready for ten. We had to take care of any and all who came, but we were amply repaid in the joy of seeing new faces and contacting with the outside world once more. On one occasion we had two very distinguished guests from London. And it was amusing and a joy to hear the enthusiastic remarks of the elder gentleman as he stood at the threshold of our home. "Why," he exclaimed, "I am astonished! How charming; how cozy; and a piano!" Our home was too simple for so much appreciation, but that we were comfortable at all, so far from the mainland, was more than he had expected to find. We often had gentlemen from Boston and New York, for they were "the Company," financing the prospecting of the property. I learned in those experiences valuable lessons; how to meet an emergency; and another, do your best for a guest, but never apologize.

. . .

One more experience, the most exciting and fearsome of all the months on the Island. Then I shall close this perhaps too long and rambling memory. One Sunday morning, while we were at service in our little church, one of the men came in and whispered something to one of the men in the congregation. He stood up and said, "The dock is on fire and every man here is asked to go to the rescue." All with one accord responded. The minister finished the service and we women and children left for our homes, not dreaming that the fire would mean much.

My husband had taken the tug to Hancock the day before, to attend to some business matters. I did not expect him back before Tuesday night at the earliest. About three o'clock that Sunday afternoon some boys came up from the dock to tell us the fire was gaining and the men were "almost done for" from hunger and thirst. I was crushed at my seeming thoughtlessness, but I had supposed the fire was out and the men had gone to their various abodes, for there was no one in our home to report. I sent the boys to several houses to ask the women to spread bread, make coffee, and gather up all the food they could. I did likewise, all of us in our homes working hard and fast. We made a great picnic coffee pot full of strong coffee and packed in baskets all the food we could find. The only man who was not down fighting the fire was the minister. I went to his boarding place to ask him to go with us to help carry the food. No one could harness the horses because they were so spirited. And I remembered, too, hearing how terrified horses were of fire. I knew it would not be safe to take them out. But our minister refused to go and went on reading. I gave him my opinion of his behavior, and left. My young brother sawed off a broomstick and we slipped it through the bail of the coffee pot. I pressed into service boys to carry the food, and, unlike the parson, they were overjoyed to go. Other women went, too, and we really in an incredibly short time had a fair amount of food, but we had two and a half miles to walk.

When we arrived what an appalling picture we found! Men black with smoke and sweat, eyes bloodshot, breath coming in gasps. It was awful! We never dreamed of what they had been enduring. Such gratitude and such heartfelt "God bless yous" as came from their parched throats! A few were lying to one side, having been overcome with fatigue and smoke. All of our officials were there directing, working by the side of the men. They were fighting to keep the flames away from the powder magazine. Oh, if only our tug had been there we could have gone onto it, made more coffee, prepared more food, and done so much more in general. What we did helped a lot and the men in command, realizing this was to be a big fight of indefinite length, organized the men into "shifts" and sent home for a few hours of rest, sleep and food those who were most exhausted.

It was two days and nights of hardship and terror, not only for the men who had to make the physical effort to fight the fire and hope against hope they might stop its further progress; but the women, too, had their hardships in preparing food for the men and in caring for their families, beside great mental anguish as to the outcome. Not one grown man on the Location; though don't forget the parson, who still sat in his rocker.

The only road out was at the dock and the fire was roaring up the road through the woods right toward our Location. The only way out was a trail to the north, a mere footpath winding through that pine forest. No horse and vehicle could get through. The poor women were getting things together for flight. My own family consisted of my mother-in-law, my baby, my own mother, who was far from well and found walking very difficult; then my brother in his early teens, and two sisters quite a few years younger.

Then, how to carry food and blankets, and where to get food when that was gone. For if we reached the shore eight miles away there wasn't a man at the mine to go with us or even to consult with. But my predicament was only that of all the other women on the Location. Some of them went around clothed in two dresses and their best hats on their heads. Poor things, they wanted to save something. At one time, when some of the men came up to rest they put our piano in the mouth of the mine shaft. Fortunately, it began with a very gentle slope. I locked my flat silver and my table linen in the piano, not attempting to save anything else.

My family was calm, my two mothers standing pat. By this time the roar of the fire was warning us of its nearness and blazing embers blown by the wind fell on our roofs and into our woodpiles. Often these embers were a foot and more in length and five or six inches around. Small boys helped my brother keep the roofs cleared and pulled them off the woodpiles all over the Location. These boys deserved no small praise, for certainly without their valiant efforts the whole settlement would have gone.

This was our condition. I knew we must soon, very soon, start on our march or the flames would overtake us, but it was so awful to contemplate. Yet to go by fire was worse. This was Tuesday afternoon. We prayed; oh, how we did pray! And we scanned the heaven until I think our looks and prayers must have rent it open; for during the day the wind changed, the heavens opened up and the only thing that could save us came—rain! We all dropped with exhaustion of mind and body, too thankful, too grateful, to say words of praise and thanksgiving, but it poured forth in wordless feeling. The rain came down in torrents and lasted all through the night and the next day, and ended all menace of fire.

The next noon the tug came in. My husband had been delayed and knew nothing of what we had been enduring on the Island.

There is not much more to tell. One narrow escape of our tug from being shipwrecked, coming from Hancock with a party of interested mining men from the east, and also several very close friends of ours. Our Siskiwit Bay was not easy of approach even under the best of conditions, and that afternoon a fearful storm was raging. On an upper landing of the staircase was a window that gave a glimpse of the lake, I knew the tug was intending to come over and I was uneasy. I made several trips to the stair landing even after dark. Summer was nearing its end. I stood there and heard the whistle of the tug. It sounded several times. I ran downstairs and told the three men of our household, but I was laughed at and my statement scorned. "It would have been impossible to hear it at that distance. Besides, the tug would not have ventured out from Hancock." I knew it was the tug, but, being a "mere woman," I said no more. Hours after the tug came in. She could not make the passage through our bay and had to go at least twenty miles up the Island and come in through the inner channel to our dock. The men of our mine who were sent out onto the dock to help haul her in had to be lashed with ropes to the piling and other men stood by to haul in such as fell and were in danger of drowning by being washed off the dock. The tug had whistled about five o'clock as she passed by. I really felt quite important and would have gloated more, but to hear the story of the very, very narrow escape of the men from drowning was too harrowing for gaiety. "Uncle Seth" North was one of the passengers and the one we knew best. They said he sat perfectly still on that bit of plank between them and the awful water, calm, courageous, a great strength to the others, who also were brave, as men are always in time of danger.

I must pay tribute to our tug. So many times she had come safely into port. Captain Cook, too, who was almost the entire crew, though during the busy summer season he had a mate and a negro cook. It was not a tiny tug, such as we see running about the Chicago River, for instance, but a tug nevertheless. There was a tiny cabin in the depths of the hull, in the middle a narrow table for our meals, and four bunks along the sides, with built-in benches to step on to get into bed or sit on when at table. There was a ladderlike set of steps to get down to the cabin. One had to be too seasick to care before they would go into that hole. I know, for I was a victim several times. Not the last time, however; I was too frightened to be seasick!

Then in early October we left the Island, almost the last to go, and a stormy and dangerous trip it was. We had in tow a big scow piled high with valuable lumber. (There was a small sawmill on the Island.) All of our family had left early in September; only the baby, my husband and I on board. It was so rough the Captain was concerned about the scow. It was valuable and he wanted to get it over to the mainland, but we were in great danger of being pulled under by it. Finally the Captain had his helper, a young fellow of about seventeen, stand by the rope attached to the tug, knife in hand, and, at command from the Captain, he was to cut it from the scow. Well, of course, we did get over with the scow still in tow.

Thus ended our year of life on beautiful Isle Royale.

FROM THE JOURNAL OF EMMA BAYLIS
(1872-1884)
Emma Baylis

MANY OF THE WOMEN who travelled to the frontier went as missionaries to the settlers or to the Indians. J. Raleigh Nelson's novel, *Lady Unafraid* (1952) describes his mother's work at the Native mission on L'Anse Bay in Michigan's Upper Peninsula, but it is a fictionalized account written after the fact by a worshipful son. Emma Baylis's diary is altogether different, and hardly so sanguine. Baylis was a missionary for the Canadian Congregational Indian Missionary Society who spent her summers from 1870 to 1884 running a school and offering church services at Spanish River on the Ontario shore north of Manitoulin Island. She came and left her post by steamboat, usually alone in the early 1870s; later other single women joined her to help provide companionship.

When Baylis describes it, Spanish River was a summer mill settlement, set up at the mouth of the river to process the logs that were floated down in the spring drives. Logs that had been cut in the north in winter were driven down the river, and the Native men followed the drives south and set up bark tepees for their families while they worked in the mill during summer. When summer was over, the Indian families moved back into the forest for another season.

Baylis ran a daily school for the children of the Indian and white mill workers, initiated a temperance society, held four services on Sundays, and visited the various Native encampments by canoe and sailboat during the week. She contended vociferously with the Catholic priest for souls, supplied clothing to her young pupils so they could come to school, and after she returned to Montreal for the winter, raised money tirelessly for the Indian missionary efforts.

The bureaucracy of the Congregational Church was sometimes as great a hurdle for her as the poverty of her students and her own inability to speak (or learn) their language. The Canadian Congregational Indian Missionary Society had begun in 1860 because the supervising Congregational Missionary Society in London, England, refused to provide monies for missionary work to "non-heathen" peoples such as North American Native Peoples. As a result, the Indian Missionary Society was left on its own to raise funds to support missionaries in the field. Baylis yearly canvassed churches between Toronto and Montreal, one year producing and selling an "autograph" quilt for $50.00.

Baylis's journal, which is now in the United Church Archives in Toronto, is a record only of her summer work. She worked as a missionary until 1884 when her journal abruptly ends. In that year the Congregational Church disbanded the Indian Missionary Society and left the field to the Jesuits who, in later years, founded a school for Indian children at Spanish River. (Basil Johnston, the noted Canadian Native ethnographer, describes his education there in *Indian School Days* [1988]). When the Congregational Church later founded a Woman's Missionary Society, Baylis's name is conspicuously absent, as are any activities among the Canadian Native Peoples by other missionaries.

Her journal was obviously intended to be a public document, much as the log books of lighthouse keepers. Yet like those log books, what is provocative is not only the day-to-day recording of her activities, but the irruptions of her emotions into the text she prepared for the church elders. At one point she notes stridently that women should not be sent alone to missions like Spanish River, a recognition that what she was doing taxed her courage and abilities. Another year she inserts a note about the ordination of a Native man as a minister, certainly her comment on the prejudice of the church governing board she must have experienced when trying to garner more funds for her work. Her description of being "chased" by a threatening priest in the woods was clearly calculated to raise denominational emotions among the Protestant community in Montreal.

Emma Baylis's record, and our lack of knowledge about who she was and why she labored as she did, are emblematic of many women's lives on the frontier. The biographies of male ministers in the same places are often recorded in detail; of Emma, we know only what she left in a small, leather-bound book, written in a crabbed hand when she was tired, in order to satisfy the men who determined whether or not she would once again, next summer, be able to continue her work.

⊷⊨◉⊜⊰⊷

1872

May—Spanish River Indian Mission

I am again in the Mission. All my last summer's journal was burnt at [the] Marchmont fire. I have nothing left on record of my work. I now commence a new journal. After spending a week in Owen Sound, yesterday and today I have been occupied cleaning my schoolroom and arranging my books and scripture texts 'round the room. After I had finished, twelve little Indians and French children gathered in. I played some music for them and they sang some hymns which I was glad to hear they had not forgotten, "Happy Lands" especially, which is a great favorite with them and "Come to Jesus." An Indian girl called Lin-Lin had been looking for me ever since the boats began to run. They told me she would go down every time the boat came and when she found I was not there would say "Baylis Bah! Bah!"

I received a hearty welcome back. Those who shook hands with me said they were glad to see me back. A white woman asked me if I would have a Mother's prayer meeting again.

May 31—

Commenced school today. Ten Indian and French children. I questioned them to ascertain how much they remembered from last summer and found they had remembered quite a number of texts and part [of the] hymns "Happy Lands" and "Jesus Loves Me." I asked a half-Indian boy for a text and he gave me "God is love." A French child said "God sees me"; another "I am the good shepherd . . . ." This afternoon I went across the Bay and called on the Indian families and invited them to the school.

Saturday. Invited the people to come to a Bible reading on Sunday morning, and also to Sunday School. One young man who I asked to come said he would thankfully have attended a Sunday School in the States, but not since he came to Canada.

Sabbath Morning. I had ten present at my Bible reading—grown people. Sunday School—twenty-two men, women, and children, Indian, French, English. I revived the School and last summer's lessons—the children remembered a number of verses and some hymns. . . . After Sunday School three of the men asked me if I would not have some reading in the evening for them. I consented and fourteen came. Took for my reading parable of "lost sheep." Read the "old story." The meeting was great and solemn. I had singing and prayer. Thus passed my first Sabbath this season. I hope profitable to all.

Wednesday, June 12—

School as usual. Eighteen yesterday, mostly Indians and French children. I had a long conversation with a half-Indian woman today. They tell me a good deal of the manners and customs of the Indians. She said they camp far inland in the winter, walking three or four hundred miles, moving frequently about from place to place, carrying their birch-bark tent with them, also blankets and provisions, little children walking with them. When children get tired they camp for a few days to rest. They are a very improvident people, wasting a great deal. One Indian had about $1000 for food. He spent it in provisions visiting the camp of Indians to feast with him. In this way they become poor. She said they tear up their blankets and leave them behind. They sometimes bury their provisions in the ground for some future use. When one of their members dies, they are put in a coffin, a very large one, with all the clothes they possess. They also put in a small canoe and cooking utensils for them to use in Indian Spirit Land, also guns and powder. When shut in the coffin their friends make three large holes in the coffin, then fire a gun three times in the air, they say to make the spirit depart quickly away and not return to annoy them. They say the spirit has to cross a river walking over a narrow plank. If it looks back it falls into the hell. By firing the gun they say it passes quickly over safely. Poor deluded people, how much [they] need to have the gospel preached to them.

Saturday, June 15—

Yesterday I commenced a prayer meeting for women. Had three: two Protestant, one Catholic. After meeting I went and visited two Indian families. Spoke to one of the way of salvation. Three were Catholic. In the evening went twenty-two miles in the "Tug" to the "Light house."

June 17—

Yesterday Sabbath. I had morning meeting, eight present. Sunday School, twenty-three. Evening meeting, nineteen. Today school, twelve [in the] morning. Sewing class [this] afternoon, seven.

Tuesday evening Reverend Mr. Hurlburt made me a visit, had a meeting of the women. I commenced [the] same afternoon a reading class for the women. School the rest of [the] week. Been sick for two days with [a] sore throat.

Saturday, June 29—

I returned late last night from "Sha-She-Wasining"; been away two days— first night had to camp—arrived at "Sha" seven o'clock in the morning. Reverend Mr. Clark and Mr. Robinson had service from nine to eleven. The Chief then made a very interesting speech. . . [ended] by asking for a missionary. It was then decided that I should go for one month this summer. We took our departure and visited a another Indian place but did not find any Indians. I am very much bitten by mosquitos and black flies. My face, hands, and eyes are all swollen.

July 1—

Yesterday Sabbath. Reverend W. Clarke preached in [the] morning, twenty present. Afternoon, Reverend Robinson [preached] to the Indians through Mr. Walker. Eight Indians present. [In the] Evening Mr. R. preached in English, thirty-two present. I have had school today: twelve present. The school door has been repaired by Mr. Robinson and Walker. Mr. Clarke has been quite ill since he has been here. They all left this morning for "La-Cloche". . . In honour of Dominion Day I hoisted an addition to the mission flag: the British.

Some of the children who attended school last summer don't come this, I think through the influence of the priest.

July 6—

School every day—small—I visit the Indians almost daily. Yesterday Sabbath, small meeting: eight [in the] morning—Sunday School eight—evening meeting, four. I thought the evening meeting interesting. They do not seem to take as much interest in the meetings as last summer. A different class of men. Today after school I went across the Bay to see the Indians, two of my schoolboys accompanying me. Invited them to come to the school and meetings. Had a conversation this morning with an Indian—he said he knew something about the Savior—but when I asked him where he would [go] to after death he said he did not know—

July 10—

School as usual. This afternoon at mother's meeting only two. The reading class for women seems to be a failure. This evening I visited a poor sick Indian who I think will soon die. He said he does not know anything about the future. Through my interpreter I talked to him about Jesus and we even had a short prayer—Afterwards talked with Indian and his wife—read a portion of Scripture and gave woman part of New Testament and promised her one in Indian.

July 11—

School all day after visiting the Indians. Went to see the man who is suffering with lameness in his leg. Same that I visited last summer—has been lying ever since. He was glad to see me. I read the Scriptures to him through my interpreter; he said he hoped I would come often. He remembered what I had said to him last summer. He is a pagan. Took him some biscuits. I read to him Matt. 11, [verses] 28 to 30—and prayed and sang "Come to Jesus."

July 15—

Yesterday Sabbath. Rev. Hurlburt preached morning and evening in English. . . . I enjoyed the sermons very much. It is quite a rest for me to have some one take the Sabbath sermons off of me and I think the change is appreciated.

July 17—

School in the morning. Afternoon visiting the Indians [and] found that some of them could read. One of them had been taught by Mr. Ketchin. I gave away an Indian Testament to someone who could read. That evening read and talked to the sick man through my interpreter—spoke of Christ's willingness to save him, taught him a short prayer. He seemed sad and depressed [to] know he will die "Forsaken his state of nature is." He has had no instruction. I pray that the Lord will enlighten his mind. I do not think I am doing any good here. I cannot talk to them myself and cannot always get my interpreter when I need him. I feel isolated and alone and trials to bear—

July 18—

Today in school I promised a prize to the boy who would make the best figures—also to the one that learned to read the soonest and also to the one who gave me the least trouble. . . .

July 29—

Today I have been visiting the Indians. Had a long talk with [a] reading and prayer and singing with the man who has the lameness. He said he would like to have me come often and read with him, that he was beginning to understand religion better. I read Christ healing the sick of the palsy.

August 7—

Returned from a visit of a few days from La Cloche. Sunday went to church at The Current [and] heard Reverend Mr. Hill. Went in a sail boat . . . going and coming. Monday visited Indian Burying ground. Odd looking graves—in some of the children's graves were the play things which they had used during life—in one was a tin "patty pan jews harp," bottle stopper, piece of tin, bow and arrow—in another, a doll, a wooden sword . . . . The graves are covered with bark in the shape of Pyramids. At the top is a table to place the offerings on and a small fire is sometimes kept burning for the accommodation of the spirit when it comes to the grave—

"An Indian Story" as I heard it from an eye witness: About twenty-five years ago there lived in one of the Bay's families an Indian girl. One day an Indian visited the family and asked this girl to be his wife. She refused; he said she would be sorry before sundown. The girl had an old mother living outside the "fort" in a tent alone. The girl used to carry food to her daily. That evening the family was aroused by the loud barking of the dogs outside. The men rushed out, taking their guns with them. On reaching the tent of the old woman, they found her murdered—literally cut to pieces—lying in a pool of blood from where her hands had been cut off. It was in this way that the Indian showed his revenge on the girl for refusing to marry him.

Yesterday while at La Cloche I saw two squaws dressed alike—the wives of one man. One was old, the other young—he had a short time since sent another old one away. I hear that they are some times cruel to the old people; they sometimes leave them to starve, or shift for themselves. I heard of an old woman being left in a tent alone. When women passed by she would cry out to them and say, "Daughter, bring me a little water."

August 14, Wednesday—

School every day. The priest has been influencing the people against me—telling the children they must not take any more books from me, though they still come to the school. Mrs. Cameron's baby died last night. It is to be buried tomorrow at the "Current." I gave it some medicine but could not save it. . . .

August 17—

Yesterday I gave the children the "Christmas Tree": twenty children present, three absent. I cannot do much with the Indians at their camp—I have no interpreter. The children were greatly delighted with their "tree" and presents. Today my interpreter told me the priest had forbade her to interpret for me, giving her a good scolding for doing so. As she is a Roman Catholic, my work with the Indians seems to be at an end. Today gave material to make dresses for two little girls to come to school.

August 19, Monday—

Saturday evening. I was told the sick Indian was dying. I went to see him and was told that the priest had told them not to let me come near them nor believe anything I said. A Catholic woman was kneeling over him chanting, but I took my place beside him and sang "Come to Jesus." The Catholic woman went out of the tent. The priest said I was telling them lies and that if they believed me they would go to the bad place.

August 26—

School all week as usual. Saturday the sick Indian died, a Catholic as they suppose. A coffin was made and he was put in with the small crucifix placed in it and the bottle of holy water. They took him away to a native burying ground. Poor man, I saw him a short time before he died. I asked him if he believed in Jesus. He said, "Kah" and showed me the crucifix. I think if the priest had not interfered he might have become an enlightened man.

I feel discouraged and grieved. Yesterday Sabbath and scarcely anyone attended the meetings, nearly all were Sabbath-breaking. Morning meeting, three white men, ten Indians. Sunday School, ten. Evening, four, two white men and two squaws. What could have possessed them I cannot tell. It has grieved and pained me very much since I lost my interpreter. I go to the tents myself and read to the Indians as well as I can.

August 31, Saturday—

School all the week. I have visited a poor old squaw several times, given her some clothes and food—she is very sick. Yesterday an Indian came and asked me to go and see his sick child. I went, and gave it some medicine and prayed with the family and those in the tent. Going now to see it.

The child died at four o'clock this afternoon. It looked very nice dressed in a little white dress, tied with ribbons. Three deaths during the last few weeks. The parents of the baby are Protestants. The father speaks English. I had a long talk with him about his children. Told him to think of his child in heaven.

September 9—

Indian families nearly all left. The school is very small. Yesterday I had readings after the morning meeting, four. Sunday school, five. They have fallen off of late from coming to the meetings. I do not know the reason. There appears to be some evil influence at work somewhere. Yesterday [on the] Sabbath a vessel arrived for [?]. Saturday eve before she arrived two of the sailors were drowned—fell from the rigging.

September 23—

I closed my school on Friday. . . I closed the school with a general examination of the summer lessons. I gave a book as a prize to a little English girl for repeating and remembering hymns and Bible verses. I gave a parting advice to all present and [the] classes left singing "Here we meet to part again. In heaven we part no more. . . ." Today I have been packing away books.

1873

Toronto, May

Why art thou cast down, oh my soul, and why so dispirited? I do indeed feel sad. I do not feel joyous about going this summer. I know not why. However the big cloud which I seem to see in the distance may possibly burst with blessings on my work. God only knows. Perhaps the Lord may take me away this summer. Oh that he would take me to himself forever. I long to be with him and see him. Oh that I may be permitted to see his face in glory. If he should spare my life I shall labor for him. I leave all things in his hands.

August 22—

School morning. Feeling quite indisposed. Yesterday morning Mr. and Mrs. Robinson arrived on their way to "Sha Wasaning." They only stayed a few hours. I think the people are disappointed and think it strange that Mr. Robinson does not stop and preach. Ministers of other denominations come and preach, which makes it awkward for me.

August 23, Saturday—

This afternoon I visited all the Indian camps. Read hymns and invited the Indians to come tomorrow morning to meeting. They said they would engage in interpreter, a man. I have just been selecting tomorrow's readings.

I feel tired. I had to climb and walk over the rocks and through the brushwoods. On my return an Indian brought me across the water in his bark canoe. I then visited all the Indians in the settlement. I returned to the Mission House through the woods and over the rocks. When about half-way home I turned round and looked back and saw an old "priest" about twelve yards behind me, walking very stealthily with his eyes fixed on me with not a very pleased look. I took no notice of him, but hurried home, which I thought was wise. He had evidently seem me going about among the Indians and had followed me into that lonely place with some intent of "ill." I think it must have been his intention to come up slowly behind and strike me down. No one would have been the wiser of who had done the deed. He left at night by steamer for the "Sault." I was thankful when I heard he had left. He was only here one day. The Lord has delivered me out of many dangers this far—

August 24—

Sabbath. Last night my dreams were altogether of the priest and then Indians. Today I am alone in my little sitting room. It is pouring rain. Well would I like to have a peep [of] home or at some dear familiar face . . . .

August 25—

I had school [this] morning. First I went around to the camps and tried to find the Indian children, but could not get them to come to school. Some of them were going away. I feel almost hopeless about getting the Indian children into the school this summer. . . .

September 15—

Yesterday Sabbath. Indians did not come; they are nearly all gone. . .

This morning only five white children in school. The work is now looking discouraging. It is also cold, rainy, and bleak. The time seems long that I am all alone. I do not think I should like to undertake another summer under the same circumstances. Last Friday night the people were very much frightened by a man frantic with drink, running about bursting open their doors and smashing windows. The watchman found him at my house; he had been trying my door. If I had been sleeping in the house I have no doubt the fright would have made me very ill. I think only married missionaries should undertake mission work. They are protection and company for each other, especially in a place like this. It is a den of wickedness. Some of the white people here are very wicked. Liquor is the cause of it all.

1874

Arrived May 29—

Received a hearty welcome from all. The Indians have not come yet. The weather has been very cold. Saturday morning found a student has come with the intention of preaching on Sabbath. Immediately after my arrival I had the boards taking down from the windows, swept out the school room, and I had two services on Sabbath. This week I have been occupied unpacking and getting the house cleaned.

June 19—

School as usual. Thirteen scholars. Indians engaged an interpreter for Sunday. I told him to invite the Indians to come Sunday morning. Fitted out four girls with clothes for school. They have just been in to see me with their old clothes on. They take the new clothes off when they go home so as to keep them clean for school.

1875

July 6—

Since I last wrote I have been away four days, boat travelling, visiting pagan Indians, and selecting suitable places for schools. We have engaged Mr. Nawagesheick from Serpent River and we have another place in view. We had some very interesting meetings with the Indians. On Sabbath we had three camp meetings in different places. . . . They listened to the gospel proclaimed to them through an interpreter. I visited all the women and gave them a little present each. We invited the Chief to tea. He came—we gave some tea to his wife, who is blind. We had our tea as usual spread on the ground. I slept in the boat at night alone. ["alone" is crossed through here; ed note] We returned yesterday and had a meeting with the Indians and white people in the evening.

September 20—
Received for teaching the white children $2.85. Used it for mission expenses.

October 6—
Closed up the Mission House and left for this season. Went as far as Little Current and spent ten days with Mrs. Absey. Arrived in Toronto October 19th. While at Little Current I saw a number of Indians. Made inquiries about a school for them. I think there will be an opening for part of the summer at "Sucker Creek," a place where Mr. Walker once taught. The women would like a teacher to come again.

Remarks: I feel somewhat discouraged in regard of the work this summer. Very few Indians settled at Spanish River this summer. One interesting feature of the work is Mr. Nawagesheick offering himself for the Mission work and being accepted by the Board. It has pleased and gratified me very much. I pray and trust that he Lord will make him faithful and bless him abundantly in his work.

> *Toronto*
> *October 20, 1875*
> *Emma Baylis*

1876

August 8th—
School all week [but] few Indian children in the place. The people are busy picking berries. They take the children with them to help bring the berries back and sell them at the store. It is their harvest now. They come to see me after they have disposed of the berries. I have my room generally [filled] every day with squaws and Indians. I show them scripture pictures and read and sing Indian hymns so they generally remain over a Sabbath. I have had very large gatherings every Sunday morning. Mr. Nawagesheick is here sometimes but often I am alone. We occupy the time in singing hymns and prayer. Yesterday he did not come. Twenty-five Indians came in. They stayed quietly for an hour.

August 14—

School all the week, though few Indian children. The work is very discouraging. The people do not care for religion.

I have passed through a severe trial. My interpreter has asked to go on a pleasure trip on a Sabbath afternoon instead of coming to Sunday School. When I was expecting him, [the] poor man yielded and went, but I think repented sincerely. I talked to him very kindly, but faithfully.

1877

July 11—

Sabbath morning. I have been very ill for two or three days and passed through severe trials with two of the people. . . Mr. Dyke and Mr. Forest, Catholics. Mr. Forest came into my house yesterday and said I had to shut down this school and go away and that if I did not the people would make me, that they did not want me here because I was teaching religion in school and that the children were not learning anything from me, and that I made a fool of myself in school in having prayer in school and reading the Bible which was not allowed. I told him it was allowed in our school as it was not a government school, but a Mission school. He got into a great rage and said I would have to quit the place as they intended to have a government school in the place and that he would go round to the people and get them to drive me out. I made inquiries of the people and they said, most of them, they did want me there and that the children were learning well and they would send them to my school and that the man had told me a lie. The Lord has instructed me and given me the strength and fortitude under the trials, all glory be to his name. . . .

I am glad they accuse me of [teaching religion]. It was for that I came. In the evening I walked amongst the Indian camp and found some of the pagan women making a bark canoe. Told them it was now Sabbath and that God would be angry and so put it away and work on the morrow.

PROFILE:
CONSTANCE FENIMORE WOOLSON
1840-1894

Courtesy Rollins College Archives

WHEN WOOLSON COMMITTED SUICIDE in Venice in 1894, she was fifty-four, a well-known and successful writer. She had come far from her beginnings in Cleveland, penning romantic frontier adventure tales set on the Great Lakes, including the lakes' first shipwreck fiction. Woolson had gotten her first publishing break writing this sort of "local color" fiction, stories about curious characters in remote regions of the United States that captivated Eastern magazine readers after the Civil War. Because this fiction depended on a detailed knowledge of place, women were not excluded from writing it as they often were from the more "serious" subjects of politics or theology. Readers enjoyed it because it was an escape from the insistently real problems of massive immigration and the accelerating Industrial Revolution, which may have been local but was hardly colorful.

Woolson was lucky that her abilities coincided with the marketplace, for she had to support herself, and later her mother. When Mrs. Woolson's health failed, the mother and daughter emigrated to St. Augustine, where Woolson became the first Northerner to describe the Reconstruction South in fiction and travel narratives. When her mother died, she moved on to Europe to become part of the ex-patriot American community that included Henry James, who became her life-long friend and companion. Woolson continued to write "local" stories and travel pieces once in Europe, describing the Americans who had come there to escape problems at home or to find a better life, much as she had.

Although her novels always sold well, particularly *Anne*, a national best-seller which inspired decades of sentimental pilgrimages to Mackinac Island, Woolson did her best work in the short story. Taking the limited forms of saccharin romance and overly-quaint local color Woolson had to work with to be published, she created lasting works of art that few have equalled. Her Great Lakes stories are collected in *Castle Nowhere* (1875), her Southern Sketches in *Rodman The Keeper* (1880), and her European stories in *The Front Yard* (1896) and *Dorothy and Other Italian Stories* (1896).

She has often been called a literary pioneer because she was the first women realist writer after the Civil War and paved the way for other women such as Edith Wharton. While the other great pioneers of the realistic movement in fiction, all men, gathered in Boston and New York and supported each other, Woolson worked alone in the Midwest and Florida. For her Great Lakes stories, she drew on her memories of the world she had first discovered as a child when her family moved from New York, where she was born, after three older sisters died of scarlet fever. Once settled in Cleveland, she accompanied her father on his trips around the lakes, and the family summered at Mackinac Island in the years when memories of the fur trade were still fresh. The great summer hotels with their the swarms of tourists were far in the future, and Woolson memorized the wild and pristine landscapes of the Great Lakes just before the massive and unrestrained development began after the Civil War. She never forgot what she had seen, and the landscapes of her stories are as sensitive and finely detailed as any in the fiction of her time.

Her love of place is evident in the short story that follows, "St. Clair Flats," which she named one of her favorites. The great sweeps of uninhabited wild places that often occur in her lakes stories are here, as is her typical Great Lakes figure: a singular, strong, self-supporting woman holding out against the memory of sorrow. Because Woolson had no mentors in life, she created them in her fiction, describing women on high places or precipices like towers of strength against the elements and against their memories of the past.

She never married, and as she grew older, deafness cut her off from society. Although she often wrote of her longing to return to the lakes, she refrained, perhaps because she knew the frontier landscapes she had loved no longer existed. She remained in Europe, a disciplined and productive writer until, beset by illness and depression after finishing a novel, she opened the window of her third-floor bedroom and flung herself to the pavement. She was buried in the Protestant Cemetery in Rome in a simple grave bordered by a low, stone coping and planted with violets.

ST. CLAIR FLATS

(1873)

Constance Fenimore Woolson

AT FIRST READING "St. Clair Flats," from *Castle Nowhere: Lake-Country Sketches*, appears to be another example of the post-Civil War vogue for "local color" fiction. But Woolson seldom indulged in the condescension of many local colorists, and here she is interested here in portraying a genuinely regional dilemma: what happened to women who followed their husbands west to settle the frontier. Many found rewarding lives and happiness after leaving the East, but many did not, often because they were unprepared for what they found. The emigrant's guides and sentimental women's novels painted the frontier as a garden where little work was needed to make a living, a welcome escape from the industrialized East.

When Woolson created the character of Roxana, she was sensitive to what Roxana had lost when she followed her crazed religious husband west, but Woolson also described the freedom and accomplishment Roxana was able to achieve by making the watery world of the old St. Clair Flats near Detroit her own. There is nostalgia here for the Flats that were channeled and drained after Woolson first knew them, and there is also sadness at Roxana's isolation. But Woolson subtly implies this may be temporary. By alluding to the Greek myth of Ariadne, who helped her lover Theseus escape the trackless maze of palace of the Minos on the island of Crete with a ball of golden twine that unwound to mark the passage, Woolson suggests Roxana is a modern Ariadne. Once out of the maze, Theseus abandoned Ariadne, but she was later rescued by Bacchus, given a crown, and became the mother of several children.

Woolson's use of the Greek myth in this story highlights her situation as a serious woman artist in the 1870s. Long sentimental stories filled with poetry where the heroine married well and lived happily ever after were demanded by the reading public, but as an artist, as well as a popular writer, Woolson rebelled at such simplistic endings. She also knew that her audience would recognize references to Greek literature. She overcame her dilemma by crafting a realistic story, then leaving the ending for the reader to finish. If readers believe Roxana is an Ariadne figure, the story is positive, providing we believe the frontier is an Edenic world like the golden age of Greece. If readers are less sanguine, the ending is darker and Roxana becomes another nameless settler who is lost to history on the frontier, despite her superficial resemblance to a figure of Greek myth. Woolson's subtly here was nearly her undoing, for she had trouble placing the story. Readers wanted a joyous ending with wedding bells, which Woolson refused to provide. Neither did she patronize Roxana as most local color writers would have by sentimentalizing her situation, perhaps by having her die in the end. Instead she created a wonderful story of life on the frontier that refuses to allow readers to fall back into their comfortable assumptions of what should happen to someone whose frontier experience has not matched the national myth.

⟶⟩══◉◉══⟨⟵

IN SEPTEMBER, 1855, I first saw the St. Clair Flats. Owing to Raymond's determination, we stopped there.

"Why go on?" he asked. "Why cross another long, rough lake, when here is all we want?"

"But no one ever stops here," I said.

"So much the better; we shall have it all to ourselves."

"But we must at least have a roof over our heads."

"I presume we can find one."

The captain of the steamer, however, knew of no roof save that covering a little lighthouse set on spiles, which the boat would pass within the half hour; we decided to get off there, and throw ourselves upon the charity of the lighthouse-man. In the meantime, we sat on the bow with Captain Kidd, our four-legged companion, who had often accompanied us on hunting expeditions, but never before so far westward. It had been rough on Lake Erie—very rough. We, who had sailed the ocean with composure, found ourselves most inhumanly tossed on the short, chopping waves of this fresh-water sea; we, who alone of all the cabin-list had eaten our four courses and dessert every day on the ocean-steamer, found ourselves here reduced to the depressing diet of a herring and pilot-bread. Captain Kidd, too, had suffered dumbly; even now he could not find comfort, but tried every plank in the deck, one after the other, circling round and round after his tail, dog-fashion, before lying down, and no sooner down than up again for another melancholy wandering about the deck, another choice of planks, another circling, and another failure. We were sailing across a small lake whose smooth waters were like clear green oil; as we drew near the outlet, the low, green shores curved inward and came together, and the steamer entered a narrow, green river.

"Here we are," said Raymond. "Now we can soon land."

"But there isn't any land," I answered.

"What is that, then?" asked my near-sighted companion, pointing toward what seemed a shore.

"Reeds."

"And what do they run back to?"

"Nothing."

"But there must be solid ground beyond?"

"Nothing but reeds, flags, lily-pads, grass, and water, as far as I can see.

"A marsh?"

"Yes, a marsh."

The word "marsh" does not bring up a beautiful picture to the mind, and yet the reality was as beautiful as anything I have ever seen—an enchanted land, whose memory haunts me as an idea unwritten; a melody unsung, a picture unpainted, haunts the artist, and will not away. On each side and in front, as far as the eye could reach, stretched the low green land which was yet no land, intersected by hundreds of channels, narrow and broad, whose waters were green as their shores. In and out, now running into each other for a moment, now setting off each for himself again, these many channels flowed along with a rippling current; zigzag as they were, they never seemed to loiter, but, as if knowing just where they were going and what they had to do, they found time to take their own pleasant roundabout way, visiting the secluded households of their friends the flags, who, poor souls, must always stay at home. These currents were as clear as crystal, and green as the water-grasses that fringed their miniature shores. The bristling reeds, like companies of free-lances, rode boldly out here and there into the deeps, trying to conquer more territory for the grasses, but the currents were hard to conquer; they dismounted the free-lances, and flowed over their submerged heads; they beat them down with assaulting ripples; they broke their backs so effectually that the bravest had no spirit left, but trailed along, limp and bedraggled. And, if by chance the lances succeeded in stretching their forces across from one little shore to another, then the unconquered currents forced their way between the closely-serried ranks of the enemy, and flowed on as gayly as ever, leaving the grasses sitting hopeless on the bank; for they needed solid ground for their delicate feet, these graceful ladies in green.

You might call it a marsh; but there was no mud, no dark slimy water, no stagnant scum; there were no rank yellow lilies, no gormandizing frogs, no swinish mud-turtles. The clear waters of the channels ran over golden sands, and hurtled among the stiff reeds so swiftly that only in a bay, or where protected by a crescent point, could the fair white lilies float in the quiet their serene beauty requires. The flags, who brandished their swords proudly, were martinets down to their very heels, keeping themselves as clean under the water as above, and harboring not a speck of mud on their bright green uniforms. For inhabitants, there were small fish roving about here and there in the clear tide, keeping an eye out for the herons, who, watery as to legs, but venerable and wise of aspect, stood on promontories musing, apparently, on the secrets of the ages.

The steamer's route was a constant curve; through the larger channels of the archipelago she wound, as if following the clew of a labyrinth. By turns she headed toward all the points of the compass, finding a channel where, to our uninitiated eyes, there was no channel, doubling upon her own track, going broadside foremost, floundering and backing, like a whale caught in a shallow. Here, landlocked, she would choose what seemed the narrowest channel of all, and dash recklessly through, with the reeds almost brushing her sides; there she crept gingerly along a broad expanse of water, her paddle-wheels scarcely revolving, in the excess of her caution saplings, with their heads of foliage on, and branches adorned with fluttering rags, served as finger-posts to show the way through the watery defiles, and there were many other hieroglyphics legible only to the pilot. "This time, surely, we shall run ashore," we thought again and again, as the steamer glided, head-on, toward an islet; but at the last there was always a quick turn into some unseen strait opening like a secret passage in a castle-wall, and we found ourselves in a new lakelet, heading in the opposite direction. Once we met another steamer, and the two great hulls floated slowly past each other, with engines motionless, so near that the passengers could have shaken hands with each other had they been so disposed. Not that they were so disposed, however; far from it. They gathered on their respective decks and gazed at each other gravely; not a smile was seen, not a word spoken, not the shadow of a salutation given. It was not pride, it was not suspicion; it was the universal listlessness of the travelling American bereft of his business, Othello with his occupation gone. What can such a man do on a steamer? Generally, nothing. Certainly he would never think of any such light-hearted nonsense as a smile or passing bow.

But the ships were, par excellence, the bewitched craft, the Flying Dutchmen of the Flats. A brig, with lofty, sky-scraping sails, bound south, came into view of our steamer, bound north, and passed, we hugging the shore to give her room; five minutes afterward the sky-scraping sails we had left behind veered around in front of us again; another five minutes, and there they were far distant on the right; another, and there they were again close by us on the left. For half an hour those sails circled around us, and yet all the time we were pushing steadily forward; this seemed witching work indeed. Again, the numerous schooners thought nothing of sailing overland; we saw them on all sides gliding before the wind, or beating up against it over the meadows as easily as over the water; sailing on grass was a mere trifle to these spirit-barks. All this we saw, as I said before, apparently. But in that adverb is hidden the magic of the St. Clair Flats.

"It is beautiful—beautiful," I said, looking off over the vivid green expanse.

"Beautiful?" echoed the captain, who had himself taken charge of the steering when the steamer entered the labyrinth— "I don't see anything beautiful in it!—Port your helm up there; port!"

"Port it is, sir," came back from the pilot-house above.

"These Flats give us more trouble than any other spot on the lakes; vessels are all the time getting aground and blocking up the way, which is narrow enough at best. There's some talk of Uncle Sam's cutting a canal right through—a straight canal; but he's so slow, Uncle Sam is, and I'm afraid I'll be off the waters before the job is done."

"A straight canal!" I repeated, thinking with dismay of an ugly utilitarian ditch invading this beautiful winding waste of green.

"Yes, you can see for yourself what a saving it would be," replied the captain. "We could run right through in no time, day or night; whereas, now, we have to turn and twist and watch every inch of the whole everlasting marsh." Such was the captain's opinion. But we, albeit neither romantic nor artistic, were captivated with his "everlasting marsh," and eager to penetrate far within its green fastnesses.

"I suppose there are other families living about here, besides the family at the lighthouse?" I said.

"Never heard of any. They'd have to live on a raft if they did."

"But there must be some solid ground."

"Don't believe it; it's nothing but one great sponge for miles.—Steady up there; steady!"

"Very well," said Raymond, "so be it. If there is only the lighthouse, at the lighthouse we'll get off, and take our chances."

"You're surveyors, I suppose?" said the captain.

Surveyors are the pioneers of the lake-country, understood by the people to be a set of harmless monomaniacs, given to building little observatories along-shore, where there is nothing to observe; mild madmen, whose vagaries and instruments are equally singular. As surveyors, therefore, the captain saw nothing surprising in our determination to get off at the lighthouse; if we had proposed going ashore on a plank in the middle of Lake Huron, he would have made no objection.

At length the lighthouse came into view, a little fortress perched on spiles, with a ladder for entrance; as usual in small houses, much time seemed devoted to washing, for a large crane, swung to and fro by a rope, extended out over the water, covered with fluttering garments hung out to dry. The steamer lay-to, our row-boat was launched, our traps handed out, Captain Kidd took his place in the bow, and we pushed off into the shallows; then the great paddlewheels revolved again, and the steamer sailed away, leaving us astern, rocking on her waves, and watched listlessly by the passengers until a turn hid us from their view. In the meantime numerous flaxen-haired children had appeared at the little windows of the lighthouse—too many of them, indeed, for our hopes of comfort.

"Ten," said Raymond, counting heads.

The ten, moved by curiosity as we approached, hung out of the windows so far that they held on merely by their ankles.

"We cannot possibly save them all," I remarked, looking up at the dangling gazers.

"O, they're amphibious," said Raymond; "webfooted, I presume."

We rowed up under the fortress, and demanded parley with the keeper in the following language:

"Is your father here?"

"No; but ma is," answered the chorus.— "Ma! ma!"

Ma appeared, a portly female, who held converse with us from the top of the ladder. The sum and substance of the dialogue was that she had not a corner to give us, and recommended us to find Liakim, and have him show us the way to Waiting Samuel's.

"Waiting Samuel's?" we repeated.

"Yes; he's a kind of crazy man living away over there in the Flats. But there's no harm in him, and his wife is a tidy housekeeper. You be surveyors, I suppose?"

We accepted the imputation in order to avoid a broadside of questions, and asked the whereabouts of Liakim.

"O, he's round the point, somewhere there, fishing!"

We rowed on and found him, a little, roundshouldered man, in an old flat-bottomed boat, who had not taken a fish, and looked as though he never would. We explained our errand.

"Did Rosabel Lee tell ye to come to me?" he asked.

"The woman in the lighthouse told us," I said.

"That's Rosabel Lee, that's my wife; I'm Liakim Lee," said the little man, gathering together his forlorn old rods and tackle, and pulling up his anchor.

> "In the kingdom down by the sea
> Lived the beautiful Annabel Lee,"

I quoted, sotto voce.

"And what very remarkable feet had she!" added Raymond, improvising, under the inspiration of certain shoes, scow-like in shape, gigantic in length and breadth, which had made themselves visible at the top round of the ladder.

At length the shabby old boat got under way, and we followed in its path, turning off to the right through a network of channels, now pulling ourselves along by the reeds, now paddling over a raft of lily-pads, now poling through a winding labyrinth, and now rowing with broad sweeps across the little lake. The sun was sinking, and the western sky grew bright at his coming; there was not a cloud to make mountain-peaks on the horizon, nothing, but the level earth below meeting the curved sky above, so evenly and clearly that it seemed as though we could go out there and touch it with our hands. Soon we lost sight of the little lighthouse; then one by one the distant sails sank down and disappeared, and we were left alone on the grassy sea, rowing toward the sunset.

"We must have come a mile or two, and there is no sign of a house," I called out to our guide.

"Well, I don't pretend to know how far it is, exactly," replied Liakim; "we don't know how far anything is here in the Flats, we don't."

"But are you sure you know the way?"

"O my, yes! We've got most to the boy. There it is!"

The "boy" was a buoy, a fragment of plank painted white, part of the cabin-work of some wrecked steamer.

"Now, then" said Liakim, pausing, "you jest go straight on in this here channel till you come to the ninth run from this boy, on the right; take that, and it will lead you right up to Waiting Samuel's door."

"Aren't you coming, with us?"

"Well, no. In the first place, Rosabel Lee will be waiting supper for me, and she don't like to wait; and, besides, Samuel can't abide to see none of us round his part of the Flats."

"But—" I began.

"Let him go," interposed Raymond; "we can find the house without trouble." And he tossed a silver dollar to the little man, who was already turning, his boat.

"Thank you," said Liakim. "Be sure you take the ninth run and no other— the ninth run from this boy. If you make any mistake, you'll find yourselves miles away."

With this cheerful statement, he began to row back. I did not altogether fancy being left on the watery waste without a guide; the name, too, of our mythic host did not bring up a certainty of supper and beds. "Waiting Samuel," I repeated, doubtfully. "What is he waiting for?" I called back over my shoulder; for Raymond was rowing.

"The judgment-day!" answered Liakim, in a shrill key. The boats were now far apart; another turn, and we were alone.

We glided on, counting, the runs on the right: some were wide, promising rivers; others wee little rivulets; the eighth was far away; and, when we had passed it, we could hardly decide whether we had reached the ninth or not, so small was the opening, so choked with weeds, showing scarcely a gleam of water beyond when we stood up to inspect it.

"It is certainly the ninth, and I vote that we try it. It will do as well as another, and I, for one, am in no hurry to arrive anywhere," said Raymond, pushing the boat in among the reeds.

"Do you want to lose yourself in this wilderness?" I asked, making a flag of my handkerchief to mark the spot where we had left the main stream.

"I think we are lost already," was the calm reply. I began to fear we were.

For some distance the "run," as Liakim called it, continued choked with aquatic vegetation, which acted like so many devil-fish catching our oars; at length it widened and gradually gave us a clear channel, albeit so winding and erratic that the glow of the sunset, our only beacon, seemed to be executing a waltz all round the horizon. At length we saw a dark spot on the left, and distinguished the outline of a low house. "There it is," I said, plying my oars with renewed strength.

But the run turned short off in the opposite direction, and the house disappeared. After some time it rose again, this time on our right, but once more the run turned its back and shot off on a tangent. The sun had gone, and the rapid twilight of September was falling around us; the air, however, was singularly clear, and, as there was absolutely nothing to make a shadow, the darkness came on evenly over the level green. I was growing anxious, when a third time the house appeared, but the willful run passed by it, although so near that we could distinguish its open windows and door.

"Why not get out and wade across?" I suggested.

"According to Liakim, it is the duty of this run to take us to the very door of Waiting Samuel's mansion, and it shall take us," said Raymond, rowing on. It did.

Doubling upon itself in the most unexpected manner, it brought us back to a little island, where the tall grass had given way to a vegetable-garden. We landed, secured our boat, and walked up the pathway toward the house. In the dusk it seemed to be a low, square structure, built of planks covered with plaster; the roof was flat, the windows unusually broad, the door stood open—but no one appeared. We knocked. A voice from within called out, "Who are you, and what do you want with Waiting Samuel?"

"Pilgrims, asking for food and shelter," replied Raymond.

"Do you know the ways of righteousness?"

"We can learn them."

"Will you conform to the rules of this household without murmuring?"

"We will."

"Enter then, and peace be with you!" said the voice, drawing nearer. We stepped cautiously through the dark passage into a room, whose open windows let in sufficient twilight to show us a shadowy figure. "Seat yourselves," it said. We found a bench, and sat down.

"What seek ye here?" continued the shadow.

"Rest!" replied Raymond.

"Hunting and fishing!" I added.

"Ye will find more than rest," said the voice, ignoring me altogether (I am often ignored in this way), — "more than rest, if ye stay long enough, and learn of the hidden treasures. Are you willing to seek for them?"

"Certainly!" said Raymond. "Where shall we dig?"

"I speak not of earthly digging, young man. Will you give me the charge of your souls?"

"Certainly, if you will also take charge of our bodies."

"Supper, for instance," I said, again coming to the front; "and beds."

The shadow groaned; then it called out wearily, "Roxana!"

"Yes, Samuel," replied an answering voice, and a second shadow became dimly visible on the threshold. "The woman will attend to your earthly concerns," said Waiting Samuel.— "Roxana, take them hence." The second shadow came forward, and, without a word, took our hands and led us along the dark passage like two children, warning us now of a step, now of a turn, then of two steps, and finally opening a door and ushering us into a firelighted room. Peat was burning upon the wide hearth, and a singing kettle hung above it on a crane; the red glow shone on a rough table, chairs cushioned in bright calico, a loud-ticking clock, a few gayly flowered plates and cups on a shelf, shining tins against the plastered wall, and a cat dozing on a bit of carpet in one corner. The cheery domestic scene, coming after the wide, dusky Flats, the silence, the darkness, and the mystical words of the shadowy Samuel, seemed so real and pleasant that my heart grew light within me.

"What a bright fire!" I said. "This is your domain, I suppose, Mrs.— Mrs.—"

"I am not Mrs.; I am called Roxana," replied the woman, busying herself at the hearth.

"Ah, you are then the sister of Waiting, Samuel, I presume?"

"No, I am his wife, fast enough; we were married by the minister twenty years ago. But that was before Samuel had seen any visions."

"Does he see visions?"

"Yes, almost every day."

"Do you see them, also?"

"Oh, no; I'm not like Samuel. He has great gifts, Samuel has! The visions told us to come here; we used to live away down in Maine."

"Indeed! That was a long journey!"

"Yes! And we didn't come straight either. We'd get to one place and stop, and I'd think we were going to stay, and just get things comfortable, when

Samuel would see another vision, and we'd have to start on. We wandered in that way two or three years, but at last we got here, and something in the Flats seemed to suit the spirits, and they let us stay."

At this moment, through the half-open door, came a voice.

"An evil beast is in this house. Let him depart."

"Do you mean me?" said Raymond, who had made himself comfortable in a rocking-chair.

"Nay; I refer to the four-legged beast," continued the voice. "Come forth, Apollyon!"

Poor Captain Kidd seemed to feel that he was the person in question, for he hastened under the table with drooping tail and mortified aspect.

"Roxana, send forth the beast," said the voice.

The woman put down her dishes and went toward the table; but I interposed.

"If he must go, I will take him," I said, rising.

"Yes; he must go," replied Roxana, holding open the door. So I ordered out the unwilling Captain, and led him into the passageway.

"Out of the house, out of the house," said Waiting Samuel. "His feet may not rest upon this sacred ground. I must take him hence in the boat."

"But where?"

"Across the channel there is an islet large enough for him; he shall have food and shelter, but here he cannot abide," said the man, leading the way down to the boat.

The Captain was therefore ferried across, a tent was made for him out of some old mats, food was provided, and, lest he should swim back, he was tethered by a long rope, which allowed him to prowl around his domain and take his choice of three runs for drinking-water. With all these advantages, the ungrateful animal persisted in howling dismally as we rowed away. It was company he wanted, and not a "dear little isle of his own"; but then, he was not by nature poetical.

"You do not like dogs?" I said, as we reached our strand again.

"St. Paul wrote, 'Beware of dogs,'" replied Samuel.

"But did he mean—"

"I argue not with unbelievers; his meaning is clear to me, let that suffice," said my strange host, turning away and leaving me to find my way back alone. A delicious repast was awaiting me. Years have gone by, the world and all its delicacies have been unrolled before me, but the memory of the meals I ate in that little kitchen in the Flats haunts me still. That night it was only fish, potatoes, biscuits, butter, stewed fruit, and coffee; but the fish was fresh, and done to the turn of a perfect broil, not burn; the potatoes were fried to a rare crisp, yet tender perfection, not chippy brittleness; the biscuits were light, flaked creamily, and brown on the bottom; the butter freshly churned, without salt; the fruit, great pears, with their cores extracted, standing whole on their dish, ready to melt, but not melted; and the coffee clear and strong, with yellow cream and the old-fashioned, unadulterated loaf-sugar. We ate. That does not express it; we devoured. Roxana waited on us, and warmed up into something like excitement under our praises.

"I do like good cooking," she confessed. "It's about all I have left of my old life. I go over to the mainland for supplies, and in the winter I try all kinds of new things to pass away the time. But Samuel is a poor eater, he is; and so there isn't much comfort in it. I'm mighty glad you've come, and I hope you'll stay as long as you find it pleasant." This we promised to do, as we finished the potatoes and attacked the great jellied pears. "There's one thing though," continued Roxana, "you'll have to come to our service on the roof at sunrise."

"What service?" I asked.

"The invocation. Dawn is a holy time, Samuel says, and we always wait for it; 'before the morning watch,' you know,—it says so in the Bible. Why, my name means 'the dawn,' Samuel says; that's the reason he gave it to me. My real name, down in Maine, was Maria—Maria Ann."

"But I may not wake in time," I said.

"Samuel will call you."

"And if, in spite of that, I should sleep over?"

"You would not do that; it would vex him," replied Roxana, calmly.

"Do you believe in these visions, madam?" asked Raymond, as we left the table, and seated ourselves in front of the dying fire.

"Yes," said Roxana; emphasis was unnecessary—of course she believed.

"How often do they come?"

"Almost every day there is a spiritual presence, but it does not always speak. They come and hold long conversations in the winter, when there is nothing else to do; that, I think, is very kind of them, for in the summer Samuel can fish, and his time is more occupied. There were fishermen in the Bible, you know; it is a holy calling."

"Does Samuel ever go over to the mainland?"

"No, he never leaves the Flats. I do all the business; take over the fish, and buy the supplies. I bought all our cattle," said Roxana, with pride. "I poled them away over here on a raft, one by one, when they were little things."

"Where do you pasture them?"

"Here, on the island; there are only a few acres, to be sure; but I can cut boat-loads of the best feed within a stone's throw. If we only had a little more solid ground! But this island is almost the only solid piece in the Flats."

"Your butter is certainly delicious."

"Yes, I do my best. It is sold to the steamers and vessels as fast as I make it."

"You keep yourself busy, I see."

"Oh, I like to work; I couldn't get on without it."

"And Samuel?"

"He is not like me," replied Roxana. "He has great gifts, Samuel has. I often think how strange it is that I should be the wife of such a holy-man! He is very kind to me, too; he tells me about the visions, and all the other things."

"What things?" said Raymond.

"The spirits, and the sacred influence of the sun; the fiery triangle, and the thousand years of joy. The great day is coming, you know; Samuel is waiting for it."

"Nine of the night. Take thou thy rest. I will lay me down in peace, and sleep, for it is thou, Lord, only, that makest me dwell in safety," chanted a voice in the hall; the tone was deep and not without melody, and the words singularly impressive in that still, remote place.

"Go," said Roxana, instantly pushing aside her halfwashed dishes. "Samuel will take you to your room."

"Do you leave your work unfinished?" I said, with some curiosity, noticing that she had folded her hands without even hanging up her towels.

"We do nothing after the evening chant," she said. "Pray go; he is waiting."

"Can we have candles?"

"Waiting Samuel allows no false lights in his house; as imitations of the glorious sun, they are abominable to him. Go, I beg."

She opened the door, and we went into the passage; it was entirely dark, but the man led us across to our room, showed us the position of our beds by sense of feeling, and left us without a word. After he had gone, we struck matches, one by one, and, with the aid of their uncertain light, managed to get into our respective mounds in safety; they were shake-downs on the floor, made of fragrant hay instead of straw, covered with clean sheets and patchwork coverlids, and provided with large, luxurious pillows. 0 pillow! Has any one sung thy praises? When tired or sick, when discouraged or sad, what gives so much comfort as a pillow? Not your curled-hair brickbats; not your stiff, fluted, rasping covers, or limp cotton cases; but a good, generous, soft pillow, deftly cased in smooth, cool, untrimmed linen! There's a friend for you, a friend who changes not, a friend who soothes all your troubles with a soft caress, a mesmeric touch of balmy forgetfulness.

I slept a dreamless sleep. Then I heard a voice borne toward me as if coming from far over a sea, the waves bringing it nearer and nearer.

"Awake!" it cried; "awake! The night is far spent; the day is at hand. Awake!"

I wondered vaguely over this voice as to what manner of voice it might be, but it came again, and again, and finally I awoke to find it at my side. The gray light of dawn came through the open windows, and Raymond was already up, engaged with a tub of water and crash towels. Again the chant sounded in my ears.

"Very well, very well," I said, testily. "But if you sing before breakfast you'll cry before night, Waiting Samuel."

Our host had disappeared, however, without hearing my flippant speech, and slowly I rose from my fragrant couch; the room was empty save for our two mounds, two tubs of water, and a number of towels hanging on nails. "Not overcrowded with furniture," I remarked.

"From Maine to Florida, from Massachusetts to Missouri, have I travelled, and never before found water enough," said Raymond. "If waiting for the judgment-day raises such liberal ideas of tubs and towels, I would that all the hotel-keepers in the land could be convened here to take a lesson."

Our green hunting-clothes were soon donned, and we went out into the hall; a flight of broad steps led up to the roof; Roxana appeared at the top and beckoned us thither. We ascended, and found ourselves on the flat roof. Samuel stood with his face toward the east and his arms outstretched, watching the horizon; behind was Roxana, with her hands clasped on her breast and her head bowed: thus they waited. The eastern sky was bright with golden light; rays shot upward toward the zenith, where the rose-lights of dawn were retreating down to the west, which still lay in the shadow of night; there was not a sound; the Flats stretched out dusky and still. Two or three minutes passed, and then a dazzling rim appeared above the horizon, and the first gleam of sunshine was shed over the level earth; simultaneously the two began a chant, simple as a Gregorian, but rendered in correct full tones. The words, apparently, had been collected from the Bible:—

> "The heavens declare the glory of God—
> Joy cometh in the morning!
> In them is laid out the path of the sun—
> Joy cometh in the morning!
> As a bridegroom goeth he forth;
> As a strong man runneth his race.
> The outgoings of the morning
> Praise thee, O Lord!
> Like a pelican in the wilderness,
> Like a sparrow upon the house-top,
> I wait for the Lord.
> It is good that we hope and wait,
> Wait—wait."

The chant over, the two stood a moment silently, as if in contemplation, and then descended, passing us without a word or sign, with their hands clasped before them as though forming part of an unseen procession. Raymond and I were left alone upon the house-top.

"After all, it is not such a bad opening for a day; and there is the pelican of the wilderness to emphasize it," I said, as a heron flew up from the water, and, slowly flapping his great wings, sailed across to another channel. As the sun rose higher, the birds began to sing; first a single note here and there, then a little trilling solo, and finally an outpouring of melody on all sides,— land-birds and water-birds, birds that lived in the Flats, and birds that had flown thither for breakfast,—the whole waste was awake and rejoicing in the sunshine.

"What a wild place it is!" said Raymond. "How boundless it looks! One hill in the distance, one dark line of forest, even one tree, would break its charm. I have seen the ocean, I have seen the prairies, I have seen the great desert, but this is like a mixture of the three. It is an ocean full of land,—a prairie full of water,—a desert full of verdure."

"Whatever it is, we shall find in it fishing and aquatic hunting to our hearts' content," I answered.

And we did. After a breakfast delicious as the supper, we took our boat and a lunch-basket, and set out.

"But how shall we ever find our way back?" I said, pausing as I recalled the network of runs, and the will-o'-the-wisp aspect of the house, the previous evening.

"There is no other way but to take a large ball of cord with you, fasten one end on shore, and let it run out over the stern of the boat," said Roxana. "Let it run out loosely, and it will float on the water. When you want to come back you can turn around and wind it in as you come. I can read the Flats like a book, but they're very blinding to most people; and you might keep going round in a circle. You will do better not to go far anyway. I'll wind the bugle on the roof an hour before sunset; you can start back when you hear it; for it's awkward getting supper after dark." With this musical promise we took the clew of twine which Roxana rigged for us in the stern of our boat, and started away, first releasing Captain Kidd, who was pacing his islet in sullen majesty, like another Napoleon on St. Helena. We took a new channel and passed behind the house, where the imported cattle were feeding in their little pasture; but the winding stream soon bore us away, the house sank out of sight, and we were left alone.

We had fine sport that morning among the ducks,-wood, teal, and canvas-back,—shooting from behind our screens woven of rushes; later in the day we took to fishing. The sun shone down, but there was a cool September breeze, and the freshness of the verdure was like early spring. At noon we took our lunch and a siesta among the water-lilies. When we awoke we found that a bittern had taken up his position near by, and was surveying us gravely:—

> "The moping bittern, motionless and stiff,
> That on a stone so silently and stilly
> Stands, an apparent sentinel, as if
>   To guard the water-lily,"

quoted Raymond. The solemn bird, in his dark uniform, seemed quite undisturbed by our presence; yellow-throats and swamp-sparrows also came in numbers to have a look at us; and the fish swam up to the surface and eyed us curiously. Lying at ease in the boat, we in our turn looked down into the water. There is a singular fascination in looking down into a clear stream as the boat floats above; the mosses and twining water-plants seem to have arbors and grottos in their recesses, where delicate marine creatures might live, naiads and mermaids of miniature size; at least we are always looking for them. There is a fancy, too, that one may find something,—a ring dropped from fair fingers idly trailing in the water; a book which the fishes have read thoroughly; a scarf caught among the lilies; a spoon with unknown initials; a drenched ribbon, or an embroidered handkerchief. None of these things did we find, but we did discover an old brass breastpin, whose probable glass stone was gone. It was a paltry trinket at best, but I fished it out with superstitious care,—a treasure trove of the Flats. "Drowned," I said, pathetically, "drowned in her white robes—"

"And brass breastpin," added Raymond, who objected to sentiment, true or false.

"You Philistine! Is nothing sacred to you?"

"Not brass jewelry, certainly."

"Take some lilies and consider them," I said, plucking several of the queenly blossoms floating alongside.

> "Cleopatra art thou, regal blossom,
>   Floating in thy galley down the Nile,—
> All my soul does homage to thy splendor,
>   All my heart grows warmer in thy smile;
> Yet thou smilest for thine own grand pleasure
>   Caring not for all the world beside,
> As in insolence of perfect beauty,
>   Sailest thou in silence down the tide.
>
> "Loving, humble rivers all pursue thee,
>   Wasted are their kisses at thy feet;
> Fiery sun himself cannot subdue thee,
>   Calm thou smilest through his raging heat;
> Naught to thee the earth's great crowd of blossoms,

    Naught to thee the rose-queen on her throne;
  Haughty empress of the summer waters,
    Livest thou, and diest, all alone."

This from Raymond.

"Where did you find that?" I asked.

"It is my own."

"Of course! I might have known it. There is a certain rawness of style and versification which—"

"That's right," interrupted Raymond; "I know just what you are going to say. The whole matter of opinion is a game of 'follow-my-leader'; not one of you dares admire anything unless the critics say so. If I had told you the verses were by somebody instead of a nobody, you would have found wonderful beauties in them."

"Exactly. My motto is, 'Never read anything unless it is by a somebody.' For, don't you see, that a nobody, if he is worth anything, will soon grow into a somebody, and, if he isn't worth anything, you will have saved your time!"

"But it is not merely a question of growing," said Raymond; "it is a question of critics."

"No; there you are mistaken. All the critics in the world can neither make nor crush a true poet."

"What is poetry?" said Raymond, gloomily.

At this comprehensive question the bittern gave a hollow croak, and flew away with his long legs trailing behind him. Probably he was not of an aesthetic turn of mind, and dreaded lest I should give a ramified answer.

Through the afternoon we fished when the fancy struck us, but most of the time we floated idly, enjoying the wild freedom of the watery waste. We watched the infinite varieties of the grasses, feathery, lance-leaved, tufted, drooping, banner-like, the deer's tongue, the wild-celery, and the so-called wild-rice, besides many unknown beauties delicately fringed, as difficult to catch and hold as thistle-down. There were plants journeying to and fro on the water like nomadic tribes of the desert; there were fleets of green leaves floating down the current; and now and then we saw a wonderful flower with scarlet bells, but could never approach near enough to touch it.

At length, the distant sound of the bugle came to us on the breeze, and I slowly wound in the clew, directing Raymond as he pushed the boat along, backing water with the oars. The sound seemed to come from every direction. There was nothing for it to echo against, but, in place of the echo, we heard a long, dying cadence, which sounded on over the Flats fainter and fainter in a sweet, slender note, until a new tone broke forth. The music floated around us, now on one side, now on the other; if it had been our only guide, we should have been completely bewildered. But I wound the cord steadily; and at last suddenly, there before us, appeared the house with Roxana on the roof, her figure outlined against the sky. Seeing us, she played a final salute, and then descended, carrying the imprisoned music with her.

That night we had our supper at sunset. Waiting Samuel had his meals by himself in the front room. "So that in case the spirits come, I shall not be there to hinder them," explained Roxana. "I am not holy, like Samuel; they will not speak before me."

"Do you have your meals apart in the winter, also?" asked Raymond. "Yes."

"That is not very sociable," I said.

"Samuel never was sociable," replied Roxana "Only common folks are sociable; but he is different. He has great gifts, Samuel has."

The meal over, we went up on the roof to smoke our cigars in the open air; when the sun had disappeared and his glory had darkened into twilight, our host joined us. He was a tall man, wasted and gaunt, with piercing dark eyes and dark hair, tinged with gray, hanging down upon his shoulders. (Why is it that long hair on the outside is almost always the sign of something wrong in the inside of a man's head?) He wore a black robe like a priest's cassock, and on his head a black skull-cap like the *Faust* of the operatic stage.

"Why were the Flats called St. Clair?" I said; for there is something fascinating to me in the unknown history of the West. "There isn't any," do you say? you, I mean, who are strong in the Punic wars! you, too, who are so well up in Grecian mythology. But there is history, only we don't know it. The story of Lake Huron in the times of the Pharaohs, the story of the Mississippi during the reign of Belshazzar, would be worth hearing. But it is lost! All we can do is to gather together the details of our era,—the era when Columbus came to this New World, which was, nevertheless, as old as the world he left behind.

"It was in 1679," began Waiting Samuel, "that La Salle sailed up the Detroit River in his little vessel of sixty tons burden, called the *Griffin*. He was accompanied by thirty-four men, mostly fur traders; but there were among them two holy monks, and Father Louis Hennepin, a friar of the Franciscan order. They passed up the river and entered the little lake just south of us, crossing it and these Flats on the 12th of August, which is Saint Clair's day. Struck with the gentle beauty of the scene, they named the waters after their saint, and at sunset sang a Te Deum in her honor."

"And who was Saint Clair?"

"Saint Clair, virgin and abbess, born in Italy, in 1193, made superior of a convent by the great Francis, and canonized for her distinguished virtues," said Samuel, as though reading from an encyclopedia.

"Are you a Roman Catholic?" asked Raymond.

"I am everything; all sincere faith is sacred to me," replied the man. "It is but a question of names."

"Tell us of your religion," said Raymond, thoughtfully; for, in religions, Raymond was something of a polyglot.

"You would hear of my faith? Well, so be it. Your question is the work of spirit influence. Listen, then. The great Creator has sowed immensity with innumerable systems of suns. In one of these systems a spirit forgot that he was a limited, subordinate being, and misused his freedom; how, we know not. He fell, and with him all his kind. A new race was then created for the vacant world, and, according to the fixed purpose of the Creator, each was left free to act for himself; he loves not mere machines. The fallen spirit, envying the new creature called man, tempted him to sin. What was his sin? Simply the giving up of his birthright, the divine soul-sparkle, for a promise of earthly pleasure. The triune divine deep, the mysterious fiery triangle, which, to our finite minds, best represents the Deity, now withdrew his personal presence; the elements, their balance broken, stormed upon man; his body, which was once ethereal, moving by mere volition, now grew heavy; and it was also appointed unto him to die. The race thus darkened, crippled, and degenerate, sank almost to the level of the brutes, the mind-fire alone remaining of all their spiritual gifts. They lived on blindly, and as blindly died. The sun, however, was left to them, a type of what they had lost.

"At length, in the fullness of time, the world-day of four thousand years, which was appointed by the council in heaven for the regiving of the divine and forfeited soul-sparkle, as on the fourth day of creation the great sun was given, there came to earth the earth's compassionate Saviour, who took upon himself our degenerate body, and revivified it with the divine soul sparkle, who overcame all our temptations, and finally allowed the tinder of our sins to perish in his own painful death upon the cross. Through him our paradise body was restored, it waits for us on the other side of the grave. He showed us what it was like on Mount Tabor, with it he passed through closed doors, walked upon the water, and ruled the elements; so will it be with us. Paradise will come again; this world will, for a thousand years, see its first estate; it will be again the Garden of Eden. America is the great escaping-place; here will the change begin. As it is written, 'Those who escape to my utmost borders.' As the time draws near, the spirits who watch above are permitted to speak to those souls who listen. Of these listening, waiting souls am I; therefore have I withdrawn myself. The sun himself speaks to me, the greatest spirit of all; each morning I watch for his coming; each morning I ask, 'Is it to-day?' Thus do I wait."

"And how long have you been waiting?" I asked.

"I know not, time is nothing, to me."

"Is the great day near at hand?" said Raymond.

"Almost at its dawning; the last days are passing."

"How do you know this?"

"The spirits tell me. Abide here, and perhaps they will speak to you also," replied Waiting Samuel.

We made no answer. Twilight had darkened into night, and the Flats had sunk into silence below us. After some moments I turned to speak to our host; but, noiselessly as one of his own spirits, he had departed.

"A strange mixture of Jacob Boehmen, chiliastic dreams, Christianity, sun-worship, and modern spiritualism," I said. "Much learning hath made the Maine farmer mad."

"Is he mad?" said Raymond. "Sometimes I think we are all mad."

"We should certainly become so if we spent our time in speculations upon subjects clearly beyond our reach. The whole race of philosophers from Plato down are all the time going round in a circle. As long as we are in the world, I for one propose to keep my feet on solid ground; especially as we have no wings. 'Abide here, and perhaps the spirits will speak to you,' did he say? I think very likely they will, and to such good purpose that you won't have any mind left."

"After all, why should not spirits speak to us?" said Raymond, in a musing tone.

As he uttered these words the mocking laugh of a loon came across the dark waste.

"The very loons are laughing at you," I said, rising. "Come down; there is a chill in the air, composed in equal parts of the Flats, the night, and Waiting Samuel. Come down, man; come down to the warm kitchen and common-sense."

We found Roxana alone by the fire, whose glow was refreshingly real and warm; it was like the touch of a flesh-and-blood hand, after vague dreamings of spirit companions, cold and intangible at best, with the added suspicion that, after all, they are but creations of our own fancy, and even their spirit-nature fictitious. Prime, the graceful raconteur who goes a-fishing, says, "firelight is as much of a polisher in-doors as moonlight outside." It is; but with a different result. The moonlight polishes everything into romance, the firelight into comfort. We brought up two remarkably easy old chairs in front of the hearth and sat down, Raymond still adrift with his wandering thoughts, I, as usual, making talk out of the present. Roxana sat opposite, knitting in hand, the cat purring at her feet. She was a slender woman, with faded light hair, insignificant features, small dull blue eyes, and a general aspect which, with every desire to state at its best, I can only call commonplace. Her gown was limp, her hands roughened with work, and there was no collar around her yellow throat. O magic rim of white, great is thy power! With thee, man is civilized; without thee, he becomes at once a savage.

"I am out of pork," remarked Roxana, casually; "I must go over to the mainland to-morrow and get some."

If it had been anything but pork! In truth, the word did not chime with the mystic conversation of Waiting Samuel. Yes; there was no doubt about it. Roxana's mind was sadly commonplace.

"See what I have found," I said, after a while, taking out the old breastpin. "The stone is gone; but who knows? It might have been a diamond dropped by some French duchess, exiled, and fleeing for life across these far Western waters; or perhaps that German Princess of Brunswick-Wolfen-something-or-other, who, about one hundred years ago, was dead and buried in Russia, and travelling in America at the same time, a sort of a female wandering Jew, who has been done up in stories ever since."

(The other day, in Bret Harte's "Melons," I saw the following: "The singular conflicting conditions of John Brown's body and soul were, at that time, beginning to attract the attention of American youth." That is good, isn't it? Well, at the time I visited the Flats, the singular conflicting conditions of the Princess of Brunswick-Wolfen-something-or-other had, for a long time, haunted me.)

Roxana's small eyes were near-sighted; she peered at the empty setting, but said nothing.

"It is water-logged," I continued, holding it up in the firelight, "and it hath a brassy odor; nevertheless, I feel convinced that it belonged to the princess."

Roxana leaned forward and took the trinket; I lifted up my arms and gave a mighty stretch, one of those enjoyable lengthenings-out which belong only to the healthy fatigue of country life. When I drew myself in again, I was surprised to see Roxana's features working, and her rough hands trembling, as she held the battered setting.

"It was mine," she said; "my dear old cameo breastpin that Abby gave me when I was married. I saved it and saved it, and wouldn't sell it, no matter how low we got, for someway it seemed to tie me to home and baby's grave. I used to wear it when I had baby—I had neck-ribbons then; we had things like other folks, and on Sundays we went to the old meeting-house on the green. Baby is buried there—Oh baby, baby!" and the voice broke into sobs.

"You lost a child?" I said, pitying the sorrow which was, which must be, so lonely, so unshared.

"Yes. Oh baby! baby!" cried the woman, in a wailing tone. "It was a little boy, gentlemen, and it had curly hair, and could just talk a word or two; its name was Ethan, after father, but we all called it Robin. Father was mighty proud of Robin, and mother, too. It died, gentlemen, my baby died, and I buried it in the old churchyard near the thorn-tree. But still I thought to stay there always along with mother and the girls; I never supposed anything else, until Samuel began to see visions. Then, everything was different, and everybody against us; for, you see, I would marry Samuel, and when he left off working, and began to talk to the spirits, the folks all said, 'I told yer so, Maria Ann!' Samuel wasn't of Maine stock exactly: his father was a sailor, and it was suspected that his mother was some kind of an East-Injia woman, but no one knew. His father died and left the boy on the town, so he lived round from house to house until he got old enough to hire out. Then he came to our farm, and there he stayed. He had wonderful eyes, Samuel had, and he had a way with him—well, the long and short of it was, that I got to thinking about him, and couldn't think of anything else. The folks didn't like it at all, for, you see, there was Adam Rand, who had a farm of his own over the hill; but I never could bear Adam Rand. The worst of it was, though, that Samuel never so much as looked at me, hardly. Well, it got to be the second year, and Susan, my younger sister, married Adam Rand. Adam, he thought he'd break up my nonsense, that's what they called it, and so he got a good place for Samuel away down in Connecticut, and Samuel said he'd go, for he was always restless, Samuel was. When I heard it, I was ready to lie down and die. I ran out into the pasture and threw myself down by the fence like a crazy woman. Samuel happened to come by along the lane, and saw me; he was always kind to all the dumb creatures, and stopped to see what was the matter, just as he would have stopped to help a calf. It all came out then, and he was awful sorry for me. He sat down on the top bar of the fence and looked at me, and I sat on the ground a-crying with my hair down, and my face all red and swollen.

" 'I never thought to marry, Maria Ann,' says he.

" 'O, please do, Samuel,' says I, 'I'm a real good housekeeper, I am, and we can have a little land of our own, and everything nice—'

" 'But I wanted to go away. My father was a sailor,' he began, a-looking away off toward the ocean.

" 'Oh, I can't stand it,—I can't stand it,' says I, beginning to cry again. Well, after that he agreed to stay at home and marry me, and the folks they had to give in to it when they saw how I felt. We were married on Thanksgiving day, and I wore a pink delaine, purple neck-ribbon, and this very breastpin that sister Abby gave me,—it cost four dollars, and came 'way from Boston. Mother kissed me, and said she hoped I'd be happy.

" 'Of course I shall, mother,' says I. "Samuel has great gifts; he isn't like common folks."

" 'But common folks is a deal comfortabler," says mother. The folks never understood Samuel.

"Well, we had a chirk little house and bit of land, and baby came, and was so cunning and pretty. The visions had begun to appear then, and Samuel said he must go.

"Where?" says I.

"Anywhere the spirits lead me," says he.

"But baby couldn't travel, and so it hung along; Samuel left off work, and everything ran down to loose ends; I did the best I could, but it wasn't much. Then baby died, and I buried him under the thorn-tree, and the visions came thicker and thicker, and Samuel told me as how this time he must go. The folks wanted me to stay behind without him; but they never understood me nor him. I could no more leave him than I could fly; I was just wrapped up in him. So we went away; I cried dreadfully when it came to leaving the folks and Robin's little grave, but I had so much to do after we got started, that there wasn't time for anything but work. We thought to settle in ever so many places, but after a while there would always come a vision, and I'd have to sell out and start on. The little money we had was soon gone, and then I went out for days' work, and picked up any work I could get. But many's the time we were cold, and many's the time we were hungry, gentlemen. The visions kept coming, and by and by I got to like 'em too. Samuel he told me all they said when I came home nights, and it was nice to hear all about the thousand years of joy, when there'd be no more trouble, and when Robin would come back to us again. Only I told Samuel that I hoped the world wouldn't alter much, because I wanted to go back to Maine for a few days, and see all the old places. Father and mother are dead, I suppose," said Roxana, looking up at us with a pathetic expression in her small dull eyes. Beautiful eyes are doubly beautiful in sorrow; but there is something peculiarly pathetic in small dull eyes looking up at you, struggling to express the grief that lies within, like a prisoner behind the bars of his small dull window.

"And how did you lose your breastpin?" I said, coming back to the original subject.

"Samuel found I had it, and threw it away soon after we came to the Flats; he said it was vanity."

"Have you been here long?"

"O yes, years. I hope we shall stay here always now,—at least, I mean until the thousand years of joy begin,—for it's quiet, and Samuel's more easy here than in any other place. I've got used to the lonely feeling, and don't mind it much now. There's no one near us for miles, except Rosabel Lee and Liakim; they don't come here, for Samuel can't abide 'em, but sometimes I stop there on my way over from the mainland, and have a little chat about the children. Rosabel Lee has got lovely children, she has! They don't stay there in the winter, though; the winters are long, I don't deny it."

"What do you do then?"

"Well, I knit and cook, and Samuel reads to me, and has a great many visions."

"He has books, then?"

"Yes, all kinds; he's a great reader, and he has boxes of books about the spirits, and such things."

"Nine of the night. Take thou thy rest. I will lay me down in peace and sleep; for it is thou, Lord, only, that makest me dwell in safety," chanted the voice in the hall; and our evening was over.

At dawn we attended the service on the roof; then, after breakfast, we released Captain Kidd, and started out for another day's sport. We had not rowed far when Roxana passed us, poling her flat-boat rapidly along; she had a load of fish and butter, and was bound for the mainland village. "Bring us back a Detroit paper," I said. She nodded and passed on, stolid and homely in the morning light. Yes, I was obliged to confess to myself that she was commonplace.

A glorious day we had on the moors in the rushing September wind. Everything rustled and waved and danced, and the grass undulated in long billows as far as the eye could see. The wind enjoyed himself like a mad creature; he had no forests to oppose him, no heavy water to roll up,— nothing but merry, swaying grasses. It was the west wind,— "of all the winds, the best wind." The east wind was given us for our sins; I have long suspected that the east wind was the angel that drove Adam out of Paradise. We did nothing that day,—nothing but enjoy the rushing breeze. We felt like Bedouins of the desert, with our boat for a steed. "He came flying upon the wings of the wind," is the grandest image of the Hebrew poet.

Late in the afternoon we heard the bugle and returned, following our clew as before. Roxana had brought a late paper, and, opening it, I saw the account of an accident,—a yacht run down on the Sound and five drowned; five, all near and dear to us. Hastily and sadly we gathered our possessions together; the hunting, the fishing, were nothing now; all we thought of was to get away, to go home to the sorrowing ones around the new-made graves. Roxana went with us in her boat to guide us back to the little lighthouse. Waiting Samuel bade us no farewell, but as we rowed away we saw him standing on the house-top gazing after us. We bowed; he waved his hand; and then turned away to look at the sunset. What were our little affairs to a man who held converse with the spirits!

We rowed in silence. How long, how weary seemed the way! The grasses, the lilies, the silver channels,—we no longer even saw them. At length the forward boat stopped. "There's the lighthouse yonder," said Roxana. "I won't go over there tonight. Mayhap you'd rather not talk, and Rosabel Lee will be sure to talk to me. Good by." We shook hands, and I laid in the boat a sum of money to help the little household through the winter; then we rowed on toward the lighthouse. At the turn I looked back; Roxana was sitting motionless in her boat; the dark clouds were rolling up behind her; and the Flats looked wild and desolate. "God help her!" I said.

A steamer passed the lighthouse and took us off within the hour.

Years rolled away, and I often thought of the grassy sea, and intended to go there; but the intention never grew into reality. In 1870, however, I was travelling westward, and, finding myself at Detroit, a sudden impulse took me up to the Flats. The steamer sailed up the beautiful river and crossed the little lake, both unchanged. But, alas! the canal predicted by the captain fifteen years before had been cut, and, in all its unmitigated ugliness, stretched straight through the enchanted land. I got off at the new and prosaic brick lighthouse, half expecting to see Liakim and his Rosabel Lee; but they were not there, and no one knew anything about them. And Waiting Samuel? No one knew anything about him, either. I took a skiff, and, at the risk of losing myself, I rowed away into the wilderness, spending the day among the silvery channels, which were as beautiful as ever. There were fewer birds; I saw no grave herons, no sombre bitterns and the fish had grown shy. But the water-lilies were beautiful as of old, and the grasses as delicate and luxuriant. I had scarcely a hope of finding the old house on the island, but late in the afternoon, by a mere chance, I rowed up unexpectedly to its little landing-place. The walls stood firm and the roof was unbroken; I landed and walked up the overgrown path. Opening the door, I found the few old chairs and tables in their places, weather-beaten and decayed, the storms had forced a way within, and the floor was insecure; but the gay crockery was on its shelf, the old tins against the wall, and all looked so natural that I almost feared to find the mortal remains of the husband and wife as I went from room to room. They were not there, however, and the place looked as if it had been uninhabited for years. I lingered in the doorway. What had become of them? Were they dead? Or had a new vision sent them farther toward the setting sun? I never knew, although I made many inquiries. If dead, they were probably lying somewhere under the shining waters; if alive, they must have "folded their tents, like the Arabs, and silently stolen away."

I rowed back in the glow of the evening across the grassy sea. "It is beautiful, beautiful," I thought, "but it is passing away. Already commerce has invaded its borders; a few more years and its loveliness will be but a legend of the past. The bittern has vanished; the loon has fled away. Waiting Samuel was the prophet of the waste; he has gone, and the barriers are broken down. Farewell, beautiful grass-water! No artist has painted, no poet has sung your wild, vanishing charm; but in one heart, at least, you have a place, O lovely land of St. Clair!"

MARSH, HAWK

(1978)

Margaret Atwood

Diseased or unwanted
trees, cut into pieces, thrown
away here, damp and soft in the sun, rotting and half-
covered with sand, burst truck
tires, abandoned, bottles and cans hit
with rocks or bullets, a mass grave,
someone made it, spreads on the
land like a bruise and we stand on it, vantage
point, looking out over the marsh.

Expanse of green
reeds, patches of water, shapes
just out of reach of the eyes,
the wind moves, moves it and it
eludes us, it is full
daylight. From the places
we can't see, the guttural swamp voices
impenetrable, not human,
utter their one-note
syllables, boring and
significant as oracles and quickly over.

It will not answer, it will not
answer, though we hit
it with rocks, there is a splash, the wind
covers it over; but
intrusion is not what we want,

we want it open, the marsh rushes
to bend aside, the water
to accept us, it is only
revelation, simple as the hawk
which lifts up now against
the sun and into
our eyes, wingspread and sharp call
filling the head/sky, this,

to immerse, to have it slide
through us, disappearance
of the skin, this is what we are looking for,
the way in.

MARGARET ATWOOD (1939-) is the author of numerous novels and collections of poetry, including *Surfacing* (1970), fiction about a young woman's coming of age in her family's cabin in the north woods, and *The Journals of Susanna Moodie* (1970), poetry based on *Roughing It In the Bush* (1852). Atwood wrote the first guide to Canadian literature, *Survival: A Thematic Guide to Canadian Literature* (1972). "Marsh Hawk" and "Marsh Languages" (page 320) are from her books *Two-Headed Poems* and *Morning In the Burned House.*

Women Travellers on the Great Lakes

Travellers on the Great Lakes
Frances Benjamin Johnston

WOMEN TRAVELLERS ON THE LAKES

IN 1818 FRANCES WRIGHT, an independently wealthy English propagandist for democracy, travelled to the United States and then wrote about her experiences with great enthusiasm, emotion, and personal detail. *Views of Society and Manners in America . . . during the years 1818, 1819, 1820* (1821) was the one of the first accounts by a woman traveller to break the mold set by men's exploration narratives which often concentrated on the dry delineation of facts. With her book Franny Wright created a new mode of travel writing and opened the form to women who, like herself, were interested in transgressing the approved topics on which women were allowed to write.

It may be difficult for readers in the late twentieth century to comprehend the rigid social expectations that confined early nineteenth-century women writers, who were usually limited to discussing topics related to home, church, and charitable work. Travel literature, however, offered a lucrative public forum for women writers to make their opinions known on national and international issues, to suggest alternative models for women's place in society, and to challenge the tradition of men's travel and exploration narratives. Women established a female-oriented genre that allowed them to express otherwise unacceptable opinions through their response to landscape and Native cultures. After Wright, the travel narrative became a way for women writers to comment upon national and international events and concerns without broaching the boundaries of what was considered ladylike and decorous.

Many used the form of the travel narrative as a kind of autobiography by which they could respond to two forces of power that affected what they wrote: the male-dominated culture from which they came, and the white patronization of Native peoples they observed. Still, their writing is often constrained by gender and class and by readers' expectations of how Native peoples could be described. The most clever writers, such as Anna Jameson in *Winter Studies and Summer Rambles* (1837), were able to transcend all traditional limits. Jameson used a subversive technique in which she asked a number of questions with which readers could agree until she led them to an inescapable conclusion of her choice. In her book, part of which is reprinted here, she leaves readers little choice but to agree with her observation that the Indians she observed were more honest than whites and that Indian women had equal rights that white women did not have: both revolutionary statements for her time.

Because the travel narrative was an elastic form that women writers appropriated to publicize their concerns, these books are some of the most fascinating writing by women in the nineteenth century. Mrs. Trollope's *Domes-*

tic Manners of the Americans was so blunt about American lack of manners it created a scandal that lasted a generation. After she published it in 1832, no writer could avoid commenting on her example, as does Isabella Lucy Bird. Bird was only twenty-five when she wrote her book, and she illustrates that age and experience were no bar to writing. All the writer needed was the social and economic freedom to travel and the courage to record her observations truthfully.

There were some topics, however, that were required, primarily descriptions of Niagara Falls. By the twentieth century the attractions of Niagara had paled, but in the nineteenth, when descriptions of sublime scenery were a mark of the writer's ability and sensitivity, no book was complete without a set-piece delineating the affect of the Falls on the viewer. These descriptions are as predictable as the round of tourist excursions the writers took: they all saw the same features and their greatest task became to write something new about a familiar place. One of the most interesting is included: the infectiously enthusiastic account of the twelve-year-old Victoria Stuart-Whortley who was travelling North and South America with her mother.

Travel narrative is not only a capacious, generous form that allows women writers to adapt it to their own purposes, but it is a durable one as well. It can be fictionalized and romanticized to sell vacations, turned into poetry, and recreated afresh for each era from sailing ships to speed boats. *The Women's Great Lakes Reader* concludes with a chapter from the most recent lakes' travel narrative by a woman, *Deep Water Passage* (1995), which reflects the concerns women face in the late twentieth century. In addition to describing Lake Superior, Ann Linnea's narrative illustrates how her kayaking trip changed her in ways she did not expect, making it impossible to accept the old life she had once lived. Many women travellers have had the same experience. Once free of confines of their former lives, able to take risks and succeed in doing things they had never thought they could, they were unwilling to once again become confined by others' expectations. Most of the travel narratives collected here marked a time of great growth in their writers' abilities and confidence, and contributed to their determination to make successful careers for themselves once their journeys, emotional as well as physical, were complete.

FROM A YOUNG TRAVELLER'S JOURNAL OF A TOUR IN NORTH AND SOUTH AMERICA DURING THE YEAR 1850 (1855)

Victoria Stuart-Wortley

VICTORIA STUART-WORTLEY'S mother, Lady Welby, developed a passion for travel before her marriage. When her husband died, she took Victoria, who had been born eleven years before in 1837, with her to the United States, Canada, Mexico, and South America. They continued travelling, to Spain, Morocco, Turkey, Palestine, and Syria, until Lady Welby died in Beruit after being kicked by a mule when Victoria was eighteen. Lady Victoria Stuart-Wortley returned home to become Maid of Honor to Queen Victoria, her namesake and Godmother, and married Sir William Welby in 1863. After raising her family, she became interested in the philosophical problems of language and meaning, or semiotics, and published several monographs and books on the subject before her death in 1912.

Her mother published extensively, both poetry and travel narratives, so young Victoria grew up with a strong model of female achievement. It was natural that she should keep a journal of her first long trip with the plan of turning it into a book for other young people. While there are thousands of accounts of visits to Niagara Falls, few are written by travellers as young as Victoria Stuart-Welby, and fewer still are as interesting to read. Her youth and irreverence spare nothing, and her account still delights readers who are no longer interested in what the Falls looked like, but in what one young woman thought important to record, including mice.

NIAGARA

IT MAY SEEM PRESUMPTUOUS in so youthful a traveller, (having only attained her twelfth year a week before starting for America), to put her everyday and naturally childish impressions and observations in print. This little book, however, is not destined to become a candidate for the honours of books of travels in general; since it is intended for children,—those of her own age, for instance, whom it is her highest aim to amuse, and, to a certain degree, instruct. Her little volume, therefore, lays no claim to the attention of the public farther than its character as a child's book may deserve.

May 22d, evening, Falls of Niagara—On leaving Buffalo soon after dawn, we passed some very pretty scenery. Its general character was rather Scotch; the "burns" and glens, rocks, and clouds, and frowning hills answered to all the descriptions, all the pictures I have ever read or seen of that much-admired land. As we penetrated farther into the interior, however, the whole aspect of the country was completely changed; I could do nothing but exclaim in astonishment at the bewilderingly vast forests. They seemed to me perfectly endless, and of an extraordinary uniform character. Maples, beeches, and pines, seemed to me to be kings of the forest; other trees—if there were any—were comparatively small and few, looking like strangers to the soil. By the bye, I must mention the account of an English friend of ours (whom we had met on the *Canada* in crossing the Atlantic) of his first sight of a real Americanism. He was walking leisurely in one of the greatest thoroughfares of Albany when a large building attracted his attention. The lower story seemed almost all open, nothing but slender frames indicating the presence of windows. A long row of boots (of which he could only see the soles) was seemingly placed on a transverse bar of the supposed window frames, nearly six feet above the level of the ground. Naturally thinking it to be some immense boot-shop he approached a little nearer. When what was his astonishment to discover that the supposed bootshop was nothing less than a large and popular cafe, and that the boots he saw were then under the process of wearing, their owners being only enjoying their after-dinner siesta and daily lounge! It was a natural mistake to make, however, when it is remembered that, as I said before, the boots were at least five or six feet from the ground. It was late at night when we arrived at Buffalo, and having found tolerably comfortable apartments, we prepared to rest.

Starting the next morning at eight o'clock, we arrived at the village of Manchester at half-past ten a.m. The said village is only about two or three hundred yards from the American cataract. When our train arrived, there arose (as is often the case in the United States, and even in Europe, as travellers sometimes know to their cost) a quarrel between the porters of the different hotels as to who should have the privilege of disposing of our persons and luggage—a privilege which none ultimately possessed, for we immediately made arrangements for crossing the river to the Canadian side by the ferry. As it required some little time, however, for our luggage to be packed on the ferry-boat, we turned our steps toward a jutting-out and barren rock above the American fall. Here we had our first view of the two cataracts. Perhaps my readers expect me to describe my first impressions of the falls; if so I fear they must be disappointed, for I cannot tell them what they were. They were certainly neither admiration or disappointment; perhaps they more resembled bewilderment. The fact is—I have since found it out—that one cannot take in all its magnificence and grandeur at a single glance, but must see it for a long time, hour after hour, day after day;—it grows upon you. One thing, however, that puzzled me was the apparent disparity between the height and volume of the cataracts, and the intensity of the noise. I could not help remarking aloud to mamma that the noise was not really so very loud; she did not hear me, and, to my infinite astonishment, I was obliged to repeat it, in a louder voice, two or three times before she did so. A negro who happened to be standing close to my elbow at the time, taking my observation to be intended for him, suddenly bawled in my ear, "Yes, marm, him mackee mush noise more, far, farder down the river." I cannot answer for the truth of this, but certainly it was bewildering to find that what one was actually saying was at the same time practically contradicted! By this time the ferry was waiting for us, so jumping into the boat, we were rowed across, amid such a shower of spray that we got wet almost to the skin. On arriving at the Canadian shore, we had to ascend in a primitive carriage the steep face of the abrupt and precipitous banks of the river in order to arrive at Clifton House. Its situation could not have been better chosen; it is only about half a mile from the Horse-shoe, or Canadian Fall, having a delightful view of both cataracts from the broad piazzas with which it is surrounded.

26th.—Today I have been doing many wonders, among which, perhaps going under Niagara may be ranked as one of the most notable. I fear, however, that, as it is an excursion daily becoming more popular, it will, ere a year has passed, become an every-day affair. Having made the necessary arrangements and preparations, in the shape of putting on oilskin dresses, and somewhat recovered from the fits of laughing which the sight of our extraordinary costume aroused in us, we (that is, the most courageous of our two maids, and I) proceeded to Table-Rock, and, descending a crazy and creaking staircase found ourselves under the high and projecting crag so called. Winding our way along a narrow path, rendered slippery by clouds of spray, we suddenly came in sight of the giant, which, though as yet nearly a hundred yards from us, seemed as though it was actually pouring on our devoted heads. Just at that moment we had a foretaste of what was coming, from a small brook that, trickling down from Table-Rock, drenched us as we passed under it. We were now approaching the cloud, or rather sheet of spray, which effectually hid from our sight the "mysteries within." Once on the other side, we wiped our eyes, and with difficulty I succeeded in half-opening them, and giving a rapid glance around, notwithstanding the injunctions of the guide "not to look up by no means, as that there cat'rackt as is so wet, 'ud send all the wawter down yer throat, mess!" Scarcely had that been accomplished, when I was obliged speedily to shut them again, for the water (pouring down from my forehead and oilskin cap) got into them in undesirable quantities. In that hasty glance, however, I certainly saw all that could be seen, except the eels, which I was afterwards told were slipping about in great numbers. Strange, I thought, was the man who could thus look at eels while Niagara was before him!

We were in a spacious hall: the water-roof of our rocky palace seemed as though formed of rainbows; its tint, or rather tints, were as lapis lazuli, emeralds, and sapphires; these again, decorated with the most delicate arabesques of silver, formed by the glittering foam and spray. Glittering, I say, because the sun was at the moment shining through it; and that was also in some measure the cause of the lovely playing colours we beheld. But it was now time to return; so after another drowning, we passed through the silvery spray-curtain, and found ourselves once more in the open air. Mamma and one of the maids were standing on Table-Rock watching for our return, and were soon after satisfied by seeing us arrive at the top of the spiral ladder. One would naturally think that such a cold and plentiful shower-bath would have left a chill behind, but, on the contrary, it was succeeded by a most agreeable warmth, and we felt quite refreshed.

27th.—Last night I woke up just at twelve o'clock, and as a faint glimmer in the room announced that it was moonlight, I arose and looked through the Venetian jalousies. Certainly the soft and lovely, mingled with the magnificent, had rarely, if ever, been so beauteously presented to my eyes. The mellow moonlight was gently playing with, and kissing, as it were, the sparkling water; the moon quiet and silent;—not so its thundering playmate! The thousands of stars in the clear sky were reflected in the comparatively still water a little lower down the river, while the moon mirrored herself in a long glistening trail. The roar of the mighty cataract seemed to be mellowed into gentleness by the shower of smiling rays descending upon it, instead of thundering its own dirge. Strolling today, with my maid, towards the suspension-bridge, I was surprised to be warned of bears. I believe they really, every now and then, are seen in the winter, but I should not have thought a meeting with one was much to be dreaded at this season of the year.

23d.—Today we visited the Suspension Bridge, Whirlpool, and Burning springs. Having ordered a carriage, we proceeded to drive through a forest, enriched with wild flowers, and occasionally enlivened by a settler's clearing, or a glimpse of the now foaming and agitated river. Our driver was a great chatter-box, and amused himself and us by describing, with impromptu eloquence, every cart or carriage, every tree or bend of the river, which we passed, not omitting to find ingeniously something in each in which to praise himself. The following is a poor specimen of his dialogue:—

"You can't think, marm—you can't think, that 'ere whiler-pool is parfectly

spleendid, and there han't a part of ladies and gentlement as doesn't be enchanted; and I assures ye, marm—I assures ye, there *is* some people that
likes the Suspension Bridge and the barnin' Springs better than the Falls;
and them always takes me, marm, they *does* (with solemn emphasis). I's al'ays
prefeered!"

We passed several dogwood-trees; their blossom is large and white, having a sweet smell. It is not unlike an English dog-rose, or apple-blossom. It is
hardly necessary to describe the Suspension Bridge, except that it was certainly an immense height from the river. The whirlpool rather disappointed
us all, except the coachman. It is a very dangerous spot, no doubt, and may
be very wonderful; but I think in outward appearance, at least, that it does
not fully realise the description sometimes given of it. The scenery around,
however, is very striking, consisting of high and rocky banks, clothed only
with gloomy firs, whilst an almost unexplored forest forms the background.
The whirlpool, we were told, is caused by the force of the water on the upper
side, which, forming a huge rapid, descends with great force on the circular
basin, and, suddenly meeting with a rival current, darts under it with tremendous power, thus creating the whirlpool, which is ever changing the
place of its vortex; so that if you throw a large stick into the boiling water it
will swing round and round for a little time in the same place, then it will
suddenly plunge and disappear, reappearing a moment afterwards at a different place, and re-commencing its rapid twirlings.

The Burning Springs are quite in a different direction from the whirlpool; they are about a mile above the Falls. We drove the whole way along
the lake-like river, with its blooming islands, in some places white with foaming rapids, which are sometimes almost like little cascades, caused by banks
of rock stretching across the river, over which the water rushes in a *slant*.
Several of the smaller islands, even those quite near the shore, have never
been trodden by a living being, so strong is the current between them and
the shore. Between two and three hundred yards above the Horse-shoe Cataract the water rushes at the speed of thirty-six miles and hour! The bridge
springs themselves are, I believe, composed of sulphurous water, from which
a great quantity of gas escapes, which is collected in a barrel placed at the top
of the tank, surmounted by a pipe, out of which, on a torch being applied,
there burnt a clear bright flame. One would think that this might be made
very useful, as a source for supplying the ill-lighted, or, rather not-lighted
towns that surround Niagara; and I can not help wondering that some "cute"
Yankee or enterprising Englishman has not already take the business in hand.

31st.—The house was crowded yesterday with the inmates of a Canadian boarding-school not far from here, who were having, I suppose, their
annual fete. I fear I cannot say much in praise of their manners in general, if

they may be judged of from their conduct on this occasion. They stared in at our window from the verandah with such impudence and pertinacity, that we were obliged to pull the window-blinds down; and in the evening they made a noise as if to deafen one, with talking, giggling, laughing, playing, singing, or rather screaming, and dancing antediluvian quadrilles, all in bad time. They, however, afterwards quite gained mamma's heart by singing "God Save the Queen." I am now trying to collect the seeds of wild flowers here, before we start again for New York.

June 1st.—It has been very sultry to-day; scarcely a breath of air was stirring, except in the woods, which are always cool. This morning we walked out, but found the heat so great that we were glad to take refuge in the silent forest. Our walk was interrupted with no brushwood; there was hardly a blade of grass on the ground. We looked through the forest miles and miles, without other obstruction than the bare, slender trunks of the maples and beeches. Occasionally a dogwood or balm of Gilead tree diversified with its gay blossoms the monotony of the scene. The *roof*, however, that the thick and verdant foliage seems to make, though effectually preventing the appearance of a single ray, does not shield the ground beneath from the furious rains which, in due season, water the land. Hence frequent bogs, or small marshes, sometimes render walking quite a difficult accomplishment; they appear so very deceptive in the sombre light of the forest, that it becomes far from easy to escape them. I myself one day was thus placed in a dilemma, for, having with some difficulty crossed a small bog, I landed on a tiny island, the mud apparently environing me on all sides, and it was only with the assistance of my maid that I managed to get out. Passing through a small village, on our return home, I was astonished to see a respectably dressed young woman sitting at the door of a large and tidy-looking cottage *smoking a pipe!* I found a very beautiful specimen of moss to-day, it closely resembled a miniature forest (about four inches high) of very light green firs, or, more properly, larches, with thick and tangled underwood. I attempted to preserve it, but found it impossible, it was so delicate.

June 2d.—To-day we visited Iris, or Goat Island. We walked down to the ferry, and, engaging a boat, crossed to the American side. It seems we had chosen a lucky moment, for the spray did not once touch us during the transit. We sat down on the edge of the rock above the American falls, after having clambered at least two hundred steps up the almost perpendicular face of the rock, to rest ourselves. We then walked along the edge of the water, until we reached—must I say it?—a saw-mill! The industrious Americans could not rest, of course, until they had made "that 'ere big Fall of some use to mortal man!" No, it would have been sacrificing their "cuteness." We crossed over the whirling river by an ingenious wooden bridge, probably the work of the same "smart" personage who built the mill. Goat Island is very lovely; it is covered almost entirely with forest, which serves to hide from the sun many beautiful flowers, among which two are my great favourites. One is like a large single camellia, quite white, and very wax-like (I believe it is called the "white death-flower"); the other is a flower rather like a large lily of the valley, only pink. We followed a small path in the wood, till we came to the Hog's Back, and stood by the trunk of an old tree, which stretches out from the very farthest point of the island towards the American Falls. It almost dips one of its old arms into the ribbon Cascade, so named from the comparative smallness of it size from the others. A very small island, with hardly room for three trees to grow upon it, separates it from the American Fall. We crossed a little bridge, not more than seven feet wide, and stood on the end of Luna Island. This, in my opinion, is the finest view of the American Fall. Close to where we stood, the water was very shallow, only a few inches deep; and H— could hardly help observing, that she thought she could, with safety and without help, stand where we had only been told a minute before no man, standing on dry land, could have prevented a boat from being washed over. We then went to the Tower, which is erected on a group of small rocks, which extend to the very edge of the Horse-shoe Fall. A small bridge, poised at intervals upon the rocks (which would almost form a rough bridge of themselves), stretches to the land. Not long ago, it was considered safe to mount the Tower, which, indeed, was the purpose it was originally intended for; but as it was never a very strong edifice, it could not long stand the wear and tear of the continual and violent shaking produced by the cataract. Of this, perhaps, some faint idea may be given, when I mention, that at Clifton House, which I should think was at least three-quarters of a mile from the Horse-shoe, and nearly half a mile from the American cataract, the vibration is so violent, that I almost invariably at night wake up and fancy myself, for several moments, in rather a rough-going steamer. The view from the foot of the Tower is overwhelmingly magnificent; the spray, which almost always inclines more towards the American side than towards the Canadian, hides from you the bottom; and, without any stretch of the imagination, you can easily fancy, that if there is any at all, the bottom must be an unfathomable depth below you. We amused ourselves by throwing in pieces of wood at a little distance off, and then watching how they increased, more and more, their headlong pace, until they flew over the edge, shivered for a second in the snowy spraydrops, and were seen no more. So occupied were we in looking with fixed eyes upon the Cataract, that it was nearly sunset ere we reached home.

3d.—Last night there was one of the grandest thunderstorms I ever saw. The last glow of the sunset had hardly faded away when it began to lighten faintly. Even then it was very beautiful; a rose-coloured light seemed to cover the sky for a second, with a little white globe on the horizon. As it grew darker, the flashes increased in brilliancy, though always presenting the same curious form. Having first ascertained that it was only sheet-lightning, I ascended to the verandah of the third story, and from the window of my servant's room, which opens on the balcony, enjoyed an extensive view of the magnificent storm, and having enveloped ourselves in warm shawls (for the night was rather damp) we stepped out. Hardly had we done so, however, than a flash of an extraordinary character and brilliancy burst upon us. I think I must describe it, that my readers may see what sheet lightning in America sometimes is. The whole sky was apparently covered with a resplendent gold colour, intersected with small clouds of the most brilliant whiteness. Exactly behind the Horse-shoe was a kind of globe of intense, fiery red. From this there shot in every direction broad, zig-zag streams of liquid fire, every one a flash in itself. This lasted for about half a second, but reappeared (only fainter) several times in the space of a minute, till, at last, it died away. The last coruscation was immediately followed by a loud clap of thunder, which, announcing the approach of a terrific storm, made us glad to retire. And it was a terrific storm! It continued the whole night with such violence, that the noise of the Cataracts was drowned for the time, and the house seemed to totter to his foundations.

5th, Wednesday.—We had a delightful drive this afternoon. I attempted to sketch the Horse-shoe from behind the Fall; but, as it was almost my first attempt at sketching landscapes, it may be easily supposed that it was not very like it. Sambo, our Negro waiter (an exceedingly obliging and civil man, by the way) was guilty today of a funny breach of etiquette. During dinner, while engaged in a interesting conversation, all of a sudden (thinking, I suppose, that we were rather long) his black face presented itself at a corner of the window, from the balcony. Observing this, I gave him rather a reproving glance. He then came round, supposing that we had finished, though we had always told him not to come until we rang, with the rest of the dinner. When he found he had to take it all away again, his face turned a most extraordinary colour, which, had he been white, would no doubt have been scarlet. There are, by the way, a great many mice in our drawing-room, which are very tame, and they scamper about, in the evening, in search of crumbs. As I am very fond of mice, anywhere but in a bedroom, they are a great amusement to me.

FROM THE ENGLISHWOMAN IN AMERICA

(1856)

Isabella Lucy Bird

FOR MUCH OF HER LIFE, Isabella Bird, born in 1831 to an Edinburgh Church of England clergyman, was an invalid. She was also the first woman elected to the Royal Geographical Society and the author of a number of popular nineteenth-century travel narratives, including *Six Months in the Sandwich Islands* (1875), *The Hawaiian Archipelago* (1875), *A Lady's Life in the Rocky Mountains* (1879), *Unbeaten Tracks in Japan* (1880), *Among the Tibetans* (1894), *Journeys to Persia and Kurdistan* (1891), *The Yangtze Valley and Beyond* (1899), and *Chinese Pictures* (1900). The cause of her poor health was a chronic spinal ailment; when she was eighteen she had surgery to remove a fibrous tumor. Like many convalescent cases in her time, a long sea voyage and travel were recommended to help her recover. Once on board ship bound for North America and free from the stifling constraints of Victorian rectory gentility, Bird discovered not only health, but freedom. She never looked back, happy to spend nearly the rest of her life travelling, usually under far more difficult conditions than she encountered on her first trip. Although she lamented throughout her travels that she missed her home and sister Henrietta, she spent little time there. After Henrietta's death, Bird married her physician and attempted to put down roots. When Dr. Bishop died a few years later, Bird began travelling and writing again. When she died in 1904 her bags were packed for a return trip to China.

Bird had prepared herself for her first trip, to North America, by reading all the travel books about Canada and the United States she could obtain. Once enroute, she kept a detailed journal so that she might join the legions of other women travelling in the United States and Canada who hoped to publish their accounts. Many of these narratives are eminently forgettable, but Bird's book is still interesting, perhaps because it is an irreverent collection of observations and opinions of a highly intelligent, direct young woman who admitted she came to America to dispel her prejudices that "Yankees . . . are famous for smoking, spitting, [eye] 'gouging,' and bowie-knives—for monster hotels, steamboat explosions, railway collisions, and repudiated debts." The sections reprinted here describe Great Lakes steamboat travel, including a terrifying voyage on Lake Ontario which Bird, who enjoyed rough weather more than any other North American traveller, calmly, if a bit sarcastically, relates.

LAKE ONTARIO

AFTER STAYING SOME little time with my friends at Toronto, I went to pay a visit to some friends at Hamilton. The afternoon was very windy and stormy. The lake looked very unpromising from the wharf; the island protected the harbour, but beyond this the waves were breaking with fury. Several persons who came down, intending to take their passage for Hamilton, were deterred by the threatening aspect of the weather, but, not having heard anything against the character of Lake Ontario, I had sufficient confidence in it to persevere in my intention. I said to the captain, "I suppose it won't be rough?" to which he replied that he could not flatter me by saying so, adding that he had never seen so many persons sick as in the morning. Dinner was served immediately upon our leaving the harbour, but the number of those who sat down, at first about thirty, soon diminished to five, the others having rushed in a most mysterious manner to state rooms or windows. For my own I part cannot say that the allowed excellence of the cuisine tempted me to make a very substantial meal, and I was glad of an excuse for retiring to a state-room I shared with a lady who had just taken leave of three children. This cabin was very prettily arranged, but the movements of things were rather erratic, and my valise gave most disagreeable manifestations of spiritual agency.

The ship was making little way, and rolling and pitching fearfully, and, knowing how very top-heavy she was, I did not like at all like the glimpses of raging water which I with difficulty obtained through the cabin windows. To understand what followed it will be necessary for the reader to recollect that the saloon and state-rooms in this vessel formed an erection or deck-house about eight feet high upon the deck, and that the part of the saloon where most of the passengers were congregated, as well as the state-room where I was sitting, were within a few feet of the bow of the ship, and consequently exposed to the fury of the waves. I had sat in my state-room for half an hour, feeling very apathetic, and wishing myself anywhere but where I was, when something struck the ship, and the wretched fabric fell over on her side. Another and another—then silence for a second, broken only by the crash and roar of winds and waters. The inner door burst open, letting in an inundation of water. My companion jumped up, shrieking, "Oh, my children! We're lost—we're lost!" and crawled, pale and trembling, into the saloon. The vessel was lying on her side, therefore locomotion was most difficult; but sea-sick people were emerging from their state-rooms, shrieking, some that they were lost—others for their children—others for mercy; while a group of gentlemen, less noisy, but not less frightened, and drenched to the skin, were standing together, with pale and ashy faces. "What is the matter?"

inquired my companion, taking hold of one of these men. "Say your prayers, for we are going down," was the brutal reply. For the first and only time during my American travels I was really petrified with fear. Suddenly a wave struck the hapless vessel, and with a stunning crash broke through the thin woodwork of the side of the saloon. I caught hold of a life-buoy which was near me—a gentleman clutched it from me, for fright makes some men self-ish—and, breathless, I was thrown down into the gurgling water. I learned then how quickly thoughts can pass through the mind, for in those few seconds I thought less of the anticipated death-struggle amid the boiling surges of the lake, and of the quiet sleep beneath its gloomy waters, than of the unsatisfactory manner in which those at home would glean the terrible tidings from the accident columns of a newspaper. Another minute and I was swept through the open door into a state-room—another one of sus-pense, and the ship righted as if by a superhuman effort. There seemed a respite—there was a silence, broken only by the roar of winds and waves and with the respite came hope. Shortly after, the master of the ship ap-peared, with his hat off, and completely drenched. "Thank God, we're safe!" he said, and returned to his duty. We had all supposed that we had struck a rock or wreck. I never knew the precise nature of our danger beyond this, that the vessel had been thrown on her beam-ends in a squall, and that, the wind immediately veering round, the fury of the waves had been spent on her.

Many of the passengers now wished the captain to return, but he said that he should incur greater danger in an attempt to make the harbour of Toronto than by proceeding down the open lake. For some time nothing was to be seen but a dense fog, a storm of sleet which quite darkened the air, and raging waves, on which we mounted sometimes, while at others we were buried between them. In another hour the gale had completely subsided, and, after we had changed our drenched habiliments, no token remained of the previous storm but the drowned and dismantled appearance of the sa-loon, and the resolution on my own mind never to trust myself again on one of these fearful lakes. I was amused to observe that those people who had displayed the greatest symptoms of fear during the storm were the first to protest that, "as for them, they never thought there was any danger." The afternoon, though cold, was extremely beautiful, but owing to the storm in the early part of our voyage, we did not reach Hamilton till nightfall, or three hours after our appointed time.

I do not like these inland lakes, or tideless fresh-water seas, as they may more appropriately be termed. I know Lake Ontario well; I have crossed it twice, and have been up and down it five times. I have sojourned upon its shores, and have seen them under the hot light of an autumn sun, and un-derneath a mantle of wintry snow; but there is to me something peculiarly oppressive about this vast expanse of water. If the lake is rough, there are no harbours of refuge in which to take shelter—if calm, the waters, though blue, pure, and clear, look monotonous and dead. The very ships look lonely things; their hulls and sails are white, and some of them have been known in time of cholera to drift over the lake from day to day, with none to guide the helm. The shores, too, are flat and uninteresting; my eyes wearied of following that interminable boundary of trees stretching away to the distant horizon.

[Bird continued to travel in Canada and once again found herself leaving Toronto on a steamship.]

FROM CHAPTER XII

THE *ARABIAN* BY WHICH I left Toronto, was inferior to any American steamer I had travelled in. It was crowded with both saloon and steerage passengers, bound for Coburg, Port Hope, and Montreal. It was very bustling and dirty, and the carpet was plentifully sprinkled with tobacco-juice. The captain was very much flustered with his unusually large living cargo, but he was a good-hearted man, and very careful, having, to use his own phrase, "climbed in at the hawse-holes, and worked his way aft, instead of creeping in at the cabin door with his gloves on." The stewards were dirty, and the stewardess too smart to attend to the comforts of the passengers.

As passengers, crates, and boxes poured in at both the fore and aft entrances, I went out on the little slip of deck to look at the prevalent confusion, having previously ascertained that all my effects were secure. The scene was a very amusing one, for, acting out the maxim that "time is money," comparatively few of the passengers came down to the wharf more than five minutes before the hour of sailing. People, among whom were a number of "unprotected females," and juveniles who would not *move on*, were entangled among trucks and carts discharging cargo—hacks, horses, crates, and barrels. These passengers, who would find it difficult to elbow their way unencumbered, find it next to impossible when their hands are burdened with uncut books, baskets of provender, and diminutive carpet-bags. Horses back carts against helpless females, barrels roll upon people's toes, newspaper hawkers puff their wares, bonbon vendors push their plaster of Paris abominations almost at people's eyes, yet, strange to say, it is very seldom that any accident occurs. Family groups invariably are separated, and distracted mamas are running after children whom everybody wishes out of the way, giving utterance to hopes that they are not on shore. Then the obedient papa is sent on shore to look after "that dear little Harry," who is probably all the time in time in the ladies' saloon on some child-fancier's lap eating bonbons. The board is drawn in—the moorings are cast off—the wheels revolve—the bell rings—the engine squeals, and away speeds the steamer down the calm waters of Lake Ontario. Little children and inquisitive young ladies are knocked down or blackened in coiling the hawser, by "hands" who, being nothing but hands, evidently cannot say, "I beg your pardon, miss." There were children, who always will go where they ought not to go, running against people, and taking hold of their clothes with sticky, smeared hands, asking commercial gentlemen to spin their tops, and corpulent ladies to play at hide and seek. I saw one stern-visaged gentleman tormented in this way till he looked ready to give child its "final quietus." There were angry people who had lost their portmanteaus, and were ransacking state-rooms in quest of them, and indolent people who lay on sofas reading novels and chewing tobacco. Some gentleman, taking no heed of the printed notice, goes to the ladies' cabin to see if his wife is safe on board, and meets with a rebuff from the stewardess, who tells him that "gentlemen are not admitted," and, knowing that the *sense*, or as he would say, the nonsense of the community is against him, he beats a reluctant retreat. Everybody seems to have lost somebody or something, but in an hour or two the ladies are deep in novels, the gentlemen in the morning papers, the children have quarreled themselves to sleep, and the captain has gone to smoke by the funnel.

PROFILE:
ANNA BROWNELL MURPHY JAMESON
1794-1860

Courtesy Metropolitan Toronto Reference Library

ANNA JAMESON BEGAN supporting herself as a governess when she was sixteen. Her father was an impoverished Irish miniature painter to the English Court who had his daughter well-educated because he feared she would need to take care of herself and perhaps her sisters. Indeed she did, and except for a brief period shortly after her marriage, she was responsible for herself and her extended family for the rest of her life. She had worked as a governess for years when, after a long and troubled courtship, she married the man who would become Chancellor of Canada. Only then was she free to write. When she came to Toronto in 1837 to help Robert Jameson improve his chances for promotion, she had already published six books, but she suspected her marriage was doomed. A desolate winter in Toronto confirmed her unhappiness; as soon as spring came she set out on a long trip up the lakes to escape. She left Toronto immediately after returning from her voyage, having negotiated a settlement with her husband for a separation and annual stipend that, depending on his alcoholism, he sometimes paid and sometimes did not.

But she was free to return to Europe, her friends, and her career. Jameson was one of the more determined feminists of her era, but fearing that stridency would alienate her audience, she developed a subtle technique whereby she asked readers a series of seemingly easy questions, leading them question by question to the inescapable conclusions she wished to advance. In popular books such as *Memoirs of Celebrated Female Sovereigns* (1831), *The Beauties of the Court of King Charles the Second* (1833), and *The Heroines of Shakespeare* (1846) she quietly but tenaciously argued for equal rights for women. In her travel books, including the famous *Winter Studies and Summer Rambles in Canada* (1838), she became more forthright about women's problems, including the exploitation of governesses and the causes of prostitution, neither of which was a great problem in Canada, but she used every opportunity to argue for women's rights and education. In later life she became an authority on art and with *Sacred and Legendary Art* (1857), her reputation as the first female art historian was assured.

Jameson never had children and did not remarry after her husband's death in 1854. She continued her life-long friendship with Ottilie von Goethe, the daughter-in-law of the famous poet to whom she had addressed her letters in *Winter Studies and Summer Rambles in Canada*, and with her poet-friends Elizabeth and Robert Browning. When the Crimean War began in 1853 and Florence Nightingale began her "experiment" of using women as nurses, Jameson gave public lectures in her support and visited hospitals on the Continent to try to persuade England to adopt similar practices. Shortly afterwards she wrote to Ottilie:

I believe that the Gospel of Christ recognises mankind, male and female, as one body, one church, both sexes being *equally* rational beings with improvable faculties, *equally* responsible for the use or abuse of the faculties entrusted to them, *equally* free, to choose the good and refuse the evil, equally destined to an equal immortality; and I insist that any human and social laws which are *not* founded in the recognition of this primary law, are and must be false in the general principle, and in the particular application and in result, equally injurious to both sexes.

Anna Jameson died in 1860 of bronchial pneumonia after having walked in a snowstorm from the British Museum to her rooms, where she was assembling the final volumes of *Sacred and Legendary Art*, titled *The History of Our Lord*.

FROM WINTER STUDIES AND SUMMER RAMBLES
(1838)

Anna Jameson

THE NARRATIVE JAMESON created about her Great Lakes trip became one of the more famous nineteenth-century travel narratives, the first by a woman who travelled part way in the lakes' wilderness with only her male guides. Jameson also took the opportunity in this book to address a number of other controversial social and political issues on which women were not supposed to have opinions: the Canadian Rebellion for independence in 1837, prostitution, and the miserable working conditions of governesses and maids. *Winter Studies and Summer Rambles* purports to be a description of Toronto and the Great Lakes, but there are repeated interruptions in the descriptions of the countryside and the people she met to discuss topics that have little relevance to Canada but were problems in England and on the Continent where the majority of her readers were.

Jameson was privileged to spend time with the Ojibwa/Irish Johnston family in Sault Ste. Marie where she became the first white woman to shoot the rapids of the St. Mary's River in a canoe. Her account inspired a small industry of "rapids pilots" who ferried travellers down the rapids for decades, although later travellers were not baptized with a new Indian name to celebrate their courage. What is most interesting about Jameson's account, however, is the sympathy and understanding she brings to her experiences with the Indians. Jameson wrote during a time when Indians and mixed-blood persons were considered savages who lived in filth and were doomed to disappear, preferably sooner rather than later. But Jameson refuses to judge. Instead, she uses the egalitarian position of Indian women in their society to castigate the diminished position of women in her own, a radical stance for her time but a preview of her later works devoted to bettering conditions for women. The section reprinted here describes Jameson's trip from Mackinac Island to the Sault with Jane Johnston Schoolcraft and her children to visit her mother, the daughter of a Chippewa chief who was married to the Irish trader John Johnston, and Jameson's baptism by the tribe.

⤛⬤⬤⤜

July 29th.

Where was I? Where did I leave off four days ago? O—at Mackinaw! that fairy island, which I shall never see again! and which I should have dearly liked to filch from the Americans, and carry home to you in my dressing-box, or, perdie, in my toothpick case—but, good lack! to see the ups and downs of this (new) world! I take up my tale a hundred miles from it—but before I tell you where I am now, I must take you over the ground, or rather over the water, in a proper and journal-like style.

I was sitting last Friday, at sultry noon-tide, under the shadow of a schooner which had just anchored alongside the little pier—sketching and dreaming—when up came a messenger, breathless, to say that a boat was going off for the Sault Ste Marie, in which I could be accommodated with a passage. Now this was precisely what I had been wishing and waiting for, and yet I heard the information with an emotion of regret. I had become every day more attached to the society of Mrs. Schoolcraft—more interested about her; and the idea of parting, and parting suddenly took me by surprise, and was anything but agreeable. On reaching the house, I found all in movement, and learned, to my inexpressible delight, that my friend would take the opportunity of paying a visit to her mother and family, and, with her children, was to accompany me on my voyage.

We had but one hour to prepare packages, provisions, everything—and in one hour all was ready.

This voyage of two days was to be made in a little Canadian bateau, rowed by five voyageurs from the Sault. The boat might have carried fifteen persons, hardly more, and was rather clumsy in form. The two ends were appropriated to the rowers, baggage, and provisions; in the centre there was a clear space, with a locker on each side, on which we sat or reclined, having stowed away in them our smaller and more valuable packages. This was the internal arrangement.

The distance to the Sault or, as the Americans call it, the Sou, is not more than thirty miles over land, as the bird flies; but the whole region being one mass of mingled forest and swamp, infested with bears and mosquitoes, it is seldom crossed but in winter, and in snow shoes. The usual route by water is ninety-four miles.

At three o'clock in the afternoon, with a favourable breeze, we launched forth on the lake, and having rowed about a mile from the shore, the little square sail was hoisted, and away we went merrily over the blue waves.

For a detailed account of the voyageurs, or Canadian boatmen, their peculiar condition and mode of life, I refer you to Washington Irving's *Astoria*: what he describes them to have been, and what Henry represents them in his time, they are even now, in these regions of the upper lakes. But the voyageurs in our boat were not favourable specimens of their very amusing and peculiar class. They were fatigued with rowing for three days previous, and had only two helpless women to deal with. As soon, therefore, as the sail was hoisted, two began to play cards on the top of a keg, the other two went to sleep. The youngest and most intelligent of the set, a lively, half-breed boy of eighteen took the helm. He told us with great self-complacency that he was captain, and that it was already the third time that he had been elected by his comrades to this dignity—but I cannot say he had a very obedient crew.

About seven o'clock we landed to cook our supper on an island which is commemorated by Henry as the Isle des Outardes, and is now Goose Island. Mrs. Schoolcraft undertook the general management with all the alertness of one accustomed to these impromptu arrangements, and I did my best in my new vocation—dragged one or two blasted boughs to the fire—the least of them twice as big as myself—and laid the cloth upon the pebbly beach. The enormous fire was to keep off the mosquitoes, in which we succeeded pretty well, swallowing, however, as much smoke as would have dried us externally into hams or red herrings. We then returned to the boat, spread a bed for the children (who were my delight), in the bottom of it with mats and blankets, and disposed our own, on the lockers on each side, with buffalo skins, blankets, shawls, cloaks, and whatever was available, with my writing-case for a pillow.

After sunset, the breeze fell; the men were urged to row, but pleaded fatigue, and that they were hired for the day, and not for the night, (which is the custom). One by one they sulkily abandoned their oars, and sunk to sleep under their blankets, all but our young captain; like Ulysses when steering away from Calypso—

Placed at the helm he sat, and watched the skies,
Nor closed in sleep his ever watchful eyes.

He kept himself awake by singing hymns, in which Mrs. Schoolcraft joined him. I lay still, looking up at the stars and listening; when there was a pause in the singing, we kept up the conversation, fearing lest sleep should overcome our only pilot and guardian. Thus we floated on beneath that divine canopy— "which love had spread to curtain the sleeping world": it was a most lovely and blessed night, bright and calm and warm, and we made some little way, for both wind and current were in our favour.

As we were coasting a little shadowy island, our captain mentioned a strange circumstance, very illustrative of Indian life and character. A short time ago a young Chippewa hunter, whom he knew, was shooting squirrels on this spot, when by some chance a large blighted pine fell upon him, knocking him down and crushing his leg, which was fractured in two places. He could not rise, he could not remove the tree which was lying across his broken leg. He was in a little uninhabited island, without the slightest probability of passing aid, and to lie there and starve to death in agonies, seemed all that was left to him. In this dilemma, with all the fortitude and promptitude of resource of a thorough-bred Indian, he took out his knife, cut off his own leg, bound it up, dragged himself along the ground to his hunting canoe, and paddled himself home to his wigwam on a distant island, where the cure of his wound was completed. The man is still alive.

Perhaps this story appears to you incredible. I believe it firmly; at the time, and since then, I heard other instances of Indian fortitude, and of their courage and skill in performing some of the boldest and most critical operations in surgery, which I really cannot venture to set down. *You* would believe them if I could swear that I had witnessed them with "my own two good-looking eyes," not otherwise. But I will mention one or two of the least marvelous of these stories. There was a young chief and famous hunter, whose arm was shattered by the bursting of his rifle. No one would venture the amputation, and it was bound up with certain herbs and dressings, accompanied with many magical ceremonies. The young man, who seemed aware of the inefficacy of such expedients, waited till the moment when he should be left alone. He had meantime, with pain and difficulty, hatched one of his knives into a saw; with this he completed the amputation of his own arm; and when his relations appeared they found the arm lying at one end of the wigwam, and the patient sitting at the other, with his wound bound up, and smoking with great tranquillity.

Mrs. Schoolcraft told me of a young Chippewa who went on a hunting expedition with his wife only; they were camped at a considerable distance from the village, when the woman was seized with the pains of child-birth. This is in general a very easy matter among the Indian women, cases of danger or death being exceedingly rare; but on this occasion some unusual and horrible difficulty occurred. The husband, who was described to me as an affectionate, gentle spirited man, much attached to his wife, did his best to assist her; but after a few struggles she became insensible, and lay, as he supposed, dead. He took out his knife, and with astonishing presence of mind, performed on his wife the Cesarean operation, saved his infant, and ultimately the mother, and brought them both home on a sleigh to his village at the Sault, where, as Mrs. Schoolcraft told me, she had frequently seen both the man and woman.

We remained in conversation till long after midnight; then the boat was moored to a tree, but kept off shore, for fear of the mosquitoes, and we addressed ourselves to sleep. I remember lying awake for some minutes, looking up at the quiet stars, and around upon the dark weltering waters, and at the faint waning moon, just suspended on the very edge of the horizon. I saw it sink—sink into the bosom of the lake as if to rest, and then with a thought of far-off friends, and a most fervent thanksgiving, I dropped asleep. It is odd that I did not think of praying for protection, and that no sense of fear came over me; it seemed as if the eye of God himself looked down upon me; that I was protected. I do not say I *thought* this any more than the un-weaned child in its cradle; but I had some such feeling of unconscious trust and love, now I recall those moments.

I slept, however, uneasily, not being yet accustomed to a board and a blanket; ça viendra avec le temps. About dawn I awoke in a sort of stupor, but after bathing my face and hands over the boat side, I felt refreshed. The voyageurs, after a good night's rest, were in better humour, and took man-fully to their oars. Soon after sunrise, we passed round that very conspicu-ous cape, famous in the history of north-west adventure, called the "Grand Detour," half-way between Mackinaw and the Sault. Now, if you look at the map you will see that our course was henceforth quite altered; we had been running down the coast of the mainland towards the east; we had now to turn short round the point, and steer almost due west; hence its most fitting name, the Grand DeTour. The wind, hitherto favourable, was now dead against us. This part of Lake Huron is studded with little islands, which, as well as the neighbouring mainland, are all uninhabited, yet clothed with the richest, loveliest, most fantastic vegetation, and no doubt swarming with animal life.

I cannot, I dare not, attempt to describe to you the strange sensation one has, thus thrown for a time beyond the bounds of civilised humanity, or indeed any humanity; nor the wild yet solemn reveries which come over one in the midst of this wilderness of woods and waters. All was so solitary, so grand in its solitude, as if nature unviolated sufficed to herself. Two days and nights the solitude was unbroken; not a trace of social life, not a human being, not a canoe, not even a deserted wigwam, met our view. Our little boat held on its way over the placid lake and among green tufted islands; and we its inmates, two women, differing in clime, nation, complexion, strang-ers to each other but a few days ago, might have fancied ourselves alone in a new-born world.

We landed to boil our kettle, and breakfast on a point of the island of St. Joseph's. This most beautiful island is between thirty and forty miles in length, and nearly a hundred miles in circumference, and towards the centre the land is high and picturesque. They tell me that on the other side of the island there is a settlement of whites and Indians. Another large island, Drummond's Isle, was for a short time, in view. We had also a settlement here, but it was unaccountably surrendered to the Americans. If now you look at the map, you will wonder, as I did, that in retaining St. Joseph's and the Manitoolin islands, we gave up Drummond's Island. Both these islands had forts and garrisons during the war.

By the time breakfast was over, the children had gathered some fine strawberries; the heat had now become almost intolerable, and unluckily we had no awning. The men rowed languidly, and we made but little way; we coasted along the south shore of St. Joseph's, through fields of rushes, miles in extent, across Lake George, and Muddy Lake; (the name, I thought, must be a libel, for it was as clear as crystal and as blue as heaven; but they say that, like a sulky temper, the least ruffle of wind turns it as black as ditchwater, and it does not subside again in a hurry), and then came a succession of openings spotted with lovely islands, all solitary. The sky was without a cloud, a speck—except when the great fish-eagle was descried sailing over its blue depths—the water without a wave. We were too hot and too languid to converse. Nothing disturbed the deep noon-tide stillness, but the dip of the oars, or the spring and splash of a sturgeon as he leapt from the surface of the lake, leaving a circle of little wavelets spreading around. All the islands we passed were so woody, and so infested with mosquitoes, that we could not land and light our fire, till we reached the entrance of St. Mary's River, between Nebish island and the mainland.

Here was a well-known spot, a sort of little opening on a flat shore, called the Encampment, because a party of boatmen coming down from Lake Superior, and camping here for the night, were surprised by the frost and obliged to remain the whole winter till the opening of the ice, in the spring. After rowing all this hot day till seven o'clock against the wind, (what there was of it), and against the current coming rapidly and strongly down from Lake Superior, we did at length reach this promised harbour of rest and refreshment. Alas! there was neither for us; the moment our boat touched the shore, we were enveloped in a cloud of mosquitoes. Fires were lighted instantly, six were burning in a circle at once; we were well nigh suffocated and smoke-dried—all in vain. At last we left the voyageurs to boil the kettle, and retreated to our boat, desiring them to make us fast to a tree by a long rope; then, each of us taking an oar—I only wish you could have seen us— we pushed off from the land, while the children were sweeping away the enemy with green boughs. This being done, we commenced supper, really half famished, and were too much engrossed to look about us. Suddenly we were again surrounded by our adversaries; they came upon us in swarms, in clouds, in myriads, entering our eyes, our noses, our mouths, stinging till the blood followed. We had, unawares, and while absorbed in our culinary operations, drifted into the shore, got entangled among the roots of trees, and were with difficulty extricated, presenting all the time a fair mark and a rich banquet for our detested tormentors. The dear children cried with agony and impatience, and but for shame I could almost have cried too.

I had suffered from these plagues in Italy; you too, by this time, may probably know what they are in the southern countries of the old world; but 'tis a jest, believe me, to encountering a forest full of them in these wild regions. I had heard much, and much was I forewarned, but never could have conceived the torture they can inflict, nor the impossibility of escape, defence, or endurance. Some amiable person who took an especial interest in our future welfare, in enumerating the torments prepared for hardened sinners, assures us that they will be stung by mosquitoes all made of brass, and as large as black beetles—he was an ignoramus and a bungler; you may credit me, that the brass is quite an unnecessary improvement, and the increase of size equally superfluous. Mosquitoes, as they exist in this upper world, are as pretty and perfect a plague as the most ingenious amateur sinner-tormentor ever devised. Observe, that a mosquito does not sting like a wasp, or a gad-fly; he has a long proboscis like an awl, with which he bores your veins and pumps the life-blood out of you, leaving venom and fever behind. Enough of mosquitoes—I will never again do more than allude to them; only they are enough to make philosophy go hang herself, and Patience swear like a Turk or a trooper.

Well, we left this most detestable and inhospitable shore as soon as possible, but the enemy followed us, and we did not soon get rid of them; night came on, and we were still twenty miles below the Sault.

I offered an extra gratuity to the men, if they would keep to their oars without interruption; and then, fairly exhausted, lay down on my locker and blanket. But whenever I woke from uneasy, restless slumbers, there was Mrs. Schoolcraft, bending over her sleeping children, and waving off the mosquitoes, singing all the time a low, melancholy Indian song; while the northern lights were streaming and dancing in the sky, and the fitful moaning of the wind, the gathering clouds, and chilly atmosphere, foretold a change of weather. This would have been the comble de malheur. When daylight came, we passed Sugar Island, where immense quantities of maple sugar are made every spring, and just as the rain began to fall in earnest, we arrived at the Sault Ste. Marie. On one side of the river, Mrs. Schoolcraft was welcomed by her mother; and on the other, my friends, the MacMurrays, received me with delighted and delightful hospitality. I went to bed—oh! the luxury!—and slept for six hours.

• • •

One of the gratifications I had anticipated in coming hither—my strongest inducement perhaps—was an introduction to the mother of my two friends, of whom her children so delighted to speak, and of whom I had heard much from other sources. A woman of pure Indian blood, of a race celebrated in these regions as warriors and chiefs from generation to generation, who had never resided within the pale of what we call civilised life, whose habits and manners were those of a genuine Indian squaw, and whose talents and domestic virtues commanded the highest respect, was, as you may suppose, an object of the deepest interest to me. I observed that not only her own children but her two sons-in-law, Mr. MacMurray and Mr. Schoolcraft, both educated in good society, the one a clergyman and the other a man of science and literature, looked up to this remarkable woman with sentiments of affection and veneration.

As soon, then, as I was a little refreshed after my two nights on the lake, and my battles with the mosquitoes, we paddled over the river to dine with Mrs. Johnston: she resides in a large loghouse close upon the shore; there is a little portico in front with seats, and the interior is most comfortable. The old lady herself is rather large in person, with the strongest marked Indian features, a countenance open, benevolent, and intelligent, and a manner perfectly easy—simple yet with something of motherly dignity, becoming the head of her large family. She received me most affectionately, and we entered into conversation—Mrs. Schoolcraft, who looked all animation and happiness, acting as interpreter. Mrs. Johnston speaks no English, but can understand it a little, and the Canadian French still better; but in her own language she is eloquent, and her voice, like that of her people, low and musical; many kind words were exchanged, and when I said anything that pleased her, she laughed softly like a child. I was not well and much fevered, and I remember she took me in her arms, laid me down on a couch, and began to rub my feet, soothing and caressing me. She called me Nindannis, daughter, and I called her Neengai, mother, (though how different from my own fair mother, I thought, as I looked up gratefully in her dark Indian face!) She set before us the best dressed and best served dinner I had seen since I left Toronto, and presided at her table, and did the honours of her house with unembarrassed, unaffected propriety. My attempts to speak Indian caused, of course, considerable amusement; if I do not make progress, it will not be for want of teaching and teachers.

After dinner we took a walk to visit Mrs. Johnston's brother, Wayish,ky, whose wigwam is at a little distance, on the verge of the burial ground. The lodge is of the genuine Chippewa form, like an egg cut in half lengthways. It is formed of poles stuck in the ground, and bent over at top, strengthened with a few wattles and boards; the whole is covered over with mats, birch-bark, and skins; a large blanket formed the door or curtain, which was not ungracefully looped aside. Wayish,ky, being a great man, has also a smaller lodge hard by, which serves as a storehouse and kitchen.

Rude as was the exterior of Wayish,ky's hut, the interior presented every appearance of comfort and even elegance, according to the Indian notions of both. It formed a good-sized room: a raised couch ran all round like a Turkish divan, serving both for seats and beds, and covered with very soft and beautiful matting of various colours and patterns. The chests and baskets of birch-bark, containing the family wardrobe and property, the rifles, the hunting and fishing tackle, were stored away all round very tidily; I observed a coffee-mill nailed up to one of the posts or stakes; the floor was trodden down hard and perfectly clean, and there was a place for a fire in the middle: there was no window, but quite sufficient light and air were admitted through the door, and through an aperture in the roof. There was no disagreeable smell, and everything looked neat and clean. We found Wayish,ky and his wife and three of their children seated in the lodge, and as it was Sunday, and they are all Christians, no work was going forward. They received me with genuine and simple politeness, each taking my hand with a gentle inclination of the head, and some words of welcome murmured in their own soft language. We then sat down.

The conversation became very lively; and, if I might judge from looks and tones, very affectionate. I sported my last new words and phrases with great effect, and when I had exhausted my vocabulary—which was very soon—I amused myself with looking and listening.

Mrs. Wayish,ky (I forget her proper name) must have been a very beautiful woman. Though now no longer young, and the mother of twelve children, she is one of the handsomest Indian women I have yet seen. The number of her children is remarkable, for in general there are few large families among the Indians. Her daughter, Zah,gah,see,ga,quay, "The Sunbeams Breaking Through a Cloud," is a very beautiful girl, with eyes that are a warrant for her poetical name—she is about sixteen. Wayish,ky himself is a grave, dignified man about fifty. He told me that his eldest son had gone down to the Manitoolin Island to represent his family, and receive his quota of presents. His youngest son he had sent to a college in the United States, to be educated in the learning of the white men. Mrs. Schoolcraft whispered to me that this poor boy is now dying of consumption, owing to the confinement and change of living, and that the parents knew it. Wayish,ky seemed aware that we were alluding to his son, for his eye at that moment rested on me, and such an expression of keen pain came suddenly over his fine countenance, it was as if a knife had struck him; and I really felt it in my heart, and see it still before me—that look of misery.

After about an hour we left this good and interesting family. I lingered for a while on the burial-ground, looking over the rapids, and watching with a mixture of admiration and terror several little canoes which were fishing in the midst of the boiling surge, dancing and popping about like corks. The canoe used for fishing is very small and light; one man (or woman more commonly) sits in the stern, and steers with a paddle; the fisher places himself upright on the prow, balancing a long pole with both hands, at the end of which is a scoop-net. This he every minute dips into the water, bringing up at each dip a fish, and sometimes two. I used to admire the fishermen on the Arno, and those on the Lagune, and above all the Neapolitan fishermen, hauling in their nets, or diving like ducks, but I never saw anything like these Indians. The manner in which they keep their position upon a footing of a few inches, is to me as incomprehensible as the beauty of their forms and attitudes, swayed by every movement and turn of their dancing, fragile barks, is admirable.

George Johnston, on whose arm I was leaning, (and I had much ado to *reach* it,) gave me such a vivid idea of the delight of coming down the cataract in a canoe, that I am half resolved to attempt it. Terrific as it appears, yet in a good canoe, and with experienced guides, there is no absolute danger, and it must be a glorious sensation.

Mr. Johnston had spent the last fall and winter in the country, beyond Lake Superior, towards the forks of the Mississippi, where he had been employed as American agent to arrange the boundary line between the country of the Chippewas and that of their neighbours and implacable enemies, the Sioux. His mediation appeared successful for the time, and he smoked the pipe of peace with both tribes; but during the spring this ferocious war has again broken out, and he seems to think that nothing but the annihilation of either one nation or the other will entirely put an end to their conflicts; "for there is no point at which the Indian law of retaliation stops, short of the extermination of one of the parties."

I asked him how it is that in their wars the Indians make no distinction between the warriors opposed to them and helpless women and children?—how it could be with a brave and manly people, that the scalps taken from the weak, the helpless, the unresisting, were as honourable as those torn from the warrior's skull? And I described to him the horror which this custom inspired—this, which of all their customs, most justifies the name of *savage!*

He said it was inseparable from their principles of war and their mode of warfare; the first consists in inflicting the greatest possible insult and injury on their foe with the least possible risk to themselves. This truly savage law of honour we might call cowardly, but that, being associated with the bravest contempt of danger and pain, it seems nearer to the natural law. With regard to the mode of warfare, they have rarely pitched battles, but skirmishes, surprises, ambuscades, and sudden forays into each other's hunting grounds and villages. The usual practice is to creep stealthily on the enemy's village or hunting-encampment, and wait till just after the dawn; then, at the moment the sleepers in the lodges are rising, the ambushed warriors stoop and level their pieces about two feet from the ground, which thus slaughter indiscriminately. If they find one of the enemy's lodges undefended they murder its inmates, that when the owner returns he may find his hearth desolate; for this is exquisite vengeance! But outrage against the chastity of women is absolutely unknown under any degree whatever of furious excitement.

This respect for female honour will remind you of the ancient Germans, as described by Julius Caesar: he contrasts in some surprise their forbearance with the very opposite conduct of the Romans; and even down to this present day, if I recollect rightly, the history of our European wars and sieges will bear out this early and characteristic distinction between the Latin and the Teutonic nations. Am I right, or am I not?

To return to the Indians. After telling me some other particulars, which gave me a clearer view of their notions and feelings on these points than I ever had before, my informant mildly added,— "It is a constant and favourite subject of reproach against the Indians—this barbarism of their desultory warfare; but I should think more women and children have perished in one of your civilised sieges, and that in late times, than during the whole war between the Chippewas and Sioux, and that has lasted a century."

I was silent, for there is a sensible proverb about taking care of our own glass windows: and I wonder if any of the recorded atrocities of Indian warfare or Indian vengeance, or all of them together, ever exceeded Massena's retreat from Portugal,—and the French call themselves civilised. A war-party of Indians, perhaps two or three hundred, (and that is a very large number), dance their war-dance, go out and burn a village, and bring back twenty or thirty scalps. They are savages and heathens. We Europeans fight a battle, leave fifty thousand dead or dying by inches on the field, and a hundred thousand to mourn them, desolate; but we are civilised and Christians. Then only look into the motives and causes of our bloodiest European wars as revealed in the private history of courts"—the miserable, puerile, degrading intrigues which set man against man—so horridly disproportioned to the horrid result! and then see the Indian take up his war-hatchet in vengeance for some personal injury, or from motives that rouse all the natural feelings of the natural man within him! Really I do not see that an Indian warrior, flourishing his tomahawk, and smeared with his enemy's blood, is so very much a greater savage than the pipe-clayed, padded, embroidered personage, who, without cause or motive, has sold himself to slay or be slain: one scalps his enemy, the other rips him open with a sabre; one smashes his brains with a tomahawk, and the other blows him to atoms with a cannon-ball: and to me, femininely speaking, there is not a needle's point difference between the one and the other. If war be unchristian and barbarous, then war as a science is more absurd, unnatural, unchristian, than war as a *passion*.

This, perhaps, is putting it all too strongly, and a little exaggerated.

God forbid that I should think to disparage the blessings of civilisation! I am a woman, and to the progress of civilisation alone can we women look for release from many pains and penalties and liabilities which now lie heavily upon us. Neither am I greatly in love with savage life, with all its picturesque accompaniments and lofty virtues. I see no reason why these virtues should be necessarily connected with dirt, ignorance, and barbarism. I am thankful to live in a land of literature and steam engines. Chatsworth is better than a wigwam, and a seventy-four is a finer thing than a bark canoe. I do not *positively* assert that Taglioni dances more gracefully than the Little-Pure to-bacco-smoker, nor that soap and water are preferable as cosmetics to tallow and charcoal; for these are matters of taste, and mine may be disputed. But I do say, that if our advantages of intellect and refinement are not to lead on to farther moral superiority, I prefer the Indians on the score of consistency; they are what they profess to be, and we are *not* what we profess to be. They profess to be warriors and hunters, and are so; we profess to be Christians, and civilised—are we so?

Then as to the mere point of cruelty;—there is something to be said on this point too. Ferocity, when the hot blood is up, and all the demon in man is roused by every conceivable excitement, I can understand better than the Indian can comprehend the tender mercies of our law. Owyawatta, better known by his English name, Red-Jacket, was once seen hurrying from the town of Buffalo with rapid strides, and every mark of disgust and consterna-tion in his face. Three malefactors were to be hung that morning, and the Indian warrior had not nerve to face the horrid spectacle, although,

> "In sober truth the veriest devil
> That ere clenched fingers in a captive's hair."

Thus endeth my homily for to-night.

The more I looked upon those glancing, dancing rapids, the more reso-lute I grew to venture myself in the midst of them. George Johnston went to seek a fit canoe and a dexterous steersman, and meantime I strolled away to pay a visit to Wayish,ky's family, and made a sketch of their lodge, while pretty Zah,gah,see,gah,qua, held the umbrella to shade me from the sun.

The canoe being ready, I went to the upper end of the portage, and we launched into the river. It was a small fishing canoe about ten feet long, quite new, and light and elegant and buoyant as a bird on the waters. I reclined on a mat at the bottom, Indian fashion, (there are no seats in a genuine Indian canoe); in a minute we were within the verge of the rapids, and down we went with a whirl and a splash!—the white surge leaping around me—over me. The Indian with astonishing dexterity kept the head of the canoe to the breakers, and somehow or other we danced through them. I could see, as I looked over the edge of the canoe, that the passage between the rocks was sometimes not more than two feet in width, and we had to turn sharp angles—

a touch of which would have sent us to destruction—all this I could see through the transparent eddying waters, but I can truly say I had not even a momentary sensation of fear, but rather of giddy, breathless, delicious excitement. I could even admire the beautiful attitude of a fisher, past whom we swept as we came to the bottom. The whole affair, from the moment I entered the canoe till I reached the landing-place, occupied seven minutes, and the distance is about three quarters of a mile.

My Indians were enchanted, and when I reached home, my good friends were not less delighted at my exploit: they told me I was the first European female who had ever performed it, and assuredly I shall not be the last. I recommend it as an exercise before breakfast. Two glasses of champagne could not have made me more tipsy and more self-complacent! As for my Neengai, she laughed, clapped her hands, and embraced me several times. I was declared duly initiated, and adopted into the family by the name of Wah,sàh,ge,wah,nó,quà. They had already called me among themselves, in reference to my complexion and my travelling propensities, O,daw,yaun,gee, "The Fair Changing Moon," or rather, "The Fair Moon Which Changes Her Place": but now, in compliment to my successful achievement, Mrs. Johnston bestowed this new appellation, which I much prefer. It signifies the bright foam, or more properly, with the feminine adjunct *qua*, "The Woman of The Bright Foam," and by this name I am henceforth to be known among the Chippewas.

LAKE SUPERIOR

(1968)

Lorine Niedecker

In every part of every living thing
is stuff that once was rock

In blood the minerals
of the rock

•

Iron the common element of earth
in rocks and freighters

Sault Sainte Marie—big boats
coal-black and iron-ore-red
topped with what white castlework

The waters working together
            internationally
Gulls playing both sides

•

Radisson:
'a laborinth of pleasure'
this world of the Lake

Long hair, long gun

Fingernails pulled out
by Mohawks

(The long canoes)

'Birch Bark
  and white Seder
    for the ribs'

　　◆

Through all this granite land
the sign of the cross

Beauty: impurities in the rock

　　◆

And at the blue ice superior spot
priest-robed Marquette grazed
azoic rock, hornblende granite
basalt the common dark
in all the Earth

And his bones of such is coral
raised up out of his grave
were sunned and bird bark-floated
to the straits

Joliet

Entered the Mississippi
Found there the paddlebill catfish
come down from The Age of Fishes

At Hudson Bay he conversed in latin
with an Englishman

To Labrador and back to vanish

His funeral gratis—he'd played
Quebec's Cathedral organ
so many winters

    •

Ruby of corundum
lapis lazuli
from changing limestone
glow-apricot red-brown
carnelian sand

Greek named
Exodus-antique
kicked up in America's
Northwest
you have been in my mind
between my toes
agate

Wild Pigeon

Did not man
        maimed by no
                stone-fall
mash the cobalt
        and carnelian
                of that bird

    •

Schoolcraft left the Soo—canoes
US pennants, masts, sails
chanting canoemen, barge
soldiers—for Minnesota
Their South Shore journey

as if Life's—
The Chocolate River
  The Laughing Fish
and The River of the Dead

Passed peaks of volcanic thrust
Hornblende in massed granite
Wave-cut Cambrian rock
painted by soluble mineral oxides
wave-washed and the rains
did their work and a green
running as from copper

Sea-roaring caverns—
Chippewas threw deermeat
to the savage maws
'Voyageurs crossed themselves
tossed a twist of tobacco in'

  Inland then
beside the great granite
gneiss and the schists

to the redolent pondy lakes'
lilies, flag and Indian reed
'through which we successfully
          passed'

  ✦

The smooth black stone
I picked up on true source park
    the leaf beside it
once was stone

Why should we hurry
    home

I'm sorry to have missed
      Sand Lake
My dear one tells me
      we did not
We watched a gopher there

Unlike the well-traveled, cosmopolitan Anna Jameson, Lorine Niedecker (1903-1970) was a fisherman's daughter who lived all her life on Black Hawk Island in the Rock River in Wisconsin. Whereas Jameson earned her living writing books that would appeal to everyone, Niedecker worked at odd jobs and wrote intellectual, experimental poetry in the "objectivist" manner: condensed poems concentrating on precision, clarity, and intensity with all imprecise feeling stripped away. Her spare and lovely language is musical and visual, her poems evocative of the world they create in as few words as possible; what she called the "hard, clear image." Although she traveled very little, she read the explorers' and naturalists' accounts of the Great Lakes region, and in "Lake Superior" interweaves their accounts with the physical characteristics of the landscape to suggest a world in which the masculine experience of exploration and conquest is only one part of an interconnected world. The poem is part of her book *North Central*.

THE SUMMER GIRL.

"*The Summer Girl*"

A HUSBANDLESS VACATION

(1915)

Grace Margaret Wilson

WHEN THE DETROIT & CLEVELAND Navigation Company, which operated passenger and package freight steamships for years between Buffalo and Detroit, decided to initiate service up Lake Huron to their new investment on Mackinac Island, the Grand Hotel, in 1882, the company directors had a problem. The market for passengers did not exist automatically as it did on Lake Erie, it had to be created. The question was how? Their solution was a brilliant one, decades ahead of its time, known as "subjective" advertising, a campaign that concentrated on the benefits of having a product, rather than on the product itself. Steamships there were aplenty, and they were all hardworking coastal steamers with small cabins and deck passengers eating from paper bags. But the director of the company had risen through the ranks from a ticket clerk, and he knew what advertising executives wouldn't realize until after World War I: women made most of the purchasing decisions. And what women wanted was romance.

Thus began a decades-long tradition on the Detroit & Cleveland ships—a new romantic novel or collection of short stories distributed free every season. Not only could the writers describe the delights of the company's ships, Mackinac Island, and the Grand Hotel, but they could do so in the context of romantic escape literature where it never rained, children were non-existent, no one ever got seasick, and women were in complete control of men. As the decades passed, the story elements changed to incorporate modern inventions like the telegraph and changes in women's status like the professional "New Woman" of business, but the ending was infallible. A vacation sailing up Lake Huron to Mackinac and a stay at the Grand Hotel cured everyone's problems. Including the company's, since the Lake Huron route always ran in the black, even though the sailing season ended in October when the Grand closed.

The little romantic story that follows, part of a volume called *Waterway Tales*, is a forerunner of twentieth-century sociodrama advertising, a technique still widely used. The author, a frequent contributor who also wrote children's literature and romances, has created a slightly daring story for the time, but the hidden message is clear. Since divorce was still difficult to obtain before World War I, if your husband was crabby, run away to Mackinac. Grace Margaret Wilson ignored a number of significant facts—children, the lack of paid vacation time for most workers, and the cost of staying at the Grand—but she wasn't selling reality. Like the illustration of "The Summer Girl" that accompanied the romances for years, mirroring popular fantasies and fulfilling nonrational yearnings was the way to open buyers' wallets. It still is.

⊷═◉═⊷

AMONG THE DISPERSING people on the dock, a sullen-faced man gazed somberly after the departing D. & C. steamer that was making its way majestically toward mid-stream. The Detroit River wore its usual summer air of "busyness" and gaiety. Excursion boats plied hither and thither. The big lumber boats seemed bearing dangerously down upon the white-winged yachts that flirted coquettishly in their path. The sky was very blue overhead, and a slowly gathering radiance in the west gave promise of a picturesque sunset.

Sitting aft on the deck of the Mackinac steamer that was now headed north, two young women chatted joyously as they looked out over the busy river scene. The dark-haired one, with big, brown eyes and charmingly flushed cheeks, seemed especially animated.

"I'd like to get up and dance, Nita!" she exclaimed. "Do you think the other passengers would object?"

"Probably not," replied her fair-haired companion, smiling at her friend's high spirits. "But perhaps just now you had better calm down and tell me how you managed your escape, Polly dear."

The other sobered instantly, and composed herself with a long sigh. "Nita, it was just awful!" she answered solemnly. "I know just how the slaves felt before the war. I have never been away from Dick before, in all the ten years since we've been married. Think of it!—I tell you, I've felt like a prisoner behind bars, or a wild animal in a cage, at times. I had just made up my mind to do something desperate, when your letter came proposing this trip. It had come to the breaking point, Nita. I'm tired of being a 'possession,' owned body and soul. Without giving myself time to think about it very much, I organized a great rebellion—and I carried it through, though it nearly killed me!"

"You poor little thing! Was he so very fierce about it?" asked her friend sympathetically.

"Fierce, and stubborn, and—O well, what's the use of going over it all now? He cut short his western trip, gave up a hunting excursion he had planned, and took the first train home, after I had written him about what I was going to do. He thought, of course, that he could stop me. I really think he would have tried to prevent me by force, at the last minute, if he hadn't been so dazed by my obstinacy. I never had the courage to stand out against him before."

"You see, Nita," she added, in a half-apologetic manner, "I was only six-teen when I eloped with him, and he broke my will from the very start. He began by ruling me like a child, and he has kept it up ever since—though I'm twenty-six now. He has never allowed me to do anything or go anywhere without him. For a long while I didn't realize what a caged thing I was. But something waked me up, a year or so ago, and I've been growing more and more restless and unhappy until—well, something seemed to snap in my soul, and—here I am, free, free, free for two heavenly weeks—if he will only stay away from me that long."

"Yes, but do you think he will, dear?" Nita asked skeptically.

"O, hush, Nita—don't let's even consider such a possibility! Let me for-get, and at least play I'm free for a little while."

"You poor, abused thing! Go ahead and 'play.' Laugh, and flirt and carry on just as much as you please. I won't even chaperone you. Have your fling, and make hay while the sun shines."

"You chaperone me—you blessed unmarried girl! My stars, Nita—how happy and grateful you ought to be! Why, you're as gloriously free as one of those airy, white gulls up there in the blue. Nita, I just want to be a care-free girl again. I'm young, really—yet I feel a thousand years old, sometimes."

"Draw a good, long breath of this glorious air, and forget your troubles, Polly dear," said Nita dreamily, propping her feet up on the chair in front of her, and leaning back with a sigh of luxurious happiness. "Business is my jailer, and I am going to make the most of my escape from him—it—during the next few weeks, I assure you. Why, if it isn't—no, yes, it is—Perry Minot, as sure as you live! He's got some good-looking chap with him, and they're headed this way, Polly."

"Look here, Nita,—if you are going to introduce me to anyone, I'm going to be incog. on this trip. I'm not going to be Mrs.—anybody. I've put my wed-ding ring in my purse, and I am going to know the thrill of being a blessed, unattached girl again. Look, they're almost here. Remember, Nita—I'm Polly Lawrence. 'Mrs. Richard Larramie' is dead—for two weeks, at least!"

"Gracious, Polly—I don't know. Well, all right, if you want to shoulder the responsibility. But you know some man may fall in love with you—"

"Pooh! If he does, it will be Fate, and my name won't make the least bit of difference anyway. Here they are—now don't forget, Nita!"

The young men, whose approach had been halted once or twice by the greetings of acquaintances, now came up with lifted caps and the shorter of the two, smiling jovially, shook hands enthusiastically with Nita, and forth-with presented his companion, a tall, fair-haired young fellow with a certain boyish charm in his face and manner. Nita, with a little gasp only half-concealed by a sudden cough, proceeded to introduce her friend— "Miss Lawrence—Miss Polly Lawrence."

After half-an-hour's chat in a cozy corner of the deck, the four young people might have known each other all their lives. Pretty Polly was the liveliest of them all. Like a rare butterfly just emerged from its chrysalis, she radiated life, and joy, and color. To the two young fellows not long out of college, she was as their first taste of champagne. The more quiet Nita was a delightful comrade, a charming "pal"; but this joyous young woman, bubbling over with rapturous enthusiasm, was a new experience. Both of them openly adored her from the first, and attached themselves to her with a persistence that would have bored or annoyed most girls. But Polly revelled in it. It meant that she was a different being for a little while, free from the hand-cuffs of marital jealousy—free to be adored by the whole world, if the whole world chose.

The big steamer was carrying a large and assorted load of passengers northward, but it so chanced that none of them were friends or acquaintances of Polly. She was practically alone among strangers. Nita didn't count— dear, good-natured Nita, who was ready to go to almost any length to please her friend.

At dinner that evening, the four young people sat together, and their merry laughter, while not loud or noisy, was so infectious that many responsive smiles and envious glances were directed toward their table.

"Who in the world are those pretty girls that Perry Minot and Ned Farrell have picked up?" asked Mrs. Nicholas Merrivale of her daughter "The dark-haired one is a little witch! They seem to be traveling alone. Really, it's a scandalous way the young girls go about, these days."

"I don't know, I'm sure, mamma," replied Lena Merrivale, rather crossly. "They're not in my set, so I don't see where those boys met them."

"Well, they are good, clean chaps, both of them—so I guess they'll come to no harm," said Lena's father, stirring his coffee meditatively. "They are certainly having a lot of fun over there—and the dark-haired girl seems to be the center of it."

And it was true. Free, untrammelled laughter was such a new-found joy to Polly that she laughed just for the pure ecstasy of it.

For ten years she had had at her elbow, wherever she went, a rather sulky, domineering man, practically devoid of a sense of humor, and always on the lookout jealously for any sign of what he termed "flirting" on her part. Heavens! She would have been terrified at the very thought of flirting in his presence.

So, tonight, her merry, laughing eyes roved joyously and innocently in search of new adventures, with the result that every man in the dining-room was metaphorically at her feet before the dinner was over. And the two fortunate young men were besieged, the rest of the evening, for introductions, whenever one of their masculine acquaintances succeeded in cornering one or both of them.

Certain it is there were no opportunities for moonlight tete-a-tetes on the deck that evening. The four soon became the center of an increasingly large group, until, at ten o'clock, Nita declared it was high time for bed, as the lake air had made her hopelessly sleepy.

"Say, Polly," she yawned, as she boosted her friend into the upper berth at the latter's request— "if you're going around like this all the time, with a train of men after you, you'll have to engage a few extra chaperones. Really, I don't feel that I'm equal to the task."

"O, Nita darling, it's such fun," cooed Polly happily. "I feel just like a jolly little kid again, with nothing to do but play. Goodnight, dear; don't you worry—I won't do anything naughty. I'm just shaking my wings like one of those big, white gulls, and drifting—drifting—"

The next thing Polly knew, the sun was shining into her eyes with a dazzling challenge, the tramp of feet was heard on the deck, and, as she peered out over the top of the blind, she saw miles of blue water dancing and coquetting with the morning breeze.

The long, golden day that followed was like a dream to Polly. Northward the steamer continued to bear her and her fellow-passengers, between the two expanses of infinite azure—cloud-flecked above, snow-crested below. Now and then they stopped at busy ports, but most of the time were speeding past stretches of pine-wooded shore, now green against the blue, now lifting gaunt, dead arms stripped by forest fires.

Ever a trail of white gulls followed the steamer—the birds that were to Polly symbol of herself in her new-found freedom.

Perry and Ned, Polly and Nita formed a lively quartette that all eyes followed. Whether feeding the gulls from the deck, taking brisk promenades in the bracing air, or swapping yarns in some sheltered nook, they were a center of such care-free joyousness as made many a man and woman sigh for their vanished youth.

So strong grew their comradeship that the two clean-hearted boys actually proved a barricade against the undesirable attentions of certain older and more dangerous men, who hovered within the enchanted zone of Polly's smiles. For, despite her ten years of married life, Mrs. Richard Larramie was still a very child-hearted and unsophisticated young woman. Constant confinement within the narrow cell of her jailer-husband's narrow existence had kept her as innocent of many of the world's lures and pit-falls as a convent-bred debutante.

Nita Halstead, a bright young business woman of about the same age as Polly, knew much more of life than her young married friend and was secretly glad that they had fallen in with two such nice boys as Perry Minot and his chum, instead of with that other and far more numerous type of male which she had learned to know and dread.

The four sat watching the sunset as the steamer was towed out of the long canal at Cheboygan, and turned its prow toward a misty shape that gradually took outline in the distance—the enchanted island toward which they were speeding.

"Where are you girls going to stop on the island?" Asked Ned Farrell, as the Great Turtle grew more and more distinct in the golden glow of the sunset.

"We're going to be real 'sports' and put up at the Grand," Nita answered. "By the way, Polly, if you will watch that point over there, you'll soon see the lights of the Grand."

"Is this your first visit to Mackinac, Miss Lawrence?" asked Perry Minot.

"My very first—and I can hardly wait! Nita has told me such wonderful stories of its loveliness."

"Well, I guess they're all true," Ned Farrell chimed in eagerly. "And I hope you will give me the pleasure of showing you some of the 'points of interest.' I've been here half-a-dozen times at least. Oh, I say—do your girls ride horseback?"

"I never did—but I'm sure I could learn, and I would just love to," Polly exclaimed happily.

"Well, I never did, and I haven't the slightest desire to begin," said Nita. "I know it would scare me to death, even if I didn't actually fall off and kill myself."

"Nonsense, Nita; you'll just have to come if I do, you know," urged Polly, eagerly.

"O, we'll make up a jolly little party, and I'll take care of Miss Nita, myself," Perry announced enthusiastically.

"And—will you look after stupid me, Mr. Farrell?" Polly asked, turning to that young man with an enchanting smile.

"Well, you just bet I will!" was the convincing reply.

"Look—there are the lights of the Grand!" Nita exclaimed suddenly.

Whatever the two young men's original intentions may have been with regard to a stopping-place, their baggage went up to the big hotel with the girls', and before seeking their rooms to dress for the evening, they had asked and received permission to take Nita and Polly to the dance in the ball-room at nine o'clock.

It seemed to Polly, a little later, that she had never been so radiantly happy in her life. Charmingly gowned, with a handsome young man for a partner, and her pulses bounding in time to the delicious sway of the music, she felt like another being, free as air, her monotonous married life a dream from which she had awakened, and life stretching before her in a long, golden vista of unexplored joys.

Presently she found herself strolling on the great piazza in the moon-light, with Ned Farrell, and with Nita and Perry not far behind them. Never had Polly seen so wonderful a view. High above a dense forest of pines, she looked out over the silver straights across which the full moon was tracing a path of gold. A great steamer, jewelled with lights, was making its majestic way across that track of radiance. And softly from within the hotel floated the amorous, intoxicating strains of "Un Peu d'Amour."

It was hard to leave all this loveliness, but, about midnight, the girls tore themselves away at last, with a promise to Perry and Ned to explore the island's delights with them in the morning.

"Polly," asked Nita, half an hour later, as she threw herself rather wearily on the bed— "how long to you think this dream of bliss is likely to last? Do you really think he's going to keep away very long? I mean Dick, of course."

"I don't know, Nita," answered Polly vaguely from the window, where she was taking a last look at the beautiful picture she had seen from the piazza below. "I have a strange feeling tonight, that he has never really ex-isted, and that I'm just emerging from the nightmare of a fever."

"Don't you fool yourself with any such mental opium-draughts as that, child," warned Nita yawningly. "I strongly advise you to be prepared for the worst, and not be taken off your guard. There's no telling what may happen, if he should drop down suddenly from the blue, and find you disporting yourself with a couple of strange young men!"

"Pooh, Nita—they're only boys, after all. There isn't a particle of harm in having them for playmates while we're here."

But Nita only murmured something unintelligible on the verge of slum-ber, and Polly soon followed her friend into the land of Nod.

Three days of such happiness as Polly could not remember to have known since she was a very little girl sped by with incredible swiftness. On the second afternoon, as the young people were returning from a drive, Polly encountered an acquaintance on the hotel piazza. It was Mrs. Paul Masters, wife of an elderly physician of Detroit, whom Polly had occasion to call on at various times during her residence in that city.

On seeing that Mrs. Masters had recognized her, Polly excused herself to her companions, and went over to the white-haired woman, who greeted her eagerly.

"My dear, yours is the first familiar face I've seen here yet. How long are you staying? And—where is Mr. Larramie?"

For one swift instant, Polly considered, then decided to take this kind-faced woman into her confidence. Somehow Mrs. Masters did not seem to find it hard to understand the pathetic little story, and she assured Polly that she and the Doctor would not "give her away," as long as she wanted to keep on with the masquerade.

"I believe it's an innocent enough thing, Paul," she said, a little later, to her husband, as she told him of Polly's "adventure." "Having known Richard Larramie, I can quite comprehend that poor child's desire to have a few days' freedom from his haunting, relentless espionage. She means no harm, and I'm sure those nice boys don't either. Let the poor young thing get back her lost youth and freedom, for a few days, if she can."

"I think I agree with you, mother, even though it does seem a bit risky," answered the Doctor. "There's Richard, himself, to be considered, you must remember. Is it likely he will leave her in peace very long?"

"Probably not," responded Mrs. Masters with a sigh. "And it's never men like that who are removed by a kind Providence," she added musingly.

But the third day came and went, and the fourth dawned full of bright promise. The sunshine in Polly's heart was as sparkling as the sun which danced on the blue water of the straits, as she and Nita rode forth for their first horseback ride with Perry Minot and Ned Farrell. On the previous days they had explored the beautiful island on foot and in carriages, and had circled it in a gay little steamer, both by daylight and moonlight. Now, to Polly, had come the supreme "adventure." She was astride a gentle but spirited horse, and with Ned to instruct and watch over her, she was going to thread those bewitching little bridle-paths through the heart of the Mackinac woods.

In and out they wound, through acres of green silence,—now in the solemn cathedral of the pines, now in some fairy forest of birches, and presently into the wilder denseness of the beeches and maples. Polly felt no fear of the splendid creature she rode, and was rapidly learning to guide and control him.

She was riding a little ahead of Ned, and the others were following, when the path suddenly broadened out to meet a carriage-drive. And, still more suddenly, there appeared directly in front of Polly, a man on horseback, who was staring straight at her with a white, set, furious face.

Polly gave an involuntary start and a short scream. That was all, but it was enough for the spirited animal she rode. With a nervous lunge he was off down a narrow by-path; Polly clung for a moment, then the low-hanging branches struck her sharply in the face, and one bough, heavier than the rest, swept her off as the horse plunged under it.

There was a low cry from Nita, a hoarse shout from Richard Larramie, and three men simultaneously leaped from their horses and ran toward the little figure that was lying so still upon the ground.

When Ned and Perry reached the spot, the other man was bending over the prostrate form. His face was wild, and as white as the one on the ground. "For God's sake, ride for a doctor!" he cried.

Without a word, Perry turned and sprang into his saddle, and in another moment was well on his way back to the hotel.

"You had better let me help you carry her to the nearest road," young Farrell said. "There's sure to be a carriage along, any minute, that will carry her to the hotel. She's—not dead, is she?" he whispered.

By this time, Nita was on her knees beside her friend. "No, no," she cried; "her heart beats. I'm sure she's only unconscious. See, she must have struck her head against that rock, as she fell."

Then sitting up suddenly, she looked Richard Larramie straight in the face, and exclaimed fiercely, "You did this! You mean, contemptible spy!"

"Yes," blurted out Ned, in his ignorance of the meaning of the situation. "What the devil did you mean by jumping out like that, right in the path of a woman's horse?"

"O," cried Nita, with passionate sarcasm, "he had a perfect right to; he's her husband!"

"Her hus—for the love of Mike! Do you mean it, Miss Nita?"

"Listen—there comes a carriage now," Nita exclaimed. "Go stop it, Mr. Farrell."

And so, a little later, they bore Polly Larramie, still unconscious, into the hotel, where Dr. Masters hurried to meet the distressed little party, having just been found returning from a stroll by the shore.

"Yes, she will recover," he announced, presently, to Richard Larramie, in tones more stern than sympathetic. "It was a pretty bad blow on the head, but she will regain consciousness soon, and I believe—so far as I can tell now—there are no internal injuries."

Larramie was still deathly pale, and very quiet. He made no comment upon the doctor's statement, but went over to the window, and stood staring out over the straits with unseeing eyes.

A few moments later, Polly slowly opened her eyes, gazed about in a bewildered fashion, and then looked up at the doctor with a little anxious smile. "I fell—or something—didn't I?" she asked tremulously.

"Yes, my dear, you had a pretty hard bump, but you're going to be all right presently," he replied cheerily.

Then Polly looked up and saw her husband's white face staring down at her. Something like a nervous spasm crossed her face; then she closed her eyes, shuddered again, and deliberately turned away her head.

"I think you had better leave her alone for a while," Dr. Masters said coldly to the man. "She will need perfect quiet, and nothing to excite her for several hours."

Larramie bowed assent, and half stumbled out of the room.

Three days passed. Polly was up, now, and sitting by the window in a becoming negligee. She was still pale, but would have been considered quite well and unharmed by her accident, had it not been for a queer symptom that baffled the doctor. She appeared not to know her husband, treated him like a stranger, and shrank away without a word, if he approached.

Dick Larramie tried pleading; he tried sternness; in desperation, at last, he resorted to the old, passionate love-making of their long-ago courting days. Each method proved equally in vain. Polly only drooped listlessly in her chair, and stared fixedly out of the window. If he attempted to touch her, she pushed him away and looked so wild that Dr. Masters grew alarmed and told Larramie he must let her alone, if he did not wish to make a complete wreck of his already distraught young wife.

After another day or two of this, with no apparent change in Polly's attitude toward her husband, although to others she spoke quietly and altogether sanely, Dick Larramie followed Dr. Masters to a remote corner of the long veranda, and demanded to know what must be done.

"Important business is calling me home, sir," Larramie said brusquely, "and you will have to make her understand that she must come along. Heaven knows what I'll do with her when I get her home—but she can't spend the rest of her life staring out of that hotel window. I've done and said everything I can think of—you know that. Now I'm at the end of my string, and you'll have to help me decide what's best to do with her. Again let me ask you, how long is this fit of 'nerves' or whatever it is, likely to last?"

Dr. Masters stood looking, for a moment, at the wonderful view, in silence. Then—

"I'm going to give you plain talk, Dick Larramie. Things have come to a pass where it's necessary to do so. Frankly—I am not certain, yet, whether there is anything wrong with your wife's brain, or whether this is merely a temporary mental state induced by nervous shock and the blow which she received on the head. But of one thing I am certain—she needs complete rest from you and the nervous excitement which your presence seems to bring to her in her present condition."

Larramie's face flushed a dull red, but he choked back his anger and asked, coldly, "You would suggest—a sanitarium?"

"I would suggest, on the contrary, that Mrs. Larramie remain here, on this island. There is no more health-giving spot in the world than Mackinac, and no more restful place for one suffering from disordered nerves. O, not in this big, gay hotel, of course. But there are many cozy, comfortable little cottages on this island. Let Mrs. Masters and me take her to one of these, and keep her with us for a few weeks at least; perhaps for the rest of the summer. I firmly believe it will make a new woman of her, Larramie."

As Larramie remained silent, chewing the end of his cigar, Dr. Masters laid a hand on his shoulder and said, with quiet firmness:

"The trouble is, man—you have tried to cut that young thing off from all human society but your own, and I much fear you have not always made that very attractive. But Nature has a law against that sort of thing. She won't allow one human being to monopolize another, without either a rebellion or a collapse on the part of the one so victimized. Your wife attempted the first—and now is on the verge of the second. For heaven's sake, Larramie, why couldn't you let her have a little vacation from you? All husbands and wives need an occasional change; they need to see each other from a new view-point once in a while. Poor little Polly Larramie wanted her youth back— the girlhood of which you robbed her. She was enjoying an innocent taste of all this, when you came and nearly killed her."

Larramie did not answer at once. At last, turning partly away, he mut- tered in a low voice: "All right, Doctor; you've got the upper hand of me just now, I guess. Go ahead; do what you think is best for Polly. —I'll leave her here with you. —Don't see what else I could do, in fact."

"One thing more, Larramie," said Dr. Masters. "You must give me your word to stay away from her until I consider her well enough to go home. Then I'll bring her back to you. Is that a go?"

"As I said before, Doc—you've got it on me, this time. Have the thing your own way. I promise to leave her alone till you tell me she's ready and willing to come back. Is that enough?"

"It is—and I don't think you will regret it," Dr. Masters replied, with a great relief in his heart.

Richard Larramie left Mackinac the following day, on the noon D. & C. steamer for Detroit. He did not stand on deck, with the other passengers, to see the last of the beautiful island, but went at once to the smoking room, and buried himself in a newspaper.

Dr. Masters, who had gone down to see him off, stood on the dock until quite a wide strip of water intervened between it and the departing steamer, and the faces on deck had become indistinguishable. He was musing, a little anxiously, over the responsibility he had assumed.

Suddenly, directly behind him, he heard a gay little laugh—such a familiar laugh that he turned with a jerk, and almost bumped into Polly Larramie. But not the pale, listless Polly he had left sitting by the window in the big hotel. The cheeks of this Polly were flushed, her eyes were dancing, and her lips were parted in smiling excitement. Her whole attitude was that of a mischievous child not in the least afraid of being punished.

Dr. Masters did not permit himself to smile in response, however. He looked long and searchingly into the bright eyes, and finally said, quietly,— "Well, Polly?"

Her face sobered a little, but it was still full of animation as she looked, first, up into the wide expanse of blue sky above her, and then out over the sparkling water of the straits. Presently she flung out her arms, and took a long, deep breath of ecstasy—of freedom.

"Doctor, dear," said Polly— "I had to do it. It was the only way. The plan came to me like an inspiration, when I opened my eyes after that unconscious spell, and saw him standing there—and realized what was before me. I couldn't go back to it, Doctor—the old imprisonment—after that glorious taste of freedom I had. Don't you see that I couldn't?"

"But Polly—what do you mean by 'not going back?' Do you mean— never?"

"No, Doctor. I mean that I am not going back to Dick until I have gained the moral strength to resist and defy his will; until I feel mentally and spiritually capable of asserting my rights as a human being. O, it is all going to come to me. I feel sure of it, now. I have played my hand for just such a breathing-spell as this; and you helped me win it! Some day, I'll be able to thank you properly. Now I'm just going to beg you to stick by me a little longer in the game that I'm playing for such high stakes. Will you, Doctor man?"

Her sweet, eager, pleading face would have been irresistible to a far harder heart than Dr. Masters. He hesitated only a moment, then clasped her little hand in both his big ones, and said:

"You took a pretty strenuous method, little lady. But I believe you are right in what you are trying to accomplish—and I'll stand by you. But— what are we going to write to your husband about you? I don't like lying."

"It won't be lying, Doctor, to write him about once a week, that I am steadily improving, but that you insist upon his keeping his promise to stay away until you consider me quite ready to go home."

"But meanwhile, my dear—there's to be no flirting or carrying on with young men!"

"O, I solemnly promise not to make eyes at a single masculine creature but you, Doctor! That is, not without asking your permission first. Anyway, those two nice boys have gone—and I'm afraid of the older men, who take things seriously. No, Nita has promised to stay and keep me company for a week or so, if her business firm will give her a longer leave of absence, and we'll have a beautiful time exploring the secrets of this fascinating fairyland."

Turning slowly, Polly lifted dreaming eyes to the old white fort that towered above her.

"I think there is healing, here, for the tired, bruised soul of me," she added softly. "And do you know, Doctor—as I begin to 'find myself' again, I believe I'm going to find, too, a spark of real honest affection, deep down in my heart, for that poor, misguided Dick of mine."

FROM IN THE WAKE OF THE GEMINI
(1962)
Ann Davison

AFTER SAILING THE ATLANTIC single handed, the first woman to do so, getting married, and surviving brain cancer, Ann Davison (1914-1992) decided she needed a real challenge, so she chose the Great Lakes. She outfitted a seventeen-foot outboard cruiser, renamed the *Gemini*, with twin thirty-five horsepower motors she named Castor and Pollux after the sons of Jupiter and Leda who make up the constellation Gemini, and set off from Florida up the Intracoastal Waterway. Her goal was to make a circuit up the Waterway, through the Great Lakes, and down the Mississippi to the Gulf of Mexico, then write about her trip to make money. As she tells it, "when I see bottom through the royalties it is time to think of a new venture. . . ." and this time it would be the States. With a cheerful British aplomb reminiscent of Anna Jameson, Davison defied storms, chartless Great Lakes passages, and American stereotypes about women sailors to create a fascinating account of modern lakes travel. Her book is long out-of-print, so I have selected from it a section describing her travels in Georgian Bay and the North Channel which will amuse every sailor—woman or man, armchair or active—who reads it.

LAKES

THE WONDERLAND, STORYBOOK quality that pervades the Trent Waterways persists into Georgian Bay, although there it is of sterner stuff. The Trent has a serenity about it even in its most rugged moments. It belongs to the land, where man is at home. But Georgian Bay is more like the sea, where man is not at home, only temporarily on it by a courtesy that is often quickly revoked. I found it very hard to believe that Georgian Bay was an inlet off a lake. It looked like the sea and behaved like the sea and gave one the same feeling of its being a sleeping tiger, beautiful, unpredictable and dangerous. It was extraordinary to see fresh-water fish idling round barnacle-free pilings, and the lack of salt in the spray was quite shocking. I had not felt this way about Lake Ontario, which is also big and can certainly be rough enough to look sealike, because there the shores are such as one might expect to find

round a lake; but the shores on Georgian Bay are seashores, and wild northern seashores at that.

It was baffling, but I could not go so far as the Yorkshire woman I met
with her husband in one of the snug little harbors with which the bay abounds.
Recently emigrated, they had come from one of the stern little fishing ports
on the northeast coast of England which is continuously under assault from
the cold gray North Sea. One would have thought they would have welcomed the change, for Georgian Bay, with its rich red rocks and dark blue
waters, at least looks a warmer and more congenial place. But when I asked
how they liked it the wife said, "I dunno. It's all right. Kids like it. But I miss
the salt. The air was salty at home. You could taste it." She looked out across
the narrow harbor entrance to where a ribbon of bay could be seen shimmering in the afternoon sun, and sighed, "It's lovely, of course, but no salt. It
doesn't seem like proper water, somehow."

I know how she felt, though not wholly agreeing with her; for to my
mind any water that'll float a boat and lead it to somewhere new cannot fail
to be proper water.

Georgian Bay is roughly rectangular in shape, lying northwest-south-
east, with Port Severn in the southeastern corner and Killarney (whither I
was bound) in the northwestern corner, a distance of about 120 miles, across
a bay sixty miles wide. This was altogether too much open water for a seventeen-foot boat to take in one fell swoop. So I elected to drive up along the
coast through the Thirty Thousand Islands to the Byng Inlet and make a
sixty-mile open-water crossing from there.

I haven't seen the Thousand Islands of the St. Lawrence, but I've glimpsed
a few of the Ten Thousand Islands on the Gulf Coast of Florida, and I can't
help feeling that it is pretty niggling to allow only 30,000 for all those islands
on the east coast of Georgian Bay. Either that or careless counting. Or perhaps there is a size limit for islands, like fish, and you put the small ones
back. So at what point does a rock become an island?

My Crusoe complex is very strongly developed. An island is an immedi-
ate challenge to me and I want to explore it on sight. I've lived on a few small
islands and am not disillusioned. I look forward to living on several more.
Even without the threat of that long crossing I would not have been able to
resist a journey through the Thirty Thousand Islands. However, when I looked
at the chart I was appalled.

In Norfolk, Virginia, I had been at the receiving end of one of those
unlooked-for, unlikely, long-lost-uncle-remembers-you-in-his-will sort of
gestures that happen every once in a while to perpetuate the belief in Santa
Claus. The owner of a large ketch southward bound from the Great Lakes
dumped into my lap a huge roll of charts saving: "You might as well have

these. I'll never be going that way again."

Charts are a big item on a trip like mine and they are as indispensable for the safety and comfort of a voyage as the face mask is for a skin diver. The massive gift roll covered all the Great Lakes areas that I proposed to travel, and more, except for the Trent (the ketch being too big for this waterway), but I did not examine the Georgian Bay charts until I got to Peterborough. Then I cried in dismay, gift horse or not, "Oh, no! There must be something better than this!"

I was in the Outboard Marine offices at the time and it was generally agreed that the charts were pretty horrible and that there would surely be better ones available. Not, however, in Peterborough, as it turned out.

No matter, there was a boat works at Honey Harbor in Georgian Bay, only twelve miles from Port Severn, that had everything, I was assured. If clear, legible, up-to-date charts were to be got anywhere, that's where they'd be.

My charts were not clear nor legible and certainly not up-to-date. They were made from surveys conducted in the [eighteen] nineties and preserved in the original manner of their printing. (I must make it clear that no reflection is intended on the generosity of the donor. The charts were the only kind available, as I found out.) They were printed without color differentiation between land and water, and where land and water intermingle to the extent they do in the Thirty Thousand Islands this can be very confusing. The print was very small, black on a white ground. Black dots depicted figures relating to the depth of water, rocks, channel markers, buoys, lights, islets, and fly specks. Black lines outlined the shores and islands, so indented they looked like the outside edges of jigsaw pieces, and the overall effect was of someone having upset the black pepper on the tablecloth.

Large areas left white bore a legend reading succinctly "numerous rocks and islands." So numerous, in fact, that the surveyors had gotten fed up and gone home. Large areas left white without any legend indicated the surveyors hadn't gotten round to even thinking about them. The attitude conveyed by the charts was that those who knew the waters wouldn't need one and those who didn't shouldn't be there.

Ah well, I thought, I'll get this cleared up at Honey Harbor (a most appealing place-name).

There was of course the little matter of getting to Honey Harbor. And that, according to my chart, was impossible.

It allowed you to pick a way through a rock-field out of Port Severn until the rocks were so thick the printer's ink ran and there the channel gave up. Supposing one's boat at this point to be a helicopter, one could fly over that bit to clear water, land, and sail on in the ordinary way to the Honey Harbor approaches, where, according to the chart, the fun began again. More rocks, and only a hint here and there of a marker. Nothing convincing in the way of a channel at all. In fact the original cartographers thought so little of the necessity of strangers being able to get to Honey Harbor that they printed the compass rose slap over the area, otherwise leaving it in pristine purity for the stranger to guess at the water's depth and what might lie submerged.

Yet from all I heard, Honey Harbor was a busy bustling place with boats going in and out all the time, and not all the boatmen using the harbor can have been born with a built-in fathometer and range-finder.

Perhaps I would be able to get a chart at Port Severn for Honey Harbor.

But I could not. I discussed the problem with local fishermen in Port Severn who looked at my chart uncomprehendingly and embarked on detailed directions along the lines of "turn left where the old red barn used to be and bear right at Tom's new pasture," interspersed with brief exchanges relating to complicated short cuts and finally condensing to a simple agreement that it would be all right if I went slowly and followed the bull's-eyes.

"Bull's-eyes?" I admit there is a lot I don't know about navigation.

"Yes," they affirmed, nodding vigorously, "on the rocks. Bull's-eyes." (I *had* heard right the first time.)

If I had been appalled by the sight of the chart, it was nothing to what I felt at the sight of the real thing.

It was a very lowering sky that frowned on my departure from Port Severn that morning. I tiptoed down the channel, out into the bay and to a vista that was hard to believe even looking directly at it. As if flung by giant handfuls, rocks lay scattered in the water with barely a boat's breadth between them, and were spread thus for miles. They were not rough and jagged as sea rocks are, but rounded and smooth, which by increasing the giant pebble illusion and giving a feeling of being lost on another world seemed to make them more menacing.

Good heavens, I thought, I'll never get through that lot. But by careful observation it was possible here and there to discern an occasional red or black stake, and sure enough, where it was not feasible to plant a stake, a bull's-eye was painted on a rock, with a black or red center to indicate on which side one was supposed to pass.

It took me two hours to get to Honey Harbor picking my way from marker to marker through the rocks. Knowing what I know now, I guess I could make it in an hour and fifty-five minutes. I would not stop to gasp.

Honey Harbor is as delightful as its name. It is a village of islands. There must be some mainland about somewhere but I was not aware of it. Hotels, houses, churches and stores all seemed to have their own islands.

A low-lying outcrop of rock a few yards long with a stunted shrub in the middle of it bore a "For Sale" sign, and when I remarked on this at the village store, itself an island, there was a burst of laughter.

"The joke of it is," I was told, "the water's four feet lower than normal this summer. That's why the island is there. Usually most of it is under water."

"But surely it is not being offered for sale seriously?" I asked.

"Oh, yes. Islands are all the thing now. Everyone wants one. Some visitor will probably fall for it, and get a surprise when the water comes up again."

Honey Harbor is a summer resort, but the Despoilers haven't got there yet with their eternal gripes and insatiable demands, and it still has the atmosphere of a thriving country village. A Venice amongst villages, where the outboard takes the place of the bicycle and the jeep.

The water is full of little boats sizzling about importantly. Everyone drives an outboard, it is the only way of getting about; and it was pleasantly novel to see them being responsibly driven by schoolchildren, housewives out shopping with babies and baskets beside them, and little old ladies in prim churchgoing hats. Most of the boats were open, skiff type, and built of wood. Fiberglas construction was rare. *Gemini* came in for quite a bit of attention. "Is that one of those plastic boats?" I was asked.

The Honey Harbor Boat Works, a very active concern, owned and operated by the Milner family, did not have anything new to offer in the way of charts, but did have a nice line in hospitality.

Despite the fact she had just undergone the treatment at Peterborough, *Gemini* was freshened up with a light overhaul and a new set of plugs, and given an overnight berth, all on the house. And I was asked to tea. A lovely tea-pot tea at Mrs. Milner's.

Tea is a very British institution, as I hardly need say, but it is one of the better minor ones. It takes care of the tag end of the afternoon when energies flag and it is too late to get started on anything else, and it recharges the batteries for the evening. If you have tea you don't gobble dinner as if you haven't seen food for a week and consequently you stay awake later. Also, it is useful for informal noncommittal social occasions.

The only snag about it, so far as I am concerned, is that I don't like tea. That is, unless I can make it myself, or get someone else to make it weak enough. Which is practically impossible, as there appears to be a social taboo on weak drinks, especially weak tea. People ask you how you like your tea and when you tell them they say, "Oh no, you can't possibly drink that," and hand you a cup of lye that removes the entire lining of your stomach in one swallow. Years ago in self-defense I learned to drown the tea in milk. Anyone can under stand your wanting more milk, whereas they find incredible your wanting more hot water.

However, Mrs. Milner made splendid tea, and along with her daughters was eager to tell of the recent great occasion of the opening of the St. Lawrence Seaway and the Queen's visit. "You should have made your trip then," said Mrs. Milner, her eyes alight with the memory of an event already assuming legendary proportions. Everything that could float, she said, was taken out to greet the Queen, and I was shown photographs of the crush of boats round the Royal Yacht. It looked just like the Jersey Waterways on Sunday afternoon.

Charts are like kitchen space or cupboards. No matter how much or how many you have, you always want more.

Looking them over for the North Channel area, where I was soon to be cruising, I found more detailed ones were needed for the north side of Manitoulin Island. There were none available at the Boat Works, but Mr. Milner said they could be obtained at the Board of Trade Offices at Parry Sound, which was on my way. Then I found that in the journey from Honey Harbor to Parry Sound there was a twenty-mile gap in the black peppers for which no cartographic bridge was available. In view of the pilotage involved, I was rather dismayed. True, the charts were little better than moral support, but that is always better than nothing.

Mr. Milner was reassuring. "There's an inside channel," he said, "all the way to Parry Sound and it is so well marked you'll never need to look at a chart. They even use road signs," he added. "You can't possibly miss it."

It sounded like famous last words to me at the time but it was true enough. The road signs made their appearance near Parry Sound, and whilst a little startling at first, they seemed eminently sensible, especially in an area where innumerable streams all looking like the main channel lead off in every direction round innumerable islands and peninsulas. A curve sign on a point leaves no doubt as to which way the channel goes, and a SLOW sign by a narrows takes you through with a warning thrown in.

And despite the gap in the charts, there was no difficulty in getting to Parry Sound.

The boating boom had made such an impression on the Board of Trade (Canadian Department of Transport) that it had with commendable and unusual fervor and imagination set about improving conditions in order that boats would be encouraged to boom there in ever greater numbers and from ever farther afield.

The inside passage from Honey Harbor to Parry Sound was a result of these endeavors, a scenic and sheltered run in which one is never out of sight of a marker of some sort. Bull's-eyes, day-marks, lights, stakes are all there in profusion. It will be impossible to miss the channel when charts come out to match the buoys and one knows what they all mean. Such charts, I learned at the Board of Trade offices, were being made, but not knowing what they all meant certainly added zest to *my* pilotage.

The passage winds north through the Thirty Thousand Islands, islets, rocks, reefs and bars, with every so often channels branching off to small ports tucked away in the hinterland to the east. One would come round an island, islet, or some other thirty thousand obstruction and light on a single marker. It might be black or red, but only one, and just what did it mean? Was it part of the northbound channel, or one of those leading off into the interior? The answer was fairly important in waters which a survey-boat captain has described as being "sixty feet on the fathometer amidships and pounding on the bow."

Again, one might come on a pair of markers, a black and a red, but this did not necessarily denote a channel or that one should pass between them. They might be marking the outer edges of a shoal. . . .

These are the things that keep you young.

And, as I have said, there was really no difficulty in getting to Parry Sound. I took my cues from day-marks, which showed up clearly as white blobs in the distance. When in doubt over the position of a marker I looked round for an island with a white blob on it and took my direction from that, thus making fairly good time to Parry Sound.

There, at the Board of Trade wharves where I stopped to pick up the North Channel charts, I had an interesting conversation with the grizzled skipper of a surveyboat. He recited with exquisite detail every inch of the way of the passage from Parry Sound to Pointe au Baril. At Pointe au Baril I intended to "go to sea" and continue along the coast outside for fifteen miles or so to the Byng Inlet, where, if the weather was right, I would make my departure for Killarney on the other side of Georgian Bay. There was no point in following the coast round, because from the Byng Inlet onwards the shores were wild, shoal, and to all intents and purposes uncharted—practically, one might say, unchartable. An exciting coast to explore, but not one on which to be caught out.

I had hoped to make Pointe au Baril after leaving Parry Sound, charts in hand, landmarks in head, and eyes wide for day-marks, but a few blustery squalls with curtains of rain slowed me down and I stopped for the night in a cove appropriately named Snug Harbor. There the civilizing hand of man was only manifest in a dilapidated boathouse and a strong wooden jetty. It was quiet and still, an ideal spot to rest up and get ready for the crossing next day.

I ate supper, put things away in case the going was rough across the bay, and did a little work on course and distance calculations. I was about to turn in when there was a bumping alongside and a thunderous rapping on the cabin top.

I looked out, and in the dark made out three figures in a small fishing skiff. Two, muffled to the ears, crouched amidships. The other, standing authoritatively in the stern, was getting ready to deliver another fusillade which my appearance happily forestalled. He wore a black patch over one eye which gave him a piratical air.

"You can't come to Snug Harbor and just sit there," he announced. "You had better come back with us. It'll be much more fun."

"No doubt," said I, "but I'm off to Killarney tomorrow and want to make an early start. Thank you kindly, but I don't really want to go out tonight." (It sounded as though I was turning down an invitation to make a round of the local night spots.)

The Pirate wouldn't take no for an answer and called upon the other two to back him up.

"We won't keep you late," they promised. "We have to get up early, too. Come on." So I went.

We took off at high speed and went through a long cavernous creek where the rock walls rose sheer on either side and so closely as to muffle the motor. Finally we slid into a boathouse, left the boat there and climbed into a log cabin perched above, where oil lamps threw long shadows and a mellow golden light. Two college boys sat at a table demolishing a monumental feast.

"Now," said the Pirate, unwinding a long woolen scarf from around his neck, "we know who you are. But you don't know us. I am Alan Acres." He unwound the last of the scarf with a flourish and waved the end of it at the other two who had been in the boat and were now busily unmuffling themselves. "May I present Mr. and Mrs. Parr. They own that big fishing boat we passed on the way, only you couldn't see it on account of the dark. A pity, for it is a fine boat, and who knows when she'll sail again, commercial fishing being what it is. All the fish are gone from the lake and Mr. Parr is working for the Board of Trade. You must have passed some of his handiwork on the way to Parry Sound. Didn't you love the road signs? This is Roger, by the way"—one of the boys looked up from his diminishing plate and nodded—"and that's Gordon. They're on vacation. Roger does the cooking. To good effect, as one can see. Now, Miss Davison, what will you have to drink?"

"Well, I'll be darned," I said, "you do know who I am. But I don't see how. And no one knew I was coming here. I didn't myself, until I came."

"Smoke signals," said Alan. "You're out in the wilds now. Never underestimate the power of the bush telegraph. It knows what you are going to do sooner than you do yourself. Parr saw you at the Board of Trade today and recognized your boat when he came home tonight. You didn't say what you'd like to drink?"

From there the conversation naturally gravitated to smuggling, moonshine, shipwreck, and murder.

"We're a lawless lot here, you know," said Alan with the satisfaction one can afford when the lawlessness is kept within certain gentlemanly bounds.

The evening passed quickly. When I got up to go Alan said, "You are writing a book, of course. Well, you've come to the right place, there's material here for a library, though you won't get any of it rushing through like this. However, if you must go in the morning you had better have breakfast with us first. I'll come by at half past six—early enough?—to pick you up and bring you here. You may not find this place otherwise, it is off the beaten track. Roger will cook breakfast and then we'll see you on your way. There are one or two places round here that are rather difficult when you don't know them, rocks you can't see and ranges hard to follow. Oh, and incidentally, don't get the bird sanctuary signs confused with the day-marks. Lots of people do and get into no end of trouble. The National Park people put them up to show which islands are strictly for the birds, if you'll excuse the expression. They're white boards like the day-marks, only a different shape. They all look alike in the distance."

"Oh." White blobs in the distance. "Would they be oblong sort of boards?" I asked.

Alan nodded.

Looking back over my trip along Georgian Bay through the Thirty Thousand Islands, I would say at a rough guess I must have navigated about sixty miles, all told, on bird sanctuary signs. At twenty miles an hour.

MACKINAC ISLAND

(1984)

Paulette Jiles

This is where the English came and fortified
themselves against Lake Michigan, Indians, wolves,
the French, rebellions. The walls are white as
the Caribbean, the water is the same blue
but more glacial. Young men walk around in
pipe-clayed britches and fire off muzzle-loaders.
People scream. Everything is like it was.

In the bay below the walls, our boat nods
like a gull in the middle of expensive
racers, ocean-goers, hundred-footers.
We stopped talking somewhere
around Sault Ste. Marie.

On the docks men are using wagons and
big Belgian horses to off-load ice cream
and asphalt. No cars are allowed on this
island. You're waiting for me to ask what's
the matter. I played that game already. So
has everybody. No surrender.

I'm glad we sailed here; there are all kinds
of lessons about people who
guard themselves behind walls and are
defeated by treachery, they get you
when your guard is down, the night watch
hopes his cigarette will burn his lips if
he falls asleep, the innocent enemy playing lacrosse
in front of the gates, then the bloodshed
and men hiding in pork barrels.

If only we could arrange to leave each
other simultaneously, without the war, with
a small, sharp noise like a halyard parting in
mid-wind, if only we knew how to make love,
piece by piece, out of common household materials.

If we knew how the pieces fit, how
it worked. War is easier. One or the
other will win, leave first, sign things,
move out.

You build the walls first. After the
fortifications are ready, then you get
your French, your wolves, your
Indians and rebellions. No chance to
get the message through, the runners wash
up on the shore months later.

We sail past the ferryboat, the only
sound is the wind's slow whistle,
the boom of the evening cannon, and
a crowd of people presenting arms.

"Mackinac Island" is part of the book *Celestial Navigation,* which won the Governor General's Award, the most prestigious literary prize in Canada, in 1984. Jiles was born in Missouri in 1943, but after graduating from college left for Toronto, and eventually the sub-arctic and the Arctic. She wrote radio plays, novels (*Sitting in the Club Car Drinking Rum and Karma Cola: A Manual of Etiquette for Ladies Crossing Canada by Train* [1986]), and five books of poetry.

Women's Work

Women's Work

IN *How Women Can Make Money* Virginia Penny described the ways women could be self-supporting in 1870s, including working as stewardesses on passenger steamers. Penny's book reflects a new reality insistently making itself felt in the latter half of the nineteenth century. An earlier world of family farms and small town entrepreneurship was disappearing, and with it the familiar roles men and women had occupied since Europeans came to the New World. Where once an entire family had worked to produce what they needed on farms or in small shops and businesses, or on the Great Lakes in the family schooner, with the advent of industrial capitalism and massive immigration, many families could no longer support themselves without resorting to outside work for hire. Those jobs went mostly to men and women became limited to domestic responsibilities. In addition to the economic displacements, the mortality rate of men in the Civil War in the United States had ensured that many women would not be able to marry and would need to find ways to support themselves.

The problem was that the few occupations women without educations could pursue—sewing, working as housemaids, working in factories, or later in offices—enabled them to earn a living wage, particularly if they had to support minor children or other family members. In the Great Lakes region a number of women who were forced to work outside the home had historically found employment in the maritime industry. Because of the Civil War, the booming construction of heavy industry, and the opening of more land to settlement with the Homestead Act, positions that men would normally have filled before the 1860s, such as lightkeepers, sometimes went to women. Other women cooked on the ships plying the lakes or sailed as chambermaids and stewardesses. During some periods when having a woman cook was fashionable, there were more positions open than women, preferably attractive young farm girls, could be found to fill them. At other times, usually when the wives of officers complained publicly, women were driven off the lakes. Even when jobs were available, women sailors were usually the lowest-paid crew members and often subjected to abuse, probably because they were considered lower class and not worthy of respect. Without male relatives aboard to protect them, they were at the mercy of the crew. The news clippings collected in "The Fickle Fortunes of Female Cooks" are a small sample of the problems wage-earning women faced and do not include reports of women's lawsuits for lost wages and rape. Nevertheless, maritime work earned more than unskilled and uneducated women could earn ashore, and many took advantage of this, despite the dangers.

In the 1870s, however, the first of the great "panics," or depressions, that were to reoccur until World War I began, and pressure grew to force women from positions, such as lightkeeping, that could be held by men. At the beginning of this decade, one of every five lighthouse keepers or assistant keepers on lakes was female. Most had come to their positions like Elizabeth Whitney Williams, who took over the light when her husband died. In *A Child of the Sea*, portions of which are reprinted here, Williams describes her commitment to the service, but she also notes that she had to support herself and her mother.

Women had been keeping lakes' lights for decades. The first was Rachel Wolcott, who succeeded her husband after his death at the Marblehead, Ohio, light in 1832. By 1877 there were 143 lighthouses on the US portion of the lakes, ten kept by women. In addition, there were seventeen assistant keepers, who were usually the wives or daughters of the keepers, sometimes men who were too ill or infirm to do the physical work required and so kept their lights in name only. Their families did most of the work. But the true situation of women lightkeepers, and symbolically all women working in the world of the merchant marine on the lakes in the 1870s and 1880s, is revealed in the correspondence between the district lighthouse service supervisors on the lakes and the Treasury Department in Washington, DC.

When Barney Litigot, the keeper of the Mama Juda light in the Detroit River, died, his assistant keeper and wife, Caroline, applied for his job. But it was 1874, and many men wanted the secure government position she had nominally filled for a number of years while she took care of her invalid husband, who probably had been given the post of lightkeeper as a reward for his Civil War service. A letter written by the lakes' district supervisor to his superior in Washington, DC, is testimony to her skill as well as to the government's attempts to deny her the job:

Honorable B. H. Bristow
Secretary of the Treasury
Detroit, July 24, 1874

Dear Sir:

I telegraphed you on the 18th inst. to suspend action on the removal of Mrs. Litogot, Keeper of the Light House at Mama Juda. My reasons for doing so are these: the Light has been nominally kept by her husband for some time before his death, but in fact by Mrs. Litogot, her husband being disabled from wounds received in the war from the effects of which he died, leaving his wife and two children penniless and with no means of support except what she receives as a Light Keeper.

The vessel men all say that she keeps a [MS burned] excellent light, and I think it very hard to remove a woman who is faithful and efficient, and throw her upon the world with her children entirely destitute when her husband lost his life in defense of the union, and I can give as adequate [MS burned] so, when I have been told by her numerous friends and sympathizers, many whom are masters and pilots of vessels, competent to speak of the manner in which she has kept the light and who pass it frequently.

I therefore earnestly hope that she may be allowed to remain.

Very Resply,

Z. Chandler

By 1897 only four women had managed to retain their lights on the Great Lakes, among them Harriet A. Colfax and Elizabeth Whitney Williams. Many who had been listed as keepers or assistant keepers in the 1870s had been dismissed. A fire in the US Treasury Department in the 1920s destroyed or damaged most of the documents that would give evidence of what happened, but enough remain to suggest that as economic conditions deteriorated and the service became professionalized, women were forced out. Letters from the 1880s are revealing.

On July 12, 1882, Chairman Rear Admiral R. W. Wyman wrote to the Superintendent of Lights in Port Huron, Michigan, regarding the nomination of Mrs. Jane E. Sinclair as assistant light keeper for her husband:

. . . on acct of the importance and isolated position of this light, and the operation of a steam fog signal there, [the Board] thinks that the vacancy could be better filled by the appointment of a man and that the appointment of Mrs. Sinclair would not provide the station with an assistant keeper possessing the requisite qualifications."

On October 20, 1882, Naval Secretary Commander Henry F. Pickering wrote to the Superintendent of Lights in Grand Haven, Michigan:

Sir: The nomination of Mrs. Hattie Hanson, wife of the Keeper, to be assistant keeper at Grand Point au Sauble, Michigan submitted by you on the 16th *instant* has been received.

Referring thereto the Board has to say that in addition to a desire to adhere as strictly as possible to Paragraph 53 of the Lighthouse Regulations which provides that members of a keeper's family could be appointed only in rare and exceptional cases, it does not believe it to be a good policy to appoint women as keepers or assistant keepers where it can be avoided. Furthermore in the particular instance it is not thought that the appointment of Mrs. Hanson at Grand Point au Sauble would supply that station with an assistant as efficient as its importance and location demand, especially in case of an accident.

The Board would be glad therefore if you will substitute for the nomination of Mrs. Hanson, a suitable man. . . .

In 1883 Mrs. Nellie Buzzard was rejected for the assistant keeper's position of the Saginaw River Range Light in Michigan. The Superintendent of Lights at Port Huron protested. Commander Pickering relented, but wrote

"The Board hopes, however, it may not be called upon to make a similar exception. . . ."

Undoubtedly there had been some abuses and featherbedding of relatives in the Lighthouse Service. In addition, when steam fog horns were introduced, many women would not have been physically able to handle the equipment, which included shoveling coal to feed the boilers. (The installation of steam fog apparatus was delayed at Michigan City until Harriet Colfax retired.) What also appears to have happened is what took place on all North American frontiers: as they became more settled, and as economic conditions became less open, opportunities for women diminished. The need for a pair of hands, no matter what the gender, became less important as more laborers were available; then women's contributions became defined by the boundaries of home. As the nineteenth century progressed, the discrimination against women became more pronounced. This occurred despite the emerging rhetoric of the "New Woman" bandied about in the press that championed the movement of women into the world outside the home. But working against this popular fantasy was another, equally powerful, rhetoric that denied women commercially lucrative work. If they were not to be "angels in the house," they could be the saviors of culture through charitable work, the church, and volunteerism. They could do unpaid work for the good of society and for the world their children would inhabit. If they had to earn money, they could take in laundry and boarders.

What industrialization and the concomitant restructuring of society required was that women's spheres of influence and men's spheres of action be separated. As men became the sole economic providers for their families, homemaking became a social and cultural activity rather than a natural one, a situation that would not change, except for World War II, until the 1970s. The problem was, however, that many women—some historians estimate thirty to forty percent—still had to provide for themselves and, if they were married, for their families if their husbands died or became incapacitated or lost their jobs. But the popular rhetoric of domesticity and economic realities prevented women from earning equal pay for equal work and from entering most professions. One result of this dilemma was a rise in prostitution; others were abandoned children, domestic violence, and poverty.

As the Great Lakes changed from a maritime frontier to an industrial heartland the world of work changed dramatically. Men who had once owned their own ships and took their families along as crew could no longer compete against the newer, bigger, more efficient iron and steel ships owned by corporations and sailed by professional crews. The lighthouse service and the life-saving service became professionalized as well; civil service examinations determined who was appointed. The coming of the railroads, and later automobiles, undermined the monopoly of lakes shipping. Vertical integration, which encouraged large, efficient steel ships owned by a few companies, replaced small wooden schooners operated by independent captains and their families. For those who did not own farms or successful small businesses, the late nineteenth century was a time when many, particularly women, often experienced a narrowing of opportunity.

Still, some women persevered. Williams and Colfax managed to outwit the bureaucracy and keep their jobs, largely because of their superior records and the testimony of powerful men. Other, less fortunate, women continued sailing on passenger ships once the corporate-owned bulk carriers were closed to them. A few women pioneers were able to make careers for themselves as wreck divers and captains if they were lucky enough to have supportive families. Women who were part of lighthouse families worked without pay or acknowledgment unless they accomplished something heroic, as did two young women who earned medals for their bravery. But the frontier Great Lakes world, where many women handled rowboats as confidently as modern women drive a car and where most travel was by water, was gone and would not be replaced. Certainly there were exceptions, but for most women, work would be on land. Given the difficult climate of the lakes and the isolation they enforced during the frontier period, this change was welcome, but at the same time, women lost the opportunity to prove themselves in a physically demanding landscape and work at jobs that sometimes required great courage and paid well.

The result has been a region surrounded by watery landscape where few women are comfortable. Although many women scuba dive for recreation, few do it as a profession. All the lighthouses are automated. The fishing industry has virtually disappeared, and with it the chance for women to learn that craft. After decades of discrimination, women crew now work in the merchant marine and earn the same pay as men; often a chief cook will earn nearly as much as the captain. Women graduate from maritime academies and pursue careers as officers on lakes ships, but still problems of discrimination remain. While many women sail for pleasure, the majority do not. Recreational boating, now the most common form of maritime activity on the lakes, is primarily a male hobby, as are the yacht races, perhaps because few women have the money or the freedom from other responsibilities. Great Lakes maritime history is researched, written, and published primarily by men about men. "Women's Work" is in some respects a eulogy for the possibilities both men and women had, but it is also an attempt to correct the overwhelming historical focus on men's activities on the lakes. Women made history here too: they earned life-saving medals, they kept their lights in difficult conditions, and they persevered in the face of discrimination. Their courage and dedication were remarkable.

MADAME LA FRAMBOISE, FUR TRADER

FROM REMINISCENCES OF EARLY DAYS ON MACKINAC ISLAND

(1898)

Elizabeth Thérèse Baird

MADAME MARGUERITE MAGDELAINE Marcot La Framboise, born in 1780 to Jean Baptiste Marcotte and Marie Neskesh, was by all accounts a beautiful, intelligent, commanding presence. She was also, like many citizens of Mackinac Island, the daughter of a French fur-trader father and an Odawa mother, and therefore conversant with both Indian and French culture, skills that were necessary when her husband was murdered at the start of winter operations and she assumed control of their fur-trading operation as bourgeois in 1806. She had accompanied her husband, Joseph, on his winter expeditions for years, and rather than selling out or remarrying after his death, she used her intelligence and ability to trade to amass a small fortune for her children and to seriously hinder the operations of John Jacob Astor's fur traders in her territories. After failing to compete against her, the American Fur Company hired her in 1818. Because she did not learn to read until late in life, she left no autobiographical account before her death in 1846. This description of her life was written by her great niece, Elizabeth Thérèse Baird.

->≔⊚⊂≕<-

Madame La Framboise

JOSEPH LA FRAMBOISE, a Frenchman, father of Josette La Framboise, dealt largely with the Indians. He was a firm, determined man, and moreover was especially devout, adhering to all the rites and usages of the Catholic Church. He was especially particular as to the observance of the Angelus. Out in the Indian country, timed by his watch, he was as faithful in this discharge of duty as elsewhere. Whenever in any town where the bells of his church rang out three times three,—at six in the morning, at noon, and at six in the evening,—he and his family paid reverent heed to it. Madame La Framboise, his widow, maintained this custom as long as she lived, and it was very impressive. The moment the Angelus sounded, she would drop her work, make the sign of the cross, and with bowed head and crossed hands would say the short prayers, which did not last much longer than the solemn ringing of the bells.

In 1809, La Framboise left Mackinac with his wife and baby-boy (the daughter being at Montreal, at school) for his usual wintering place on the upper part of Grand River, in Michigan. They traveled in Mackinac boats, or bateaux. There were two boats, with a crew of six men to each. They were also accompanied by their servants,—old Angelique, a slave, and her son, Louizon—all of whom made a large party. At the last encampment, before reaching Grand River, La Framboise, while kneeling in his tent one night saying his prayers, was shot dead by an Indian, who had previously asked for liquor and had been refused. The widowed wife, knowing that she was nearer Grand River than her own home, journeyed on, taking the remains of her husband with her, and had them buried at the only town in that vicinity, which was near the entrance of the river—the present Grand Haven, Mich. Now was developed the unselfish devotion of her servant, Angelique, whose faithfulness was displayed in many ways through the deep affliction which had fallen upon her mistress. She greatly endeared herself to Madame La Framboise, and was ever after her constant companion in all journeyings, Madame becoming in time very dependent upon her; the tie that bound them together remained unbroken until the death of the mistress.

After Madame La Framboise had laid away her husband, she proceeded to her place of business. Here she remained until spring, trading with the Indians. Then she returned to Mackinac and procured a license as a trader, and added much to her already large fortune. In the course of that winter the Indians captured the murderer of La Framboise, and, bringing him to her, desired that she should decide his fate,—whether he should be shot or burned. Madame addressed them eloquently, referring, in words profoundly touching, to her dead husband, his piety, and his good deeds. Then, displaying in her forgiving spirit a most Christ-like quality, she continued: "I will do as I know he would do, could he now speak to you; I will forgive him, and leave him to the Great Spirit. He will do what is right." She never again saw that man.

Madame La Framboise would in June return with her furs to Mackinac. The servants whom she left in care of her home there, would have it in readiness upon her arrival, and here she would keep house for about three months and then go back to her work. Among these servants was one notably faithful, Geneviève Maranda, who remained with her until her death.

Madame La Framboise was a remarkable woman in many ways. As long as her father, Jean Baptiste Marcotte, lived, his children, when old enough, were sent to Montreal to be educated. But she and her sister, Grandmother [Thérèse] Schindler, did not share these advantages, they being the youngest of the family, and the father dying when Madame La Framboise was but three months old. Her mother was of chiefly blood, being the daughter of

Kewinaquot, "Returning Cloud," one of the most powerful chiefs of the Ottawa tribe. She had no book-lore, but many might be proud of her attainments. She spoke French easily, having learned it from her husband. All conversation in that day was as a rule held in French. Robert Stuart, a Scotchman, who was educated in Paris, used to say that her diction was as pure as that of a Parisian. She was a graceful and refined person, and remarkably entertaining. She always wore the full Indian costume, and there was at that time no better fur trader than she. She had both the love and respect of the Indians that her husband had before her. She, indeed, had no fear of the Indians, no matter what their condition; she was always able to control them.

Now to return to Josette La Framboise's marriage to Capt. Benjamin K. Pierce, commandant of Fort Mackinac (and brother of the President). This marriage took place at the home of a great friend of the young lady's. An officer's widow, in writing her husband's military life, speaks of his being ordered to the command of Captain Pierce, at Fort Mackinac, in 1816, and says that the captain there met a half-breed girl whom he addressed and married. This "half-breed girl" was a highly educated and cultivated woman. Her graceful demeanor was a charm. She was small in person, a clear brunette with black eyes and very black, wavy hair. She was both handsome and agreeable. What wonder was it, that a young man should be won by so winsome a maiden?

In May, 1817, Madame La Framboise arrived in Mackinac by bateau with her furs. She then hired a birch-bark canoe and Indian crew to take her to Montreal, where she went to place her boy in school. Her daughter was to be married that summer, but had to await her mother's return. As soon as the mother did return, the wedding took place. As Madame could not have time to open her house and make preparations at that late date, the home of Mrs. Mitchell, previously mentioned, was insisted upon, by her whole family, as being the place for the wedding. The friendship between the families was sincere, and in this home, famed for its handsome weddings, another was added to the list. To this wedding, none but the officers and families of the garrison, and only two families of the town, were invited. The mother and aunt (Madame Schindler) were present in full Indian costume.

After the marriage, the captain took his wife to the fort, and Madame La Framboise departed to resume her winter's work. Mrs. Pierce did not live long. She died in 1821, leaving two children. The son did not long survive his mother. Captain Pierce was ordered from Mackinac that winter. The following spring he came for his daughter, Harriet. From that date, Madame La Framboise closed her business with the American fur Company, and remained at home. She at this time left her old house and went into that which Captain Pierce had, with her means, built for her. Both houses are yet standing. I have stated that Madame La Framboise was a remarkable woman. When she was between forty and fifty years of age, she taught herself to read. It was no indifferent piece of work either, as she became able to read any French book she could obtain. She was a devoted Catholic, and worked for the church as long as she lived, greatly to the satisfaction of the poor, for whom she did much. It had been her practice to take girls, or any young woman who had no opportunity to receive instruction in church matters, and have them taught by persons whom she herself hired. In this way she began to teach herself. It was not long before she could instruct children in their catechism. It was through her, mainly, that the priest was supported. Among her gifts to the church at Mackinac was the lot on which the church now stands, and she and her daughter lie buried beneath that edifice.

The former home of Madame La Framboise was within a few rods of the home of her sister, Madame Schindler. The pleasures of that home for the few weeks she remained there, are vividly recalled; yet they were pleasures that one can hardly understand at the present time. The pleasures of past times cannot readily be made real in the minds of the younger generation. There being no children at Madame's home, and being fond of her sister's grandchild [the author], she begged that the little girl might stay with her while at Mackinac, to which they all agreed. But as she was an only and a spoiled child, it turned out that she had more than one home during that summer. The child was a precocious one, and afforded much amusement to her great-aunt. Old Angelique petted the little one greatly, and yet essayed to teach her some of the kinds of work in which she was proficient. Among the lessons imparted was that of waxing and polishing furniture. No one could tell who was the prouder, teacher or pupil. Angelique lived to see and play with the children of this petted and only child. She was an excellent house-keeper; she died at the residence of her son, Francois Lacroix, who had married and moved to Cross Village, where his descendants now live. When he became of age, Madame Schindler gave him his freedom. His younger brother, Louizon, married, and with his family left Mackinac in a schooner in 1834, to go to Grand River. The vessel was wrecked on the way and all on board were lost. Angelique's daughter, Natishe, lived to be an old woman. She was the nurse of the spoiled child.

Madame La Framboise lived in her new home for several years. It was there that I and my children were made happy in after years. To visit at that home, also, came Madame's grand-daughter, Miss Harriet Pierce, who after-wards married an army officer. She, too, died young. Her daughter, who is still living, is the wife of an officer in the army. The son, who was placed at school at Montreal, came home in due time and became a fur trader, married out in the Western country, and died there about 1854, leaving a large fam-ily. Madame La Framboise died April 4, 1846, aged 66 years.

HOW A MENOMINI WOMAN EARNS MONEY
(1920-1921)
Maskwawanahkwatok

"RED CLOUD WOMAN," or Louise Dutchman, was an informant for the ethnologist Leonard Bloomfield during his work among the Menominee in Wisconsin. She was also his adopted mother and language teacher, and he lived her and her husband Charles at their home in the traditionals' village of Zoar for many weeks. When Bloomfield collected narratives from the Menominee they had long been settled on their reservation, which was established in 1854, but Maskwawanahkwatok had obviously thought about her options if she could no longer farm.

HOW A MENOMINI WOMAN EARNS MONEY.
(mʌskwawā'nahkwʌtōk)

ni'nah kī'spin kʌn mō'nahaman, pʌs nitō'sihtunan anā'hkyʌnan misik tatā'ʔtakuku'ʌtsikan; misik mē'kehsē'hseh pas nitō'sihaw; misi'k nayī'wapit pas nikiw-awēh-kisē'ʔnitsikäm, sū'nien as a-kʌtäw-wī'hkihtawan. anā'hkiʌnan mā'wa niw pas niki-tepāhā'käm. misi'k kā'hkupinā'kanan pas nitō'sihtunan. meʔsi'h kēs-kē'sihtawan, mā'wa niw pas nitä'pahakäm. ini'ʔ pas wä'htinaman meʔsi'h sū'nyen. mē'kehsē'hseh pas nitä'pahakäm; tatā'ʔtakuku'ʌtsikan pas nitä'pahakäm. ahpä'n niw meʔsih sū'nyen pas nitä'htanan. anō'hkanak ahpä'n niw pas nnä'winem s a-tipā'hākä'yan. ini'ʔ pas ä'siʔta'yan ni'nah, kʌn mō'nahaman. ini'ʔ ninah kiw-isē'ʔtayan.

If I were not farming, I should make mats and quilts and beadwork, and I should go to Neopit to do washing, so as to earn money. I should sell all the mats. Baskets too I should make. When I had made a great quantity, I should sell them all. From this I should obtain much money. I should sell beadwork; I should sell patchwork quilts. I should always have a great deal of money. I should always gather raspberries and sell them. That is what I should do, if I did not farm. That is the way I do.

J. Kitty Schaefer, cook of the Lyman M. Davis, c. 1922

THE FICKLE FORTUNES OF FEMALE COOKS

The fates of cooks in the lakes' merchant marine can often be read in the columns of the maritime newspapers published in port cities. The following clippings from *The Daily Inter Ocean* of Chicago, a business newspaper giving coverage of maritime affairs, are a small, but representative sample of hundreds of news articles in the nineteenth and early twentieth centuries, and reflect the varying attitudes toward women on shipboard. During some years it was a status symbol to have a woman cook and captains competed furiously for the best ones. At other times, particularly in the American fleet in the twentieth century, no women were allowed on board. In the nineteenth century, many cooks were related to crew members, often the wives of captains or mates, but many others were women who just needed a job. How they fared was often a matter of luck, and as these news clips suggest, sexual harassment and manipulation in the media flowed both ways.

⋅⇒●⊕●⇐⋅

AN OUTRAGE ON SHIPBOARD
October 15, 1875

U.S. Revenue Steamer *Fessenden*
Port Huron, October 15, 1875

THE UNITED STATES Revenue Cutter *Fessenden*, while proceeding up the St. Clair River on the afternoon of the 12th ult., was attracted by the cries of distress on board the schooner *Harvest Home* of Cleveland, and in tow with the tug *Quayle*. The *Fessenden* ran alongside of the *Harvest Home* to ascertain the trouble, and found the master, James Green, beastly intoxicated, and that he had brutally beaten the cook, a poor defenseless woman named Jennie Simmons, dragging her over the deck by the hair of her head and kicking her until she was a mass of bruises. She had appealed in vain to the mates of the schooner to protect her. Either through cowardice or policy they laughed at her. The woman was taken on board the *Fessenden* and kindly cared for and furnished means to proceed to her home in Cleveland.

Looking to the interests of the owners of the schooner, and not wishing to detain her in order to hand the offender over to the civil authorities, the commander of the *Fessenden* permitted the *Harvest Home* to proceed to her destination.

SAVED BY A FEMALE COOK

July 8, 1878

(From the Oswego Palladium, *July 5)*

The steamer *Hastings* arrived here about 9 a.m. yesterday with an excursion, most of the party remaining to see the celebration. She left at 10 a.m. with another party of between 300 and 400 people, a large number of whom were from Syracuse, bound for Kingston, and was due here on the return at 9 p.m. She did not arrive then, however, nor til 7 a.m. today—and she perhaps never would have arrived at all except for the favorable circumstance of clear and calm weather, and the fact that there happened to be a woman there who knew more about navigation than anybody else on board. The *Hastings* left Kingston about 5 p.m. When about 15 miles from Oswego, she sighted the light of the N[orthwest] T[ransportation] propeller *City of Toledo*, bound for Kingston, which left here at 8 p.m. Taking it to be the Oswego light, she followed it back to the Ducks, or thereabouts, and at daylight found herself somewhere in the vicinity of Mexico Bay, whereupon she put about, and reached here at 7 a.m. From all obtainable accounts, there was no one aboard competent to navigate the steamer, and she was finally taken in charge by a woman, who ascertained her situation and was practically in command.

Martha Hart, an Oswego woman, who has sailed the lakes as a cook at various periods for the past ten or twelve years, happened to be aboard. Following is her statement to a *Palladium* reporter:

"We left Kingston at 5:30 p.m.; between 11 and 12 p.m. they spied the light of an N. T. boat and followed her down the lake until they got below the Galloup Islands and about four miles from shore; there they let her lay to the mercy of the waves, had there been any, and if there was any all would have been lost; we stayed here till the morning star made its appearance; the wheelsman point her for it; there was no captain, mate, nor sailor to be seen all night; he run her for the morning star, running wild until we saw land at Nine Mile Point, about half-past five; the wheelsman run her; no captain nor mate giving any orders; we reached the dock about half-past seven; at 2:30 a.m. I told them they were near Sackett's Harbor, below the Galloup, and told them to point south, and pointed out the direction to Oswego; I made use of marine glasses which I had borrowed, the boat's glasses not being good for anything; I told the passengers if they set the table to go for it; but they didn't set any table; we didn't have a bite to eat and couldn't buy it; neither could we even get a bunk to sleep in; the passengers were very much excited and alarmed, and anxious to get home."

The statement that no one appeared to be competent to navigate the steamer is corroborated by other passengers. This woman further says that there was no chart aboard. Before, or soon after they started to follow the N. T. boat, she saw the Oswego light and pointed it out, but the wheelsman thought he knew better and refused to steer for it. She also relates that when she became satisfied that they were getting dangerously near land, she went down and told the engineer that they would soon be ashore and that he then stopped the engine after which they floated around indiscriminately. . . .

⤙⥱◉⥱⤚

MYSTERY OF THE BISSELL

The Death of the Young and Beautiful Stewardess of the Vessel on Lake Michigan
May 26, 1882

THE FOLLOWING LETTER is from a prominent gentleman at Sturgeon Bay, where the schooner *Harvey Bissell* landed the corpse of the female cook who came to her death from a pistol wound on board that vessel while outside on Lake Michigan on the passage from Chicago to Escanaba, and where the remains were buried. In justice to Captain Brock, who is known as a straight-forward gentleman, it may be repeated here that the Coroner's jury declared the case to be one of suicide, but assigned no cause.

Green Bay, Wis., May 22—Sir: Observing a number of articles in your paper referring to the suicide of Mrs. Mary Gorman, of the schooner *Harvey Bissell*, I am moved to contribute another myself, believing that the feeling of many private individuals in regard to that matter should be made public as thereby the cause of justice may be served. It is the feeling here among many that the inquest was not conducted with due care by those who had it in charge, and who, of course, now feel a reluctance in acknowledging that they were at all remiss in duty, and are bound in asserting that their somewhat hasty verdict positively settled that it was a case of suicide. The very superficial investigation made by the Justice of the Peace and his assistants, who viewed the body as it lay in the captain's room on the schooner, taken in connection with certain facts known to those who saw the body after it was brought to the town to be prepared for burial, must make it apparent to any fair-minded person that the matter was *not properly investigated*. The following facts will explain the occasion of these remarks:

The men who conducted the inquest had with them a physician who, in probing the wound to find the ball, did not succeed in reaching the ball, but (if report may be believed), announced that it had taken a direction downward, and from the left side toward the right, making it apparent that if Mrs. Gowan fired the revolver herself, she was a left-handed person.

Still it does not appear that any inquiry was made to ascertain whether she really was left-handed. The many who saw the wound assert that it would have been impossible for her to have fired the revolver herself with either hand, for the reason that the ball entered so high in the chest that, if held by either of her hands, it must have taken an upward directions instead of doing downward.

The condition of the rings which were on Mrs. Gowan's hand would seem to indicate that there may have been some rough handling of her before her death, for one was broken completely in two and the other was so badly bent in against the finger that it was difficult to remove it, and it is not to be supposed that she wore it right along in that condition for it must have occasioned pain to the finger.

If two suitable physicians could be appointed to have the body disinterred, and to ascertain beyond a doubt the direction and whereabouts of the ball, it would settle the question of the possibility of her having fired the revolver herself, and would save the officers of the *Harvey Bissell* from disagreeable remarks and imputations, and if Captain Brock is the upright gentleman he is believed to be no doubt he will be as anxious as any one that the matter should be set at rest.

No one here has heard from Mrs. Gowan's relatives (if she has any), but a person living in Cleveland, Ohio, a Mrs. Carrie Smallwood, 302 Viaduct Street, has written, claiming an acquaintance with Mrs. G. of one year, and giving no clew to any other acquaintance or relative except a child of 7 or eight years, who is in an industrial school on Detroit Street, in Cleveland, and belongs to Mrs. G's first husband, who died. Mrs. Smallwood mentioned having received a communication from Captain Brock, previous to the letter of inquiry sent from here. She says also that Mrs. G. was devoted to her second husband, who, nevertheless, had taken a dislike to her little boy, to whom she was much attached, and from whom she did not wish to part; and further, that Mrs. G. has instituted proceedings for a divorce from her husband, on the ground of infidelity.

Justice Sherman has tried to communicate with William Gowan, or Gowman, but has failed to hear from him. The Justice has also received a letter from Mrs. Smallwood's husband, requesting to have Mrs. G.'s effects forwarded for him, to receive in trust for the child. It does not appear what right he has to undertake such a trust.

I would remark that Mrs. Gowan, or Gowman, was a fine-looking woman, apparently about 25 years of age; and in closing would inquire: Is it, or is it not, customary in such cases as this to have more than one physician to conduct the examination of injuries?

⊷⊜⊷

THE FESTIVE FEMALE COOK
Another Good Man Gone Wrong
July 25, 1882

KENOSHA, WIS., JULY 24—It appears that the female cook on the fast sailing packet *Maria* kicked the dust off the heels of her boots on the first day of last week, and took the cars for the great city at the foot of the hill. The scarlet gown and the sunflower hat that she left in the cabin of the vessel was merely dust for the master's eyes, untruthfully indicating suicide, or return of the truant to the post of duty. As the sun, day after day, chased away the shadows of the preceding night, the master kept watch and ward for the returning footsteps of the fair deserter. On the third day after the occurrence of that untoward event the master sought repose, and during a brief period went into dream-land on the pool table at the bridge saloon. While occupying that position he voiced several songs, and the chorus of each song went tremblingly along the air as follows:

> "To north, to south, to west, or to the east,
> Whichever way mine weary eyes may look,
> O, may they never, never cease to feast
> Upon a whisky shop and female cook."

The words of the song your correspondent threw into the artesian well, and when the same come to the surface they will be fitted to the tune known as "Captain Jinks, of the Horse Marines."

The combined influences of song and strong drink failed to tranquilize the master's mind, and he procured a six-shooter at the hardware store of M. C. Dewey and took the fast express train for Chicago. He went forth, indeed, with a heroic determination to conquer fate or die.

The prolonged absence of the master brought at last disorder to the minds of the crew, and two of the number were deputed to proceed to Chicago with the hope of finding the living form of the captain on the avenues of travel, or, alas! his inanimate remains at the public morgue in that city. The search proving fruitless of event, the owners of the *Maria* came to Kenosha and placed the mate in charge of the vessel. The late female cook of that vessel continues to occupy the position of a distant moon, and the ex-master of the same vessel is preparing to lecture against prohibitory legislation.

⊷⊨⊜⊯⊷

April, 1883

From the letter of the wife of a captain:

" . . . Several years ago you brought happiness to many homes along the lakes by driving female cooks off the lakes. Now I want to post you. Captains are sneaking in these women again. They destroy all discipline on shipboard, and the assertion by captains to owners that they are cheaper than men cooks and save money to the vessel, is all false. Then, in a storm, men cooks can take hold and help, while a woman is only in the way, or worse, for she often unnerves the crew by her alarm. Besides all this the mate wants to love the woman cook as well as the captain does, and there is often trouble between these two commanding officers. A great grain fleet is about leaving Chicago for below, and I want you to drive the women off these vessels. My husband's schooner is among the rest."

⊷⊨⊜⊯⊷

"MARY ANN! MARY ANN! I'LL TELL YOUR MA!"
The Great Question of Female Cooks on the Grain Fleet
April 30, 1883

ON INQUIRY AROUND shipping agents and others, it is learned that there has been very little demand from the grain vessels this spring for men cooks. Almost every vessel wanted a female cook, and this great demand cornered the supply to such an extent that the only way girls enough to go around could be obtained was by advertising. Old ladies were not in demand at all, and country girls were preferred over those from the city. It is learned to a certainty that of the grain fleet now about to sail, fifty have female cooks and many others are to have them. The day after the fleet sails, *The Inter Ocean* will publish an accurate list of the craft whose cabins are graced by calico cooks. Meanwhile space will be given in these columns to all communications on the subject. By the way, some additional letters have already come to hand:

Threats, Low and Deep

April 28—You better have your marine reporter shut up on his female cook nonsense. It is a slander. If you don't, you won't have any marine reporter. I swear by all that's good and great that if he prints me, I'll kill him. Yours, in dead earnest, VESSEL CAPTAIN.

P. S.—You have no right to print the private affairs of any one. Because my wife (I am divorced from her), writes to your paper it is no reason you should print it. To tell the truth, she is crazy. There is insanity in her family for a fact. Her mother died in insane.

The Girls in Danger

April 29—As a woman, interested in the general welfare of women, I studied up the subject of female cooks on lake vessels several years ago when *The Inter Ocean* agitated the subject, and I, with a majority of the ladies of our society, concluded that a single female out at sea, with only men for companions, was in the greatest possible danger, no matter how strong her ideas of right might be. And instances of the forced debauchery of a female cook on a sailing vessel are not wanting. Certainly *The Inter Ocean* has exposed a sufficient number of such cases in the last five years to indicate to the girls themselves and to their families the danger they are in. If a captain sees fit to employ force what is to prevent him? Of course, there are lots of captains who are honorable, virtuous men, but it is of the scoundrels that I write, and there are lots of them, too. The undeniable fact is that no young girl should accept such a berth as a cook on a sailing vessel. Mrs. B.

Respectable, Yes

April 29—Do I understand you to intimate that women who ship on lake vessels as cooks are not respectable? Captain.

Full Faith but Watchful

April 28—I hope you will show up the female cook business thoroughly. It cannot fail to do good. I have full faith in my husband, but I propose to be on board until the tug lets go of her. If the wives would be a little watchful, they might drive these women off the fleets themselves.

An Argument for Women

April 28—I am not an interested party, but I can tell you that female cooks are a great saving to a vessel. The women can cook better and do the work better, and they are not wasteful like men. Isn't a woman cook and waiter much better anywhere than a man? I'll leave it to yourself. How would you like to have a greasy, dirty man to do your cooking and wait on your table?

⊷═◦═⊷

But Here's Richness

A LADY CAME into *The Inter Ocean* office yesterday afternoon and, asking for the marine reporter, explained to him that she resided in Cleveland; that her husband sailed, and that his vessel was now grain loaded and ready to leave Chicago for below; that she had reason to believe that a young woman, who had already caused trouble in their family, was on board the vessel, and that she (the wife) proposed to expose the whole matter. She gave her husband's name, the name of the vessel, and the name of the woman on board, and asked that all be published. The reporter told her that for a few days this could not be done, but that her wishes would be complied with if her husband did not send the woman ashore and mend his ways. Leaving two letters with the reporter, the lady withdrew, saying that during the night she and her father and a policeman would give "a surprise party" on the schooner.

The two letters left by the lady, as among the evidence of her husband's perfidy, are given below. They were found in the pockets of a coat that the Captain forgot when he was leaving Cleveland for Chicago. The letter from the Captain was sealed and stamped, and was not mailed, for the reason in all probability that he got the letter from the woman on the same day he wrote his:

The Captain to "Mary Ann"

My own Mary Ann: you have not written for some time. It is more than three weeks—three long weeks—since one of your bright, welcome letters came to hand. You are cruel, darling. I hope nothing has occurred. Are you well? I don't know what to think of your silence just at this time when I had hoped that we would so soon be reunited. In my last I sent a ticket and asked you to meet me here and we would proceed to Chicago together. The vessel is there and she will be chartered this week and I am ordered there. Darling, I hope your love for me has not grown cold. I wouldn't give you up for anything in life. Without you life would indeed be dreary. Darling be sure and come on the first train. Oh, I want to see you so bad. Never have a doubt about me. I am yours till death. You shan't do a thing on the ship but be a lady. You were born to be a queen. Be sure you come. I want to see you here and make arrangements.

"Mary Ann" to The Captain

Dearest R.—I will meet you in Chicago. I will be there by April 15. I am a little afraid that if I come to Cleveland your royal wife will suspect something. I long to be near you. Since you were here I have not been out anywhere. I have been awful lonesome. Good-by. Your own Mary Ann.

A SENSATION IN MARINE CIRCLES
May 1, 1883

FEMALE COOKS FORMED the absorbing topic of conversation in marine circles yesterday. The "Mary Ann" case proved a perfect bombshell. A number of the masters soon learned who the captain concerned was, and the matter created a great sensation. In the offices of vessel and insurance agents, on 'Change, at the tug offices, at the ship chandleries, and on Central Wharf, at the lumber market, every one was discussing female cooks and poking fun at the Cleveland man—who, however, was not to be seen in any of these haunts. Some of the captains got very hot over the matter. They darned the eyes of "that reporter of *The Inter Ocean*" in his absence, and then wanted to buy him cigars when they met him.

The Cleveland man's love letter was generally admired, and a number of the masters who were sending away marked papers said they wanted the papers solely on account of that letter; that is was the finest thing they had ever seen in English literature; that they might want to put it into their own hand-writing at some future time, etc. It is suspected that some of these masters expect, by sending marked papers to their wives, and joining in the fun at some one else's expense, to throw suspicion away from themselves.

The Reporter Surprised

During the afternoon the reporter foolishly ventured into a shipping office were several female cooks were sitting waiting for berths. The agent was mad at him and told the women who he was, and a war of words was immediately begun on him. He pleaded all sorts of excuses, but the women would not hear him and he finally beat a hasty retreat. One of the gentle beings said in all earnestness that "the calico cooks proposed to hold a mass meeting, and that *The Inter Ocean* office would be mobbed." It seems that the demand for female cooks was not good yesterday, and that several who had been engaged had been replaced by men.

The "Surprise Party"

The "surprise party" announced by the wife of the Cleveland captain, to take place on his schooner in the harbor Sunday night, "came off in fine style." The attendance was "small but very select," and the captain and Mary Ann "did all the dancing," while the enraged wife and her father "made the music." Three policemen and two other captains, invited by the wife, played wallflowers. In a word, the wife's worst fears were verified. It was midnight when the unwelcome guests boarded the schooner, and Mary Ann was found in an apartment she should not have been in. "When the cruel war was over," Mary Ann, bag and baggage, went ashore with the policeman, and later, at her own option, took a train for her home in Lorain, Ohio. The wife and her father left the vessel at the same time and returned to their hotel. The lady was asked last evening what course she now intended to pursue. She said her father wanted her to break up housekeeping, and bring her two children to the paternal roof, but that, as yet, she had not fully made up her mind. She had changed her mind about exposing the matter, however, and begged that all the names be suppressed.

Mary Ann's real name is Margaret Ann Dudly. She is single and her parents are reputable, well-to-do people in Lorain, Ohio. She is 22 years of age and is described as "a beautiful blonde, with a wealth of curling hair and large, fine eyes."

Calico Cooks Scattering
May 2, 1883

Numerous letters and telegrams were received in Chicago yesterday from the owners of vessels about to leave, instructing the captains to employ men cooks. . . . As a result there was a great scattering of the calico cooks and a corresponding demand for men cooks. Three vessels that are known of could not get men cooks up to last night, and rather than sail with the female on board, they remained in port until to-day.

To the Editor of The Inter Ocean:
May 4, 1883

I see that you are waging war on the female vessel cooks, and as one of them, and a subscriber to *The Inter Ocean*, I want to say a word in their defense. I have been cooking for three seasons for one party, and in all that time received no surprise parties, and, moreover, conducted myself, and should continue to, in such a manner as to have no fears of them. Please allow me to state that there are just as honorable women cooking on vessels as in any other calling, and I don't think it is right for you to single them out. I believe, however, that all this hue and cry is made by "incompetent" men cooks, jealous sweethearts, and over-zealous wives, who perhaps may need as much looking after as the women whom they see fit to censure and condemn. I will say in conclusion, that all that will prevent my going on the water this season will be my failing to get a situation.

Yours most humbly,
"Calico Cook"

FROM NOT BY BREAD ALONE
(1941)
Mary Francis Doner

MARY FRANCIS DONER (1893-1985), the daughter of a lakes captain, grew up in a port town and devoted much of her professional life to writing about the men and women in the merchant marine. During her long career she wrote twenty-nine novels and nearly 300 hundred short stories. Many of the latter were sentimental romances published in pulp fiction magazines, although her better work appeared in the *Toronto Daily Star* and women's magazines. Her novels set on the Great Lakes are her finest work though, because when Doner describes the pain of families left for the season she writes from personal experience. Her vision of those who ship out to earn a living is free from men's needs to prove themselves in command—as captains' autobiographies always do—and so she could create, in *Glass Mountain* (1942), one the least romanticized portraits of what it means to command a ship in the literature of the lakes.

In *Not By Bread Alone* (1941), from which a chapter follows, Doner traces the lives of three generations of women who marry for love, rather than common sense, and find themselves responsible for the men they married. The first is a cook on a lakes freighter, and in delineating the portrait of Maggie Killean and her kind but hapless husband Joe, Doner creates for readers the life of a woman cook on a bulk carrier at the turn of the century. She does not pity her character; neither does she judge. But in the small details—Maggie's work-roughened hands, her worn winter coat, her sorrow about her children left on shore with their grandmother—Doner details of the conflicts of women who must sail for a living because there is no better job they can find. This is the best record of women who, like Maggie Killean, gave up, and still give up, their lives ashore to sail.

⊷⊶⊙⊜⊷⊶

Chapter Three

Asleep, Maggie?
"She's rollin', ain't she?" The muffled voice assumed drowsiness.
"A bit of a gale," Joe said. "Lucky you don't get seasick."
"Um-hm. What time is it?"
"Near three."
"Only three?"

"Maggie, you're gettin' off at St. Gabriel. I got it figured out. Me and Benny can run it. We'll be takin' on an extra porter below, anyway, on account of the passengers."

"What's there to get off for?" Not anger in that tone, but terror masked as anger. And who would bake the bread, Joe? And the pies? Who'd know when the meat was done, the gravy thick enough? Are you asking for them to find out you don't know any more about cooking than the lad Benny, who can't fry an egg without breaking it? "I ain't crossin' the bridge till I come to it."

"They're sick, Maggie. Your ma was afraid to write."

She was glad the darkness hid his eyes, for she could feel the anguish there, the fear and humiliation, the pity and the love. But for him, he knew, she would be home with her children where she belonged.

"Most likely we'll get a letter at the Soo," she said. "Go to sleep, Joe. The days are long enough."

"This ain't no place for a woman," he groaned. "Not a woman, anyway, with two young ones at home. We've got to figure it out some other way, Maggie. It ain't fair to you. I'll find something on shore to do."

"What could you find to do—like this?" she demanded. "Ain't no opportunities in St. Gabriel for a man with—with ability. This job was made for you. Who could run a kitchen like you do, Joe? And order and pick out meat? Captain Graham says since he sailed this is the best grub. And you feed them cheap, too, Joe. Look what you've pared it down to for a meal!"

"Did he say that, Maggie? Did the old man say that to you?"

"Course! When he went into the refrigerator the other day he said it smelled sweet for a ship's cold box. And he's a man of few words. You know that yourself."

"Yeah." Joe's voice was warm with pride.

Soon then she heard him breathing easily, steadily. Asleep. Her eyes followed the rocking stars through the porthole. Her wide, frightened eyes. Typhoid fever. . . . Someone she'd known once had died of it in St. Gabriel. Charlie Mains. Handsome Charlie, they'd called him. And at the end it hadn't been Charlie but a strange, shriveled creature. A rigid hand against her lips stifled the cry that came mounting, mounting as if to rend the tiny cabin from end to end.

Above the slap of the waves, along the crest of the wind, voices: "Hello, Mama! Hello, Papa! I'm a good girl, Mama. I like my new shoes. Grandma lets me wear my roller skates on Saturday."

Kate. Cora. A golden head hot and wet against a white pillow. Dark hair framing a pale sick face in the night.

If you only knew the truth. If there were only some way. . . .

I'll get off at Port Huron. I'll get a rig to take me down to St. Gabriel. Just for a few days. I can go on then. Just one day, one minute even. Maybe Joe and Benny could make out alone. Simple food. I'd figure it out beforehand. I'd—Maggie, you fool! If it were only as easy as that! If you go Joe goes. Could he stay a minute but for you? Face it. You're like an actress, Maggie Killean, praising Joe up to the captain and passing the captain's praise along to Joe, words that you put in his mouth. There's one you're not fooling. It's Benny. He's got an eye in his head and he knows enough to keep his mouth shut. You can be thankful for that.

But maybe Joe's right. Maybe there's a job back home he could get now. People look up to Joe since he's on the *Tinkham*. His step is different. His ways. Proud-like and sure. Like a flower that's opened all of a sudden—a fine, strong flower that never seemed to bloom before. Want to take it away from him so soon? Want to see that old haunted look in his eyes again and feel his silent pain going through you like a knife? You've given him something and you can't be taking it away, Maggie. No matter what it costs you. The Lord picked you out to lead Joe Killean down the road, and lead him you must if it takes the last drops of blood in your veins. But in the leading, Maggie, go slow and easylike, so he won't suspect it's him and not you that's doing the following. That's your job too. . . .

Wash of waves against that steel wall just beyond. Wash and slap of waves, jerk of ship in the wind and the starry dome above Lake Superior dipping and rocking there in the ever-changing disk of porthole. Creak of bunk and dip of curtain with the rhythm of the roll as the ship plunged down, righted itself and climbed back up to the crest of another wave. Home. . . .

You're not the only woman that's had to face a thing like this, Maggie Killean. Ain't what you've had been worth it? The love and the laughter and kisses, the bearing of his children—days and nights together with a rightness and a glory of living, a feeling of touching the stars sometimes and burning your fingers on happiness that leaves no scars? What's there to compare with the comfort this minute of knowing he's there within reach of your hand; yours before God, clean and loving and complete, with no thought in his head of another woman or the things men often hanker for? No thought in his head but for you; to be near you, to love you and watch over you like a dove in the nest. Ain't you expecting pain, Maggie, to pay for it? For the children he's given you, the faithfulness and the song that's in your heart from the dawn of the day till night comes and through it in your sleep, music so soft you don't know it's there, almost. You have to stop and listen to hear it, because it's become part of you. It's in the beat of your heart, in the bend of your finger, in the steps you take and the words you say. And he's made the music there, Maggie. Is it that you're questioning God about the payment, now and then, when the paying time is at hand?

His breath came evenly, the steady, deep breathing of the tired man. Sleep then, Joe. God rest you. I'll be figuring it out, somehow. A bit of praying won't do no harm. And if the Almighty don't listen this time, then it's the first He's turned a deaf ear. I won't ask favors. I'll say, "Thy will be done." I'll just ask if He'll be letting me keep going through the days like as if I wasn't afraid or worrying and thinking, but contented and glad enough here with you, and I'll turn the two of them over to Him and know He'll be dealing fair with me. . . .

Dawn streaked the dipping disk of porthole with gray, and the glow of a rose-gold sun spread across the rolling waters in a fantastically beautiful panorama. It's easier when the darkness goes. . . .

She slipped quietly out of the bunk, dressed, found the old box of writing paper and laboriously began to write. Hugh Burke was getting off at the Soo. He'd take a letter back with him to St. Gabriel. She'd make it sound brave and sure, as if she wasn't worried. If things got serious she would go, somehow. She would fly. But God would not forget her. There was a job to do. Not for her alone, but for them all. . . .

At eleven o'clock that night Hugh Burke went over the side of the *Tinkham* at the Soo locks. He slipped her letter in his breast pocket.

"Don't fret, Hugh." Her hand was strong and firm in his. "Just pray. While there's life there's hope. Maybe when she sees you Nettie will perk up. Maybe she's lonesome too," she reminded him.

He said, "I'll look in on your ma and the kids, Mis' Killean. I'll give her your letter."

She smiled and nodded because she could not trust her voice again. You will see them. You will know. . . .

Hugh waved an unsteady hand in farewell.

"Don't you worry, Hugh." Joe tried to comfort him. "Like as not we'll see the *Westcott* pullin' out in the river to put you back aboard at Detroit."

Maggie shivered, drew the worn blue sweater close about her shoulders. The night seemed dark and strange. She went inside quickly. There had been no letter for her from St. Gabriel in the mailbag put aboard at the Soo.

No singing on deck that next evening. The leaden hours dragged by. Midnight found her there against the rail as the *Tinkham* passed the lighthouse at Port Huron and slipped once more into the eddies and currents of the St. Clair River. One more hour downstream! All the familiar spots swept by. Stag Island. Marysville. The broad river road with its lovely homes clustered on the sloping greenness that swept down to the water's edge. Yankee Street stretching back through the country toward winding Pine River. The old Somerville Hotel with the beach cottages nestling down close to the water, the bend—and then St. Gabriel.

Did she imagine it, or were there more lights than usual in the grouped houses there on the hill? Her eyes strained to catch, fatuously, a sight of a house back some blocks from the river, hidden so well by trees. Were there lights in those windows? Kate, can you hear me, pet? Kate, honey—is this terror for nothing? Cora—not you, either; sturdy little Cora. There's health in your fat legs and strong arms—and your lungs, Cora. You could scream with the best of them.

The street lights out along Front Street. There—that was the waterworks now. Whose fault was it, she flamed, that the pipe burst? Whose carelessness? The park now—the salt block. . . . The *Tinkham* swung toward midstream, and St. Gabriel was a shadow in the distance.

She stood looking back, as if she would tear the night apart with her two hands to find a sign from home, assurance, hope.

"You'd better get some sleep, Maggie." Joe put an arm around her shoulders.

"Um-hm." She laid her tired head for a moment against his heart. "You're always lookin' after me, ain't you?"

"Come along," he said tenderly. "Come along, Maggie."

She felt the damp spots on his shirt. Tears were for the darkness. . . .

Long before they passed Belle Isle at five o'clock the next morning Maggie had been about her day's duties. Maybe there'd be a letter at Detroit. The busy Detroit River teemed with traffic, with passenger ferries and car ferries lacing back and forth between Detroit and Windsor, with freighters passing up and down and small river craft bobbing about.

As they neared Detroit's Third Street and the mail boat came nosing toward them, Maggie could contain herself no longer "Here, Benny! I'll watch those fried potatoes. Run up to the captain with the watchman as he delivers the mailbag and tell him I'm expectin' a letter—an important letter. And bring it back with you right away, remember!"

Benny took one look at the wild, hungry eyes and fled up the deck.

She moved swiftly, mechanically, pouring coffee, dishing up fried potatoes and eggs, an automaton in calico.

He came at last with the letter. And for the first and only time in her three years of sailing she dropped a plate of food on the floor. As she went into their tiny cabin and closed the door she was not even aware of Joe's sick eyes following her.

Benny had already begun to scrub the pantry when she returned. Joe sat at the table in the officers' dining room with lists spread out before him. Stores were replenished at the lower ports, and with passengers expected at Cleveland, the task was doubly difficult. He got to his feet as she appeared, white-faced, in the doorway.

"What's the news?"

"Kate's got it."

"Bad?"

"Maybe."

"And—Cora?"

"Not so bad."

"You goin' home, Maggie?"

"There's work here."

"You're goin' home," he said sternly.

Her eyes had a faraway look. "They'll be all right, Joe. We ain't goin' to worry. Doctor Carlson's lookin' after 'em fine. He ain't scared—yet."

"I can't let you stay, Maggie."

"Are you forgettin' that Ma nursed her own family through every kind of sickness under the sun? And she ain't lost the trick of it. I'll bet on Ma any time. . . ."

"But, Maggie—"

"Better take a minute now, hadn't we, to check over those lists for Hausheer? His grocer will be comin' out in a boat to meet us when we hit the break wall at Cleveland, lookin' for the order." She was talking quickly, as one, unsure, gives lines from memory. "I wouldn't take his job for a lot—ridin' around that smelly old Cuyahoga River. Maybe that's why he practically comes out into the lake to meet us, eh, Joe? He wants to get some fresh air." She groped for a chair, pulled the lists toward her and examined them carefully. But her blurred eyes saw nothing.

"Maybe," Joe said. "Maybe that's it. . . ."

July. Only yet July. . . . Could she face it again? Slowly, beginning with the small finger of her right hand, she began to press secretly against her knee. July. August. September. . . .

September and the equinoctial storms, when the thought of Saginaw Bay could even now make you feel the terrible pitch and plunge of the ship. October, November, December—when Lake Huron forgot its summer friendliness and became a frenzied demon under the wild lashings of the gale; when Lake Superior's waves swept to mountainous heights, and sometimes you held your breath, wondering if the ship would ever right itself and go on; when Lake Michigan fought to get the *Tinkham* in its trough and battered away mercilessly at cabin and hull.

Five long months between her and reunion with Kate and Cora, even if things went all right. If. . . .

Her hand clenched on the table, unclenched slowly. She picked up the pencil.

"I don't see rice here," she said, "and we're all out." Steadily, laboriously, she wrote the word.

IN GRANDPA'S WAKE

(1953)

Ester Rice Battenfeld

ATTORNEYS WITH AN INTEREST in admiralty law seldom spend time as porters (maids) on lakes vessels, even if sailing is a family occupation as it was for Ester Rice Battenfeld (1915-1970). Nor do cooks or porters, whatever their family history, often write about their experiences in the galley. Therefore, Battenfeld's short autobiography of her attempt to sail the lakes in her grandfather Frank Rice's footsteps is unique. When she "went sailing" in the 1940s there were few positions open to women and those were only in the galley. Although this has changed and women are now admitted to merchant marine academies, as yet there is only one women captain in the Canadian fleet and none in the American. Most women admitted to merchant marine training programs do not finish; worse, many of those who graduate leave the profession after a few years. Fortunately, the blatant sexism Battenfeld describes is beginning to disappear.

What she does in this short piece is what women autobiographers have done for centuries: use the form and content of autobiography—both of which were first determined by men—for her own purposes. Battenfeld wrote this essay for *Inland Seas*, a historical journal which was, and still is, devoted to Great Lakes shipping history. To make her piece palatable to her readers, she employs self-deprecating humor and describes her experiences as a lark. But lurking beneath her words is another story, a subtext, that most women will understand immediately: discrimination against women in the merchant marine was overwhelming, conditions were deplorable, and Battenfeld was lucky to escape them only because she had a profession to which she could return. Regular galley crews would be less fortunate. Underneath every joke she cracks is a grim reality she does little to disguise, knowing that male readers, having never experienced this sort of discrimination, would not comprehend. She uses a subtle technique to undermine the typical male description about life aboard ship and replace it with her own story, which is far less humorous than it first appears. In fact, she deliberately uses her charm and considerable wit to demolish the very patriarchy of the merchant marine she appears to reverence in her grandfather. What she learns, she tells us, is that sailing as a woman is quite different than sailing as a man. Since Battenfeld is obviously as intelligent and capable as her grandfather, perhaps moreso, the unstated question she insistently poses is why couldn't she have become a captain like he?

⊷══◉══⊷

I'VE DONE A LOT of crazy things in my life from my mother's point of view. Still, she wasn't prepared for my *sotto voce* announcement last spring that I was going to seek a job as porter on a Great Lakes freighter, carrying coal up to the head of the Lakes and hauling iron ore back down to the steel mills.

"Give up a perfectly good career to—to wash dishes in a galley, and—and everything like that?" She meant scrub bathrooms and their appurtenances.

"Yes."

"Just because when you were born your grandfather wired home from the Soo what your name should be is no reason you have to dedicate your life to the Great Lakes!"

In a way I was dedicated to the lakes. But it really wasn't going to be my fault if I were forced to run away from home to sail our midwestern inland seas. The blame would fall on grandpa, who at ninety eight drank his whiskey from a soup bowl and held title as the oldest retired master in the entire Great Lakes region from Sackett's harbor, New York, to Duluth, Minnesota. At times this must have amazed United States Steel, who, I imagine, hadn't counted on paying him a retirement pension for so many years.

Grandpa raised me on the lore of the lakes, spinning a net of wanderlust around my spirit until I was trapped by a mesh of nautichosis. I used to consider having my malady psychoanalyzed away, only I feared no substituted neurosis would prove half so exciting.

Back in grammar school, one of my teachers, who merely wanted me to learn to read the hands of the clock correctly instead of guessing, reached for her wig when I revealed to the class that fifteen degrees of longitude equals one hour of time. Arithmetic was never dull if I could side-track the pupils into listening to one of my lectures with blackboard illustrations on the secret of boxing a compass or how to lose a day in the Pacific or the Atlantic. I often got confused, but nobody in 2-B knew the difference.

Later I absorbed the rules of navigation from grandpa along with lessons on just-less-than-cheating checkers and cribbage. More years passed, and I joined a yacht club, religiously entering my small sailing craft every Sunday morning in the club races. Still later I was admitted to practice in federal court as a proctor in admiralty. But because I'd been born a granddaughter instead of a grandson I couldn't be a sailor. Then one day I discovered there was a chance—I mean, to be a sailor. A few freighters on the lakes carried women in their galleys!

Immediately I turned over my legal files to the law firm partners, and hurried to the Marine Hospital for a lung x-ray and Wassermann test so that the Coast Guard would certify to my eligibility as a food handler. Now, I thought, I was ready to sign on a crew's list the same as any old tar.

Among lake freighting circles it is well known that porters classify as itinerant labor. They are more or less picked up down in the local bowery, often work a few trips, maybe just one trip or a half-trip, then pay off or simply jump ship without their salary. So it goes all season. But my case required three interviews by appointment with the vessel personnel manager and another interview with the cook aboard the boat, which being without cargo was sitting high in the water. I wanted to believe that I was climbing right into heaven to reach the deck of my dream-boat, but I looked down at my soot-coated gloves and realized I was still in the flats alongside Cleveland's muddy Cuyahoga River.

For these interviews I didn't know whether to play the peasant with a babushka tied around my head or dress like officer material in a pressed navy blue suit and crisp white blouse, so I varied the motif from meeting to meeting. Unluckily for me, my Uncle Ed had to be the master of one of the company's boats—the only company hiring women. I learned that he had advised Mr. Vessel Personnel Manager I had been a teacher, a fashion model, even a defeated candidate for the state senate. To off-set this distorted impression of my portering potential, fast-talk became necessary on how I'd only taught a year and never suffered with mal de mer. From my haggard expression, Mr. V. P. Manager must have gained assurance that my fashion modeling days were over and there was not a chance I'd corrupt a single crew member, for finally (I'm sure only after a meeting of the "board") I was ordered to report to work Easter Monday at 7:00 A. M.

Due to boiler trouble, we remained alongside the dock for a whole week, but nothing mattered, since I'd be sailing soon. Every evening at 7:00 P. M., after having polished the chromiumed and stainless steel galley for the last time that day, I taxied home, sat in a nice, warm tub of water to ease muscular wear and tear, and called out to my mother through a crack in the bathroom door how wonderful it was to be a sailor. You could have all you wanted to eat and no responsibility. (I never mentioned—even to myself—that two porters already had quit that season during fit-out. One had broken her arm placing a new mattress on a top bunk!) Well, the bunks were all mattressed now; and all I had to do was watch out for flying knives! The cook, I'd observed, had the temperament of an artiste. When he began the ceremony of baking bread, a hush fell upon the galley. Nobody dared to speak, not even rattle a dish. I knew it counted as a crime for an officer to strike a man. That should even include with a frying pan. But it would do little good to seek punishment of the offender once my skull was split. I'd just have to remember what grandpa said about self-preservation being the first law of nature, and be on constant guard.

My nightly bath gave me courage; and I'd taxi back to Suicide Bend, crawl into my bunk with even my heels aching, and contemplate the cab company as the holder of most of my day's earnings. For some reason, though, I still wouldn't have changed places with the president of that cab company.

The night cook had the bottom bunk in the small cabin which we shared and which we couldn't both fit into at the same time unless one of us remained prostrate on her bunk (which position we dropped into with exhaustion most of our "off" hours anyway). So there was no problem there.

From the beginning, however, I felt the curiosity of the three other women on board. Somebody had found out and broadcast that my Uncle Ed was my Uncle Ed. Besides, I took at least one shower a day and my uniforms were always clean, although I couldn't take them home but had to wash and iron them myself when we were on the run. Those other three women, being old at the game, probably were laying bets on how long I could keep this up. When my hands, down in the sink regions, turned to raw beef, looks were exchanged. When my hands healed and I stayed on, I was aware of my colleagues' surprise. I even stayed on after the cook threw a box of soap chips at me with such force that it hit my chest and bounced up to split my lip. I really had only myself to blame, for I had barged into the galley in the middle of the bread-making ceremony (Russian rye and raisin) to ask for those soap chips. The life agreed with me. I wrote to grandpa every night and each week when we got down to Cleveland to unload our ore, I'd have time to run home for an hour or so if I weren't on duty. Regardless of how they complained, my family was pleased with the new glow of health and the hippage I was acquiring.

I was seeing my Great Lakes as a sailor—just like grandpa had, if I discounted the fact that I was some 600 feet aft of the pilot house. Sometimes, while gooey in the galley constructing elaborate banana splits, I could only glance now and then through a "dead-head" to note our rapid descent from Lake Superior as we locked down through the Soo. Then again, against military regulations, only half dressed, I would open my cabin door a few inches to snap an unpermitted colored photograph of Sault Ste. Marie. Up at the head of the Lakes, if I weren't submerged in the lower depths of the ice box, complete in buttoned-up refrigerator coat, struggling to hang up a half a cow without hanging myself by the sleeve, I might climb down onto the bum boat which had tied up beside us and have a Coke.

In my "off" hours, I washed and ironed clothes, and read by the light of a twenty-five watt bulb, cramped up in my top bunk. Frequently I read *Alice* in *Wonderland* to maintain the proper perspective; the ceiling above my bunk hung not with webs, but with the strands of my hair torn out by splintered ply-wood when I turned over in my sleep.

My colored slides, a documentary account from fit-out and our first trip to Duluth through the ice, were mounting. Here was another set of pictures to add to my trail-gazing collection, which I planned to enjoy from my rocking chair some day in the old folks' home. I had enough pictures to remind me of my sailor days on fresh water. I had enough —period.

I was so fat from our impeccable cuisine that I'd soon need a derrick to hoist me ashore. Still, my weight wasn't my chief problem. Once I returned to a world of worry and responsibility it would melt away. But could I ever cast off the sea hag personality I was acquiring in this galley? Everything from spearing peas to swearing was just like second nature!

If it was within the cook's power to keep me aboard when we were in or near Cleveland, he did so. I always returned too happy after a visit home. But then there came the time when we went up to Duluth with a load of coal, which would necessitate our being in port for a day or longer because several boats were ahead of us. I reported for duty that morning to discover that both the second cook and the other porter, who lived in the vicinity, were hurrying ashore to a full day of freedom. Furthermore, in addition to the usual routine of all the chores which would be left for me, there was dirty laundry to count, piles of clean linen to put away, cases of groceries to stow, and a bride and groom as passengers on board who had nothing better to do than play a game of who could think up more extra services to telephone back to the galley department for! This morning I wasn't singing in the galley, as was my custom. My repertoire might vary from "The Old Rugged Cross" clear through to "Jealousy," but I usually sang. Today I couldn't.

The cook commanded a performance. I informed him that my contract didn't require me to sing. I don't know whether he was angry because he had given two of his staff a free day or because this time I wasn't accepting his unfairness with a smile on my lips and a song in my heart.

The extra work I would have done, but when he demanded, "Smile and be happy in this galley," I slammed a tray of dishes down on the counter, stalked right up forward to the captain's quarters with a blazing cigarette dangling from the corner of my mouth, and asked for my pay! Then I threw my uniforms overboard, and took a plane to Cleveland. I had to fly to be home in time to celebrate grandpa's birthday.

THE GIRL DIVER OF THE GREAT LAKES
(1905)
By J. Olivier Curwood

BEFORE JAMES OLIVER CURWOOD (1878-1927) became famous (and wealthy) as the author of thirty-two popular adventure novels set in the Canadian wilderness with titles like *The Honor of the Big Snows* (1911), *Kazan* (1914), and *God's Country and the Woman* (1915), he was a hard-working journalist who always had an eye for a good story he could sell about the Great Lakes, even if he had to use a feminine pseudonym to do it. The following article about an early woman scuba diver was one Curwood placed with *Woman's Home Companion*, a magazine much like today's *Good Housekeeping* or *Ladies Home Journal*. Although Curwood portrayed Frances Baker as the only woman diver of her era, Margaret Campbell Goodman, of New York, was a diver also and continued salvaging into her sixties after she was a grandmother. (News reports about her work follow this interview.) Not only was diving more exciting than teaching school or working in a store, it was also lucrative, as Curwood points out.

Diving was not the only profession women made their own during this time. From the 1890s through the 1920s, the "New Woman"—stylish and smart and daring—who worked in business and the professions, became a popular image in the media. This opening of possibilities for women coincided with the social changes wrought by World War I and booming business conditions of the 1920s. Women threw away their corsets, shortened their skirts, bobbed their hair, and began lobbying more forcefully for the right to vote. Unfortunately, a growing conservative backlash and the Crash of 1929 that led to the Depression effectively ended the possibilities for New Women by the 1930s.

⊷╾◉╼⊶

PRETTY, WELL EDUCATED, and only twenty years of age, Miss Frances Baker, of Detroit, has won the reputation of being one of the most fearless and resourceful divers along the Great Lakes, and within the last three years has accumulated almost twenty-five thousand dollars in a profession that heretofore only the most courageous and physically perfect of men have dared to follow. The story of this girl's success, of her thrilling adventures and discovery of treasure reads almost like a chapter in an exciting book of fiction, and the element of romance was completed a few months ago, when Miss Baker discovered and raised fifty thousand dollars' worth of copper from the treasure-ship *W. H. Stevens*, which sank in eighty feet of water in Lake Erie several years ago.

From Duluth to Buffalo this courageous Michigan girl is now known as the Girl Diver of the Great Lakes, and wherever she goes she is regarded as the especial protege of the lake seamen. Miss Baker's love for the wild and dangerous life of the diver is inherent. For a father she has the greatest captain of divers that ever worked in the big inland seas, a man who was never known to fail, and to whom the first alarm-calls usually come when ships need aid in Lake Erie and Lake Huron. But it is doubtful if even this great man of the lakes, Capt. H. W. Baker, has had more thrilling or romantic experiences than his daughter.

From the time she was old enough to go down to the river alone, little Fannie used to watch Captain Baker's wrecking-ship leave on its adventurous missions with longing eyes. The ambition to become a diver matured in her day by day, and as she grew older she deplored the fate that had condemned her to be a girl. But when she saw that women were becoming lawyers, architects, bankers, and even engineers, her determination to become a diver was fixed. She began making wrecking-trips with her father, and soon became an almost inseparable companion to him. She studied every part of the machinery connected in any way with diving, and in time learned to command the wrecking boat with a skill and assurance that was astonishing.

In Lake Huron a ship had gone down, a big wooden barge from the North, and it lay deep in sand fifty feet below the surface of the lake. On the wrecking-ship that went to raise it was one of the owners of the vessel, who had been on the barge when she sank. One day, before the wrecker reached the scene of operations, this man stood talking with Miss Baker.

"There is one article in that boat which I would like to secure," he said to her. "There is a diamond ring in my cabin that I prize very highly. I wonder if your father would get it for me?"

"I'll get it for you myself!" cried the young girl, impulsively.

For some time Miss Baker had been planning to make her first descent, and the following morning she prepared to go down with one of the old divers who was to be sent to inspect the ship. Her own father manned the compressed-air apparatus which meant life or death to her as she calmly walked down the ship's ladder and without a moment's hesitation disappeared under the surface of the lake. That first plunge into the new and fascinating world of the under sea left a vivid impression in the young girl's brain. It seemed at first as though some great creature with a thousand arms was pressing her gently but firmly on all sides, and for a few moments her breath came in short gasps, and a feeling of suffocation oppressed her. But the girl who was soon to become the most famous young woman on the lakes was far from frightened. Steadily she lowered one weighted foot after the other down the ladder, until she stood upon the bottom of the lake, with the shadow of the sunken barge looming up before her a dozen yards away.

At this depth the twenty pounds of lead attached to her feet seemed no heavier than ordinary soles of leather, and with a strange feeling of buoyancy she followed her companion to the walls of the sunken ship, and with his aid clambered up over them. At this point the plucky girl began to experience severe pains in her head, and she feared that her nose had begun to bleed. Undaunted still, she reached the cabin of the barge, and there laid a detaining hand on her guide's arm, signifying that she intended to enter first. Inside the cabin the electric-light the girl carried at her belt lit up the scene with weird distinctness. The discomfort caused by the pressure of the water and breathing compressed air had now become almost overpowering, and Miss Baker lost not a moment in her search. In one corner of the cabin she saw the stand described to her by the owner, and on it the small box that contained the ring. In her haste to recall it she stumbled and fell, and for one moment a thrill of fear passed through her. But it was gone as quickly as it came, and with the box in her hand the girl returned to the deck of the barge, clambered over its sides again, and a couple of minutes later stood trembling and exhausted on the deck of the wrecker, the proudest and the bravest girl that ever set her foot on a ship of the inland seas.

As a reward for this daring exploit Miss Baker was presented with the diamond ring she had rescued, and it is now in her possession. That ring marked the beginning of her fame and fortune. The girl had proved that she could live in the under sea, and to be able to do this means that a person is worth anywhere from fifty to two hundred dollars a day to a wrecking company. Ninety-nine out of every hundred men who descend fifty feet under the cold waters of Lake Erie or Lake Huron will in a few minutes begin to suffer with bleeding at the nose, which is quick death if they stay, or with head-splitting pains and suffocation. That is why all the good divers, from one end of the lakes to the other, may be counted on one's fingers and toes.

Miss Baker now began following up her first adventure with practical work. The girl early developed the fact that she was fitted to be a captain of divers instead of being a diver alone. Her plans for raising sunken ships and cargoes were daring, original, and allowed remarkable genius. Her suggestions were such as those which recently brought about the discovery of the treasure ship *W. H. Stevens*, which added five thousand dollars to her rapidly growing fortune.

It was not long after this that she had a gruesome adventure which was enough to shatter the nerves of a less courageous young woman. A schooner went down in Lake Huron, but its entire crew escaped with the exception of one seaman. Before the raising of the vessel was undertaken, divers made a search for the body of this man. One after another, several of them descended, but failed to find the missing sailor. Then Miss Baker volunteered to take a turn. Like the others, she failed in the first part of the search. Then she descended into the hold of the vessel. The light she carried illuminated the empty space for many yards ahead of her, but it disclosed nothing that might be the body of the seaman. From stern to bow she continued her hunt. Confident now that the sailor had been swept in the lake, she turned toward the open hatch. As she almost reached it and lifted her eyes, the white glare of her light revealed a horrible sight. Floating between two of the deck beams with its face staring down and its arms reaching out as if to clutch her, was the body of the dead sailor, almost directly above her head. So terrible did it look, with its arms and legs moving slightly and its face so dead-white, that the girl almost fainted. But knowing that her life depended upon her reaching the deck, Miss Baker clambered up, and giving the haul-up signal on her rope, was quickly pulled to the surface.

There came a time, however, when Miss Baker was placed for a few short moments in a more thrilling position than this. When a diver goes down, the air which he breathes comes into his helmet through a long rubber tube connected to the compressed air apparatus on the deck of the wrecker. The moment this "thread of life" is broken, the diver begins to suffocate, and unless he is instantly brought to the surface, or the working of the tube is resumed, he meets frightful end. Miss Baker was once working along the side of a sunken ship when she suffered the awful experience of having her air supply cut off. She was half leaning over, examining some part of the boat, when it seemed as if a great hand had been suddenly clapped over her mouth. In an instant she knew what had happened, and even while suffocating, through the medium of her rope she sent up that mute but thrilling call, which to every diver says, "Help! Help! Help!" There came no answering pull on the rope, but just as it seemed as though she would fall back in a death-clutch of the under sea, the fresh air began pouring into her helmet again. When Miss Baker reached the surface she found that one of the men had stumbled over the air-tube, knocking it from the compressed-air machine. As quick as a flash another of the guards above had caught the tube before it slipped over the side, and had attached it again just in the nick of time.

It was not long after this that the adventurous girl became entangled in the wreckage of a sunken boat and for twenty minutes worked furiously fifty feet beneath the surface of the sea getting her guide-rope free enough to signal for help.

But all of these thrilling experiences only served to strengthen Miss Baker's infatuation for her profession. She loved to know that at times her life depended upon her own skill and nerve, and after every few days or weeks she spent at home she longed for the free and perilous life of the wrecker again. Within two years after Miss Fannie made her first descent in Lake Huron she possessed a handsome brick mansion all her own on one of the most fashionable streets in Detroit.

Now came the work that made Miss Baker truly famous, and which brought her a check for five thousand dollars for ten days' labor.

Three years and more ago a "copper-ship" left the rich mining country of northern Michigan for Buffalo with fifty thousand dollars' worth of the red metal in her hold. She passed safely down Lake Huron, through Saint Clair, and into the Detroit River. In Lake Erie she caught fire. The boats of the doomed vessel came in with her crew, and all that night the sea grew heavier and heavier, and the wind blew a gale. And when it was found that the treasure-ship was not drifting a derelict, no man could say where she had gone down.

For many months fruitless searches were made for her. The insurance companies began first, and gave it up. It was reasoned that she might have drifted fifty miles before she went to the bottom, and that it was a hopeless task to attempt to locate her. As months and years passed, the owners of the cargo offered half of it to any man or company who would solve the mystery of its resting-place. That started the great Lake Erie hunt for treasure. Wrecking companies, sea-captains in their own vessels, and men from Buffalo, Cleveland, and Detroit, joined that search for the ship-load of copper. But all failed. The W. H. *Stevens* had seemingly disappeared as completely as if the bottom of the lake had opened up to receive her when she went down.

The mystery of the copper-ship appealed to the adventurous girl diver. For many months she investigated the details of the fire, and knew just what progress that fire had made when the W. H. *Stevens* was left to her fate that stormy night on Lake Erie. She figured the direction in which the gale was blowing, and long hours at a time the girl would imagine herself on the doomed copper-ship, slowly drifting with the storm. And each time she would stop off Point Burwell, and say, "Here is where we went down!"

With that point as a center, Miss Baker mapped out a square several miles long on each side.

"If we drag that square," she said, "just as a farmer would plow his field, we will find the copper-ship."

Last summer the *Baker* wrecking ship set out on its romantic quest. On the outer edge of that part of the sea mapped out her dragnets were dropped, and then and for several days the wrecker plowed slowly back and forth, as the captain's daughter had said it should. Nearer and nearer the center, that spot "where the girl said her copper-ship had gone down," the low black ship of the wreckers came. And when it had come within half a mile of it, early one morning the nets caught, and a shudder passed through the ship as she was brought to a stop.

"I believe it's the copper-ship," said Miss Baker, and the girl prepared to go down first.

Soundings showed that whatever had caught the nets was under eighty feet of water, a depth sufficient to test the physique of the most powerful divers. But Miss Baker allowed herself to be lowered, and no sooner had she reached bottom than with a thrill of joy she recognized the timbers of a burned ship. For ten days the wreckers worked hoisting the treasure, and when the copper was brought into port and sold Miss Baker's share came to five thousand dollars.

Margaret Goodman, Salvager

Cleveland Plain Dealer
October 30, 1922

The most noted marine salvage experts on the Great Lakes were astounded this week by the announcement of Margaret G. Goodman that May 1, 1923, she would start operations to salvage the $200,000 cargo of the New Brunswick, which sank in Lake Erie in 1859.

Miss [sic] Goodman, a mere slip of a woman, four feet four inches tall, has once before startled the mariners on the lakes and throughout the world by salvaging the valuable copper and iron cargo of the old steamer Pewabic, which sank in Lake Michigan off Thunder Bay in 1865.

Hundreds of men had tried to salvage this ship which rested in 185 feet of water, but because of the depth they were unable to accomplish their purpose.

The same thing applies to the case of the New Brunswick, which rests off Pelee Point in Lake Erie in only about fifty feet of water, but because of the shallow character of the lake at this point and the treacherous eddies there, the most expert of them have failed.

Miss Goodman was first drawn to the salvage game by watching the demonstration of a diving suit years ago. She was without money but finally succeeded in interesting such men as M. H. Gasser, head of the Gasser Coffee House of Toledo; William C. Carr, vice president of the Second National Bank; H. C. Collins, vice president of the Citizens Security & Trust Company; Dr. John V. Newton; L. W. Sullivan of the Sullivan Boat Co., and Ollie Skeldon, president of the Skeldon Salvage & Dredging Co., all of Toledo.

Under her personal direction a special diving apparatus was devised which would withstand the tremendous water pressure of 136 $\frac{1}{2}$ pounds to the square inch at 360 feet.

After five weeks of dredging the hulk was found and the divers sent down, operating under the direction of this woman. That was in 1916.

During the first season 100 pounds of copper, 100 pounds of pig iron, 136 hides and a large quantity of priceless relics were brought up in good condition, despite their half century wash day.

Rings of the Victorian period, jewelry, and clothing also were rescued, and some books and papers were found in good condition.

In one safe was found $55,000 in Civil War currency, but due to leakage of the water it was impossible to redeem it at full value.

Miss Goodman directs the work of the operation from start to the finish. When a hulk is to be salvaged she directs the dredging for its location. Then she dons a diver's suit and goes down with a crew of divers and thoroughly inspects the sunken ship herself, going over it from deck to hold and stem to stern.

Mrs. Goodman Has Contract to Recover Lumber Ship Lost in 1859
Detroit News
October 11, 1934

Mrs. Margaret Campbell Goodman, of Brooklyn, New York, known since 1917 as the only woman deep-sea diver in the country, said today that she has contracted to raise the cargo of logs, worth many thousand dollars, which was lost in Lake Erie, four miles off Point Pelee, when the schooner *New Brunswick* sank in 1859.

"I am more than 60 years old now and I won't do any of the recovery work myself but I will go under water at least once to look over the site," Mrs. Goodman said. She is in Detroit on business in connection with her venture.

"Because I am the only woman diver in the country all my dives have been exaggerated. This ship is in only about 40 feet of water and it should not be especially difficult, once we locate it. But I am not as young as I used to be and my work will be principally in directing operations."

Mrs. Goodman, who formerly lived in Detroit, retired from the underwater salvage business several years ago but has returned to the work because her husband, Charles Goodman, who formerly worked as a commercial artist, has become an invalid.

Mrs. Goodman first will view the scene of the salvaging from an airplane.

"I will fly over the approximate location with a photographer," she explained. "From a high altitude we should be able to see the wreck. If we can't see it with our eyes maybe the camera plates will catch it.

"If we have good luck we should locate the wreck and have the cargo on our barge within two weeks. The weather may turn bad on us, however."

The *New Brunswick*, which sank while enroute from Wallaceburg to Montreal with a cargo of 110,000 cubic feet of white oak and black walnut, was owned by Baron Henry Eberts. Its present owner is Newton Eberts, of Chatham, Ontario. A syndicate of Toronto businessmen is backing the salvaging work in the belief that the logs will not have been damaged by their long stay under water.

Mrs. Goodman, who is only five feet [sic] four inches tall, is a former newspaper and advertising woman. She organized the first woman's advertising club in Detroit and is listed in the British directory of "Principal Women of America."

Mrs. Goodman's most noted feat was the salvaging in 1917 of $300,000 worth of copper from the *Pewabic* which had been lying at the bottom of Lake Huron since 1865 and had defied five previous salvage attempts.

Mrs. Goodman considered trying to salvage the *New Brunswick* in 1920.

Grandmother Races Youth to Erie's Sunken Treasure
Detroit News
May 5, 1938

The lure of a sunken treasure which has lain beneath the waters of Lake Erie for close to a century again holds out its invitation for adventure. Responding to this ancient lure are two whose lives are dedicated to salvaging lost treasure—one a grandmother, the other a youth.

Both are hurrying preparations to be first inside the battered hull of the three-masted schooner *New Brunswick*, which foundered off Point Pelee in 1859 and carried to the lake bottom a fortune in oak and walnut. The grandmother, Mrs. Margaret Campbell Goodman, the only woman in the world whose business is salvaging sunken treasure, will probably be first.

Twenty years ago Mrs. Goodman, who is a slender woman of 65 years, first dreamed of wresting from Erie the quarter of a million-dollar fortune in timber that was carried to the bottom. She already had been established as a retriever of sunken treasure. During the war years she found the old *Pewabic* in the depths of Lake Huron and took from its broken hull a fortune in copper.

Not until 1934, however, was Mrs. Goodman able to locate the *New Brunswick's* graveyard. Late fall weather conditions prevented any efforts at salvaging. The *New Brunswick*, carrying its fortune in timber from the port of Wallaceburg to Montreal, foundered in the night during a storm in Lake Erie.

The schooner was one of a fleet owned by Baron Henry Eberts, whose home was in Chatham. Mrs. Goodman has a contract with Newton Eberts, his son and last remaining administrator for the Eberts estate.

Eberts, who is 84 years told, sees little romance in the venture.

"Bosh," he says. "It's just a lot of hard work and we're not sure of what we'll get when we get to the thing. Mrs. Goodman has my permission to go after it, and if anyone can salvage that cargo, she is the one.

"I remember when I was a small lad and my father and I were riding in a buggy along the shore. He pointed out over the water and told me, 'Son there's a fortune out there but try to get it.' Now, after all these years maybe the little lady can do the job.

"Understand, the lumber business went on the rocks shortly after the *Brunswick* sunk. Father sold out the fleet. I was never interested in sailing and the sale was good riddance as far as I was concerned."

Mrs. Goodman, formerly of Detroit, makes her home in New York. Less than five feet tall and weighing less than 100 pounds, this frail grandmother works under water while directing salvaging operations. She is angry with the young fellow, Jack Browne, of Milwaukee, who announced in Detroit recently that he would seek the treasure of the *New Brunswick*.

"That young fellow will not touch that ship so long as I have my contract," she insists. "I found the *Brunswick* and I've got it marked. I've done a lot of research on the condition and the value of the oak. Experts tell me the wood actually improves under water. I should be inside the hull before a month passes."

The foregoing series of newspaper clippings suggest only a small fraction of the time and effort Margaret Campbell Goodman and others expended trying to salvage a cargo of lumber from the sunken 296-ton bark *New Brunswick* from 1909 to 1980. The *New Brunswick* proved elusive to Mrs. Goodman, a writer and editor who advertised herself as the world's only female deep sea diver, not only because there were legal complications about her claim to the wreck, but because there are so many ship wrecks in the Pelee Passage area. The wreck was not definitively located until the last salvager used side-scan solar technology in the 1980s. Unfortunately, after stripping the wreck of artifacts, he ripped apart the *New Brunswick* with cranes to get the cargo, which was only white oak and not the valuable black walnut of legend. After finding few buyers for the wood, he filed for bankruptcy. The *New Brunswick*, the first large lakes' ship to carry a load of grain from Chicago to Liverpool in 1847, was completely destroyed.

Toledo Blade, June 18, 1906
TOLEDO WOMAN A LICENSED PILOT
Mrs. Grace Waite First of Sex to Become a Full-Fledged Captain Here

SHE IS MASTER OF THE VESSEL NAOMI
Has Taken Written Examination to Show Her Skill

Mr. and Mrs. George F. Waite
(Toledo Blade, June, 1906)

CAPTAIN GRACE L. WAITE, master of the coast trading vessel *Naomi* will be the only woman ever regularly licensed as a pilot in the Toledo steamboat inspection district.

Mrs. Waite, the wife of George F. Waite, owner and engineer of the *Naomi*, appeared this morning at the office of Captain C. A. Potter and William A Plietz, local inspectors, and took the written examination to demonstrate her skill in seamanship, navigation, knowledge of the pilot rules, whistle and bell signals, use of the mariners' compass and lake charts, and location and characteristics of lights and lighthouses and buoys.

The route upon which Mrs. Waite will be licensed to run is between Toledo and Port Clinton, but she will be limited to the command of gasoline freight boats not exceeding twenty-five gross tons and not carrying passengers for hire.

She has sailed with her husband several seasons and her application for license shows that she has had four years' experience as a wheelsman—one year in the sailboat *Pathfinder*, one year in the gasoline boat *Piscatory*, and two years in the *Naomi*.

Last year Eva Schmidt, of Fremont, was licensed to operate a ten-ton gasoline boat, carrying both passengers and freight for hire, but no special examination is required for the operation of such small craft. It is only necessary to satisfy the inspectors that the applicant has had some experience and a general knowledge of water craft.

Captain Waite is, therefore, the only woman pilot of a regularly inspected and documented vessel in the Toledo district.

When ashore, Engineer George F. Waite and Captain Grace Waite live at 2012 Hawthorne Street, but during the summer they spend most of their time aboard of the *Naomi*, buying produce at the country ports and selling it in the city. The *Naomi* is 56 feet over all, 14 feet beam and measures up 22 gross tons.

The Buffalo Whore

Traditional Great Lakes Folksong Collected by Ivan H. Walton

WHEREVER THERE ARE SHIPS and ports there will be brothels. The Great Lakes had, and still have, some legendary red-light districts catering to sailors, but little is known about them outside the merchant marine community. Because no lakes prostitute has yet written her memoirs, and no one has ever researched this aspect of lakes shipping, the lives of the women who plied their trade near the docks are lost except for references in newspapers, court documents, and the occasional folksong such as "The Buffalo Whore."

The maritime folksong and folklore of the Great Lakes were Professor Ivan Walton's (1893-1968) lifelong interest. During his tenure as a professor of English in the school of Engineering at the University of Michigan from 1919 to 1962, he dedicated himself to collecting and preserving the folklore of the schooner age on the lakes in interviews and recordings. Walton noted that he collected this song from Norman "Beachie" MacIvor of Goderich, Ontario, in the summer of 1934. MacIvor could not remember where he learned it, but he had heard it sung "dozens" of times by lakes sailors. Walton also writes that "the sailor boarding-house district about the harbor of the city of Buffalo, especially Canal Street, was the Mecca of sailor shore life on the Great Lakes. Located at the foot of Lake Erie, the farthest down-lake point that could be reached by the larger vessels that could not negotiate the old Welland Canal, and at the head of the Erie Canal that connected the Lakes with the Hudson River and the Atlantic, Buffalo received for transshipment by far the largest portion of the grain as well as other products sent down the lakes from the western grain-producing region; and it was also the home port of a large fleet of sailing vessels.

"Annually large numbers of ocean sailors came up to Buffalo in the spring for the opening of the navigation season on the lakes, and they and local seamen and the numerous human parasites who lived off these men made the waterfront district a lively place. Sailors were regularly paid off and went ashore when their vessel tied up in an unloading dock, and as regularly they spent their money lavishly in the many 'free and easy' saloon/theater/boardinghouses and other establishments that were awaiting them. When their money was gone—and many were fleeced in a remarkably short time—they shipped out again on any vessel that wanted a crew, and then repeated the performance on their next arrival."

THE BUFFALO WHORE

On my first trip down old Lake Erie,
With some sailors to explore,
Then I met Rosie O'Flannagan,
Pride of all the Buffalo whores.

She says, "Boy, I think I know you,
Let me sit upon your knee,
How'd you like to do some lovin'?
A dollar and a half will be my fee."

Some was singin', some was dancin',
Some was drunk upon the floor;
But I was over in a corner
A 'makin' love to the Buffalo whore.

She was slick as a boardin'-house master,
I didn't know what she was about
'Till I missed my watch and wallet,
Then, by Jesus, I struck out!

Then came the whores and sons-o'-bitches,
They came at me by the score;
You'd have laughed to split your britches
To see me flying out that door!

PROFILE:
ELIZABETH WHITNEY WILLIAMS
1842-1913

BORN ON MACKINAC ISLAND, Elizabeth Whitney Williams's earliest memories were "my love of watching the water. I remember standing with my arms outstretched as if to welcome and catch the white topped waves as they came rolling in upon the white, pebbly shore at my feet. I was not quite three years old. . . ." Her parents moved to St. Helena Island on the other side of the Straights, where her father worked as a ship's carpenter, and then to Beaver Island in Lake Michigan to take advantage of the fishing industry that was then developing on the lakes after the decline of the fur trade. She assumed command of the Harbor Point Light on Beaver upon her first husband's death in 1872, married Daniel Williams in 1875, and remained as keeper until 1884. She then requested a transfer to the newly-built lighthouse at Little Traverse Point on Little Traverse Bay, where she was keeper for twenty-nine years and wrote her autobiography, *A Child of the Sea; Or Life Among the Mormons* (1905), before she died in 1913.

At Beaver (or the Beavers, as the group of islands was commonly known), the Whitneys encountered "King" Jesse James Strang, a renegade Mormon who had lost his chance to succeed Joseph Smith to Brigham Young. Strang broke away from the church, brought his followers to Beaver Island in 1848, and built a "kingdom" that practiced polygamy and aggressive territorial expansion on the Michigan mainland. The Whitneys and other "gentiles" were driven off the island, unable to return until Strang was killed by his followers and the settlement disbanded. Williams devotes much of A Child of the Sea, to descriptions of Strang's kingdom, particularly the outrages of polygamy. Later historians have faulted her accuracy, particularly Milo M. Quaife, director of the Burton Historical Collection at the Detroit Public Library, whose book about Strang attempted to be more objective.

Williams's stories of women's hairbreadth escapes from polygamy may be exaggerated, but they highlight nineteenth-century concerns with gender, sexuality, and women's ability to determine their own lives. Any woman who transgressed the rigid sexual behavioral codes for women, even if she had no choice, would be an outcast. On the frontier, which the lakes were at this time, where gender roles were fluid and traditional markers of class had been disrupted by immigration, chastity became particularly important as a marker of gentility. It ensured women would be respected, which was often the only power they could wield. Williams's focus on women's issues on Beaver Island, which occupy much of her autobiography, are an example of the tensions in society at this time. Even though she was writing decades after the events took place, and had a respected career as a lighthouse keeper, her concern with the plight of the women Strang attempted to dominate had not diminished. Unlike autobiographies written by men on the frontier which describe conquest and settlement, storms on the lakes and shipwreck, Williams's focus remains domestic, fixed on the problems women encountered when the frontier was a place of contested beliefs and behavior.

The following section of A Child of the Sea concerns Williams's career as a lightkeeper. But once again, readers will notice that she makes the lighthouse a domestic space, a home-like haven of comfort and safety to the sailors who pass. Her independence and power are also obvious. When she remarries, she notes that "Having a desire to change my residence from the island to the mainland, I made the request to be changed. . ." leaving no doubt about who made the decisions. Had she been old enough when her family lived among the Mormons, she would have posed a formidable resistance to Strang. As an autobiographer who outlived him, she had the last word and her book is more well-known today than any other history of the Mormons on Beaver Island.

FROM A CHILD OF THE SEA;
OR LIFE AMONG THE MORMONS
(1905)

Elizabeth Whitney Williams

My Husband Appointed Lightkeeper

THE WINTER OF 1865 we spent a very pleasant winter in Northport, the next winter in Charlevoix, where we had built us a new home on Bridge street. We sold and returned again to the island, engaging in the fishing business quite extensively for a few years.

In August of 1869 Mr. Peter McKinley resigned his position as light-keeper, my husband being appointed in his place. Then began a new life, other business was discontinued and all our time was devoted to the care of the light. In the spring of 1870 a large force of men came with material to build a new tower and repair the dwelling, adding a new brick kitchen. Mr. Newton with his two sons had charge of the work. A new fourth order lens was placed in the new tower and the color of the light changed from white to red. These improvements were a great addition to the station from what it had been. Our tower was built round with a winding stairs of iron steps. My husband having now very poor health I took charge of the care of the lamps, and the beautiful lens in the tower was my especial care. On stormy nights I watched the light that no accident might happen. We burned the lard oil, which needed great care, especially in cold weather, when the oil would congeal and fail to flow fast enough to the wicks. In long nights the lamps had to be trimmed twice each night, and sometimes oftener. At such times the light needed careful watching. From the first the work had a fascination for me. I loved the water, having always been near it, and I loved to stand in the tower and watch the great rolling waves chasing and tumbling in upon the shore. It was hard to tell when it was loveliest. Whether in its quiet moods or in a raging foam.

Vessels Seeking Shelter From The Storms

My three brothers were then sailing, and how glad I felt that their eyes might catch the bright rays of our light shining out over the waste of waters on a dark stormy night. Many nights when a gale came on we could hear the flapping of sails and the captain shouting orders as the vessels passed our point into the harbor, seeking shelter from the storm. Sometimes we could count fifty and sixty vessels anchored in our harbor, reaching quite a distance outside the point, as there was not room for so many inside. They lay so close they almost touched at times. At night our harbor looked like a little city with its many lights. It was a pleasant sound to hear all those sailors' voices singing as they raised the anchors in the early morning. With weather fair and white sails set the ships went gliding out so gracefully to their far away ports. My brothers were sometimes on those ships. Many captains carried their families on board with them during the warm weather. Then what a pleasure to see the children and hear their sweet voices in song in the twilight hours. Then again when they came on shore for a race on land, or taking their little baskets went out to pick the wild strawberries. All these things made life the more pleasant and cheerful.

Death of My Husband, The Lightkeeper

Life seemed very bright in our light house beside the sea. One dark and stormy night we heard the flapping of sails and saw the lights flashing in the darkness. The ship was in distress. After a hard struggle she reached the harbor and was leaking so badly she sank. My husband in his efforts to assist them lost his life. He was drowned with a companion, the first mate of the schooner *Thomas Howland*. The bodies were never recovered, and only those who have passed through the same know what a sorrow it is to lose your loved one by drowning and not be able to recover the remains. It is a sorrow that never ends through life.

My Appointment as Lightkeeper

Life to me then seemed darker than the midnight storm that raged for three days upon the deep, dark waters. I was weak from sorrow, but realized that though the life that was dearest to me had gone, yet there were others out on the dark and treacherous waters who needed to catch the rays of the shining light from my light-house tower. Nothing could rouse me but that thought, then all my life and energy was given to the work which now seemed was given me to do. The light-house was the only home I had and I was glad and willing to do my best in the service. My appointment came in a few weeks after, and since that time I have tried faithfully to perform my duty as a lightkeeper. At first I felt almost afraid to assume so great a responsibility, knowing it all required watchful care and strength, with many sleepless nights. I now felt a deeper interest in our sailors' lives than ever before, and I longed to do something for humanity's sake, as well as earn my own living, having an aged mother dependent upon me for a home. My father had passed be-

yond. Sorrows came thick and fast upon me. Two brothers and three neph-
ews had found graves beneath the deep waters, but mine was not the only
sorrow. Others around me were losing their loved ones on the stormy deep
and it seemed to me there was all the more need that the lamps in our lighthouse towers should be kept brightly burning.

> Let our lamps be brightly burning
>   For our brothers out at sea—
> Then their ships are soon returning,
>   Oh! how glad our hearts will be.
>
> There are many that have left us,
>   Never more will they return;
> Left our hearts with sorrows aching,
>   Still our lamps must brightly burn.

Tribute to The Sailors

Oh sailor boy, sailor boy, sailor boy true!
The lamps in our towers are lighted for you.
Though the sea may be raging your hearts will not fail;
You'll ride through the rolling foam not fearing the gale.

And God in his mercy will lead you aright,
As you watch the light-house with lamps burning bright.
The wind your lullaby, as the raging seas foam;
Oh sailor boy, sailor boy, we welcome you home.

Oh sailor boy, sailor boy, sailor boy true!
Your dear darling mother is praying for you;
Your sweet bride is weeping as her vigil she keeps,
Not knowing your ship has gone down into the deep.

As she walks on the shore, her eyes out to sea,
"Oh husband, my sailor boy, come back to me!"
The wild waves dash up at her feet in a foam,
They answer, "Your sailor boy no more can come home."

In sorrow she kneels on that wave-beaten shore,
"Shall I never, see my dear sailor boy more?"

The waves whisper softly, their low moaning sound,
"You'll meet your dear sailor boy, in Heaven he's crowned."

Lightkeepers and Their Work

Our lightkeepers many times live in isolated places, out on rocks and shoals far away from land and neighbors, shut off from social pleasures. In many places there can be no women and children about to cheer and gladden their lonely lives. There is no sound but the cry of the sea gulls soaring about or the beating of the restless waters, yet their lives are given to their work. As the sailor loves his ship so the lightkeeper loves his lighthouse. Where there are three or four keepers at one station they manage to make the time pass more pleasantly. They must in many cases be sailors as well as lightkeepers, as it requires both skill and courage to manage their boats in sailing back and forth between their lights and the main-land, where mail, provisions and other necessaries are procured for their comforts. Often they are drowned in making these trips. The passing of the ships near their stations are like so many old friends to them. They learn to love the passing boats and vessels, and it is a pleasure to know our lights cheer and gladden the hearts of the sailors as the waves run high and the wild winds blow on dark, stormy nights. May the hearts of the lightkeepers, as well as the life savers in the life saving service along the great lakes and coasts, be strengthened and cheered in the grand and noble work.

As we lie in our beds so snugly and warm,
The sailors are on the sea battling the storm.
As the sailors are tramping their decks in the midnight hours,
We are trimming our lamps in our light-house towers.

Gales on Our Lakes

There were many wrecks towed into our harbor, where they were left until repaired enough to be taken to dry docks in cities. Sometimes in spring and fall the canvas would be nearly all torn off a schooner in the terrible gales which swept the lakes, many of which I have been out in, in my trips on the lakes and among the islands.

One of our pioneers, Captain Robert Roe, of Buffalo, New York, had settled on South Fox Island in 1859. He put out a dock, built a comfortable house, and bought the land the Mormons had occupied. He farmed, and furnished cord wood to lake steamers for many years. Many were the gales he sailed through in his trips passing from the island to main land. His brother was keeper of the lighthouse several years at South Fox Island.

Steamer Badger State

Of all the many steamers that came to our harbor as the years passed on, and there were many, the *Badger State* of the Union Line of Buffalo, New York, gave us the longest service, running for ten years into Beaver Harbor, never once missing a trip and most always on time. Captain Alexander Clark was master. No matter what the weather might be, how heavy the gale, the good ship *Badger State* never failed us. Thousands of barrels of fish were shipped on her to city markets, bringing the merchants' goods and merchandise. She also carried our summer mails and being a popular boat was always filled with passengers. From the spring of 1873 to the summer of 1883 the *Badger State* was a faithful friend. No one but those who reside on an island can appreciate the steamboat service or what it means to the people. We learn to love the boats, the sound of the whistle even in the midnight hours was music in our ears and brought cheer and comfort to our hearts.

•   •   •

Old Neighbors Leaving The Island

About the year 1876 Mr. James Dormer, who had done an extensive business at the Point, retired and went to his home in Buffalo, New York, renting his property to Mr. John Day of Green Bay, Wisconsin. Later Mr. C. R. Wright and son, also one of the old pioneers of the island who had carried on the fish business so many years, sold his dock property and store building, moving to Harbor Springs, still continuing in the dry goods business. About that time others of our island people moved to the main land, settling in different parts, making new homes. Several of the young men filling responsible positions as captains, mates and clerks on the lake steamers, and several of the young women being trained nurses in city hospitals.

I now married again, still holding my position as lightkeeper. Since my marriage my official title has been Mrs. Daniel Williams. Having a desire to change my residence from the island to the mainland I made the request to be changed to a mainland light station. I was soon transferred to the Little Traverse light-station at Harbor Springs, Michigan. The lighthouse just finished, the lamp being lighted the first time September 25th, 1884. The light station is situated on the extreme end of Harbor Point, at the entrance of Little Traverse Harbor.

Sad Thoughts On Leaving My Island Home

Preparations were made, goods were packed, the steamer *Grace Barker* with Captain Walter Chrysler as master, had come to take us to our new home. So often before had I left the island, passing several winters in other parts, but always returning again, and happy to get back to my neighbors and pleasant island home, with its fresh, pure air. But now I knew this was different. There would be no more coming back to live, this time was to be the last. The dear old island and I must part. I had always thought it beautiful in the many years I had called it my home; but never before had I realized what it had been to me until now. I was leaving, perhaps never more to return.

Recollections came of my childhood days when free from care and knowing no sorrow, I had wandered through the pleasant paths strewn with flowers, sending their sweet perfume upon the air, as my brothers had so often taken me with them on their hunts; and the beautiful white beach where the blue waters came rolling in where so often we had wandered together, chasing the waves as they came tumbling in upon us, or as we paddled about the shores in our canoes, and where I so often had watched to see their white sails returning to land when I had not gone with them upon the water. As all these thoughts came passing through my mind I wondered if I could leave all these memories behind, or could I carry them away to the new home, the new land as it almost seemed. Though our family was broken and no more could we gather around the hearth at evening time, some had passed over into the beyond, yet there was no place on earth where we all seemed so close together as on the island shores. We had passed through many storms, both mental and physical, but had felt the mighty power of him who rules all things to give us peace and strength. And the "lighthouse!" That had been my home so many years, I loved the very bricks within its walls. Under its roof I had passed many happy years as well as some sorrowful ones. It was filled with hallowed memories. Then came the separation from the friends and neighbors. Could their places ever be filled?

The sun shone bright, the day was fair as we stepped upon our steamer that was to bear us away from our island home. As we steamed so fast away, we looked back to watch its white shores with beautiful green trees in the background and the pretty white tower and dwelling of our lighthouse, which soon could be seen no more only in sad, sweet memories.

Just a few hours passed when we steamed into Little Traverse Harbor, and the "red light," just like the one we had left, was flashing its rays over the waters of Little Traverse Bay for the first time. The water was calm and still. The "red light" shone deep into the quiet waters, and many eyes were watching the bright rays from the light-house tower, and the wish of their hearts had been gratified in having a lighthouse on Harbor Point to guide steamers and vessels into the harbor. The evening was clear and the picture was a lovely one as we rounded the point so near the light. Some passengers said to me, "Here is your home. Don't you know the red light is giving you a welcome?" Yes, it was all one's heart could wish, yet I felt there was another I had left in the old home that was now just a little more dear to my heart.

In The New Home

We were met by friends and taken to their home for the night. Next morning we drove through the resort grounds to "Harbor Point Light House," as it is known by the land people, but to the mariner it is "Little Traverse Light House." We were soon at work putting our house in order, and the beautiful lens in the tower seemed to be appealing to me for care and polishing, which I could not resist, and since that time I have given my best efforts to keep my light shining from the lighthouse tower. Many old-time friends came to see us in our new home on Harbor Point, and though we greatly missed our island home and island neighbors, we soon felt an interest in our new surroundings. What I missed here most was not to see the passing ships and steamers, as they were constantly passing where we could see them from the island.

FROM ANNUAL REPORT OF THE OPERATIONS
OF THE UNITED STATES LIFE-SAVING SERVICE
for the Fiscal Year Ending June 30, 1889

THE CLOSE OF THIS YEAR'S awards is graced with the name of Edith Morgan, of Hamlin, Michigan, the young daughter of Captain Sanford W. Morgan, keeper of the life-saving station at Grand Point au Sable.

On the 23d of March, 1878, during a northerly gale, when a heavy sea was breaking in upon the shore, and the weather was very cold, two unfortunate men were seen three miles out upon the lake clinging to a capsized boat. The spring navigation not having opened, the crew was not yet on duty, and the only persons at the station were Captain Morgan, his two sons, one of whom was a little boy, and his daughter Edith. The surf-boat could not be launched by these four, and the rescue, it was at once decided, had to be undertaken with a fishboat. To employ all the strength available, the child, Frank, was detailed to steer, and the girl took her place with her father and elder brother at he oars. She did her part in the hard work which followed but, with so small a crew, the boat could not be forced through the opposing breakers, and by the time it reached the second bar it was nearly swamped and had to put back to land. From thence the elder brother, James, at once started for the town, to gather a crew, which Edith, in order that there night be no delay, fell to work with her father to clear a track for the launch of the surf-boat, through a great mass of logs and driftwood which covered the beach, the pair laboring with such energy that when, a short time after, the crew arrived, the work was done. The true girl then helped the men to launch the heavy surf-boat, which put out to the rescue.

Upon yet another occasion her service was no less useful and noble. It was at the wreck of the steamer *City of Toledo*, which took place a mile south of the station, on the 21st of December, 1879, after navigation was closed. The steamer, which had grounded in the night about 200 yards from land in a thick snow-storm, lay the next morning broadside on in ten feet of water, with the seas flying over her and freezing as they fell, until she resembled an iceberg rather than a vessel. The weather was so cold that the crew were unable to get out to the wreck in the boat, the oars and tholl-pins clogging up with ice so rapidly as to arrest the rowing, and the rescue had to be effected by the slow process, terribly retarded under the circumstances, involved in the use of the station hauling-lines, which the ice upon the vessel prevented from being fixed at a sufficient height above the deck to keep them from immersion in the water, where the ice formed on them so quickly as to make them hard to manage, and where they were at the same time subjected to the heavy drag of a strong current. There being scant help at hand, Edith Morgan took her stand with the few men upon the ice banks, in snow a foot and a half deep, and tugged away with them upon the whip-line for five or six hours, until every one of the eighteen persons were safely landed. It is testified that but for her assistance some of the people on the steamer must have perished.

In recognition of her conduct on these two occasions, the silver medal of the service was awarded her.

⤞⟶⊜⟵⤝

FROM HISTORY OF THE GREAT LAKES
Volume II (1899)
John B. Mansfield
"Miss Maebelle Mason Awarded Life-Saving Medal"

IT WAS DURING Captain Mason's incumbency at Mamajuda that his daughter, Miss Maebelle, a maid of fourteen years, performed an act of heroism which attracted the attention, not only of the lake marine men, but of the government officials as well. On May 11, 1890, a man in a rowboat threw a line for a tow to the steamer C. W. Elphicke, Captain Montague, while passing on the Detroit river, half between Mamajuda light and Grassy Isle. The line missed connection but caught just right to capsize the boat, spilling the unfortunate man into the river. On passing Mamajuda Light Captain Montague, who could render no assistance, signaled the lightkeeper that there was a man overboard and in danger of drowning. Captain Mason was absent with the government boat, and it therefore devolved upon the humanity and courage of Mrs. Mason and her daughter Maebelle to attempt a rescue. The only thing available in the shape of a boat was a small flat-bottomed punt, which was hauled out of the dock at the lighthouse. The mother and daughter succeeded in launching this, and it was quickly decided that the daughter should undertake the work and danger of rowing out to the aid of the perishing man. After about a mile of hard rowing she came up to him near his upturned boat and succeeded in getting him aboard of her light craft, he being nearly exhausted. She then returned to the lighthouse, towing with her the submerged boat. The stranger thus rescued from death by water was profuse in incoherent thanks. This act of heroism was rewarded by the United States Government by the presentation of a life-saving medal of the second class. . . . The Ship Masters Association also presented her with a gold life-saving medal with a Maltese cross and gold chain attached. . . . From that day all steamers carrying the pennant of the association saluted while passing the lighthouse until the young heroine was wedded June 21, 1892, to Mr. Connell, who carried her away.

FROM GRANDMOTHER'S STORIES
(1889)
Francis B. Hurlbut

A MEMBER OF THE WARD shipping family on the Great Lakes, Francis B. Hurlbut grew up near Detroit, Michigan, graduated from Michigan State Normal School (Eastern Michigan University), and died in Crescent City on North Manitou Island in 1892. *Grandmother's Stories*, Hurlbut's only publication, retells the stories of her "grandmother," Emily Ward, the sister of Eber Ward, a pioneer Great Lakes iron manufacturer, steamship owner, and keeper of the Bois Blanche Island light from 1829 to 1842. "The Fall of the Lighthouse" portrays the courage required by early lakes lightkeepers, many of whom were women although the keeper of record was a man. Here Emily tells of saving the lamps and lenses from the light before it fell into Lake Michigan during the January gale of 1838. This story gives a picture of a young woman, alone except for her adopted child, who felt responsible to save what she could so the lighthouse could be rebuilt. The equipment she rescued was a combination of lard-oil lamps, lenses, and reflectors that gave only a weak beam compared to the Fresnel lenses installed later, yet in the wild darkness of the Straights it would have been a welcome sight to men who had once sailed without it.

⋯⊱⊜⊰⋯

The Fall of the Lighthouse

IT WAS A WILD NIGHT when the lighthouse fell, said grandma, as she picked up a child's stocking she was knitting. "Father had gone over to Mackinaw two days before, intending to come back the day he went; but a storm had arisen that prevented his getting back, and instead of decreasing it had increased, until in the afternoon it was blowing a perfect gale.

"The lighthouse had originally been placed too near the water, and the encroachment made by the winds and the waves, since it was built, had brought it much nearer, so that now every heavy storm was full of peril for the old lighthouse.

"My father had long anticipated the day when some extra heavy storm would sweep the waters around its foundation, loosen it, and beat its stanch tower until it should fall; and now that day had come.

"Bolivar and I were alone in the house, and there was no one on the island but the Frenchman, who was a great coward, and his Indian wife.

"Our house was very near to the lighthouse,—so near that if it should fall a certain way it would fall upon the roof,—which made it a very unsafe shelter for us.

"It was a day of great anxiety; for if the lighthouse should be blown down, its great light would be put out, and I shuddered to think of what might happen to the vessels and their crews and passengers.

"And Eber was on the lake; and what if his boat, storm driven, should look for that friendly light and not find it? My heart was like lead as I looked out upon the boiling waves, and the roaring wind, and the driving clouds, and thought of him. So I would not take down the lamps until the very last moment.

"Early in the forenoon I had seen that the water surrounded the building, and later on, as the storm increased in violence, every great wave would dash itself to foam against its brawny sides.

"Above five o'clock I saw that if I was to save the lamps and the great reflectors I must begin at once. So putting a warm hood on my head to protect it from the rain, I started, first telling Bolivar not to stir from the house, but to stand at the window and watch for me. The poor child burst into tears and begged me not to go, but I thought it was my duty to save the government property.

"I had no sooner got out of the house than the wind, with a sudden dash, nearly took me off my feet, the rain half blinded me, and the spray wet me through; but I ran quickly, and in a moment was in the lighthouse, climbing its hundred and fifty steep steps with all the speed I could. When I reached the top what a magnificent sight met my gaze!

"Whoever has stood on a perilous height, and seen the mad waters leap and roar and dash with all their mighty force against the frail structure that supported him, can imagine the wild exaltation of soul that filled me through and through to the exclusion of all fear.

"It seemed as if then, indeed, God, in his majesty, was sweeping the earth and the seas, and I felt that I also was part of the great universe that existed under that awful power.

"I had but little time, however, to indulge myself in these thoughts, for every wave made the whole tower reel. It took all my strength to carry those great lamps and reflectors down the winding stairs; and sometimes when I would stop to take breath, and would hear the beat of the waters and feel the shock it gave the tower, it would give me a momentary spasm of terror; but it would be but momentary, for my work must be done, and I had no time for fear.

"I think I climbed those stairs five times before I got everything movable down, and each time Bolivar would implore me, with tears streaming from his eyes, not to go again, that I would surely be killed."

"Oh, grandma!" said one of the aunties, "I don't see how you dared to risk your life in that way."

"Oh," said grandma, "you see I wasn't hurt. When people are doing their duty they are not apt to come to much harm."

The children looked at each other, as if they could see that grandma did right, but that it was an awful thing to do.

"Well," pursued grandma, "after I had got everything down I changed my wet clothes for dry ones, and we ate our supper, and then took our places by the window to watch for the lighthouse to fall.

"I told Bolivar that as soon as I said the word we were to leave the house and go back into the woods, and that when the time came he was not to speak one word, but hang on to my hand tight and follow me. He said he would.

"We had not long to wait. The night had come; the rain had ceased, and the moon gave such light as scurrying and wildly driven clouds would permit. Suddenly we saw a long zigzag line run from the tower's base to its top. I said to Bolivar, 'Put on your overcoat and hat,' and I put on my warm shawl and hood. Still we stood by the window; another line shot up and around, and the tower tottered.

"'Now,' said I, 'Bolivar come!' He took my hand, and we went out the back way, shutting the doors behind us, and ran for the woods, a few rods off.

"We had scarcely got there when, with one mighty crash, down went the huge pile of masonry, and the waves washed over the place where the lighthouse once stood.

"We could see that the house had not been injured; so with thankful hearts we went back, and Bolivar was soon in bed and asleep. But I could not sleep for thinking of the ships that were in peril, and especially of Eber; and tears that I could not restrain wet my pillow that night and succeeding nights."

"Was any one lost?" inquired Portie.

"Oh, yes," said grandma; "it was one of the most awful storms ever known on the lakes, and many ships went down and many lives were lost; but no one was lost near Bois Blanc, or that I knew personally.

"When father got back he was glad to find us alive; for he had been afraid from the first that the lighthouse would fall."

FROM THE LOG OF THE MICHIGAN CITY LIGHTHOUSE
(1872-1904)
Harriet E. Colfax

BORN IN OGDENSBERG, New York, in 1824, Harriet Colfax moved to Chicago in 1851. She assumed the post of lighthouse keeper at Michigan City, Indiana in 1861, a position she held until her retirement in 1904. Readers unaccustomed to perusing the logbooks of old light stations may miss the subtle notations of political maneuvering that Colfax notes in her logs. At first glance, her logs appear to be emotionless, but compared to other keeper's logs—which usually list only times, dates, and weather in boring monotony—Colfax makes certain that her concerns were recorded so that when the logs were returned to Washington, D. C. at the close of navigation, her reactions would be read.

In the 1870s the Lighthouse Service became professionalized, part of a broadly-based national movement to upgrade the governmental maritime services, including the Life-Saving Service which manned station houses to patrol beaches to rescue shipwreck victims. Aside from mandating uniforms for personnel, the Lighthouse Service set up a system of spot inspections, regulated record-keeping and supply requisitions, and decided where lights were to be placed. It was, in short, a bureaucracy. While the worst abuses of earlier practice were corrected, the new system did not always function smoothly.

At one point Colfax notes that the Service decided to move the pier beacon from the east pier to the west pier. No reason is given. Unfortunately, not all the Captains read the "Notice to Mariners" in the papers—if they had access to the newspapers—and promptly misjudged their courses because the light had been changed and wrecked their ships. Moreover, in order for Colfax to light the pierhead beacon on the west pier, it became necessary for her to climb down the breakwater, get in a scow and row across the river to the other pier, then walk down it to the new light. This was not an easy task in bad weather, especially when her scow was destroyed by storms.

She repeatedly asks for help with the pier head beacon, and is just as repeatedly told that if she can have someone, it will be only for the fall season. Since she would be incapable of tending both the beacon and the lighthouse herself, we may surmise that this was an attempt to force her out. On April 8, 1884, she notes in the log that her request for help has been granted, but only after political connections in Washington "interest[ed] themselves in my behalf. I am deeply grateful. H.E.C." This sort of notation in a lighthouse log is extremely rare and reveals how concerned she was that she would need to give up her position.

The Service next attempted to discontinue the main light altogether, replacing it with a range light. Only after the intervention of the shipping interests in Chicago and their political connections in Washington was the light restored. But Colfax could not resist the dry notation in the log on October 14 of 1886 that she viewed the beacon light washed up on the beach, just in case her superiors hadn't noticed their plan of replacing the main light with a range light wouldn't work.

While it may be true that the problems she experienced with the Service bureaucracy were a blatant attempt to force her out and replace her with man, gender did not always help. Sumner Kimball, head of the Life-Saving Service, fared little better with Washington when he tried repeatedly to raise pay and get pensions for his surfmen and station masters to avoid the constant turnover of personnel. The reality was that after the Civil War the United States suffered several profound depressions, continuing economic deflation, and the normal political infighting and stasis that still affect government today. It is equally accurate to see Colfax as a quiet, competent woman who was willing to use powerful men with connections when she needed them to get what she wanted. And then politely, but pointedly, remind her superiors that she had prevailed.

⊸═◉═⊷

1872

August 12: Clear and warm with light winds. *US Tender Blaze* came in about 5 a.m. with supplies for the Lt. House. Commodore Murray and Lt. House inspector called at the Lt. House. Expressed himself well satisfied with everything about the establishment.

August 16: This is the day on which the comet was to strike the earth and demolish all things terrestrial—but failed to come up to appointment. The elevated walk was run into by a vessel entering the harbor and considerably damaged.

August 24: Afternoon showers. Thunder storm evening. Had walk to beacon repaired today by order of General Poe.

September 18: Cold day. Heavy Northwest gale towards night, the waves dashing over both piers, very nearly carrying me with them into the lake.

September 29: Wind blowing a westerly gale all day and still rising at 5 p.m. Four vessels entered while the gale was at its height and ran against the elevated walk, breaking it in again. Went to the beacon tonight with considerable risk of life.

October 1: Weather clear and pleasant. The captain of one of the vessels that came into port in the gale of the 29th died of consumption today—death hastened by exposure.

October 13: Northerly gale, continuing all day and all night. Weather cold with rain and hail storms. Gale perfectly fearful by nightfall—waves dashed over the top of the beacon—reached the beacon in immanent risk tonight as the waves ran over the elevated walk. Watched both lights with closest attention all night. Wrote to Commander Murray today reporting the trouble I am having with the beacon.

October 14: Gale continued all day, abating somewhat as the sun went down. My assistant's appointment came today—took him down to the beacon with me this evening and instructed him in his duties. He is intelligent and will be faithful.

1873

April 1: Warm rain and south wind. Ice all out of the harbor. Exhibited the lights tonight. They are unloading the schooner *Restless* which ran ashore and was frozen in the ice last fall. It is thought she will be gotten off with very little damage.

April 15: Rainy day. Heavy fog in the night. The beacon light not visible from the house. Took a walk at 12 o'clock to investigate. The lamp was burning brilliantly and the mainlight "under a cloud."

May 6: Pleasant weather. 3 arrivals. Mailed a letter to the Office of the Light House Engineer asking for extension of elevated walk to beacon.

May 26: Pleasant day. Hard thunderstorm in the evening. Rough time getting out to the beacon.

May 28: A terrible hurricane tonight at about the time of lighting up. Narrowly escaped being swept into the lake.

June 5: Fires comfortable. The first pile for extension of the west pier was driven tonight as I was lighting the beacon.

August 17: The supply vessel *Blaze* put in (as usual) a very unexpected appearance this morning about 7 o'clock. Commodore Murray, Lt. House inspector, Captain Davis of the Lt. House board, and Colonel Wilkins USA were aboard and came up to the house. The officers expressed themselves much pleased with the buildings, lanterns, lights, apparatus, and c. Obtained commander Murray's approval of the extension of the elevated walk up to the beach line and also of a plank walk extending from the Lt. House to the pier.

October 28: Terrific westerly gale. The waves dashing high over both piers and over my head when on my way down to light the beacon.

October 31: Mainlight and beacon both bewitched tonight requiring my constant attention during the entire night.

1874

April 1: Heavy gale. A vessel entered during the storm, ran into the elevated walk doing considerable damage.

June 9: Fierce tornado and thunderstorm about 4 p.m. Bark *Geo. S. Seavor* entered the harbor in the worst of the storm in a dilapidated condition, running into and damaging the elevated walk.

October 1: Received notice today from Major Robert, Lt. House Engineer, of the proposed removal of the beacon light to the west pier.

October 20: Petitioned the Lt. House Board for an assistant.

November 16: The beacon was removed to the west pier today.

November 23: Fearful storm. Strong westerly gale, with snow and sleet. The man in temporary charge of the beacon light was unable to reach it tonight—consequently the light was not exhibited.

November 24: The storm continues unabated. Very cold and snowing and drifting. Creek frozen across. A part of the elevated walk carried away and the beacon again unlighted.

1882

July 7: Rainy day. Sent to the Dept. a request for 4 cords of wood.

July 9: Pleasant day. Rain in the evening. Rec'd reply to request for wood. Do not allow it any longer.

July 12: Clear and warm. Mr. James rec'd his dismissal from the care of the beacon light.

September 30: Rec'd letter from Commander Watson in reply to mine asking for Mr. James's restitution if possible. Is afraid nothing can be done.

1883

February 27: Letter from the Inspector informing me that I shall not be allowed any one assist me with the beacon light during the summer months.

April 22: Strong East wind and cold rain. Reached beacon with difficulty.

April 23: Strong East wind. P. M. gale from the North. Reached beacon with difficulty.

September 10: Warm and clear. Rec'd pleasant call from Lt. Kennedy this morning. Walked to the beacon with me and has consented to my employing Mr. James to assist me.

1884

April 8: 2 inches of snow. Rec'd notice thro' letter from Captain Cook to

Collector of Customs of this port that I shall be permitted to employ "a laborer" to assist me at the beacon. Representative Calkins, and other kind friends, including the Inspector, have been interesting themselves in my behalf. I am deeply grateful. H.E.C.

1885

July 23: Light southwest wind and warm rain. Draped the Lt. House in mourning for General Grant—brave old hero.

October 26: Light South wind—light warm rain. Rec'd letter from the Inspector notifying me that the mainlight will be discontinued at close of navigation and the lens transferred to the beacon lantern.

November 14: Strong Northwest wind, now flurries—cold. Great dissatisfaction exists among citizens and sailors at the contemplated discontinuance of the mainlight.

December 4: Severe West to Northwest gale, rain and snow storm. Terrible storm increasing with the night.

December 5: Gale continues, with snow—cold. Elevated walk badly damaged and beacon damaged and light put out. The beacon cannot be repaired this fall. Telegraphed the inspector and afterward wrote him and the engineer. Telegram from the inspector to "hang a lantern" out which I did.

December 6: Gale continues, with snow—cold. 14 degrees below. Lantern carried away in the storm.

December 7: Gale subsiding. Clear and very cold. Sent a man down in a tug to light the beacon. No other way of reaching it.

December 12: Fresh East wind, flurries of snow—freezing cold. Capt. Cook arrived by early train. Instructed me to close the light as soon as it was practicable and forward bill for tug services.

December 15: Weather moderating. Evening, growing colder. Cleaned and polished lamps and other apparatus and covered them from dust and dampness in the oil room.

1886

March 22: Clear and cold. Light Northwest wind. "Notice to Mariners" appeared in Chicago morning papers that the mainlight of this port would be discontinued on the opening of navigation and a 5th order lens showing a red light placed at the end of the west pier.

March 25: Cloudy and mild. Light Southwest wind. Notice in the Chicago a.m. papers that the Lt. House Board has revoked the order to discontinue the mainlight.

October 14: Severe Southeast wind and rain storm this morning and severe westerly gale this afternoon. The beacon structure was carried away in the storm and thrown up on the beach, a wreck. The temporary light also carried away.

October 17: Clear and cool. Light West wind. Took a walk up the beach to view the wreck of the beacon.

December 9: Clear and mild—fresh south wind—cloudy and growing colder. Put up lamps and other apparatus for the winter.

December 12: Thick fog and warm rain. Reopened the light for the salt boat, *F & CM No. 2,* which was supposed to have gone into winter quarters below, but subsequently concluded to make the trip and telegraphed for the light.

December 16: Calm and clear—growing colder towards night. Packed the lamps away for the second time.

1904

October 1: Tendered my resignation of the mainlight to the Lt. House Inspector, the same to take effect October 13, 1904.

October 13: North fresh to moderate winds, cloudy to clear and pleasant. Looking over public property—signed property returns. The retiring Keeper left the station this 4 p.m. and all her personal effects.

Harriet E. Colfax died April 16, 1905

FROM A LIGHT ON THE SEAWAY
(1972)
Ethel Williamson

ALTHOUGH THE WRITINGS of women lightkeepers make dramatic reading, the typical woman who lived in a lighthouse on the lakes after the 1880s
was the keeper's wife. Ethel Williamson's impressions and experiences no
doubt parallel those of the hundreds of women before her who suddenly
found themselves "for better or worse" housekeeping in a lighthouse on the
Great Lakes. For someone who thought of herself as timid, it was not always
easy. The couple with their two sons moved to their light on the Welland
Canal, which connects Lake Ontario with Lake Erie, shortly after Cy
Williamson returned from World War II. "Light-Housekeeping" she ironi-
cally calls it, especially since the keeper's house was a wilderness of dead rats
and sticky paint and lacked running water when they first moved in. The
Williamsons persevered, however, through storms, fires, Hurricane Hazel,
their car running into the canal, and the rescues of numerous boaters. Their
light became part of the new St. Lawrence Seaway and was eventually discontinued; like many other lighthouses on the lakes, it was replaced by modern range lights. When the tower was torn down Mrs. Williamson wrote, "In
spite of the many worries and heart aches that tower light caused over the
years, I couldn't help feeling sad when it was discontinued. I do miss that
familiar, searching beam. It's like losing an old friend."

The courage she gained conquering the lighthouse stood Mrs. Williamson
in good stead. She learned ham radio and kept her license from 1949 to
1997. Born in 1907, she still writes for magazines and leads tours of her old
home, now a Coast Guard station.

⤙⟞⊙⟝⤚

We Begin Life At The Port Weller Light

Doug and Bruce, who had been reluctant and hesitant about our move
to the lighthouse, now had an entirely different outlook. They began to accept their new life with good humour. They were keen to try a hand at
everything.

"I can hardly wait for the warm weather," said Bruce. "Bet I'm the first
one to dive in the canal!"

"You'll have to get up early in the morning to beat me!" said Doug.

"I'll beat both of you!" Cy boasted.

"That lets me off the hook," I told them. "You won't get me into the water before the middle of July!"

"How about that great big sand pile up the road?" said Doug. "I can just imagine all the kids we know having a ball running up to the top and sliding down."

"I don't think we'll see many kids down here," I said, "that is, unless someone drives them down."

"They can ride down on their bicycles," Doug suggested.

"I doubt if they'll want to ride seven miles down here and back," I told them.

"We're going to do that . . ." said Bruce, "and five days a week, too." He paused a moment, then added, "what'll we do when it rains?"

"Don't worry about that, dear," I told him. "There's a bus to town, once you get to the main road. I'll drive you to catch the bus on bad days, and wait for you at the bus stop when it's time to come home." They were both visibly relieved to hear this.

Climbing the high tower was the boys' chief attraction. They teased me unmercifully, because I was afraid to try it. "Come on, Mother, it's a breeze. Just take one step at a time. You'll love the view from the top. You could even see Toronto!"

"Not I," I told them, "never, never, never!"

Finally, when Cy joined in the teasing, I was shamed into it. I reached the first landing safely, then stalled. Cy, with both arms outstretched for protection, was just one step behind me. I took a deep breath, said a quiet prayer, and climbed on. Each step was taken in terror. At last we reached the halfway platform. To go up or down, which was the more frightening?

"Come on, honey," urged Cy. "You're bent over like a pretzel; straighten up and don't look down."

I sucked in another deep breath, gritted my teeth and managed to climb to the top. There, I was above the treetops. What a wonderful sight from that lofty tower! I could see the western outline of the lake as it circled from Port Weller to Toronto, thirty miles away, and to the east was the shoreline all the way to Niagara.

The lake looked peaceful and endless as it blended into the horizon. Only one small ship could be seen—the sandsucker, *Charles Dick.*

I gazed in wonder at the main light, while Cy told me all about it. The main light with large parabolic reflector was attached to a gear-driven table which revolved in a bowl of mercury. It revolved at a pre-determined rate to identify the light as Port Weller. Flashes from the light could be seen for twenty miles on a clear night. The light was very old and had originally been driven by a clock motor powered by weights. It had now been converted to electric drive, and was operated by remote control from the Watchroom.

Cy oiled the motor, checked the light bulbs, then said, "Ready, dear?"

"As ready as I'll ever be," I answered, and, following him, turned, facing the steps, and began the long, slow descent. The boys below cheered me on but the steps felt slippery, and my hands were clammy with sweat as I gripped the metal rails. Once again on the ground, I swore, "Never again!"

It was exciting watching for the first ship to enter the canal. I saw some in the distance, heading for other ports; then, suddenly, I saw one heading right for the opening to the canal, and then it slowly sailed right past the lighthouse. I stood on the bank, waving madly, and at last one of the sailors returned my wave. The captain of this ship would be honoured in an official ceremony in which he would receive a top hat for being the first to enter the canal that season. At first the movement of lake ships was slow, due to ice conditions in Lake Erie. It was at least two weeks later when the ocean ships arrived.

One day Cy called down to me from the top of the main light tower "Look out in the lake, honey. It's the first Saltie!"

Sure enough, a short time later, a ship from The Netherlands sailed up the canal. The next one was a British ship; then one from Norway. It was easy to spot the salties from a distance, for they were quite different. They were smaller than most of the lakers, and rode higher in the water. My little camera was never far away, for I wanted to capture these exciting events on film.

Once the days grew warm, I was anxious to have a garden. The ground around the lighthouse was impossible to level by hand. We worked for days with pick and shovel to no avail. Finally, we had to give up.

"I'll have to get the canal bulldozer," said Cy. "We'll never be able to move this ourselves."

A few days later, a man arrived with his machine and levelled the ground all around. Now came the job of raking and digging. What an assortment of refuse we found! Railway spikes, nuts and bolts and sundry other items left by the canal builders! We decided to plant a vegetable garden first. How we watched for the first tender shoots of lettuce and beans to appear!

One morning, I ran outside, as usual, to note the growth, and screamed in anger, "There's nothing left!"

Cy came running, the boys close behind. "What's the trouble?" he asked. Then one glance told him. "It's those darned rabbits," he cried, "they've eaten everything!"

No matter what we planted, the rabbits ate it as soon as it showed above the ground; they even ate the bark off our rose bushes. It was hopeless to try any more. We settled for lawns and spirea bushes.

Cy was responsible for the operation of the station twenty-four hours a day. I helped him by taking the day watch, so that he could get some sleep. Except for stormy days, the boys rode to school on their bicycles. I drove into town once a week for groceries—then stopped for a short visit with our parents, for we had always lived close by our families, and I knew they missed us; especially the boys. We were told it was impossible for us to get a telephone, out on the pier, so I couldn't even call them. Sometimes the hours seemed to drag.

One day I asked Cy, "Could we have some chickens, dear?"

"What?—and have them blown into the canal the first windy day!"

It was quite true. On calm days it is so easy to forget the wild ones. When that west wind blows across the lake, it has a clean sweep of about 15 to 30 miles. Often, the bed sheets have been torn right out of my hands as I tried to take them off the clothesline.

Our house was about twenty feet from the canal, and the lake about a hundred yards to the west. No matter where we looked, we saw water. Sometimes, especially in rough weather, it was just like being aboard a ship. At least we were spared the rocking motion, but we often got the spray.

Every morning, once the porridge was made and the coffee "perking," I'd awaken the boys, then run through the woods to the lakeside. I just loved being out in the early morning air. Each day the view seemed different—the cloud formations, the various shades of colour in the sky and water. Taking deep breaths, and letting the wind blow my hair, I'd scan the horizon.

"Mother's out looking for bodies!" the boys would tease. I'd have died if I had ever seen anything as gruesome as that, but I must admit I was always on the lookout for something exciting.

The view from our pier was an ever-changing delight. From my favourite vantage point, about halfway down the pier, and looking westward, I could see, first, Port Weller Beach; then Port Dalhousie piers; and from there, the lake outlined in a giant semi-circle by the Niagara Escarpment, which shelters the whole Niagara Peninsula. During a temperature inversion, the entire shoreline, from Port Weller to Toronto, thirty miles away by lake, is clearly visible, and, at night, one can see lights all around the lake like a diamond horseshoe. The hills outlined by the sunsets, are magnificent, and the reflections from the steel furnace fires in Hamilton are the most spectacular sight of all.

One day, as I was standing there, a ship suddenly exploded! I ran screaming, into the house. "I just saw a ship blown to pieces!" I yelled to Cy. He ran outside, and, with his binoculars, could see pieces of wreckage floating about. He radioed the shore station on Toronto Island, to notify all ships.

Within an hour we were besieged by hundreds of people, including the press. Reports of the incident had been received from nearby beaches. All ships were accounted for except an oil tanker. Everyone assumed it was the casualty. Rescue planes and coastguard boats searched the area. In the debris was found a man's wallet, containing his name and address. This was the only clue to the disaster. When police called his home, they heard facts of a puzzling story. Two men, partners in a shipping business, owned an obsolete ship. They decided to take it out on the lake, set explosives, and blow it up.

After leaving the ship they pulled away in a small rowboat, and rowed to Port Weller Beach; watched the explosion, then took a taxi to their homes, unaware of the confusion they had caused, or simply unconcerned. If it hadn't been for the tell-tale wallet which had accidently fallen from one man's pocket, we may never have known the true story.

My woman's curiosity, or nose for adventure, kept me alert for any signs of unusual events: a small boat in distress; youngsters adrift on a home-made raft, or swimmers who had gone beyond their depth. These things happened all the time. Cy was always nearby, ready and willing to offer assistance, or radio for help, if it was beyond our means.

Storms seemed more frightening out there than at home in the city. They developed so swiftly, seemingly out of nowhere, and there was little time for the unwary to reach the safety of shore, but the fog was our worst enemy. It was deadlier than any storm, for it crept in without warning. A sudden change in wind or temperature caused the fog to roll its blanket in seconds. No warning instruments told us it was coming; only constant vigilance that must be maintained twenty-four hours each day.

Sometimes fog is but a momentary thing; again, it can linger for a week or so without letup. The noise of the generators, pumping air into the fog-horn, was deafening for they sat plunk in the middle of our house. The radio beacon sending code, and the foghorn's mournful bellowing, sending its warning to ships on the lake, sometimes nearly sent Cy and me out of our minds. Strangely though, the boys, who slept so close to all the machinery, vowed they never missed a good night's sleep!

Inside or outside the house, there was no escape from the noise. During a very dense fog, if there were a few moments of silence, it was almost frightening, for the silence was pregnant with hidden fears. In such a fog, even the birds were still. It took me a long time to accustom myself to these strange and awesome periods.

In time I accepted these unpleasant days and learned to carry on with my household tasks, and simply ignore the noises and the depressing feeling of claustrophobia. I never realized the extent of dampness that pervaded the house until I noticed the veneer finish peeling off the bedroom furniture!

I was by nature a very timid person, having been afraid of electric storms; going alone into dark places, and with a genuine dread of physical injury. Amazingly, this new life at the lighthouse helped me to control these fears; not all at once, but gradually, over the years.

THE BEST JOB IN THE WORLD
(1997)
Victoria Brehm

A TALL, RANGY BLONDE who had crewed on her father's sailboats since she was a child, Jeanné Vachon was seventeen the summer she shipped out as a deck officer cadet on the thousand-foot bulk carrier *Indiana Harbor* in 1982. Competent, confident of her ability to handle any ship, four years later at the tender age of 22 she was master of a passenger tour boat out of Chicago. After graduating from the US Great Lakes' merchant marine academy in Michigan, she wanted to avoid the constrained world of the bulk carriers where she knew she would not get home for weeks at a time, so she worked first on tugs and then in the passenger boat business.

"I thought I owned the world when I made captain," she laughs. But the reality was less sanguine. She found herself working from ten a.m. to four a.m., commanding crews who continually tested her to see how far she could be pushed or if she would make mistakes. Enduring profanity that was "unbelievably foul," constant harassment, and exhausting hours, she discovered the shipping line's supervisors would not support her. After the owner, an Illinois congressman, came up to the pilot house one evening, put a gun down on the chart table, and "invited" her to go out, she quit. Ten years later, still smarting from her experiences, she acknowledges that she was too young, too unprepared for the situations she had to face. Her cadet experience had been with a chivalrous captain from the American Steamship fleet who had five daughters, and "his cadets became his adopted daughters. The reality after the academy was very different," she concedes. Vachon now manages a branch bank in Wisconsin.

A decade later, Katie Gullickson Bridges, another deck officer academy graduate, was met at the top of the ship's ladder by the mate who advised her not to bother unpacking. The captain had told him bluntly, "I don't care how you do it, just get rid of her." After a month of being told to stand at the side of the pilothouse and look out the window she left, filed a grievance with the union, and went back to sailing for Interlake, the more enlightened company she had sailed with as a cadet. Her union has three harassment grievances from other women pending, but Bridges doubts they will do much to punish the offending shipping line or restore the wages she lost when she was driven off. The "girls," as one union chief refers to women officers, have had rough sailing on the lakes.

When Lillian Kluka, the first woman captain of a bulk carrier, hears stories like this her black eyes snap and she jumps out of her chair and paces. An ebullient, energetic women who commanded the flagship of Canada's Patterson fleet, and is now a pilot, she is a model and an active mentor for other women who sail. "It worries me," she says, "that we're not getting any further ahead." Women still have to prove themselves every day, still have to show many of the men they sail with that they are more than Tugboat Annie or a cook who is angling to become the captain's mistress, long the common roles women played in the maritime world of the lakes. Worse, many of the women who begin classes at the maritime academies in Michigan or Ontario never finish, or if they do, stop sailing after a year or two. In 1996 there were only about a dozen women officers sailing the lakes full time. Many quit to marry and raise families; others leave because of the long hours and separation from loved ones that sailing has always demanded.

Those who continue to sail cope not only with sexism and harassment, but sometimes with hate mail, physical attacks, and worst of all, isolation. Because they are women, they are isolated as cadets; once they become officers they are isolated because they must command. They cannot easily become friends with unlicensed women crew members to whom they must give orders, especially when modern-day cooks on lakes' ships, who often earn as much as captains, think anyone who would give up an air-conditioned galley for a hot, dirty deck is crazy. Nor, except in rare instances, can women officers go "up the street" to a bar when in port because they must set an example. As Kluka observes, "If one woman screws up, it makes it worse for the other women who follow." When they develop a good working relationship with a male officer, as most women eventually do, it will be assumed they are lovers. If two women officers are friends, they are suspected of being lesbians.

But despite all the difficulties, these women who sail the lakes professionally in the 1990s are survivors who meet the challenges of being pioneers with grace and generous good wit. When a crusty chief engineer complained to Kluka that women should be kept barefoot and pregnant, she kicked off her shoes, threw out her arms, and said, "Well, I'm ready!" He vanished without another word, she notes drily. A customs officer shown to her office with papers for her to sign waited patiently a few moments, then asked for the captain. Kluka turned from her desk and said simply, "You're looking at him." As Katie Gullickson was being married, she turned to her maid of honor, long-time roommate and engineer Kathy Luhta, and winked. "I guess this ruins our reputation as lesbians, doesn't it?" Despite the problems they still encounter, all women officers describe sailing as a wonderful job, especially because of the close friendships they make with other crew members, for lakes ships have always been, and still are, like families. After numerous practical jokes at her expense, Luhta's oilers chipped in to buy her a TV for her birthday. Kluka, who was savagely beaten one night on a Lake Superior dock when she returned to the ship after a dinner engagement, observes that now she is so protected by the crews she commands she feels suffocated.

First Mate Colleen Savage, 'Leen to her friends and shipmates on the EPA research vessel *Lakes Guardian*, has sailed the lakes as long as any other woman officer, and she is adamant that what finally matters is not your sex but how you do your job. The great, great grand-daughter of a lakes captain from Beaver Island who graduated first in her class from maritime academy, Savage is a small, spare woman with glasses and a bob haircut slightly touched by gray. She looks less like a first mate and more like the librarian she sometimes considers becoming. Since she has done her job extremely well, why then hasn't she become a captain? Is there is an invisible glass ceiling for American women on the lakes that Canadians such as Lillian Kluka do not face?

Savage believes, as do the other women, that there will be more women captains and chief engineers within a few years, since the old, patriarchal world of men who came up the hawse and saw no place for women in the pilot house or the engine room is vanishing. As more men who are academy graduates and have always worked with women become senior officers, prejudices are disappearing.

But unlike Kluka, who would be nothing else, Savage has no desire to become a captain. The hours and stress of being a mate are bad enough. "There are some wonderful moments: the Northern Lights, the weather." She has always stood the four to eight watch. "Dawnings are a nice time of day. But then you can go through days and days of fog and think that you'll be crazy before you see a buoy again."

Unlike younger, unmarried women who work the lakes, Savage has never had problems with command. She and her husband, a marine engineer, graduated from the maritime academy together and have sailed on separate ships for more than a decade, not always by choice. "I was always married. And I was older. That makes a big difference. My crews have always produced for me when I needed it. They'll give 120 percent if you ask."

But she is quick to admit that being an officer changed her in ways she did not expect. "You lose your spontaneity. You can become turned off emotionally, desensitized, because being over-friendly—touching—is misconstrued." Because the responsibility is so great— "certain choices, once made, cannot be changed, and the safety of others is always on your mind"—she found herself becoming almost cold. Bonding among the crew of any ship is much more accelerated than on shore, and more intense, which is both good and bad. As generations of men before her have learned, in order to command an officer must be a little aloof. But because she was a woman, she also became the person to whom the crew came with problems— "the Ann Landers syndrome" as she terms it—problems she could not solve and, unlike a psychotherapist, was not trained to distance herself from.

As she describes it, sailors of both sexes are a different breed. They're all non-conformists who rebel at eight-to-five jobs and have an undoctrinaire religion borne of years of living with the elements and the natural world that most professionals who work in offices never experience. They also tend to be iconoclasts who are uncomfortable joining groups or melding into society on shore. Although Savage says that "doing the job is the only thing you're there for," she is quick to add that the simple humanity of being part of a group marooned for weeks at a time aboard ship makes that more complex. "If you could choose your own crew, sailing would be the best job in the world," she laughs, "but you can't do that. Everyone thinks that sailing is so romantic, but it's not. There is no longer any behavior that surprises me." There are times, she admits, when she would just like to be able to have a cup of coffee with another woman and talk as women do, to cease being a thoroughgoing professional for a few moments, to not be a role model. Finally, to stop being a token because she is a women officer.

Talking of the requests for interviews she fields and the letters asking for information about women officers that arrive at her mailbox, she is wry. "I have more to offer than getting a boat up and down the lakes." But in the same breath she admits, like any old salt, that she knows a good bar in every port and "I can talk the line with the best of them." She's also recovered from that worst of situations, being a green third mate sailing for an inexperienced captain, and recovered from the loss of confidence and self-esteem that being a cadet caused her. "I've conquered that devil," she says briskly. But she still hates to go up in the pilot house when she visits her husband's ship and there's a cadet on board. "When I watch them, my hands still sweat." She thinks that coming up through the hawse, the traditional way of the sea until the advent of the maritime academies in the 1960s, was a better system because the sailors who started as deckhands and worked their way up knew every part of the ship, had years to learn to wheel, to become officers, before they finally took command. Maritime academy cadets have no such luxury of time.

"Cadet training is never long enough to prepare you for what you're going to face. Never. And it has nothing to do with being a woman. I used to think that I had to do a better job than men, but I've learned that it's really a matter of acceptance of you as a person and an officer, no matter what sex you are. Eventually you learn the satisfaction of taking care of all the perennial crises—all the things you can't anticipate. Until finally you surprise yourself with your own achievements."

Savage has taken a year off to care for her invalid mother and she is undecided if she will return. "The hours are killers. Twenty-four hour days are not uncommon. And it's more than that. My father and my brother died while I was sailing. That's hard. And with my husband, well, I think we've just missed too much." She laughs again and tells how Charley McGuire, a folksinger from Minnesota, wrote a song about a conversation she had over channel sixteen with her husband when their ships met in the St. Mary's River. Her marriage has been conducted by radio more often than not, and as Charley sang, "The Coast Guard says loving on the radio is a sin." Most ships now have cellular phones, but as Kluka and Gullickson point out, it's easy to spend your salary talking to loved ones every night.

"We take the lakes for granted," Gordon Lightfoot wrote in his song about the sinking of the *Edmund Fitzgerald* in 1975 which has become a theme for those who work the fresh water, but his lyric is truer than many think. Landbound ship watchers never ask, or scarcely imagine, what a price sailing on the lakes demands. In the past the men who sailed the lakes were forbidden, by gender and professional tradition, from speaking out. The numerous autobiographies of lakes captains are written in a code that silences fear or failure: technical details of sailing take precedence and danger is mentioned only before they became captains and were not accountable for error. When they write, lakes captains participate in the mythology that they are minor Gods, leaders of a life that is so romantic. But women who sail are less interested in protecting a myth and more likely to tell the truth. And the truth of sailing the lakes is the truth of the merchant marine everywhere on the globe: it pays well for interesting work, there are long vacations and good benefits, and often ships are much happier, more exciting places to work than an office or a schoolroom. Women who are willing to confront the problems of sexism and harassment are freed from playing a traditional role and dressing in an expected way. They can, as one female engineer described it, put on their underwear and their coveralls and hard hat and go to work. They also have the opportunity to do what has historically been a man's job and do it well, proving themselves to themselves. But sailing also demands a great cost in lives and spirit from those who don't see their children and lose touch with families on shore. As one woman officer put it, "My mother-in-law says she'll raise my babies, but what's the point of having them if I'm not around to see them grow up?" Those men and women who remain with the industry for many years, or for a career, are sometimes those who have little to lose on shore.

The shipping companies of the Great Lakes have integrated sailing to a degree undreamed of even ten years ago. The blatant sexual harassment Jeanné

Vachon suffered in the early 1980s in Chicago would hardly be tolerated now. Still, no company, however enlightened, can change the demands of sailing itself. The merchant marine is not a romantic, easy profession for anyone, no matter what their sex. As 'Leen Savage believes, "Women's lib is not the issue. Everyone should get a fair shake." Lillian Kluka agrees, once volunteering to give her command to a man with a family when downsizing reduced the number of commands available. With sailors like 'Leen and Lillian in the pilothouse, the traditionally masculine world of the lakes is gone. Unlike the nineteenth century, women are no longer in danger of being dragged around the deck by their hair and they don't make headlines when they earn their licenses.

Where does the merchant marine on lakes go from here? Will it be better, as Kluka believes, when there are equal numbers of men and women on every ship? Or will that cause more problems? Can that equality be achieved unless older women who have already raised their families see shipping out as an attractive mid-life career? Will those women be able to overcome not only the remaining prejudice against women, but against age as well? Colleen Savage's assessment has become the trenchant question which now must be answered when the traditional roles for men and women in Great Lakes shipping have been changed forever.

What is a fair shake?

Women's Lives, Women's Lakes

Women's Lives, Women's Lakes

Where Land and Water Meet

Portrait of My Wife and Her Best Friend
Rodney Lloyd

FEW OF US WILL make history. Fewer still will leave an autobiographical record of lives well-lived but lacking, perhaps, in historical drama. This final section, "Women's Lives, Women's Lakes," is a collection of just such writings by Everywoman, narratives that record the detailed dailiness of lives lived on the Great Lakes, a counterpoint not only to the Great Man theory of history, but to the Great Woman theory as well. Aside from a poem by Margaret Atwood, there are no texts by distinguished writers such as Jameson and Woolson here. There is no profile of a notable woman as in the other sections of *The Women's Great Lakes Reader.* Many women in this section wrote only one book or a few stories; their responsibilities to families and to communities took precedence and are the subject of their work. None participated in history-making epochs such as the settlement of the frontier. No one won any medals for bravery, or challenged the assumptions of gender in a profession, or suffered extraordinary hardships. They were all, as most of us are, average: the girl next door, the mother down the block, the teacher on a summer trip, the woman facing a difficult illness.

Their narratives are arranged to reflect the patterns of women's lives from childhood through marriage and children to old age, from a way of life that was lived on the lakes for millennia before white settlement, to the contemporary reality of the nursing home. Theoretically, such a collection could be assembled from any region of the United States or Canada, but it would not be the same. What sets these writings apart is the landscape of the Great Lakes that, even now, after they have been mapped, channeled, lumbered, mined, industrialized, and supposedly civilized, still resist control, still shape lives lived near them. Because of the lakes, these narratives acknowledge the tenuousness of life and the failures of technology to protect or heal. But they also suggest that encountering the still-wild waters of a place that knows no gender or imperatives of socialization can be immensely freeing for women who have known little else.

Even as we are shaped by the places in which we lived, so are we shaped by the languages we speak. English, like many languages, divides the world into masculine and feminine, into he and she. The languages of the American Indians who first settled the lakes, however, do not divide the world by gender. Instead, it is divided between animate and inanimate—people, trees, rocks, waters—those things which are capable of life and action and those things which are not. The lakes have always been animate, genderless, and perhaps that is why in *The Women's Great Lakes Reader* and particularly in this section, the influence of Native cultures is so strong. Here is a model, unlike the Classical world or Europe, that did not distinguish based on sex. Here also is a natural world that invites risk, and sometimes rewards it with knowledge, not only of how to live, but also of how to die.

MARSH LANGUAGES
(1995)
Margaret Atwood

The dark soft languages are being silenced:
Mothertongue Mothertongue Mothertongue
falling one by one back into the moon.

Language of marshes,
language of the roots of rushes tangled
together in the ooze,
marrow cells twinning themselves
inside the warm core of the bone:
pathways of hidden light in the body fade and wink out.

The sibilants and gutturals,
the cave language, the half-light
forming at the back of the throat,
the mouth's damp velvet moulding
the lost syllable for "I" that did not mean separate,
all are becoming sounds no longer
heard because no longer spoken,
and everything that could once be said in them has
  ceased to exist.

The languages of the dying suns
are themselves dying,
but even the word for this had been forgotten.
The mouth against skin, vivid and fading,
can no longer speak both cherishing and farewell.
It is now only a mouth, only skin.
There is no more longing.

Translation was never possible.
Instead there was always only
conquest, the influx
of the language of hard nouns,
the langauge of metal,
the langauge of either/or,
the one language that has eaten all the others.

Nodinens

324 ⊕ THE WOMEN'S GREAT LAKES READER

NARRATIVE OF NODINENS
(c. 1900)
Collected by Frances Densmore

FRANCES DENSMORE (1867-1957) was trained as a musician, but she had grown up across the Mississippi River from an Indian camp and within sound of their drums. Beginning in the 1890s she embarked on a life-long study of Indian music and culture, most famously in her two-volume work *Chippewa Music* (1910, 1913). Supported by the Bureau of Ethnology of the Smithsonian Institution, and aided by her sister who kept house (and camp) for her, Densmore published numerous studies notable for their recognition of Indian life as a living, developing culture, rather than the exotic rituals of a doomed and primitive people. More remarkable still was that Densmore began her studies of American Indian culture only three years after the Battle of Wounded Knee in 1890 when few Americans considered traditional Indian life interesting except as lost remnants of a doomed race.

The narrative of Nodinens, who was seventy-four when Densmore interviewed her shortly after 1900 for the book *Chippewa Customs* (1929), is an example of Densmore's enlightened approach to her informants and their world. Nodinens, whose name translates "Little Wind," was a member of the Mille Lac Band of Chippewa and lived on the White Earth reservation in Minnesota. She had grown up with four brothers and two sisters and, as customary, her father trained her brothers and her mother taught Nodinens and her sisters. The training appears to have been rather strict, for Nodinens related that "The first thing I can remember was my mother's saying 'always be industrious. Get up early and do your work. Do you hear me? Do you hear me? Do you understand?' She took hold of my ear and pulled it hard as she said this, and she kept on until I said that I understood. She told me that I must live a quiet life and be kind to all, especially the old, and listen to the advice of the old. . . . She said, 'Do not run after a boy. If a young man wants to marry you, let him come here to see you and come here to live with you. . . .' She taught me to make mats and bags, to make belts and moccasins, leggings, and coats for my brothers, so they would never lack for these things. I have tried to do as my mother taught me. Now, at my age, I look back and am so grateful to her for giving me this advice, and I think it is the reason I have been so blessed and prospered all my life."

◆━◉◉━◆

WHEN I WAS YOUNG everything was very systematic. We worked day and night and made the best use of the material we had. My father kept count of the days on a stick. He had a stick long enough to last a year and he always began a new stick in the fall. He cut a big notch for the first day of a new moon and a small notch for each of the other days. I will begin my story at the time when he began a new counting stick. After my mother had put away the wild rice, maple sugar, and other food that we would need during the winter, she made some new mats for the sides of the wigwam. These were made of bulrushes which she had gathered and dried. She selected a nice smooth piece of ground and spread them out.

I, as the oldest daughter, boiled basswood bark, and made cord, and grandmother made the bone needles that we would use in weaving the mats. When the rushes were ready, we laid a cord on the ground and measured the right length for the mats. My mother knew just how long they should be to go around the wigwam, and we made five long ones, four of middle size, and two small ones. The long ones were two double-arm's lengths, and the middle-size ones were about one and a half double-arm's lengths. We laid the rushes two layers deep on the ground with ends resting on the cord, and then fastened the ends of the rushes to the cord, after which we fastened the cord to the pole that was the upper, horizontal part of the weaving frame. My grandmother directed everything, and she had a large quantity of the thorns from the thorn-apple tree in a leather bag. She had been gathering these all summer but she made sure she had plenty. We all three worked hard getting ready for winter. When my mother had finished the bulrush mats she made more mats for the floor, using either fresh reeds or some that she had gathered during the summer, and she made more of the woven-yarn bags in which we kept our belongings.

My home was at Mille Lac, and when the ice froze on the lake we started for the game field. I carried half of the bulrush mats and my mother carried the other half. We rolled the blankets inside the mats; and if there was a little baby, my mother put it inside the roll, cradle board and all. It was a warm place and safe for the baby. I carried a kettle beside my roll of mats. We took only food that was light in weight, such as rice and dried berries, and we always took a bag of dried pumpkin flowers, as they were so nice to thicken the meat gravy during the winter. There were six families in our party, and when we found a nice place in the deep woods we made our winter camp. The men shoveled away the snow in a big space, and the six wigwams were put in a circle and banked with evergreen boughs and snow. Of course, the snow was all shoveled away in the inside of the wigwam, and plenty of cedar boughs were spread on the ground and covered with blankets for our beds, the bright yarn bags being set along the wall for use as pillows. In the center was a place for a fire, and between it and the floor mats there was a strip of hard, dry ground that was kept clean by sweeping it with a broom made of cedar boughs. The wigwam looked nice with the yellow birch-bark top and the bright-colored things inside. Outside the door there was a little shed made of cedar bark in which we kept the split wood for the fire, so it would not get wet and so we could get it easily in the night. Sometimes there were many of these sheds around the door of a wigwam. The men brought the logs and the women chopped the wood, and put it in the sheds ready for use.

There was a big fire in the middle of the camp, and all the families did their cooking around this fire if the weather was not too cold, but we always had a fire in the wigwam in the evening, so it would be warm for us to sleep. We always slept barefoot, with our feet toward the fire, and we loosened our other clothing. I wore a dress of coarse broadcloth, with separate pieces of the cloth to cover my arms, and I had broadcloth leggings that came to my knees, but I wore no other clothing except my moccasins and blanket. The big rack for drying meat was over the fire in the middle of the circle. During the day the women kept this fire burning low and evenly to dry the meat. When the men came home at night the rack was taken off the fire, for the men put in lots of light wood to dry their clothing. They sat around it, smoking and talking. If a snowstorm came on we spread sheets of birch bark over the meat. We did not dry it entirely—only enough so that it would keep— and the drying was finished in the sun when we reached our summer camp. The fire blazed brightly until bedtime, and then the men put on dry wood so it would smolder all night. The women were busy during the day preparing the meat, attending to their household tasks, and keeping the clothing of the men in order. Each man had two or three leather suits which required considerable mending, as they had such hard wear. We snared rabbits and partridges for food and cleaned and froze all that we did not need at the time.

My father was a good hunter and sometimes killed two deer in a day. Some hunters took a sled to bring back the game, but more frequently they brought back only part of the animal, and the women went next day and packed the rest of the meat on their backs. It was the custom for a man to give a feast with the first deer or other game that he killed. The deer was cut up, boiled, and seasoned nicely, and all the other families were invited to the feast. Each family gave such a feast when the man killed his first game. The men were good hunters, and we had plenty of meat, but every bit of the deer that was not eaten was dried for carrying away, the extra meat, the liver and heart, and even the hoofs. I remember that once a hunter heard an owl following him. When he returned to camp he said: "You must preserve every bit of deer. This is a bad sign, and we will not get any more game for a long time." The hunters went out every day, but could find nothing. We stayed there until we had eaten almost all that we intended to carry away. We were so hungry that we had to dig roots and boil them. My father was a Midé, and one day, when the provisions were almost gone, a young man entered our wigwam with a kettle of rice, some dried berries, and some tobacco. He placed this before my father, saying: "Our friend, we are in danger of starving; help us." This man was the ockabewis who managed and directed things in the camp, and his arms were painted with vermillion.

My father called his Midé friends together and they sang almost all night. The men sang Midé songs and shook their rattles. No woman was allowed to go in that direction. The children were put to bed early and told that they must not even look up. My mother sat up and kept the fire burning. My father came in late and sang a Midé song, and a voice was heard outside the wigwam joining in the song. It was a woman's voice, and my mother heard it plainly. This was considered a good omen. The next morning my father directed that a fire be made at some distance from the camp. The ockabewis made the fire, and the Midé went there and sang. They put sweet grass and medicine on the fire, and let the smoke cover their bodies, their clothing, and their guns. When this was finished, my father covered his hand with red paint and applied it to the shoulders of the men. They took their guns and started to hunt, feeling sure they would succeed. No woman was allowed to pass in front of the hunters when they were starting. The ockabewis killed a bear that day and every man got some game. They killed plenty of deer and bear, and each person boiled the breast of the animals in a separate kettle from the rest of the meat. There was a feast, and they brought these kettles to my father's lodge, and the old men ate there, sitting by themselves and eating from these kettles. After that whenever we were short of game they brought a kettle of rice to my father and he sang and the luck would return. He was so successful that we had plenty of food all that winter.

The hides were tanned with the hair on and were spread on the cedar boughs along the edge of the wigwam. Father gathered us children around him in the evening and instructed us as we sat on these soft hides. He instructed us to be kind to the poor and aged and to help those who were helpless. This made a deep impression on me, and I have always helped the old people, going into the woods and getting sticks and scraping their kinnikinnick for them. During the winter my grandmother made lots of fish nets of nettle-stalk fiber. Everyone was busy. Some of the men started on long hunting trips in the middle of the winter, and did not get back until after the spring work was done; then they rested a while and started off on their fall hunting and trapping.

Toward the last of the winter my father would say, "One month after another month has gone by. Spring is near and we must get back to our other work." So the women wrapped the dried meat tightly in tanned deerskins and the men packed their furs on sleds or toboggans. Once there was a fearful snowstorm when we were starting to go back and my father quickly made snowshoes from the branches for all the older people. Grandmother had a supply of thorn-apple thorns and she got these out and pinned up the children's coats so they would be warm and we started off in the snowstorm and went to the sugar bush.

When we got to the sugar bush we took the birch-bark dishes out of the storage and the women began tapping the trees. We had queer-shaped axes made of iron. Our sugar camp was always near Mille Lac, and the men cut holes in the ice, put something over their heads, and fished through the ice. There were plenty of big fish in those days, and the men speared them. My father had some wire, and he made fishhooks and tied them on basswood cord, and he got lots of pickerel that way. A food cache was always near the sugar camp. We opened that and had all kinds of nice food that we had stored in the fall. There were cedar-bark bags of rice and there were cranberries sewed in birch-bark makuks and long strings of dried potatoes and apples. Grandmother had charge of all this, and made the young girls do the work. As soon as the little creeks opened, the boys caught lots of small fish, and my sister and I carried them to the camp and dried them on a frame. My mother had two or three big brass kettles that she had bought from an English trader and a few tin pails from the American trader. She used these in making the sugar.

We had plenty of birch-bark dishes, but the children ate mostly from the large shells that we got along the lake shore. We had sauce from the dried cranberries and blueberries sweetened with the new maple sugar. The women gathered the inside bark of the cedar. This can only be gotten in the spring, and we got plenty of it for making mats and bags.

Toward the end of the sugar season there was a great deal of thick sirup called the "last run of sap," and we had lots of fish that we had dried. This provided us with food during the time we were making our gardens.

The six families went together, and the distance was not long. Each family had a large bark house with a platform along each side, like the lodge in which the maple sap was boiled. We renewed the bark if necessary, and this was our summer home. The camps extended along the lake shore, and each family had its own garden. We added to our garden every year, my father and brothers breaking the ground with old axes, bones, or anything that would cut and break up the ground. My father had wooden hoes that he made, and sometimes we used the shoulder blade of a large deer or a moose, holding it in the hand. We planted potatoes, corn, and pumpkins. These were the principal crops. After the garden was planted the Midé gathered together, made a feast, and asked the Midé manido to bless the garden. They had a kind of ceremony and sang Midé songs. Old women could attend this feast, but no young people were allowed. Children were afraid when their parents told them to keep away from such a place. The gardens were never watered. A scarecrow made of straw was always put in a garden.

In the spring, we had pigeons to eat. They came in flocks and the men put up long fish nets on poles, just the same as in the water, and caught the pigeons in that way. We boiled them with potatoes and with meat. We went to get wild potatoes in the spring and a little later the blueberries, gooseberries, and June berries were ripe along the lake shore. The previous fall the women had tied green rice in long bundles and at this time they took it out, parched and pounded it, and we had that for food. There was scarcely an idle person around the place. The women made cedar-bark mats and bags for summer use. By that time the reeds for making floor mats were ready for use. They grew in a certain place and the girls carried them to the camp. We gathered plenty of the basswood bark and birch bark, using our canoes along the lakes and the streams. We dried berries and put them in bags for winter use. During the summer we frequently slept in the open.

Next came the rice season. The rice fields were quite a distance away and we went there and camped while we gathered rice. Then we returned to our summer camp and harvested our potatoes, corn, pumpkins, and squash, putting them in caches that were not far from the gardens.

By this time the men had gone away for the fall trapping. When the harvest was over and colder weather came, the women began their fall fishing, often working at this until after the snow came. When the men returned from the fall trapping we started for the winter camp.

FROM Grandmother's Stories
(1889)
Frances B. Hurlbut

Going After Strawberries

"ONE DAY IN JUNE, as soon as dinner was over, Sallie, and a young woman who worked for Uncle Sam, and Uncle Sam's little boy, and I went over to the Canada side of St. Clair River to gather wild strawberries that grew there in great abundance. We crossed the river in a row-boat, and when we got on shore we pulled the boat high up on the beach, so that the waves would not carry it off.

"We had a gay time filling our pails and baskets with the ripe fruit. When we got through we were rather tired, and very leisurely took our way to the boat. We did not notice that the small boy had gone ahead of us. When we were almost to the beach he came running back to us, shouting, 'Boaty! boaty!'

"I knew in a moment that he had done some mischief, and I set my strawberries down and ran as hard as I could toward the river. Sure enough, he had pushed the boat into the water, and she was floating off with the current. I waded out clear up to my neck, but I could not reach her, and as I could not swim I had to wade back.

"By this time the girls and the small boy were on the shore, and as I came back they set up a dismal wail; for the boat was gone, and here we four were, miles away from any habitation, and with a fine prospect of spending the night in the woods, where the wolves and bears still roamed and occasionally Indians were seen.

"We sat in a very melancholy plight, the girls crying, the boy looking doleful, and I thinking of what we should do. There was an island, about a mile below, near the Canada shore, and I thought the current would carry the boat to that island and strand her on its northeastern point; but how to get to that point was the question.

"I looked around the beach, and found there was drift-wood of logs and some long poles that pioneers use in building mud chimneys. I thought that with these we could make a raft, if we only had something to tie them together with; but there wasn't a string a yard long, except those we used to hold up our stockings with, as was the fashion in those days.

"But strings or no strings, that raft had got to be made, and what were sunbonnets and aprons and dresses and skirts for, if in an emergency they wouldn't tie a raft together?

"I told the girls my plan, and they said they didn't believe I ever would get that boat again in any such manner; but they went to work with a will, because I wanted them to, and because it was the only way to get home. After a good deal of hard work a raft was completed, tied with the aforesaid material.

"Luckily the fashion of those days provided every woman with a long chemise that hung down to her ankles, and covered her much more as to her neck and arms than many a fashionable belle of these times is covered by what people are pleased to call full dress.

"You may be sure such a raft was a very frail affair to sail the waters of the great St. Clair River, and Sallie said that 'she knew we would be drowned.' It was only large enough for two, and Margaret and I went, leaving Sallie to take care of the boy.

"It required a brave heart either to go or stay; for in the distance we could hear the occasional howl of a wolf, and on the water was a little raft that looked as if it might fall to pieces at a moment's notice.

"The plan was that Margaret and I should stand up and pole the raft; but as soon as we got away from the shore Margaret was afraid to stand up, so she sat down and cried, and I did the work. The current helped us a good deal, and after a time we could see the head of the island.

"We knew there was an encampment of friendly Indians there at that time, fishing and hunting, but we were not afraid of them.

"By this time the full moon was up, and as soon as we could see the island we saw all of the Indians down at the shore gazing eagerly in our direction. They didn't seem to understand what it was that was coming towards them. But as we got nearer and nearer, and the bright moonlight shone directly on us, and they discovered it was only two forlorn girls on a crazy raft, they screamed and shouted with laughter.

"I didn't care for that, for by this time I could see our boat, that had stranded about where I thought she would.

"The Indians were very kind to us: the men went and got the boat and untied the raft, and the women wrung out the clothes and took us to a wigwam and helped us put ours on; then they assisted us into the boat and put the rest of the wet clothes in, and with many friendly grunts and exclamations they pushed our boat out into the stream, and we hastened back to Sallie and the boy.

"Here I will say that I have never yet seen an Indian treated with kindness but what he returned it by equal kindness, and he never forgets a favor, as I know from experience.

"Sallie and the boy were rejoiced when we got back, and they dried the tears that had been plentifully flowing, put on their wet clothes, and we started for home.

"We agreed amongst ourselves that we would slip into the house the back way, change our clothes, and not tell any one of our adventure, and so no one knew it for some time. But Margaret had a beau, to whom she told the story after a while; and it was such a good story that, man-like, he told it to some one else, and so every one knew it in a little time, and we were well laughed at."

"I don't see anything so very funny about it," said Golden-Hair.

"Well," said grandma, "I related that story, a good many years after, to Mr. Stanley, famous for his pictures of Indians. We were passing the island on a steamer of your uncle's, and I was telling him something of the early days of St. Clair River settlements. He remarked that the incident would make a pretty picture.

"Not long after that he brought me, on my sixtieth birthday, that picture," said grandma, pointing to one that hung in the room.

Here the children all wanted to look at it, though they had seen it a hundred times, and pointed out to each other, with great glee, grandma on the raft, the Indians, and other objects of interest, while grandma herself escaped to her writing-table.

THE LIFE OF A LAKE SUPERIOR FISHERMAN FAMILY

Ida Stafford

IDA STAFFORD (1904-1990) was in her eighties when she wrote a hundred-page recollection of her life growing up as a fisherman's daughter on Lake Superior. She had left the Upper Peninsula of Michigan when she was eighteen to work in Chicago, where she married and raised two children. She was later able to return to a summer home in Skanee, where she kept a little white and yellow wooden boat she called the *GoodEnuf*. Her daughter-in-law, Lillian Stafford, who adapted Ida's manuscript into the following narrative, remembers Ida as being always cheerful and having a wonderful sense of humor. She loved the outdoors, and even in old age would put on a wide-brimmed hat and coast her boat along the shoreline, picking berries.

⋆⇒◉〓⋆

MY DEAR FATHER, husky and strong from his life as a Finnish commercial salmon fisherman in the Gulf of Bothnia, was as blond and blue-eyed, as tall, outgoing and soft-hearted as mother was dark, small, quiet, and determined. Economic hardships brought Father to the United States in 1890, where he hoped to make a better life for himself and his family, leaving Mother and their infant son, John, behind until he could send for them.

Like many other Finnish immigrants, Father found his way to Michigan's Upper Peninsula. Vast amounts of copper had been discovered in the Keweenaw area in the beginning of the 19th century, and the "Copper Boom" attracted many job-seeking immigrants.

To a lifelong outdoorsman like Father, the open sea, the wind on his face, and the endless sky above were almost as necessary as life itself. He tried one shift in a copper mine and, feeling as if he couldn't breathe freely in the enclosed space, he escaped to the outside with a sigh of relief and declared: "There's time enough to go below when I'm dead!"

Instead, he found work at a red sandstone quarry in Jacobsville, a bustling little village near Portage Entry, the entrance to Portage Lake from Lake Superior. Fortunately, in America's fast growing cities there was a great demand for the red sandstone. Quarry work was steady with fairly good pay. After two years, Father sent for Mother and John.

The Atlantic storms were at their fiercest when Mother, at age twenty, crossed the ocean with John, about two and a half at the time. They came, as she described it, "on an old wooden sailing vessel that creaked and groaned and shuddered and I felt sure leaked like a basket."

Exhausted after a month of fearfully rough, cold, uncomfortable sailing, Mother was glad to reach land. Anxiously clutching her small child, not quite knowing what to expect in her new homeland, she joined the human wave of immigrants stepping ashore on Ellis Island, New York.

The trip to Upper Michigan by train wasn't much better than the ocean crossing; a slow, jerky ride, so crowded she stood up most of the way and gave her seat to John.

What joy for Father to have his family with him again! After the happy reunion he greeted his wife with good news: He had saved enough money and could soon buy a 25-foot fishing vessel, an open wooden sailboat, with rough canvas sails.

Finally, after more than two years in Michigan, Father was doing the work he liked best and it proved a successful venture. Eventually, Father had enough funds to construct a permanent home on the west shore of the channel, a log horsebarn, a cowbarn, and a warehouse to store winter supplies of fish, meats, flour and other staples. The buildings were located on seven acres of sandy beach property, by a cove.

He worked hard building docks and shanties for the fishing industry, and an icehouse, where he stored blocks of ice packed in sawdust, plus preserves of different kinds.

A mile away, Father purchased forty acres from which came firewood and lumber. He cleared a portion for cultivation of grains, hay, and vegetables. A dugout held potatoes and other root vegetables.

In time, other fishermen came and soon Portage Entry was a village of about a dozen families all supported by a thriving fishing industry. The copper mining towns of Keweenaw Peninsula doted on fresh salmon-red trout, delicate whitefish, herring, and pike. In summer, Father brought the fish to town (about 15 miles) by boat and in winter by horse and sleigh.

Lake Superior provided but it also took its toll. Soon after Mother and Father celebrated the birth of their second child, Arthur, death claimed John, about seven then. The tragedy struck in the winter after the ice for preserving foods and fresh fish had been cut and sawed into large blocks from the frozen bay when it was about two feet thick. This had left a space of open water which soon froze over again. The ice was about an inch thick when John and his playmate went sledding on it. John went ahead with a rope about his neck and shoulders while his friend August rode. The ice gave way and John went under. August's father saw them at that moment and dashed out, managing to grab his terrified son, but the sled slipped away and John was left in the cold water under the ice. A heavy current took him quickly lakeward.

In the spring, Father searched for his son every morning for miles along the beach when the wind was favorable for taking John to the shore. One bright morning, Mother saw him carrying the small figure towards home, and relief and grief overwhelmed her. She named her next son John Peter.

In the years following, four more sons were born, Fred, Aldrick, Edward, and Henry. Then, in 1902, a daughter, Lyla, and a few years later, in 1904, I was born. Then came two more boys, Emil and Walter, and my baby sister, Esther.

Father was hard put at times to support his large family. However, a friend from Finland, a merchant in Hancock, Michigan, loaned him money with but a handshake for bond, saying: "Lake Superior always pays me back." Later in the season, the lake did indeed pay back and Father's credit remained sound.

The homes in our village were near the shore, where docks, shanties, net reels and platforms for drying floats fronted the lake and where racks held lines, ropes, and buoys.

We children looked on with wide-eyed interest as Father and his neighbors made fires under large, water-filled wooden vats, adding chips of hemlock bark to the boiling water to dye the nets, making them less conspicuous to the fish. In a community "big wheel house," (a shanty with a large wooden wheel inside, with a lathe and handle to turn it), they built cedar floats. We children loved to ride the handle, shrieking from excitement as the big wheel turned, lifting us from the floor.

Father and the others made sinkers by melting lead in a large iron kettle suspended over an open fire. We watched fascinated as the adults poured the molten lead into casts (similar to cornbread molds but smaller.) With a sharp sizzle, they dropped the casts into a pail of cold water and when cool, removed the lead sinkers from the molds with a knife.

A most unpleasant necessity at the dock were the fish-gut barrels, heavy, covered wooden kegs of about twenty-gallon capacity. Woe unto you if you came upon such a depository uncovered! They were emptied frequently, hauled far into the woods by horse and wagon and emptied into deep pits, a great attraction for bears and other animals.

Late afternoons, Father would often set herring nets outside the breakwater and then we children went along. Our greatest delight was to haul the nets the next morning with their silvery catch. The fish were beautiful to see coming out of the clear, blue waters of Lake Superior and we thought they must be the most delicious in the world when broiled over live coals at the kitchen range.

In late fall and winter, with bone-chilling arctic winds sweeping down from Canada, setting nets under the ice was by far the most miserable work of all for a Lake Superior fisherman. Father and the older boys performed this work, often in below zero weather. They pushed the nets through a hole and under the ice, with narrow boards nailed one to the other to the length of the gang of nets, about thirteen hundred feet. The boards were visible through the clear ice (unless a snow cover made the slow, painstaking task even more difficult). The worst part was raising the nets in the forty degree water—upon reaching the surface they froze into one big mess. The men had to release the fish barehanded and then, to reset the nets, they had to break off the ice once more!

Before the ice froze in the fall, fishing was roughest with cold winds, freezing rain, and hail icing boats and men mercilessly. It was very remunerative however, and Father's and other local fishermen's favorite location was around Keweenaw Point where, despite its wild storms, they often fished. The location of rocky Manitou Island nearby provided a crucial refuge with its natural deep rock harbor and dock where Father and the boys built a driftwood cabin and shanties for storing ice and fish.

During fall trout fishing seasons, storms frequently drove Father and the other fishermen there, crowded into the small quarters. It was a fine port in a storm, however. To us children, listening with fascination to the many yarns and stories of storm captivity there, the island was special, a place of real and imaginary adventures.

Father's return from Manitou was always a big event, first to have him safe at home, then helping with unloading the boat and hearing stories of big catches and wild storms. It was not unusual to catch lake trout that weighed twenty pounds or more each. We helped by holding a lantern for him as he went about completing the chores. The smell of the fish Father and the boys brought back (salted and sealed into kegs at Manitou with only the latest catch taken home unsalted), the wet sawdust, their damp woolen clothing and the sound of ice blocks as they crushed them to preserve the fish for delivery to the markets is forever imprinted in my memory.

Mother baked plenty of bread and packed numerous crocks of butter in case of such emergencies. We didn't like any bread left over from these lake provisions since, having absorbed the fumes from the boat engine, it tasted like gasoline.

A center of activity for us children was the schoolhouse, a typical one-room country school.

A big cast iron stove stood in the center of the room, a virtual monster for devouring huge logs, which the boys who were paid janitors threw on the fire. My brothers held this job for many years.

Like many beginners at our school, we knew no English since we spoke Finnish in our home and village. First graders painstakingly pronouncing words phonetically from their primers were quite amusing to us as we grew older and more proficient in English. Father and Mother, however, like many of their generation, never learned the language of their adopted land.

Our teachers, all Finnish-speaking women, boarded in the village during the school year. One of them stayed at our home for five years and she was a great influence in our family.

In school, after the Pledge of Allegiance, and singing the national anthem or "America," we sang patriotic songs, songs of the Revolutionary and Civil Wars, and ballads, temperance songs, and hymns.

We recited poems and essays such as Lincoln's "Gettysburg Address," "Hiawatha," "Evangeline," "The Declaration of Independence," "Barefoot Boy," "The Legend of Sleepy Hollow," and "Rip van Winkle."

The schoolhouse was a center of great activity during the holidays. At Christmas, the bigger boys were dismissed to get a tree from the woods. You can be sure they made a day of it, much to the envy of the girls who stayed at school making the ornaments. One year, the boys brought an especially tall tree and in hoisting it up, pushed the top right through the ceiling. Plaster showered down on the tree which we brushed off. We left the tree standing, very secure because of the mishap.

So the season began in very high Christmas spirits as we all dispersed to return home, some with horse and sleigh, others on skis or walking, footsteps crunching in the dry, cold night.

Before Christmas, Mother and Father used to go to town for a few days of shopping in preparation for the holidays. They stayed with friends or relatives and left the children at home in care of a neighbor. We awaited their return with the keenest anticipation. What a thrill to hear, at last, the familiar tinkle of the sleighbells as they approached. Then began the scramble to unload the sleigh—with frequent warnings from Mother and Father not to open any parcels.

They would bring, to our delight, tubs of red-and-green hard candy to be shared with any neighbor children who were about. Then there were oranges, dried fruits, nuts, and cookies, and less exciting—ingredients for Mother's holiday cooking. Our Christmas gifts were of the simplest kind: a rubber ball and jacks, celluloid dolls, necklaces for the girls, hockey sticks, clothing, and occasionally a pair of skates.

We decked the rooms with evergreens and their fragrance combined with the cinnamon and cardamom yeast breads and cookies Mother baked. Traditionally Father brought home a boxful of tall candles, three or four of which we placed on each windowsill and lit on Christmas Eve and through the week following—a Scandinavian custom. Father read from a large Finnish Bible of the birth in Bethlehem of the Christ child, and we sang Finnish Christmas hymns.

There was no church in our village and Mother and Father gave us all our religious instruction. Sunday mornings were for Bible study with recitations of catechism and Bible history, all in Finnish and our only formal education in that language.

Christmas vacation and later winter months proceeded with seasonal activities: Father and the boys sawed and cut wood for next year's supply, they mended nets, and made other repairs. The women cut old clothing into strips and wove them on a home carpet loom into striped rag rugs. They did patchwork quilting, hand knitting of socks, mittens, "chooks" (winter stocking caps), and sweaters. Mother spun yarn of wool from neighboring farms with her spinning wheel (made in Finland in 1803).

As the ice in the bay extended further out with the advance of winter, we skated far past the Keweenaw Waterway lighthouse north towards the Jacobsville lighthouse in the glory of winter moonlight. Cross country skiing and sledding were our other favorite winter activities. Slopes were packed down, sometimes iced, for sliding both on skis and sleighs.

In the evenings, we built bonfires in the center of the rink for warming up and for light. Someone brought a gramophone with its cylindrical records and we skated to music "just like downtown."

Winter nights were long and dark and we would stay out until ten or later, often watching in awe the play of the Northern Lights. After skating, it felt good to go indoors for hot chocolate and niusua (Finnish cinnamon bread).

In early spring we welcomed the sight when the waterway lighthouse began its annual sentinel duty, marking the end of a long, closed season of navigation. Casting its intermittent beam through the darkness, the lighthouse was just as reassuring a sign of permanence and continuity as the season itself.

It was a joyous time after the long winter when we discovered blooms of pink or white trailing arbutus under the evergreens in the soft moss, filling the woods with their pungent fragrance. Wild fleur de lis, violets, ladies' slippers, Indian pipe, spring beauty, adder tongue, and wild anemone followed.

Commerce through the Keweenaw waterway was brisk and we girls would watch steamers make the turn around the lighthouse from our bedroom window. Fascinated, we watched the large freighters and passenger steamers carrying excursionists, immigrants, and job seekers "from below" pass by. We'd wave and hail the large steamers, calling out, "Give us a salute, Cap!" and to our delight, were rewarded by loud blasts from the huge stacks.

With a large family, cleaning and cooking were continuous in our home. Mother baked all the bread we consumed. This meant two days a week devoted to that task.

Spring cleaning was a ritual that hit the village like a storm. The women, helped by us children, tore everything apart and brought mattresses, quilts, carpets, and outdoor garments outside to air. We laundered blankets and washed, starched, and ironed curtains. We polished floors, ceilings, walls, and windows to a gloss.

Later in summer, the women washed carpets at the shore in large galvanized laundry tubs. They heated water in a big copper boiler over an open fire outdoors or on the stove in the work shanty. They laid the carpets on a board across a tub of warm water and scrubbed, then rinsed them in the lake.

In spring, much farm work also awaited. Father and the boys did it all with a one-man plow, disc, and harrow, drawn by Maude, our faithful and dependable work horse. Later we planted potatoes, rutabagas, other root vegetables, and grain.

June saw the annual end-of-school picnic, usually on the grassy slope north of the school. With the channel nearby sparkling in the sun, wind in the pines, the blue sky, what truly could be as "rare as a day in June"?

The summer progressed and haymaking began in mid-July. Father rode a sicklebar, drawn by Maude, going round and round the open field, cutting swaths of green hay and clover, daisies and buttercups. Father would circle around patches of wild strawberries for us to pick. Older boys then cut the hay with scythes in spots inaccessible to the sicklebar.

We'd bring along a picnic lunch to the field to save the mile-long trip home. Sometimes we children came to the field later in the morning with fresh-baked bread, newly churned butter, and buttermilk, a snack for the workers.

When the hay was dry, Father and the boys raked it by a horsedrawn iron rake into rolls, pitched it into piles, and brought it to the barn on a hayrack. We'd go out to the field to help hand rake the remaining hay. The men then lifted us on the rack to tramp the hay down solidly, Father and the boys pitching it up to us. How we loved the ride home high atop the stack of hay jostling over the bumpy road!

Arriving at the shore hot and sweaty, everyone—including Maude—headed down to the water for a refreshing swim.

When the haying season ended, the whole village made an annual wild-blueberry picking trip, by boat, to the Huron country across Keweenaw Bay. Blueberries thrived there in rich abundance in areas cleared by loggers and in the aftermath of forest fires. Whole colonies of tents sprang up overnight. The berries were in great demand not only in town, where they were sold for a good profit, but also by the pickers themselves for winter preservation.

They were an important staple to the year-round food supply.

The fun of living in tents and sleeping under the stars in good weather made the camping trip to Huron country one of the highlights of the year. It was in every way a free and happy time. Berrying was the reason for being there and we hurried to pick our quota before the sun was up too high and hot, then went for a plunge into Lake Superior. There we swam and shouted, all boys and girls together, had a hasty lunch, then quickly dashed back into the water until it was time to go for later afternoon berrying.

In the evenings, after a hearty meal, often some freshly caught fish prepared over an open campfire, we collected driftwood for a bonfire on the beach after nightfall. Everyone gathered around to sing songs, tell stories, and play games. When tired, we enjoyed a potato baked in the bonfire as a bedtime snack and then we were good and ready for sleep.

Autumn had its seasonal work and its special pleasures. Potato harvesting was an important time and the children were dismissed from school throughout the county to help with this work. It was dusty, dirty work, but the beautiful, cool, clear days of fall had begun and all around us the forests were aflame in autumn splendor.

By Thanksgiving, all harvesting was finished, fishing came to a close, and deer hunting season began. The men went out to hunting camps (some of the same fishermen's shelters they used during fishing season) at Point Abbeye or Big Huron River or to abandoned lumber camps in the Huron Mountain area. Both does and bucks were legal game and numerous deer were allowed per license. Later in the fall and winter they hunted grouse and rabbits.

Thanksgiving dinner was deliciously prepared venison accompanied by all the abundance of the autumn harvest: rutabagas, corn, pumpkins, potatoes, berry and apple pies, berry sauces, and puddings served with rich cream.

Father smoked or dried venison for winter use and hung it from rafters in the icehouse. He slaughtered hogs, calves and cows, and stored them, with some sold to neighbors.

Thus the years passed, times we thought endless. They were not.

In 1913, Father became ill with what was diagnosed vaguely as an intestinal ailment. In June 1915, he died at home of stomach cancer. He was in his fifties, still a relatively young man. His oldest was twenty two and the youngest was four; I was ten when I lost my father. Although his prolonged illness had prepared us for his death, the final loss was a great shock to the family. He had been the center of our lives.

The funeral was on a bright June day, quite in contrast to our downcast spirits as the cortege proceeded from our dock by boat to Chassell. There were twelve fishing boats from our village, all painted white, in the procession. They passed slowly along the waterway towards Father's final resting place.

During his illness, Father had prepared the older boys to take over his leadership in the fishing business. After his death, daily life continued as usual in our home, the necessity of work a blessing in itself. We all grew more self-reliant with time. Each had duties suited to his or her age and ability. Our background had taught us resourcefulness, self-esteem, pride in work well done, and had given us a positive and optimistic outlook.

Haymaking, Huron Bay berry picking, grain and vegetable harvesting times came and went somehow that first year, and fishing and farming continued somewhat the same for many years thereafter. Father's teaching stayed with us in good stead through the first difficult years without him and throughout our lives. Memories of his quiet serenity and steadfastness abide.

After Father's death we visited Manitou Island, as sometimes we had accompanied him there when he was alive, during good weather. In June 1920, when I was in my mid-teens, we spent several wonderful days on the island searching for agates, while Arthur and Edward set and raised nets. It was a beautiful day, a day of peace and solitude. The memory of Father lingered there: in the rough-hewn furniture he had made for the cabin, in the dock and the shanties where he had stored his fish. Gulls sailed overhead ready to be fed when evening came and the boat returned with fish. A kerosene lantern provided light as later in the evening Arthur judged our stones. He discarded most as not being agates after all.

In later years, when we return to these scenes of childhood and youth, and listen to the whispers and murmurings of the second-growth pines, we send a silent question up to them: does even an echo of the joyous shouts and laughter of those earlier days linger? We think we hear: is the imagination playing tricks? We sigh and continue on our way.

FROM OFF WATCH: YESTERDAY AND TODAY ON THE GREAT LAKES
(1957)
Anna Young

BORN IN SARNIA, ONTARIO, in 1898 Anna Young was the daughter of purser on Great Lakes passenger ships and package freighters and the grand-daughter of a salt water man. Her mother died when Anna was young, and she was raised by these two men who talked "boats for breakfast, dinner, and supper" in a house surrounded by nautical memorabilia. She attended schools in Galt, Ontario, and St. Margaret's College in Toronto. Her only other book was *Great Lakes Saga*, published in 1965. She died in 1967.

‹‹›❦‹‹›

Looking Astern

From the lofty vantage point of the purser's shoulder to the more mature reflections of these later days I have chronicled the changing scene as a sailor's daughter. As purser on several of the early passenger ships on the Great Lakes, my father, at the time of my arrival, had his headquarters in Sarnia, Ontario, a port on the Canadian shore of River St. Clair, of the Great Lakes chain. On the death of my mother a short time later, my father took me intimately into his life.

I accompanied him on many trips and when he was busily engaged I was given to the loyal concern of one Billy Brown, a coloured gentleman from Owen Sound. Billy occupied the pie-making booth off the kitchen of the *S.S. United Empire* and was always addressed, through the door, as "Mr. Brown" by the kitchen crew. Billy always welcomed my assistance and as I was no taller than the door handle such a welcome qualifies Mr. Brown's good nature. When Billy had duties to perform elsewhere I was given to the care of brother Noah Brown who supervised operations, a towel over one arm and a long-handled ladle in the other hand, by going from stove to stove, stirring one pot and pushing back another. He would ladle out a cup of cream soup for my refreshment, break in a soda biscuit, then set me up on one of the long copper-bound tables in the middle of the kitchen. There he would spoonfeed "the little missy" while we told each other the news.

On one of my first trips I escaped from Noah's protective custody and found Billy who was bringing aboard two wooden pails from the dock; one was full of blueberries, the other apples. Ranged on the dewy deck were some of the final, perishable supplies while the remainder was coming aboard in slings in what seemed to me to be enormous quantities. I wanted to watch but Noah snatched me from my point of bliss and hustled me out of the danger zone to the safety of Billy's baking counter. I had a drawer in Billy's sanctum that yielded utensils adapted to my size so, mounting the stool, I began operations under Billy's fond direction.

"You-all make blueberry pies. They's just the colour o' your dress," purred Billy. We talked and rolled and crimped for nearly an hour.

Then the whistle blew. That was the supreme moment of my young life: to race for the deck and watch the ropehandler let go the last rope with a splash. We slowly drifted farther and farther from the dock, the oily slick between the boat and dock widened and, looking up, everything about the river assumed a new look, unfamiliar, for the sky came down so far and the gulls screamed as the churning propeller interfered with their supper.

"Can we go over there?" I asked Billy from the perch of his chocolate shoulder, indicating another interesting scene of operations; the second mate was setting up the log-measuring gear on the afterdeck. We joined him as he was reeling out the log and two passengers who were passing, stopped. They enquired what he was doing, for passengers who didn't know about a ship were inclined to think the log-measuring gear was some sort of trawling fishline.

"There's a float attached to this line that is wound on a reel for gauging the speed of the ship," explained the second mate. "Sometimes we calculate the ship's position by reading the log indicator."

Other passengers joined us and the mate explained the proper way to slip into the life-belt, which was always at the stern of the ship ready for any emergency. This group of passengers was from Philadelphia and ship life was a new experience. The blue expanse of water stretched to the golden sands of the shoreline; the rhythmic throb of the engines was the pulse of the ship. Discipline soon gave an atmosphere of well-ordered routine. Above, on the bridge, the watch "spelled duty and vigilance." The lounge filled up after unpacking was attended to and a pleasant friendly glow was evident. The gong sounded, the dining-room door opened, and a gay scene ensued. There were introductions all round. The guests sat at tables for eight which were screwed to the floor and fresh flowers were on each table.

Just before I was put to bed my father and I stepped into the night, stood by the rail of the ship, and looked up for the stars. The western sky was still softly lit by sunset's afterglow. Here I was shown the evening star which always appeared first in the night sky, then I learned my directions. First to the west for the setting sun, then to the north for the big and little dippers. It took all night to cross Lake Huron and next morning Father took me to the other side of the ship to see the sun come up, so I knew the east. We were slowing down in speed as we entered the St. Mary's River. The northern atmosphere was still, sunny, and pleasantly exhilarating and I listened as he pointed out the smoke from the Ojibway Indian encampments curling skywards from the sheltered inlets where fishing and hunting still provided a livelihood for the menfolk. He told me that these Indians were part of the Algonquin tribe and the women and children would be out, at this hour, gathering sweet grass and porcupine quills to fashion the pretty baskets, boxes, whisk-holders, and button boxes which they sold to the passengers.

Berries grew wild and luxuriously the entire course of the St. Mary's River. On St. Joseph's Island there were some fine farms, while the many small summer colonies along the scenic stretches gave colouring to the beautiful setting of trees and the quiet bays where lush ferns grew to the water's edge. Father explained that in the autumn it was a hunter's paradise, with an abundance of wild duck and partridge. He added that the blueberries, blackberries, and raspberries that grew so profusely went home with the vacationists in crocks of luscious jam for wintertime.

Many smiling groups gathered at the river bends and waved and called to us as they wondered at the fortunate people who so leisurely sailed by. Occasionally a megaphone blew a friendly greeting from some cabin porch. When the big, beautiful ship suddenly rounded a sharp bend in the river it was an event they welcomed in their quiet lives. They waved and watched until we were out of sight for, whatever the time and whatever the weather, the big river and the big boat fascinated them. The Garden River Indian Encampment was the largest reserve in the district and we passed close to it just before rounding the big bend that brought the town of Sault Ste. Marie into full view. At that period the channel traversed was the one north of St. Joseph's Island. From a passenger's point of view it was one of the loveliest passages in the Great Lakes chain, but it was tortuous and there were captains who would not allow a word spoken in the wheelhouse until all its shallow muddy waters were passed. That tortuous channel has been used only by light craft and launches for many years now. The main river has been deepened, straightened, and dredged, affording up and down channels for ships just as our highways have been streamlined for cars.

Today one sees the smoky haze of industry and tall chimneys belching fire before rounding the bend and seeing that Sault Ste. Marie lies ahead. From early Canadian times this area has been a key spot in the industrial and transportation development of our land. The opening and closing of this expanse of river affects all the commerce of the Great Lakes. Its significance must have been understood long, long ago for here was the establishment of the most important Hudson's Bay Company Trading Post. Now, no wigwams adorn the rocky shores, no Indians stalk its busy streets. The sulphur works, the steel plant, and the chemical industry have supplanted them all for men of great vision built here. On the American shore is a thriving community and between it and the Canadian city of Sault Ste. Marie, Ontario, the foaming rapids splash and toss. "Pawating" the Ojibways called it, believing that here their ancestors were created. Here the Manitos blessed their tribes for Pawating was considered a sacred or holy pilgrimage and the rapids were held in great awe by all Indian tribes.

The capstan rattled as it reeled out the feet of heavy rope; everyone was in high spirits for the docking of a ship has a tremendous fascination, especially for the average landlubber. Squatting in a semicircle on the gravel and cinders fringing the dock, we found a colourful aggregation of Indian women with their handicraft. Some were young and attractive with heavy braids hanging over each shoulder; some were old and wrinkled and many had missing teeth. They all wore waists and skirts of varying colours obtained from various deals because they traded wares for the clothing and shoes they needed. Their baskets were very lovely; their boxes were usually fashioned of sweet grass ornamented with porcupine quills and they coloured the reeds with dyes made from roots and berries.

Those who knew it, in those days, can only hope this art will yet be revived among their descendants for it was a unique and very lovely collection of native craft as may be seen now in Shin-wok Home and in a few Indian centres. They came early and stayed late on boat days. They brought their wares and their children, the little papooses peeping over their shoulders with shy smiles. The Indian women were quiet, with docile faces seldom breaking into a smile unless the sale were particularly large. On the whole they seemed unconscious of cold wind or blistering sun—true daughters of nature, changeless and serene. As the town of Sault Ste. Marie progressed and expanded, the Indians kept moving farther from town and gradually receded from the commercial scene to the Garden River Encampment where some seven hundred continue to reside. For many years they provided the souvenirs, so-called, of our present day. Some of us still treasure the scent of sweet grass on a moist day from a memento, holding buttons or trinkets, in the corner of a dresser drawer. For some forty years the Indians staged the Indian play "Hiawatha" for two weeks at their encampment. They drew record crowds as it was beautifully staged in a natural setting with colourful native costume. In 1937 this was shown at the Canadian National Exhibition in Toronto.

The miracle of locking through the Sault canal is told later, as my understanding developed. At this point in my career I had a particular assignment and I took my responsibility very seriously. When the ship was moored to the dockside, waiting for the water level to rise, Father unfastened a section of the deckrail and stepped over the bare inch which existed between the waling strip of the ship and the width of the dock. Locking the rail again, he told me to hold the boat and to tell the man who handled the ropes that the purser was still ashore. He walked off toward a large red stone building on the dockside which housed the marine post office. It was common practice for the purser to go ashore at such times. Time passed and the water rose so my relief was immense when I saw Father, mail in hand, rejoin the ship on a lower deck.

Crossing Lake Superior was just sublime. We sailed hours and hours without stopping and it was beautiful to see the sunset over the water during this summer cruise. The sea was usually calm and although thunderstorms occasionally broke over the lake, the lightning could do no damage as there were neither houses nor trees for it to strike.

Arriving at Port Arthur I had a difficult choice to make. I could spend the day with friends who owned an adorable good-natured pony, whose back was never burdened by the numbers of children he carried for hours at a time, or I could see the Indians. This trip I chose the Indians who lived, in those days, at the Mission at the mouth of the Kaministiquia at the entrance to Fort William. It was noon hour when we shifted to the flour sheds so I watched the Indian settlement which was busy with the preparation of the meal. Outside their wigwam homes the women had iron pots swung over smoky fires and little ones scampered all over the place. In a few years they too retreated from the scene to the fastness and greater privacy of dark Mount McKay in the background.

All too soon the boat was ready to leave but then came the night run to Duluth. The weather was fine and the captain took the inside channel among the islands of the north shore. On this summer evening the twilight lingered long and with the dense forest coming right to the water's edge it seemed there was nothing else in the world but the ship and me. On our arrival at Duluth, next day, the passengers scattered to various tourist attractions. Father and I went half way up the hilly town to have a polish on our shoes by an ebony-faced lad who performed a clop dance, wielding two brushes and both feet together, for my entertainment. Naturally, we always patronized the same shoeshine. Father then took me for a ride up the incline railway, the only form of transportation I haven't enjoyed. After it was over I was so relieved to be on the level that for several years I seldom went ashore in Duluth, fearful lest some well-meaning parent or person would take me again on that incline railway.

As soon as we entered Whitefish Bay on the downbound trip my spirit dimmed. Only two more days of glorious blue waters and the lullaby of the ship. The prettiest part lay spread before me in the upper St. Mary's River around Pointe aux Pins and the beautiful islands. Oh, how I wished I could always be just there. Of course we seemed to go very fast because we would have to say good-bye very soon now. Thoughts of home were tender but not so tender as those of the ship that was sailing to a new or different town every day.

The next trip I made was to visit Grandfather who lived in the inland town of Galt. He had retired from the seas, having been a marine engineer in Central America. Grandfather never was old but he was eighty-six when he died. His sense of humour was priceless, his fund of true stories never-ending. He told me he wanted me to live with him because Father had earned a promotion and had an office in a big city nearby. I supposed I would have to make the best of it separated from Billy, the river, and my friends. I climbed into Grandfather's lap and he said he knew how I felt for he, too, missed his shipmates. The love of the sea united our hearts.

Grandfather always rose very early, long before anyone else. He always cooked the breakfast, lots of sailors did. They were all very kind to their womenfolk and it was comforting to have Grandfather for he seemed to know the answers to all the questions! He had been around a lot.

Holidays from school were coming up and I sensed considerable opposition from my aunts to the plan Father had. He was anxious to make his little girl independent. He felt a little girl was always safe with sailors and his confidence was always justified. It was the safest way he knew to send me to Montreal to visit Aunt Alice, so he overcame the opposition to the plan and came to escort me.

Eating an early breakfast, I sniffed the delicious anticipation of being associated with big business, going away with Papa. Later I listened to the clatter of the hoofs of the horse-drawn cab on the deserted streets as we drove to the railroad station that lovely June morning in 1909. Aboard the empty coach Hugh Young shifted the telescope valise to the upper rack, turned over the extra seat with a clang and a cloud of dust, and we settled ourselves. There were few fellow travellers to see my new gingham dress and the polished points of my new shoes. I had on the new red hair-ribbons from the Christmas tree, saved for an occasion, and this was it. Everything had a value then. . . one didn't put them on just because one had them. We never questioned thrift; we lived by it.

"Where's the boat we're going to?" I enquired.

"She's in the canal," answered Father. "We'll get her at Thorold." That was a sailor's language, I understood.

The train rattled on and the seats filled up. We changed trains at Harrisburg, then at Hamilton. I minded the baggage while Father went to the telephone booth. Emerging from it a few minutes later, putting his glasses in their case, he seemed almost to consult me on the next move.

"Let's see," he said, "guess we had better catch the T. H. and B. and get off at Lock 10; that'll be the best. All right, come on."

I carried my purse and heavy coat. There was twenty-five cents in the purse, a small fortune and a good-sized purse. The coat had to be carried because it was always expected to be "cold on the lake." It was nearly noon and I was getting hungry just when new sights loomed. Father's affiliations were with freight carriers of the package freight class. These plied between Duluth, Port Arthur, and Montreal. This would be the first freight boat I had travelled on and it was a new line for me.

We got off at a cinder crossing which was so high I nearly fell over myself. Seemingly on the edge of the field was a boat and the name on the bow said *Kenora*. She rose up, oh so high, out of the water and a ladder went up the side. It was just about here Father said very casually, "You go aboard here." The awful truth suddenly dawned . . . this time I was going alone.

"How do I go?" I asked in a trembling voice. I had seen His Majesty's mail go up the side in a pail and had an idea that maybe I went up the same way. I looked furtively up at the expanse of steel moored by hawsers to the dockside.

It was his own feelings that no doubt accounted for the sternness in his reply. "You go up that ladder and don't be a bother to anybody." He kissed me.

That was the day I learned never to look back, always look up. It is still the best way to climb.

Eventually and alone, step by step and choking back my tears, I negotiated that ladder and strange hands lifted me over the last top rungs.

Fortunately the purser greeted me and I suddenly felt familiar with him. He said the mate would bring up my things that were still on the dock. I had the purse with the twenty-five cents in it and I was off that ladder but, when the mist of tears cleared, I couldn't see Father anywhere. Fortified with a deck under my feet I followed the purser aft to the dining room. He warned me "always watch that step-over" but I had long ago learned to step over ships' doorsills. While we were eating dinner Purser Marshall asked me if I could tell the time. "Oh yes," I showed him the gunmetal watch I had got last Christmas. Then he asked me if I could manage my hair alone for I had two braids crossed and tied by my ears.

"Well, no," I admitted, "and I forgot I can't button my waist either." I suddenly realized that this was a man's world.

"Don't you trouble, girlie," said Purser Marshall with a spartan gesture.

"You get up at a quarter of eight and at five-to I'll knock on your door and finish you off." That was just how Father did it; the old familiar pattern was here after all.

The captain came in for his dinner and said that if I would wait for him he would take me up on the bridge. No one seemed surprised to see me and I at once warmed to new friends. In the pilot-house the captain took over the wheel and the wheelsman stepped out to the ship's side. He was a kindly looking, stout lad of probably twenty-two years. He told me to call him "Ab." By this time the *Kenora* was entering the lock [of the Welland Canal] and as the ship slid ever so slowly through the gates there was scarcely an inch between.

"All's well, sir," said Ab, turning to the captain.

And so it went on into the sultry afternoon.

Then! Oh then, I caught my breath! Ships in fields ahead, as if they were going downhill! They must be! They looked so low down. I touched Ab's arm and pointed in surprise.

"How do they get down there?" I asked.

He smiled his kind smile and said, "You watch, little girl, in just a little while we'll be down there too. All's well, sir."

"All's well."

Many times since has Captain A. H. Foote measured the bare inch between waling strip and ship's side. A new canal has bested the draught and dimensions of greater ships; the calibre of the men sailing them is the true worth of the contribution these feats of engineering skill have brought.

It has been the "All's well" of the navigator that spelled failure or success.

Meandering through the waving grasses and the verdant fields on a boat had a weird fascination for a little girl who had floated on the wide expanse of the Upper Lakes. The wonder of it is with me yet. I became familiar with the principle at close quarters as the years advanced, but I never lost the Alice-in-Wonderland feeling of that first afternoon. Slowly the water level dropped in the big cribbed basin. Then when the water in the next and lower lock was level with the ship a man in the control tower worked a different set of levers, the big gates rattled a bit from the changing gears, then without sensation the ship passed to a lower level. We glided slowly on to another and another; quite unconsciously I watched and listened.

Literally inch by inch the locks were passed. One slip of the controls would mean a ship's bow piercing either the canal facing or the smashing of the canal gate which would tie up the entire system for hours or days. Heavy chains across the old lock gates gave a measure of protection, but with any runaway speed in the ship it would have no effect. Wind, if not perfectly calculated, was often the cause of damage and subsequent costly delays and this was not the fault of poor navigation. A mariner could not always know when a gust of wind at a certain angle would catch the bow or stern. The same great care was maintained throughout the passage of the ship; the hazard of meeting other ships at inch-close quarters meant tireless vigilance on the part of all.

Ab went off duty and his brother Fred took over. About then the purser looked me up and we went back for supper. Heretofore I had an inside track on the menu coming up, because of familiarity with kitchen routine.

"Paste two, sunny side up," sang out the mate as I tucked my napkin in at the collar.

"Double that with a rasher," spoke the second engineer, as he swung round in his chair.

"What are they talking about?" I whispered to the purser.

"Eggs," he replied. "Don't worry, little girl, you'll catch on pretty soon." Mr. Marshall explained I could have fish or eggs and cook would fix the eggs the way I wished. I settled for fish, deciding another time, on evidence forthcoming, as to how those eggs would come in. There was an abundance of good hearty food and more flies than I have ever seen in any one place before.

"Haven't you got any sticky paper here to catch flies?" I enquired.

"Well, no," ruefully answered the purser, "but we're nearly out of the canal and, we'll lose them on the lake tomorrow, when the wind blows them away."

I found that was one of my glorious duties aboard freight boats. Night and morning I helped cook and the cabin boy swat and swish but I never saw the wind that blew them all away.

When the mate left the supper table he took a pot of tea and a plate of sandwiches "for the old man." I hadn't seen him yet. I hoped he'd be like Grandfather. The purser and I followed the mate up the deck and sat down on a hatch where several men were smoking. The tangy smell of tobacco was aboard every ship; about the first thing a sailor took up was smoking a pipe. Many engine-room personnel chewed tobacco and this was understandable because their hands were always occupied with machinery and they ran up and down the narrow iron steps, from one level of the engine-room to another, with the agility of monkeys. They always had a wad of cotton waste beside their tools, wiping this and catching the drip on that.

There was a nice breeze now as we neared the lake; the sun was going down and cattle were waiting at the bars or in barnyards for milking hour. Just then a stranger with a black valise, whom I hadn't seen before, came down the deck. I at once decided this was "the old man"; his hair was white and he wore a stand-up white collar with wings that somehow suggested a professor ashore.

"Well, my boys," he began, and then caught sight of me. "So you have passengers aboard?"

"Just one," answered the purser. "Nancy, this is Mr. Bowen; he is the sailors' minister."

I was impressed with this happy-looking man with the wonderful smile and the white hair; I thought he seemed very like an angel although I had always supposed angels were women. In no time at all he had opened his bag and out it had come a beautiful brand new book which was put into my hand and which was called *Mary Jones and her Bible*.

I hugged the book and felt I had always known this nice man. "How did you know I was here?" I asked.

"God whispered to me, 'Take this along,'" Mr. Bowen answered.

"Do you know God very well, Mr. Bowen?" I asked.

"Yes Nancy, God is always listening. He is the sailor's Friend. Let us all have a little talk with Him now, boys."

There on the hatch of a canal-boat in the midst of toil and machinery and in the soft light of the departing day, this great servant of the Master brought the love of God to the souls of those men in unique surroundings. With a conviction that was seldom, if ever, questioned by another creed, Mr. Bowen "showed them the Father." From break-up to freeze-up he seldom missed a ship. First, he had a short chat with the captain. If there was an unruly member in the crew it was only with Mr. Bowen that the captain discussed it. Perhaps Mr. Bowen would go personally to pray with a man in his bunk or he would have a tract or a book from his lending library, a gospel for a penny or as a gift. It was a blessed hour wherever Mr. Bowen went and only the heavenly ledgers record how many lives were redeemed by the years of loving sacrifice and personal witness of this great man of God. His was one of the first mission enterprises set up by the British and Foreign Bible Society in Upper Canada. I later discovered that in the winter season Rev. Mr. Bowen visited churches on behalf of his work. These congregations were not always generous, or even well-attended, and I feel that those who stayed away missed a noble chance to support a most worthy home mission work. When it was nearly dark I watched a deckhand lower the accommodation ladder at the last lock. Mr. Bowen gripped the lad's hand and gave him a kind, fatherly look as he said, "God bless you, my boy." He stepped into the night. After that evening, all my angels wore wing collars and they looked like Mr. Bowen.

No sooner had the ship left a dock than she was put in readiness for the next port. The morning swabbing of decks was a daily duty; if coal were taken on at a fueling station the decks were swabbed again. Ropes were recoiled in neat pyramids, all the twists were out of them and weak lengths were spliced. During such operations the boys discussed many subjects that made it a veritable hour of charm for me. These future master mariners showed me the intricacies of knots and line heaving. Polishing brass and chipping paint were mediocre, but when a burning heart extolled his girl friend back home there was a delicious note of romance about it. It was a proud moment when I could name the points of the compass without error, "boxing the compass" the forward crew called it. My lessons were unique but they were never dull.

Next afternoon in the wheelhouse Captain Brian and the second mate wondered when the Government would get around to the actual construction of a new and greater canal. So much time was spent, the ships were often hours awaiting their turn to ascend or descend the inadequate waterway.

"The plans are ready for approval now," said the captain, "but contracts aren't let. I figure the spring of 1913 will see the beginning."

And so it was.

Among the varied panorama of the lakes the archipelago of wooded islands of the upper fifty miles of the St. Lawrence River, known as the "Thousand Islands," was a region alive with summer joys. From Brockville to Kingston, pleasure craft of all degrees of luxury and speed purred or darted through the narrow channels between islands ranging from a few lone pines to many acres. Many luxurious homes adorned the islands and the island boat tours from Gananoque and Brockville were well patronized by tourists. The Steamers *Kingston* and *Toronto* of the Richelieu and Ontario lines did a tremendous summer business out of Toronto, especially on week-end cruises that provided beauty and relaxation that the present pace cannot compensate.

There were forty steamers on Lake Ontario and the St. Lawrence River before 1840, the first being the *Frontenac*, of 1817, which plied from York (Toronto) to Prescott. Then the Royal Mail Line was inaugurated and had a "through service" to Montreal by 1843. The *Kingston* and *Toronto* began in 1901 and continued until 1938. Then the *Toronto* was pulled off and the *Kingston* continued until 1949, when she made her last trip before being sold for scrap iron. For upwards of 110 years fine passenger ships plied the lake as far as Prescott where there was a transfer to the sturdy *Rapids Shooter, Rapids King,* or *Rapids Prince* but these were not replaced when their gear became obsolete.

Approaching the port of Kingston it still suggests the Duke of Wellington's remark that he visioned it the Gibraltar of the Lakes. Old Fort Henry is a picturesque sample of the idea of military protection of another age. Its system of Martello towers, erected to protect the harbour and settlement, suggested sixteenth-century Europe. There were many reminders of LaSalle and

Frontenac. It was from here LaSalle set out on his mission to the Great West in 1679 accompanied by Father Hennepin and the Recollect priests, the latter natives of Flanders.

The ship they sailed in carried the anchors, sails, and rigging for the *Griffon* which, with considerable difficulty, were dragged from Lewiston to Cayuga Creek. The *Griffon* was completed there and, with Father Hennepin intoning "Vexilla Regis," they entered Lake Erie with swelling canvas. It must have been a tremendous achievement in that day.

No wonder the Loyalists drew new faith and inspiration from this garden of the new world. The wooded shores and the lake vistas have been balm to many a weary soul.

As the *Kenora* headed into the St. Lawrence River there was a new voice in the wheelhouse. The pilot had boarded the ship at Kingston. He was a big man of florid complexion whose name was "Gus" and he had a tremendous capacity for food and drink. His sense of navigation was exceedingly keen but he seemed to me to be out of keeping with the usual quiet voices and well defined discipline of the *Kenora*.

On wakening early the next day I noticed there was an ominous stillness about the ship. Hurriedly I stepped out on deck to find repairs being effected at a lock gate. The vessel ahead had overestimated the distance and crashed the gate. It was one of those nuisance delays that were bound to happen in the very limited area of the canal proper.

The day wore on in monotonous, searing heat as operators worked feverishly on repairs and the line of boats increased hourly. Looking around for some deliverance the purser, the second mate, and I went down the ladder for a roam ashore. It was flat, poor country but after a leisurely stroll we sat down on a pile of stones and struck up conversation with a farmer picking tomatoes. He was generous with his fruit and the boys filled their pockets to augment the ship's supper menu. I went into a fence corner and put my little-girl petticoat on top of my dress and conveniently carried home the luscious tomatoes. Taking a shortcut back to the boat I had to navigate the fences carefully with such soft cargo in my lap. All went well until the second last step of the ship's step-ladder. Gus, the pilot, stepped out of the Chief's cabin and directed his roar at me so unexpectedly that I let go the petticoat and all the tomatoes fell into the canal. Nobody regretted his departure a few hours later.

Navigation speeded up again in the canal and Captain "Bill" Brian was the first master to negotiate the Lachine Canal after dark. A few hours later we were tied up in port in Montreal.

I slept aboard that night, fascinated as I always was, by the almost touching nearness of world commerce. There was a Belgian ship alongside. Although they spoke a strange language, there was a fraternity among the men and packages of cigarettes tossed across the decks. There were old men and young men sitting on the dockside pulling on their pipes; there was the distant hum of the great city and the booming nearness of a ship's whistle as she passed up or down the river. Lights twinkled, the darkness of the night drifted across the hatches, and the men drifted off to their bunks or to a rendezvous ashore. The river was ink; the sky was buttoned with stars. The plop of the old river against the spiles of the dock was my lullaby.

The next morning the captain put me aboard a train that delivered me to the relatives living fifty miles from Montreal.

FROM SIX ON AN ISLAND
(1956)
Uldene Rudd LeRoy

BORN IN ST. IGNACE, Michigan, in 1913, Uldene LeRoy spent her girl-hood on Marquette Island in Les Cheneaux Islands (The Snows) in upper Lake Huron. A free-lance writer of poems and short stories from age twelve, she still spends her summers at The Snows. *Six On An Island* was her first published book.

--•→=●©=•←•--

The Caretaker's Daughter

IF DAD HAD KNOWN, when he took the position as caretaker on an island in Lake Huron, that he would be there for the next thirty-odd years, he would have been astounded. At the time, it seemed only a temporary solution to the problem of what to do while recovering from an attack of "flour asthma." He had been forced to give up his baking profession because of the illness, and the caretaker job meant that he could get outdoors and give the inflamed tubes a chance to heal.

I remember the day we moved. We rode on the doubledecker excursion steamer *Lotus* through the winding, treelined channels for five miles, through the summer resort region known as "the Snows." At no time was the shore any more than a few hundred yards from the high deck of the steamer, and summer cottages dotted the shores on either side.

Our first impression of our new house was of vast, empty rooms and dark, shining floors. It was an eleven-room house, and seemed huge until the furniture was moved in.

E.J. was two, Audrey three, and I was five, the fall when we made the island our home.

The first year was a hard one for Dad and Mom. They had to get used to taking a rowboat every time they went anywhere, and had to cope with the channel in all kinds of weather. Probably the hardest thing of all, at first, was learning to be completely self-sufficient, as we had not a single neighbor from September until June.

The nearest occupied houses were those in the Indian village several miles east of us on the island. Only four or five Indian families lived there, and most of the men were employed by Dad on the club grounds. They were wizards at transplanting trees and were very fine dock-builders, too. They were usually good workmen, except on the occasions when the demon rum reared its ugly head.

Although we had no neighbors in the wintertime, we had plenty of them in the summer. Dad had more than thirty cottages to supervise, which were built in a sort of circle around a mile-long cement sidewalk, with the large hotel or clubhouse in the center. The club had its own power plant then, and its own water system and pumps, run by steam. Then there was a golf course on the mainland to be maintained and kept in condition, and two clay tennis courts which had to be swept and rolled every day. The garbage was collected daily, at first by horse and wagon and later by truck. A ferry to the mainland and to the golf course had to be operated, too. Altogether, this necessitated quite a large crew of men, which Dad hired locally.

When we first came there, the clubhouse was staffed with colored help from the South, and in the warm summer evenings they gathered on the end of the big steamer dock and sang spirituals, their soft, quavering voices floating over the water like some heavenly choir. When off duty in the late afternoon, they fished off the docks. It was more a social affair than serious fishing, because there was much shrieking, laughing, and "smooching" going on. Sometimes the men would bring a few catfish, ferocious-looking monsters, back up to the hotel to fry for their supper. The local people never ate catfish, since perch and bass were abundant and made panfish more to our taste.

The club members were from Chicago, Detroit, Louisville, Nashville, Indianapolis, Cincinnati, New York, and various other cities, but all were wealthy or socially prominent families. They were considered a rather select and exclusive group, and kept to themselves, a small world in itself. They brought their families up for a long, leisurely summer, away from the heat and noise of the cities.

We children had the opportunity of meeting and knowing many famous and important people over the years, but we were not particularly impressed at the time. To us they were just summer people, all rather peculiar in their ways and not to be taken too seriously. Senators, well-known writers and editors, heads of huge corporations, and even titled personages came and went. They were all just people to us, who knew them in their more relaxed and informal moments. We noticed only how ridiculously skinny and knobby were the legs of a certain industrialist in his swimming shorts, or remembered how the caddies always hid whenever a certain society dowager played golf; she was so hard to please and so stingy with her tips!

Childish memories are strange things; they retain such seemingly trivial incidents and forget important ones. Fresh in my memory still is the hot anger I felt when, after gathering a bushel of tiny pine cones at the request of one crotchety old dame, she offered us a penny a hundred, and demanded that we dump out the bushel of cones and count them, before she would pay us. We decided then that was earning money the hard way. The next time that she wanted a bushel of cones we were conveniently elsewhere.

She was the same dear old soul who called us to her, one summer day, and demanded to see the small coin purses which she had sent us the previous Christmas. We presented them, after a lengthy search, a little the worse for wear. She examined them carefully, and then, fixing us with an eagle eye, asked to see the pennies which had come in them, one to a purse. There we had to renege, having spent them in riotous living long since.

One old gentleman probably never knew the panic wrought in our childish hearts by his affectionate nature. Every year when he saw us for the first time, he would make a game of catching and kissing us profusely and, let's face it, sloppily! He was the bearer of many gifts, candy and pretty trifles, but we felt that we paid too dearly for them, since they meant a thank-you kiss, and another whenever he could catch us. I suppose he wondered why we children were so often absent when he made his farewell visit to the house before leaving each fall. We wouldn't have hurt his feelings for the world, but it was too much to take, so we took it as seldom as possible.

Another gentleman appointed himself monitor over my reading material. I was an avid reader, and by the time that I was twelve had read almost every book in our well-stocked bookshelves, plus a good many of those in the club library, both suitable and unsuitable.

Once I was sitting on the porch steps, deep in a novel, when he came up on the porch, asking to see one of my parents. I called Mom, then very impolitely, I'm afraid, proceeded to take up my story where I had been interrupted.

He asked to see the title, which I grudgingly displayed, and he gasped in horror. He took the book out of my hands, telling me sternly that it was "very unsuitable for a little girl to read." He launched into a lecture which lasted until Mom came out, whereupon I seized the opportunity to repossess the book, and resumed my reading under his disapproving eye. He said nothing more then, but my feelings were as deeply wounded as only a sensitive twelve-year-old's can be, and for years I disliked him intensely.

A few years ago, I happened to run across that same book, and dipped into it curiously, to see what had shocked the gentleman so grievously. To my surprise, I found that I now agreed with him completely, and would have been pretty startled to find it in the hands of my own twelve-year-old. Time marches on, and with it one's point of view.

Living on an island as we did, the water and boats played a large part in our daily lives. During those first years, rowboats were our only mode of transportation and we had a good many adventures in them. When Dad took over as manager, most of the club boats were made of tin, since his predecessor had a preference for them. The tin rowboats were light and easy to handle, but were treacherous in the extreme if they were tipped or punctured even slightly. This we discovered the hard way.

One evening, when we children were still very small, Dad was rowing us home from a trip to the Old Chimney, an Indian landmark and favorite picnic spot, a little way down the channel from the club.

Being new to the channel, Dad chanced to row over a hidden rock, and the boat lodged on the pinnacle of it. A wooden boat might have splintered a little and slid off, with only a scar to show for the encounter, but we were in a tin boat, and it punctured immediately.

Even by rocking the boat as hard as we could, we just couldn't budge it off the needle-sharp rock, and a fountain of water began shooting up from the gash. We youngsters screamed in terror, and began to scramble onto the seats to get away from the water, which was rapidly filling the small boat.

Dad tried to reassure us, saying that there was no real danger, that if we had to abandon ship he could wade ashore with us on his shoulders. That served to calm us somewhat, and we sat fairly still while Dad and Mom struggled to get the boat loose before it filled and upended in the deep boat channel.

Finally, one tremendous shove freed us, and Dad rowed furiously for the safety of the shallow water, the boat unwieldy and settling, about to sink. We just made it, and were in wading depth, when the little tin rowboat settled to the bottom. After that, Dad insisted that all the tin rowboats be replaced with wooden ones, and they soon became a thing of the past. It wasn't until years later that we thought to ask Dad just how he had planned to carry three children, and Mom, who couldn't swim either, to safety, when the water was over his own head. Dad only grinned, and changed the subject.

Although the channel was more sheltered from storms and wind than the open sweep of Lake Huron, we often had perilous crossings, especially during the equinoctial storms in spring and fall. Rain and sleet or dark of night, the channel lay between us and school, stores, post office, and church, and each time had to be conquered anew.

The trick, Dad taught us, was to keep the prow of the boat headed into the wind. To let it get broadside to the waves was to court disaster and risk swamping in the huge whitecapped waves. The current at times was as swift as a river, and it took plenty of muscle to keep on the course when both the wind and current conspired against one. We all developed oversized biceps from years of rowing, and while that may have been an advantage to E.J., we girls didn't care so much for ours.

Dad's strong arms brought us across many times when we were sure that we'd never in the world make it.

"Sit tight and keep quiet!" That was his unvarying advice, which was sometimes pretty hard to follow.

It was terrifying to watch the black water rushing by on either side of the boat, with an occasional swell pouring over the sides and drenching us. Sometimes he would row for endless periods, not gaining a foot, only managing to hold his own against the powerful current and wind. If he relaxed his effort in the least, the boat would lose way and begin to turn broadside.

After a certain position was gained, and we got into the lea of the island, the wind was not so strong and the current lessened. We always breathed easier when that point was reached, and began to have hopes of stepping onto dry land again.

I usually wept loudly and enthusiastically during such a crossing, and Mom has said that she often felt like joining me, had it not been for the effect on the crew's morale! However, Dad never let us know, either by word or look, that he had a single doubt of reaching shore safely, although there must have been times when he, too, wondered.

In later years we used motorboats, and much of the channel's power was gone. Then it was fun to skim over the whitecaps and to feel the wind tug at the boat. We no longer had to pit our muscles and skill against the elements every time that we left the island shore.

The channel was a sure-fire way to test the mettle of our boy friends when we girls reached high-school age. Of course, the mere fact of our living on an island made us taboo to some of the boys. But to other more sturdy souls, I imagine we seemed more glamorous by the obstacle course which had to be run in order to enjoy our company.

To a man, however, they objected to the habit we had of doing the rowing ourselves, making them passengers only. We could understand how they felt, but, after all, we did want to get across, and not every boy could handle the oars with any skill. We were pretty critical! Anyone in our family could get into a rowboat at the mainland dock and, after taking bearings, row across the channel without once more looking around to see where we were heading. We could glide up to our dock as smoothly and effortlessly as any of our escorts could park a car, and be out and have the boat tied fast to the dock before they had hoisted themselves up and over the side.

Occasionally, however, there would be one who insisted on taking over the rowing chore, and we would be forced to give way. Usually he would manage to splash, wobble, and meander his way across with much unwanted advice from us. In his exasperation, he would often make a worse landing than if he had been let alone.

One night, when it was foggy and very late, my date insisted on rowing me across. I argued and pleaded to no avail; he was determined to be a gentleman. So we started out into the heavy fog, which hung over the water like a gray wall, visibility zero.

We wandered far afield, visiting patches of rushes far off our course along the mainland shore, then nearly colliding with various docks and boathouses along the island side. I was furious, because I knew that I could find our dock even though I couldn't see a foot ahead. He stubbornly persisted, and finally, hours later it seemed, we more or less blundered upon our dock. I climbed out, not knowing or caring if he ever found his way home, or if he were swallowed up in the fog, never to be seen again. I was way over the limit set for our week-night dates, all because of him and his misplaced gallantry.

Dad had a way of looking twenty feet tall, with blazing neon eyes, on the rare occasions when we overstayed our curfew. E.J. had an expression for it. He called it Dad's "Cold Gray Look." Whatever it was, none of us cared to trifle with it, in spite of his usual good nature.

Not everyone, we found, realizes how voices carry over the water. Audrey and I often sat on the window seat in our bedroom and watched our dates row back across after bringing us home. They thought themselves well out of earshot, and many an interesting bit of comment we picked up that way. Sometimes we wished that we couldn't hear quite so well, proving the old adage that listeners never hear well of themselves.

Yes, Ol' Man River who just keeps rolling along had nothing on our channel. As it rolled, it brought a great deal of drama into our lives at one time or another.

The channel is shallow except in the middle, where the boat channel has been dredged to a depth of perhaps eighteen to twenty-five feet. There is where the current is the swiftest. This current keeps the ice from freezing very thick except in sub-zero weather, and a few days of thaw and mild weather usually made it necessary to test the ice "out in the middle" to see what inroads the current had made.

We always walked across on a certain path, marked out by Dad with evergreen boughs at the beginning of the winter. Walk the "strait and narrow" we did in earnest. Sometimes only a foot or so off the path, airholes would develop even in cold weather, making us wonder just how much ice there actually was under us.

In the early winter, before the snows came, the ice would be clear and blue, showing plainly the rushes and weeds in the shallow places. It never helped my peace of mind any to see the weeds rushing along in the current, just beneath the ice, or to catch the glint of a tin can lying on the bottom, far below. It was a constant source of amusement to the rest of the family, watching me "walk on eggs" on the clear ice. I felt that even a deep breath might plunge me into the icy depths below. It was a great relief to me when the snow came and covered the ice—it may not have made it any safer but it felt safer to me.

One day, in early December, I was sitting at the living room windows overlooking the lake. Dad was out testing the new ice, to see if it was thick enough for the family to walk on. He had an ice chisel, and struck the ice resounding blows every few feet as he walked along. Now and then he paused to chip a hole to measure the thickness.

He had gone about two-thirds of the way across when I happened to look out just in time to see him plunge through and disappear. Frozen to my chair, I watched his head reappear, then, my common sense asserting itself, I raced through the house to the kitchen, screaming, "Dad's gone through the ice!" I grabbed a broom, the only thing at hand, as I went through the door, and ran for the shore.

Audrey followed, sensibly stopping to get something more sturdy than my broom—an old oar, I believe.

We started out onto the ice, carrying our broom and oar horizontally, as we'd been taught to do on poor ice, our intention being to reach Dad before he lost his precarious hold on the ice.

"Go back!" he yelled at us. "I'm all right, get back to shore!"

His assurances were spoiled a little by his slipping under the water again, and having to claw for a grip on the edge of the ice. But as soon as he could speak he ordered us again to go back to shore.

That was one of the few times that we ever deliberately disobeyed him, and we kept on going, gliding rather than running on the thin surface, finally arriving at the scene without mishap.

"Lovely weather we're having," quipped our Irish dad, up to his neck in icy water. We didn't bother to return his pleasantries, being nearly scared to death at the fix he was in. We slid our makeshift poles across the ice to him so that he could grasp them. He tried to get them, but he could let go of the edge of the ice with only one hand at a time, and his weight made the ice break when he tried to reach out.

Meanwhile, some men working near the shore started out on the ice but without any poles with which to effect a rescue. Colleen, about ten then, called to them to get one of the props from Mom's clotheslines, long, sturdy birch poles, so they went back and got them.

Several of the men, not liking the looks of the ice, turned back, and only two of them came out to help. They slid the two strong poles along the surface until they extended a little over the hole where Dad was dangling, becoming more numb every minute. He carefully and slowly, so as not to break the ice, edged the weight of his body up onto the poles, a little at a time until he lay across them, and the men were able to pull him to safety.

All in all, he was in the water about twenty minutes or more. Why he wasn't made helpless from the paralyzing cold of the water is a mystery, unless it was the heavy wool clothing he wore which had protected him. As it was, he was crippled for several weeks afterward and had to walk in a very peculiar fashion because of his sore muscles.

That same winter, an Indian girl about ten years old was crossing on the ice—not on our path where it was safe, but taking a short cut across a part of the channel where the ice was poor. Her mother, a huge squaw weighing some three hundred pounds, was waiting on the island shore. The girl was about in mid-channel when she went through. She bobbed up immediately, and, keeping her head admirably, fought for a hold on the edge of the ice.

Almost at once, the huge squaw was at her side, helping her. How she had managed to get out there so fast, or why she hadn't broken through herself, no one knows. But she made it back to shore with the dripping, shivering girl before anyone had time to go to their aid. Dad rushed down to them as they came ashore and insisted that they come up to our house so that the girl could get out of her wet garments in a hurry, but the squaw refused. They disappeared down the trail toward the Indian village, proud and independent as Indians always are. The girl didn't suffer any ill effects from her ducking, evidently, because in a day or so she was crossing the ice again on her way to and from school.

We had a team of horses go through the ice, too, and for a while it looked as though they were lost. But with Dad at their sides, soothing them and urging them to help themselves, the frightened animals were cut out of their harnesses and pulled up onto safe ice. They were put in the barn and given a brisk rubdown and some warm mash to eat, and next day were as good as new.

Two pet dogs we lost to the ice, though. One was a beautiful pedigreed white collie, Laddie. He fought a valiant battle against the freezing water, but had to give up at last, too weary and numb to fight any longer. Dad was always certain that he could have rescued Laddie, had he been there, but we only knew about it from a neighbor on the mainland, who stood on the shore and watched the gallant dog go down at last. We children were broken-hearted.

And then, years later, Skippy, a gay, fluffy poodle, went for a stroll on the thin new ice, early in the winter, and never returned home. That is, not until spring, when the waves gently wafted him up on the beach in front of our house. Mom was out hanging clothes on the line near the shore and discovered the remains. Home was the Skipper, home from the sea, but Mom didn't want any dinner that night.

Dat ol' debbil channel wasn't always the villain—it did make a most wonderful playground winter and summer, during all the years of our growing up. It made a marvelous skating rink in winter, and we used it constantly. Many a hockey game we played, with a tin can for a puck, as the pale winter sun sank behind the evergreens on the hill. The ring of steel blades mingled with shouts and snatches of song on the frosty air, until the fire began to burn low—we always had a bonfire when we skated—and our hands and feet became too cold for comfort. Then we and our friends would all troop into the house, where the heavenly scent of toast and hot cocoa greeted us. Mom never failed us, and our house was a popular meeting place on week ends, winter and summer.

We played crack-the-whip, too, the game which usually ended with some poor unfortunate sailing through the air to land headfirst in a snowbank (if he were lucky) or sliding on his head or posterior along the ice until he managed to stop somewhere.

The snow on the channel near our cottage usually looked like a stamping ground for many varieties of queer varmints—what with the snowshoe and ski tracks, toboggan trails, fox-and-geese games, all crisscrossing in intricate patterns.

But summer was when the channel really came into its own. We used to get into our swim suits as soon after lunch as we dared and stay in the water or on the dock, soaking up sun, until the workmen came down to cross to the mainland, at five o'clock.

Sometimes we would become so "waterlogged" that we could hardly drag ourselves up the swimming ladder—but we loved it, and begrudged every cold or stormy day that we couldn't spend in the water.

We had an old canoe, much the worse for wear, which we often took out into the deep water and overturned for a thrill. E.J. and his friends were adept at righting the canoe in the water, emptying it, and climbing back into it again—but we girls never quite mastered the art. We would paddle out in it, overturn it and swim back to the dock, leaving it for the boys to put right side up again.

Once the canoe overturned at the wrong time. E.J. and I had been on the mainland playing golf one fall evening. We had a bag of clubs in the battered old relic of a canoe, and were dressed warmly, it being a chilly evening. As we neared our dock, I somehow dropped my paddle and foolishly leaned over to retrieve it. At the same moment, E.J. reached for it too, and, of course, the inevitable happened.

Over we went, golf clubs, heavy clothes and all. I got to shore with what dignity I could muster, which wasn't much, since we had spectators who were highly amused at my sodden retreat.

Gathering my dripping coat about me, and sloshing soggily along in my water-filled shoes, I stalked to the house, undressed and went straight to bed to nurse my wounded pride.

Meanwhile E.J. got the canoe and gear ashore with the help of a young man who had been watching the scene with much interest.

Of course, the channel made an ideal setting for romance, when nicely silvered by moonlight. With the portable "vic" in the canoe, we had a scene made to order for carrying on affairs of the heart. The dance orchestra playing in the clubhouse on the hill sounded like something out of this world, when its strains drifted over the water. Close by, it wasn't nearly so dreamy. The water softened the brassy horns and harsh drums until the quite ordinary band sounded like Guy Lombardo at his best.

During the long summer days the water was a busy thoroughfare for boats of all kinds. Sailboats, yachts large and small, speedboats and cruisers, outboards and chugging fishing launches all passed in a never-ending parade.

Once a day, the big mail steamer, the *Islander*, went through the channels, carrying freight, mail, and tourists. It stopped at the steamer dock, and everyone who wasn't doing anything else always went down to meet it. Often we would be swimming when it passed, and we got a thrill from the tide it caused, which pulled the boats tied at the docks as far as their ropes allowed, and made swirling eddies in the water. We always waved at crew and passengers alike, and once in a while the captain would give us an earsplitting salute, a blast from the ship's whistle.

We often rode the big boat to Cedarville, about five miles down the winding channel, but it really was much more fun to watch it pass and see who was aboard.

Down in the narrows that we called "the Cut" was a huge rock right on the edge of the boat lane. It was called Split Rock and was the undoing of many pleasure craft whose captains were not familiar with it. It was just far enough below the surface to be invisible but close enough to rake the bottom of any unwary small boat, or rip a hole in a larger one.

Sometimes, when the water was low, the *Islander* would bump against it, and we loved to watch and listen each time, to see if it would hit. If it did, there would be a dull thud, and the big steamer would lunge over on its side a little while the captain maneuvered it back into deep water. The passengers would all rush to that side of the deck and peer anxiously over the side, not knowing that it was a frequent occurrence and not nearly so dangerous as it seemed.

In rowboats we could pass right over the rock, and we often leaned over the side to count the different colors of paint on it, scraped from the hulls of its victims.

Naturally, we all tried our luck at fishing occasionally, usually off the docks, but none of us was a real enthusiast. We caught perch, especially in the spring when the water was cold, that tasted like nothing ever has since. Bass, too, were plentiful, but not prized so highly for panfish as the silvery perch. Often freshly caught perch were cleaned and scaled so quickly that they didn't know that they were dead! They flopped over in the frying pan as though they were still alive—very unnerving to the cook.

Fishing boats full of tourists often hauled in huge muskies and pike from the water in front of the club, but we never caught any remarkably big ones. We had too many other interests to enjoy sitting quietly for very long, and patience is a fisherman's secret formula for success.

One afternoon, Audrey and I were fishing for perch from the big dock. It was an Indian-summer-type day, the water was smooth and still and sounds carried over it very clearly. We could hear automobile horns on the Hessel road, the sound of cowbells from the mainland, and voices of passengers from an occasional passing boat.

The sounds of a loud argument caught our attention, and we saw a rowboat moving very jerkily along the mainland shore, with two men in it. One was doing the rowing, in a very amateurish manner, with much splashing, and the other was sitting in the stern seat, waving his arms in the air and now and then rising to his feet in the heat of argument.

Amused, we forgot fishing and began to watch the comedy unfold. The subject of their discussion seemed to be politics, and each was fully persuaded in his own mind; their words waxed hotter as they wavered along their uncertain course.

As we watched, the passenger again got to his feet, gesturing fiercely, and tumbled overboard.

By this time, we realized that the pair were considerably "under the influence," and we wondered if the man overboard was in any condition to swim. His companion didn't share our anxiety, it seemed, for not by word or glance did he appear to notice his friend's plight, but kept rowing his erratic course, continuing the argument in a loud voice.

The unfortunate one thrashed and splashed his way back to the boat as best he could, since it was moving away almost as fast as he could swim. With much wheezing and puffing, he pulled himself back into the boat, causing it to ship considerable water in the process, and took his place again. Still there was no comment from his companion, who hadn't missed a stroke in his rowing nor paused in his harangue. The wet one took up his sentence right where he'd left off, and the little boat wobbled its way around the bend, the voices growing fainter in the distance.

Audrey and I looked at each other, wondering if we'd dreamed it, since we seemed to be the only ones who'd seen it.

Down in the Cut, partially submerged in the water, were the remains of an old wreck, whereon hangs a tale. Many years ago, when King Strang ruled the settlement of Mormons on Beaver Island, off the shore of the northern lower peninsula of Michigan, the fishermen from the villages on both sides of the Straits had trouble with marauders from the kingdom. The Mormons, so legend has it, had an annoying habit of kidnaping the wives and daughters of the fishing villages and adding them to their already large collection of wives on Beaver Island.

The fishermen were in hot pursuit of the kidnapers after one such excursion, and the Mormons sailed their vessel into the winding channels of the Snows Islands. Hoping to cut them off, the fishermen split up into several groups, and entered the channels from opposite directions, executing a modern-day pincers movement, with the marauders in the middle.

Seeing that they were about to be trapped, the Mormons beached their large sailing vessel in the Cut, set fire to it, and escaped overland, leaving the fishermen to rescue and claim their stolen women. The boat burned only to the waterline, and, preserved by the water, which became lower with the passing years, the wreck became a historic landmark in the channel.

Whenever we passed close to it, we children had an eerie feeling, expecting no doubt to see a Mormon appear, ready to take off with us!

FROM WIDOW OF THE WAVES
(1994)
Bev Jamison

FOR EVERY MAN WHO SAILS in the Great Lakes merchant marine there's a woman left on shore, but Bev Jamison, (1934-), is the first to write about what it's like to raise a family single-handedly except for telephone calls, letters, and a little vacation during the winter. Since Jim Jamison was an engineer he spent even less time at home, for winter lay-up is when the boats are fitted out for the sailing season and that is the engineers' task. Bev met the tough challenges of being a sailor's wife with courage and good-humor and occasionally tears, but she persevered. In the early part of the nineteenth century, captains could tie up their boats and take the train home for a few days whenever they felt like it. As Bev makes clear, progress in shipbuilding and harbor construction and ice breaking have changed all that.

⇥━◉◯━⇤

The Best Laid Plans

HOLIDAYS WERE PROBABLY the toughest time to be married to a sailor. When we were married on December 17, Jim and I were sure that we'd always be able to spend our anniversary and the Christmas season together because shipping would always be over by then. Not so! As it turned out, we spent many more of those two celebrations apart than together.

We should have gotten the first clue when we had to change our wedding date from December 10 to December 17, because Jim wasn't going to be home in time. I remember so well that phone call when he broke the news to me. He listened to me cry, and I really don't remember how much conversation there was that night. Poor Jim! He told me later that one of the fellows on the ship told him that he should have written me a letter instead! What sensitivity.

Well, he got home on the 11th, we got married on the 17th and we were home from our honeymoon for Christmas. We even had our tree up and trimmed, and we did most of our shopping in that hectic week between the 11th and the 17th.

It stayed this way for the first few years that we were married. Jim was always home in time for us to do our Christmas shopping together, put up the tree, and attend kids' Christmas programs. Before too many years passed the shipping season wasn't over until just before Christmas, sometimes not

368 ⊕ The Women's Great Lakes Reader

before Christmas Eve. At those times, the fellows could usually be home until New Years and then go back to work for the lay-up and engine rebuild until February. That wasn't so bad because even if we missed spending our anniversary together, we could at least be together for the holidays.

Pretty soon thereafter the season was extended into January. As long as the locks were open, the big ships continued to make the trip up and down the lakes. Jim was still home for the holiday, but the holiday was usually Valentines Day.

I remember a year when Jim got through on the afternoon of Christmas Eve and came home on the last flight from Detroit. When I drove to the airport in Duluth that night, I thought that the terminal would be practically empty. I mean, *really*, who would be traveling on Christmas Eve? Was I mistaken! The place was like, well you know what they say about sardines. It was that crowded. When Jim's plane finally landed, we hurried home, much to the pleasure of the kids who had been waiting to open gifts. I knew the kids wouldn't have wanted to wait until the next morning, so I didn't even suggest it, but I sure wish we had. Jim was so tired from working and then rushing to meet planes and make connections. I was tired from Christmas preparations and driving to the airport. I think we were both crabby because it just wasn't the Christmas that we usually had. We had always remembered and honored the true meaning of Christmas, and maybe we didn't completely forget it that year, but I thought afterward that it just didn't seem we showed Jesus that we remembered it was His birthday. Jim and I made up our minds that the next time he didn't get home until Christmas Eve, we'd wait until Christmas morning to open gifts.

As it turned out, we never had to face that decision because the shipping season grew longer and longer, they didn't even stop sailing for Christmas. Well, one year they did when it got so cold and there was so much ice on the lake that they didn't have any other choice.

Christmas was always the toughest time of year for Jim to be away from home and family. Birthdays, Mothers Day, Fathers Day, Easter, Thanksgiving and all the other special days, even Sundays, which I traditionally think of as a family day, are lonely, but there's something worse about being away from family at Christmas.

It's hard for the families left at home, but at least we have other family members and friends. It has to be worse for the fellows who are on the ship, where the only things that make it different from any other day are a few decorations and fancier food.

There is usually a Christmas tree in the mess room, engine room, and pilot house. Some ships have a tree on the deck and I remember when there was always a tree on the ore dock, in Superior. The food can be considered really special. There is usually prime rib, turkey, ham, and crab or some other fancy entree for the main course. Then, of course, there are several choices of potato, salad, dressing, maybe a couple different vegetables, and all sorts of special extras that aren't on the table for regular meals. I'm sure, though, that most of the men would prefer to eat a hamburger or bowl of soup if it meant they could be home with their families.

Eventually, left home to handle the Christmas holidays myself, I had gone to using an artificial tree. It was easier for me and I could leave it up until Jim got home at the end of the season. One year I had a real tree and I was determined to leave it up until Jim came home. I did, but by the time that Jim got home to see it, there were very few needles left . . . on the tree that is. There were plenty of them everywhere else, though.

Our brilliant plan for spending our anniversary *and* Christmas together never worked out, but over the years, I made the best of it. I was thankful for friends and family, for being able to spend Christmas with my children around me, but I always missed Jim and looked forward to the time when we could celebrate our anniversary together, and a few days later, wish each other a Merry Christmas over the dinner table instead of over the phone.

SLEEPING BEAR

Rosalind Srb Mayberry

BORN IN 1942, ROSALIND MAYBERRY was educated in French literature at Cornell University and studied music at the Schola Cantorum in Paris. A teacher and a writer, she resides in Grand Haven, Michigan, and is completing her Ph.D in literature of the environment.

⊷⊷⊛⊷⊷

WE HAD LIVED ON THE SHORE of Lake Michigan about three years before I saw Sleeping Bear Dune. Suddenly one drizzly October day, it seemed urgent to go. The night before, the lake had boiled like sea surf over the rocky Maine coast. In the morning the waves rolled in, brown and heavy with the fine sand churned up from the bottom. So I threw some stuff together, leashed up the dog, strapped the baby into her safety seat and made my brother an offer he couldn't refuse—the opportunity to demonstrate his wilderness skills. Three hours later, we arrived in the dark. We ate steak washed down with the bottle of Rhone I'd included in the bare essentials, and survived a five-raccoon attack and a cold wet night on the lumpy floor of the pup tent.

We came upon her from the flat and forested east. I could smell the water, but the lake was somewhere hidden behind the Bear Dune, lying tawny and still under the curded gray sky. Where I walked in the sand at the foot of the dune, the sodden crust gave way and the pale dry sand trickled down. In spite of the baby in the backpack beating on my head and squawking happily, I was overwhelmed with an inexorable sadness, a sense that something tragic had happened there, the same sense that had made me shiver at Culloden many years before. In neither case did I know the story before being there, but in both cases the land spoke to me, and later I heard their stories—at Culloden, the British slaughter of the Scots clans, at Sleeping Bear, the American Indian legend of a mother's loss.

A mother bear, it seems, set off from the Wisconsin shore, her two cubs swimming on either side. A storm blew up, the fierce kind that twists ships in two and eats away at the south shore dunes. In the dark, starless night, the she-bear swam through waves whipped up by the wind off the flat expanse of Saskatchewan. The rain blew in sheets, and when the bear arrived at the shore, her cubs were no longer by her side. She lay spent at the water's edge, her deep pooled eyes staring out through the storm, searching in the white caps for the cubs. The days came and went, and the months, and the seasons. The she-bear is still there on the shore of Lake Michigan, not far from Pentwater. It is called Sleeping Bear, but she waits, sleepless, for her cubs, now forever embodied in two small off-shore islands.

I've seen those storms. They hit with a howl and whip up waves that split over the Coast Guard light house at the mouth of the Grand River. Almost every year a brash teenager ventures onto the pier and is swept off into the lake. Those nights I lie awake in bed trying to hear the settling call of the fog horn through the flapping of the Coast Guard helicopter searching the shoreline. The siren sounds over the wind and the locals drive down to line up along the shore, their high beams pointed toward the water, trying to pierce the opaque surf spray that hangs over the lake. Somewhere, a mother waits.

But the lake is mutable, often glassy clear on a summer morning before the tourists come and clutter the beach and fill the air with the heavy sweetness of coconut oil. Then the sky hovers close to the surface of the water and rolls up the shore like quicksilver. The gulls soar in and out of the fog. They land, then settle onto the dry sand. Off to the side, the brown spotted yearlings wander and jostle each other like the groups of teenagers who gather at the waterfront in the evenings. Sandpipers skitter along the shore, in and out of the lapping water, leaving drunken trails of footprints. As the fog begins to lift, the air above the lake yellows and the surface of the water, roughed by the faint day breeze, takes on the scaled pewter look of the coho that wash ashore.

Shortly after Labor Day, September winds clear the sky and push up the rhythmic breakers that roll in most autumn days. The heavier winds blow the sand continuously across itself, stirring it to song.

In late fall storms come. For hours before they hit shore the night sky lights up with a shimmering glow, and as it approaches, the jagged lightening splits the sky, crackles, and plunges into the dark water. The black water boils, a frenzy of white-capped waves smashing helter skelter into each other. It is on these nights that sailors are lost and children and bears.

FROM THE SURVIVOR OF THE EDMUND FITZGERALD
(1985)
Joan Skelton

WHEN THE EDMUND FITZGERALD sank on November 10, 1975, a new era began on the Great Lakes. If this ship could sink with all hands and without explanation, the promise that technology could master nature was no longer certain. From that tragedy, Skelton crafted a slender, feminist novel about a woman dying of an undiagnosed disease and the survivor of the sinking she meets, or imagines she meets, as she waits for death in the family cottage—colloquially called *camp*—on the frozen northern shore of Lake Superior. Gene Amort was an artist who stowed away on the *Fitz*, and even though he had seen the water in the cargo holds and knew the ship was in danger, failed to warn the captain. Instead, he escaped in an uncovered life-boat that washed up on Coppermine Point, across the bay from the woman's cottage. Skelton structures her novel as Clara's journal entries written to her family, first typed, then as she becomes progressively weaker, spoken into a tape recorder. In so doing, Clara "writes beyond the ending," leaving a record others will experience when she is dead. Skelton links the ship—and ships are always referred to as "she" no matter what their names—that was lost because of man's complacency, and Clara's death, caused by that same complacency, in a lament for our lost connection with nature. At the end, Clara's own culture having failed her, she reaches back to another, to Native culture, to give her the power that she did not know in life.

⊷⊱⊜⊰⊶

January 20

I want to explain. And oddly enough I want to tell you about something interesting, a bit of intrigue here in the wilderness of Lake Superior, a bit of mystery in which I find myself involved.

As you have guessed, I am at the cottage. At Gull Rock.

I encountered the strangest person at our favorite ridge. He was weird. I had made my way there with some difficulty, wanting to see the ridge in winter, wanting just to see the ridge perhaps for the last time.

I had difficulty getting up the steep ledge. However, nothing was going to stop me and I pulled on the branches of a protruding pine to get myself up. Out of breath, perspiring, and in pain, I pawed at the top of a billowing snowdrift to locate a large boulder in order to sit down. Where had these huge rocks come from? Hudson Bay? Russia? Quebec? They had been deposited here not so long ago in geological time by the immense Wisconsin Glacier. What was I, my silly jokes, my pedantic remarks, my short life—my suffering—in a timeframe such as that? Well, the suffering was something to me, all right.

From this height, I could see Lake Superior quite clearly through the etching of the bare branches of maple and oak. Up here on this windy lookout, there was no snow on the trees and the conifers were dark, almost shadows against the naked branches of the deciduous forest. On the lake, there were still patches of open water. They were like panes of blue glass looking out of this world of white, windows to another world.

When I saw a person emerge from the woods at the far end of the ridge, I thought I was indeed seeing a vision from another world. No one wanders in the woods at this time of year.

This person was a walking snowman. He canted from side to side as he sank into the drifted snow with each step. In places, it must have been three feet deep. Icicles hung from his hat and his beard. As he lumbered towards me, I could see his eyes were fringed with white lashes. Expecting to see a death mask, I was surprised to see a vibrant, youthful face and clear blue eyes.

"Hi, there," he said.

An anomalous greeting in the wilds of Northern Ontario. I realized I hadn't even thought of being scared. Meeting someone out in the forest would have previously scared the wits out of me. And this time, unlike before, I had no fierce dog, no gun—albeit empty or otherwise—cached in the cabin. Of course, everything had changed. Priorities are different now.

"Aren't you exhausted?" I asked. He must have walked at least two miles, maybe farther, depending on where he was staying.

"No. I am all right."

He seemed all right.

He replied he wasn't tired. He didn't want to sit down.

Through the shroud of snow that enveloped him, I could see that he was young, maybe twenty-five, with a sensitive, rather babyish face, despite the rubble of beard that looked like it had been trying to grow for some time.

"You live around here?" he asked.

I answered carefully, without saying exactly where.

He asked about the weather, about the big oak that dominated the ridge, about the depth of snow in winter, the mean temperature, on and on until I realized he was carefully controlling the conversation with his questions. Although our conversation appeared to be an interchange, a returning of the verbal ball back and forth, the verbal ball was in reality being completely controlled by this young man standing in the snow before me.

So what was new? In social conversation, I have always been so pliable, so passive, talking about whatever anyone wanted, a backboard for anyone to hit the verbal ball against, I only occasionally sending the ball spinning with a joke, an obscure piece of information, an esoteric word—see?—that I usually tried to conceal.

To hell with it, I thought.

"I seem to be answering a lot of questions," I said. "Why don't you tell me about yourself? Where are you staying? What are you doing in this part of the world?"

Without a word, he turned around and slowly lumbered back across the clearing, canting from side to side as he stepped into one deep footprint after the next.

He seemed to vanish into the snow even before he came to the edge of the woods. A white shadow against the white. A wraith . . . .

My first venture into assertiveness didn't turn out very well.

January 21

It is January cold. The temperature is fifteen below. Fahrenheit, that is. On the Celsius scale, I guess that would be about twenty-five below. Will I ever adjust to this senseless tampering with our system of measurement?

The trip to the wood pile and the root cellar is becoming more difficult. I am fortunate to have both. Some time ago, I stocked the root cellar for you kids in case of some continental or global disaster; Jeff, your father that is, has kept the wood pile forever stocked with kindling and lengths of wood because of his obsession with cutting and splitting.

I am glad I made it to the ridge yesterday. I have yet to go to the cave.

I have the typewriter on the buffet and I am now standing to type. It works well.

Yesterday, as I began this journal, I said that I wanted to explain to you, my adult children, the reasons behind my actions. I want you to understand. It is important to me that you understand.

Nevertheless, I find myself more willing to talk to you about other things . . . especially about that intriguing person I met yesterday during the storm.

I met him again today. I found out his name is Gene. Gene Amort. I met him in the parking area while I was out getting wood. There he was, covered in his shroud of snow and ice, looking as if it was he who was ready to lie down in the snow.

"Hi," he said.

"You again? You startled me."

"Sorry about that. How are you?"

"Cold. Do you want to come in for a minute?"

I thought I had taken leave of my senses actually inviting a complete stranger into the house when I was so vulnerable, so alone, so far away from anyone. Then I remembered. My priorities had changed. Besides, I thought cynically, it would be him who would be taking the chance.

You would think I was the most attractive woman in the world. Oh, I guess I am not bad. A young-looking fifty. Or I was a young-looking fifty, past tense. My once stylish blonde hair in its frizzy halo around my face is definitely showing signs of grey and it is beginning to droop. For several months now, I have been unable to put that hair-coloring goop on it that Jeff has always so insistently wanted. My figure is still about the same. Unfortunately. Although I have lost some weight, I am still as you would remember me: more than pleasingly plump.

But no matter what state of attractiveness, no matter what age, a woman never gets over the fear of molestation, of invasion. Men don't have that basic, almost primeval fear. . . .

•   •   •

I went inside and set the wood down in front of the stove. The pain engulfed me. As I stand here now, I wish I could tell you about it. It is a mind-expanding experience to know the limits of human endurance. For you, Andrew, studying medicine, it is fortunate that you, too, know what pain is because there are no words to describe pain. Words are just symbols for something, symbols that we agree on to describe an experience that seems to be mutual—but pain is no mutual experience. It is mine. I can tell you what it does to me but I cannot tell you what it is.

•   •   •

January 22

Solitude has such an interesting effect on me. It seems to drive me into myself. I don't live in the world, I live in my mind, and my surroundings become my mind; the rocks, the snowladen trees, the turquoise ice, are mine just like my memories, my thoughts. It's almost as if I am in a dream; everything is mental. I like it but I want to run from it. No yakkety-yak to people; no television; no structure or obligation into which I can lose myself. I am driven, yes driven, to be an active participant in the phantasmagoria of this spirit world. I understand that ants will die if required to live alone—but humans are not ants, or rats or white mice for that matter, a dig at the psychologists who are forever equating human behavior to their animals in the lab. I can understand why the highs of the human race come from solitudinous individuals, from maverick behavior of individuals standing alone, acting alone, thinking alone. Solitude impels action.

• • •

Along with my reading and with my writing of this journal—which is the high point of my day, the time when I get to have a conversation with you, my loves—my days are simple. In the morning, I stay nestled under the covers until forced up by the demands of nature. That's another story. We'll leave that. I put wood on the fire which by early morning is just a heap of red ashes. Each time I open the door of that stove and see that it is still going, I feel proud. No one, well, in particular your father, and I guess, myself, thought I could survive alone at the cottage. Jeff always ridiculed the idea of me coming to the cottage myself. However, I seemed to have absorbed quite a bit about survival and even your father would be astonished. The airtight stove certainly makes it easier. I rarely have to re-light it, except when I forget it like I did the other day when I stood talking to Gene in the parking lot and the darn thing almost went out. Anyway, I then check the mouse-traps. The mice are so cute. They have big ears and big black eyes, carica-tures straight out of the old Walt Disney movies. I feel badly about catching them—but mice and humans cannot coexist in the same house. I must again be a predator, a predator for land, a predator for food, a predator wherever the earth has been civilized. Does it help that I recognize this? That I try not to kill or usurp without good reason? Never wantonly? I have filled all the possible mouse holes with steel wool. I have done my best to keep them out so I won't have to kill them. Yet, I feel guilty.

I empty the mousetraps and bait them again.

I get weighed.

I sponge bath, the best I can do without running water.

Then I get dressed. I am wearing long underwear, your father's jeans and a big plaid shirt. Rather hilarious, especially considering my previous con-cern for fashion, even here. No more tight designer jeans and high heels. With sensible, flat-heeled shoes, I never knew walking could be so fluid. Despite my problem, my mobility is better. Of course, the weight I am losing helps too. I take my pill and eat something for breakfast. I am still eating a good breakfast, usually juice, egg, toast, and coffee. Occasionally, I try to drink some powdered milk. Sometimes I make a feed of pancakes or French toast; you know how much I love them. I take my vitamins. Irrational, isn't it? But a good habit is as hard to break as a bad one. Despite my eating habits, I am beginning to lose weight. Did I say that? Of course, I can afford it. I am surprised that even in these circumstances I am more agile. I think if I had realized I was losing so much agility, I would never have let myself get so heavy. How I justified having to sneak off to a podiatrist to get my toenails cut, I don't know.

When the pain-killer has taken hold, I go out again to the outhouse. I suppose I must tell you this. Medical science should see me. It would hang its collective head in shame. If I had a head-ache, arthritis, eczema, a broken leg, the medical world would be right there, ready to help. Yet faced with this, they don't know what to do. Their deity stance is threatened. And so I have been avoided or ignored. Because I didn't fly apart, cry, scream with pain before their very eyes, they simply didn't acknowledge that I had pain. Couldn't they deduce it? I guess not. I already said that earlier, didn't I? Or did I? As the pain got worse, I retreated into myself, afraid I would fly apart and never put myself together again, afraid that I would create a scene or act silly. Why didn't I? Then they would have listened to me. One doctor actually made me wait a week for a consultation. Another wouldn't return my phone call when I told the nurse the medication he gave me wasn't working. The nurse called me back and told me the doctor said to go to the emergency of the hospital. Obviously, he preferred not to face his impotence. Was it egotism that prevented referral outside the city? It was a small problem—hah!—so out of hand they didn't want any other medical group to know about it. Thank goodness, I finally had the sense to drag myself to another city. My unconscious did it, actually. I dreamed I died. I had just bought a new fur coat—predator, again—but I was so cold and I dreamed that I just sank down into the soft, dark fur of my new coat and died. The next morning, I realized I must try and find help outside the city. But it was too late. However, I was given pain killers. Oh, forget all this. What does it matter?

I get back to the cabin and usually doze for a while. Then, I straighten it up. At first, I sort of enjoyed living like a slob. I could eat without manners. Leave the cabin a mess. Do whatever I wanted, when I wanted. But then order returned. I found that despite everything, I could not escape my standards or my realization that I did not want to leave a mess for you. Each morning, I struggle around and clean up the cabin. Lint from the log walls is perpetually falling and a fine ash from the wood stove glazes everything. However, it is dirt I can see and get rid of. It is not like the so-called cleanliness of the invisible dirt of man-made chemicals and radioactivity that we can neither see nor get rid of.

After I have cleaned up the cabin, I usually take my reading to the couch and lie down. My mind by then is often too foggy to read. Words drop from my mind; nouns disappear from their syntax as if they were sucked into the black holes of space. In my writing, fortunately, it is not quite as bad as in my reading, my random thoughts, or in my conversation. What was that name? What was I about to do? What happened in the first chapter? If this is aging, it sure is the best kept secret of the century. I am only fifty. Surely it must be the pain-killers.

•   •   •

January 23

Before I forget—and it has been on my mind to say it so often—but you know what we are like in this family—the positive is expected but rarely complimented—the negative, of course, is articulated. A messy room, a bad report, a friend we didn't like, these would certainly be mentioned—and perhaps punished. Yet, so often your behavior was just downright wonderful, decorating the house at Christmas for Jeff and me to return to; Clarissa, your baking and sewing; Andrew, saving us so much money by wiring the cottage; we took it all for granted; we expected good behavior; we expected outstanding children; and we got it. But did we sufficiently praise you?

Right now I want to break tradition, break the momentum of the past, break my pattern of cracking a joke when things get serious—and say how proud I am of you. You both have turned out to be honest, hard-working, independent individuals. You are pulling your weight in society and if the world was comprised of individuals like you, there would be no trouble. Can you imagine the satisfaction a mother feels when she realizes her hard work has contributed to such excellent results?

I say contributed because I realize there are many other factors that have made you what you are today. A mother or a father can never take all the credit; your own individual strength— that unknown x factor that allows some people to profit from bad experiences while others crumple, that allows some people to grow in a good environment while others are weakened by it—your own individual strength plays an unknown and yet important part. Nurturing you has been my job and I feel satisfied and happy that my work has been successful. I have accomplished something. Something very important. I don't feel that is nothing. Yet how often have I felt worthless, second-rate, as if what I am doing is nothing. As if my job is nothing. That my children are good people, that my husband is happy and has a good environment from which he can do a good job, why is that regarded as nothing? Why do women themselves think it is nothing? Why do *I* think it is nothing ?

There are so many slights and put-downs. Eyes turned towards the husband in conversation; eyes seeking out the male; eyes turned towards the man, any man, by waitresses at fast food counters; by stewardesses on airplanes; by my friends, yes, my friends, in conversations when they know darn well I was the one who did the reading on the subject, not my husband, when they know darn well it is I who have the strong opinions. Do you know I actually had a friend ask during the midst of a high-powered discussion on a political question, she asked: "And what does Jeff think?"

Never mind, for you my reading and education has been of value, however incomplete and self-directed, however unimportant in conversation.

Even though I quit law school after the first year in order to get married and work as a legal secretary to help put your father through law, I never regretted a smidgen of my academic education. I was able to give a background and richness to three other people's lives. Does it sound smug and egotistical to say so? You must realize I am really trying to justify myself, justify my existence, justify my life. Why must I?

I saw a plane fly over today. It was a small plane soaring like a noisy gull along the shoreline. Could someone have been looking for me? The smoke from the chimney would have been a giveaway. I left many clues to a false trail, even a sealed letter to Jeff to open only if he absolutely needed to get in touch with me. It contained a plea to leave me alone, difficult I know for a husband of thirty years to do.

I have not seen Gene today. It has been so beautiful you would think today of all days he would be out rambling around. The sun shone in prisms through the frozen air over the bay. The new snow that must have fallen during the night is like goose down over the land and there is that smell, that delightful smell of winter.

I walked on the beach in front of the cabin, fluffing up the snow with my foot, exulting in the world.

I am feeling fairly good about my stay here. I am managing quite well on my own, despite my disability. In fact, my fat—uh, I have never said that before—even though it wasn't killing me, was definitely a handicap. Now, I realize it. Jeff always said I could never get along at the cottage alone. It would be too hard for me. However, I have managed to get water, keep the fire going, walk the beach, scramble over the rocks. And I'm not even afraid.

I remember before when everyone went away for the evening, I felt a cold apprehension as night began to fall. The fear of wild animals, the fear of some crazed individual, crept closer to me and wild fantasies would ravage my mind. I never learned to shoot our gun—and consequently I had nothing to rely on in case some happenstance brought a crazy across my path. And there are a lot of crazies today.

I shoved the fantasies of fear from my mind, as I shoved frustration, loneliness, insufficiency from my mind, by cooking. And then eating.

"There's Mom baking bread at night again."

But you didn't know I was baking because I was afraid of being alone while you were all out.

And when I didn't feel good about myself, when I was bored or secretly raging at my loss of self as I was inundated by my role of wife and mother, I would cook. When I felt compelled to stay in the role even when you went away to university, to stay there because it was expected of me, because my education had been interrupted—what could I do now?—and because of my own lack of gumption, I would cook. It was not only creative and pleasing to everyone—Clara is a wonderful cook—it tasted good. If no one was at home, I would eat it.

I must clarify what I said about my feelings of inundation. It was not the role of wife and mother that swamped me, it was the endless physical work. Although it was done by my body, it depleted my mind and I was too tired to read and study as much as I wanted. Why didn't we get more help ? Don't ask me. We wanted to get ahead, I guess. To save money and get ahead, whatever that means.

Clarissa, you won't make the same mistake. You won't let yourself be inundated by the home. However, you might make another mistake: you might abdicate the role of wife and mother entirely.

I must have felt some anger too about having given up a promising, stimulating career, about the drudge my supposedly brilliant mind was subjected to, about my gradual inability to keep up with legal conversations. At social gatherings, usually of lawyers and their wives, I gradually eased over to the side of the living room with the women. I must have felt anger but I don't remember it. I just remember the fatigue, the atrophying mind, the need to eat to keep up my strength. Eating, as usual, was my solution.

Needless to say, I have been cooking while I am here. I still long for certain foods, certain dishes, almost with love. I used to eat them with such gusto and vigor that Jeff couldn't stand it. He wouldn't say much but I could tell. So often I used to have my 'feed'—he hated that expression —in private.

Once I ate so much butterscotch pie I was sick.

•   •   •

I still feel constraints about writing this journal, some shyness in talking to you so openly about myself now you are adult, about disrobing my mind. For the first time in my life I have complete freedom to say what I want in adult company, to be serious instead of twisting what is serious into a joke, and yet I find this freedom difficult.

I will keep trying.

•   •   •

Dear Children: *January 31*

My house is in disorder. My clothes are filthy. I smell. I cannot wash. I cannot be bothered to wash. My standards are being eroded by pain. My brain is being eroded by pain killers. I have resorted to using the chamber. What ignominy. Someone else, probably Gene, is going to have to empty it. There are few pretensions left.

Gene is down at the lake getting water. He will soon finish his story and then I will be free, free of this body that has me trapped, free to swirl somewhere; somewhere, wherever the outdated Law of Conservation of Energy takes its energy when one form of energy changes to another.

I am so worried I will leave a mess for you. I will get Gene to promise to clean up everything. I want to leave this beautiful place unsullied by my dying presence.

Remember there are provisions in the root cellar, dried fruits, beans, freeze dried foods, and powdered milk. This can be your haven, if only for a little while, in case the world goes crazy and the last war, the unwinable war, begins. If I was a young mother I would be going berserk with worry. The lioness instinct to protect the young would be so thwarted by the invisible enemy, the enemy of disintegrating atoms. How to protect? Yet protect the lioness must. I give you then the root cellar. What a pitiable gesture. Such problems my generation has bequeathed to you. Please be wiser.

Where's that bottle of brandy? I can hear Gene's footsteps squeaking across the cold snow. Even the thermopane windows are beginning to frost it is so cold.

When Gene arrives, sets the pails of water in the kitchen, it will be more talk. Despite my dying body, my eroded mind, I find his story interesting. It has kept me alive for a few more days. It has made life worth living for a few more days. However, today, I can hardly bear to be alive. Life is a flowering outward, a reaching to others, to things, and a forgetting of self. From habit, I use the inadequate word life; I really mean spectrum. As consciousness moves along the spectrum of existence and the flower begins to wilt, there is a focussing inward, a retreat. Sometimes it is swift and traumatic. Usually it is gradual. But fast or slow, this retreat back into the ego, into the self, becomes a forgetting of self oddly similar to the forgetting of self in the flowering outward of life. Yet in death, the flower wilts inward, backward, to the nirvana of the womb, peace, entropy, stillness.

Oh, where's that bottle of brandy?

"Good morning, Gene."

"Hi, Clara. You're looking a little better, this morning. I see you got the juice and coffee I made for you. Would you like something else?"

"Just the brandy, thanks. I never thought I would be reduced to having a belt for breakfast. Put the water in the kitchen and let's get on with your story."

Gene is in the kitchen now. I can hear him putting the pails of water under the counter. Now he is tidying up the kitchen. He really doesn't realize my urgency. Perhaps he is stalling because of reticence to unfold his story. He wants to tell me but he doesn't want to tell me. Remember I told you about the strange look that I saw in his eyes one of the early times I encountered him? His eyes were sort of bugged out, with dark pupils, and constantly darting from side to side? Well, that look is back. It probably came yesterday during his story but I was too unwell to notice. It's still there this morning. I noticed it when he walked in. I have only seen that look in someone's eyes once before. When our neighbors were involved in a head-on collision where three people died, they returned from the hospital, bandaged and mis-shapen and with that look in their eyes. It left after about a month. I wonder what causes it? Terror? A dramatic escape from death? A head-on collision with death?

"Gene. Come on. For heaven's sake get in here and finish your story."

"Okay, Clara. I was just doing up these few dishes."

"Well, sit down and let's go. I can hear the wind howling over at Coppermine Point."

"That's impossible, Clara. It's too far."

It's howling, tearing at the tree tops, racing up the indentations it has worn in the rock, attacking the vertical cliff, spewing sand and foam everywhere, brutal and furious and entirely untamable. It's at Coppermine Point now and it's coming towards us. Towards me.

• • •

February

A half-dead mouse is on the floor beside the couch. It must have been caught last night and not killed outright. I can see it has gnawed the corner off the trap. Every once in a while it flutters to get free and then it lies still again. How I wish I could put it out of its misery.

I think it is morning. I have been on the couch for how long? I don't know what date it is. I believe it is February, a new month. The milk must be sour by now, the food bad, except for the provisions I stored for you in the root cellar. The storm I heard coming arrived during the night. The roof of the cottage cried as the storm rained pellets of snow and branches on it. The pressure of the wind must have been too much for the ice and a zig-zag gash has opened up in the lake. The water is dark and angry, trying to break free.

However, all seems quiet now. Could it possibly be peace? Oh, I don't want it to be peace yet. I have to get away from here.

Gene, where are you?

He was so kind to me last night. I went out to the john—I could not bear to use the chamber—and as usual, I fell. I howled with pain and there was Gene watching me. For the first time, I saw concern in his eyes. After helping me to stand, I noticed the darting look of terror had returned. He waited for me while I was in the john. Carefully, we walked back towards the cabin.

Hanging on to his arm—I walk so stooped now—I told him my plan, how he could help me. And do you know what he did? He left. He steadied me to the door of the cabin, grabbed his heavy coat and ran away. Now, how can I get away from here and leave this place unsullied for you? I have been proud of most things I have done in my life—I now realize it—I look back and see that I neither sacrificed my standards, nor acted sleazily, was at home when you needed me and always helped you despite my own endeavors. Remember that oral on Marshall McLuhan that we worked on, Clarissa? You picked my brains like a regular news hound and then put together a summary that would do a university student proud. And, Andrew, you seemed to be such a slow developer; I cried when you brought home your first report card and you had done well. Then you turned out to be a brilliant student. Would I have had such satisfaction if I had been a lawyer, smart as I supposedly was? Would I have felt anything comparable to participating in the life cycle of birth? Of nurturing a life that is the next generation, tomorrow's history? Or sitting back and just being satisfied to see you strong, competent individuals? Oh, I have carped about being regarded as a second-class citizen, about not being able to get a credit card without my husband's name, about women looking and talking to the first man that walks into a room instead of talking to me—me!—about being expected to wear back-distorting high heels and to use cancer-producing hair dyes, about my husband getting all the credit, even for what I do. But in the quiet of this room, in the quiet of my mind, I smugly feel I really did an important job and I did it well.

I hope that doesn't sound like bragging.

Nor was the job easy. When you try hard, there is always a threat of failure. When you aim high, there is guilt and remorse when you fall short or think you fall short. I was always so aware of what fragile blossoms your little lives were. Did I bruise you when I yelled at you? Did I expect too much of you? Was I too hard on you? I was so afraid of the mewling permissiveness that seemed to be producing marshmallow adults. I was so afraid my own selfish individuality would come before you. I still remember the dream I had, Clarissa, when you were a toddler. I dreamed I was experiencing the lovely joys of making love only to find that you were almost strangling in your high chair. I worried and I worried.

When I left the house for the last time, I brought along with me the file marked "Children." I had filled it with mementos of your growing up. The Mother's Day card you made for me, Andrew: "M is for the million things you gave me." And letters: remember your description of the hazing at university, Andrew, my son. My son! And Clarissa, my daughter, your first drawings as form gradually emerged from your random scribblings? Your essays: "How Life Begins," "Can You Talk to Plants?"

How proud I am of you.

And now I want to be proud of my death, my last, perhaps only really individual and free act. My eating was certainly individual but it wasn't free.

Gene, where are you?

I waited to let him tell me his story and now he is gone and I am too weak. I lie here on the couch listening to the mouse struggle against its trap. What I would like to do is to get up and walk bravely through the snow to our picnic inlet down the road. I hope you don't mind. You hardly ever go there now that we have Gull Rock. But no matter how much motivation I have, my body will barely move.

Gene, where are you?

Do you realize you have jumped ship again? You jumped ship when you ran from your success in art. You jumped ship, not when you got in the life boat on the *Fitzgerald*, but when you hid from your rescuers, when you jumped away from the recognition that you actually made a reasoned, correct choice.

And now you've jumped ship when you had the chance to be honorable and helpful to me, when you had the chance to fulfill a promise. All I wanted you to do was pull me on the toboggan down to the inlet. I didn't tell you why—I don't want you to be legally implicated—but I think you must have guessed.

You can still change your mind and come back. If those hours of talking, of listening, if those painful hours of postponing my final peace did any good, you will come back. You still have time for a second chance.

I hear the storm mounting again. The wind is stacking the ice that formed during the night on the open water into sheaves of glass along the shore. The transparent lake has become transparent glass, broken and stacked into neat sheaves along the shore. Or was that yesterday? Did Lake Superior make ice sheaves again?

I don't know how we are going to get water. But who needs water? I feel so light. I feel myself floating, no earthly body to give me pain, floating along the beach, floating over the transparent sheaves of ice, the wind mingling with my aerie spirit. The waves are huge now. Gene was right when he said they were like animals, huge, frothing dragons rearing out of the sea. Do you see that? Do you see that dragon rushing along the water, foam frothing from its crest? It is Mishipishu, the Ojibway god Manitou. There he goes, racing across the water, the wind tearing at his crest. Up he comes, rearing proudly above the waves, and then slowly, slowly submerging in a gurgle of bubbles.

You know I am blessed because Mishipishu has appeared to me. He is the most powerful Manitou of all and he is now my spirit guardian because he has appeared to me.

Great Mishipishu, guardian of this mighty lake, grant me my wish. . . .
What is my wish?

Oh yes, I wish to remove my earthly body from this place. I wish to keep this place sanctified for my children and their physical life here. Whisk me down to my inlet. There I will sit on the rocks, feel the spray on my face, drink a toast with this eau de vie as the welcome cold envelops me. I will join the memories of my children and my husband, memories of when we ran and danced on the beach, memories of when we loved and played and ate and laughed. I will join these memories and I will not be alone. We will never say goodbye.

Help me, Mishipishu. Help me get there.

I feel myself going down to the cave, the sacred place of the Ojibway. The pellets of snow are insinuating themselves into my eyes, my ears, my mouth. I am becoming part of the storm. By foot it would be difficult going because of the glaze of ice on the beach. The agates are bright from the ice, polished by the sand and glazed by the waves, frozen into place as if time had stopped, which, of course, it never does. Or does it?

I am following my usual route to the cave, up over those bulging rocks and then around and down, wending my way through the corridors of lava. The gas holes in the lava are filled with copper and quartz, polka dots of beige and turquoise like the surface of a child's toy dog. Don't you believe me? Look the next time you are there.

The waves are thundering in. The lake has broken free. As I approach the cave the roar increases, the waves reverberating against the ice in the rock grotto, etching it deeper and deeper with each thrust. The surge almost touches the tree-line—but never regularly. You'd think you were safe to walk along the rocks as the waves diminish and lap and lap away at the shore—but then without warning, one, two, three, they thrust up and over the beach and over the ice, grabbing at the trees with their watery claws.

Chunks of ice are bobbing in the open water. Soon they will be massed together on shore into voluptuous Henry Moore shapes that could easily be called icebergs. There will be dainty ice bridges and castles for these Henry Moore damsels and the ice will turn a delicate turquoise blue. Then they will all break free from the shore and float to oblivion in the cobalt blue water of Lake Superior, while the diamond tips of the iceglazed trees nod and crackle in the wind.

Mishipishu, help me float to oblivion. I can see my body on that couch, lying in its earthly mess. Old and hairy.

Remember me differently, Jeff. Remember me vibrant and young.

Oh Mishipishu, get me out of here. Help me get out of here,

"Clara. Clara. Are you all right? Wake up. Wake up. I've come back. I will help you."

"Mishipishu?"

"Clara. It's Gene."

"Gene?"

"I've been so wound up with my problems I haven't been able to think of anything else. I haven't been able to see anything else. My God, how sick you are."

"Not until today have I been able to draw. Time and time again I tried to draw your face and I just couldn't remember it. Today I saw your face—and I saw your suffering. And I could draw. You have freed me."

"Freed you? You did that. But let me look at your eyes."

"My eyes?"

"Yes. Let me see. Yes. Your eyes are okay."

"What are you talking about, Clara? Are you raving again?"

"Probably. You had a look in your eyes that bothered me. It's okay. The look has gone."

"Do you still want me to help you?"

"Oh, please, Gene. Please help me. The skis and toboggan are in the boat-house. You just have to pull me down the road to the inlet. What goes on there is my business. You don't know what that is. Right?"

"Right."

"Come back and clean up, will you? And empty the traps. But first, before we go, will you take this poor little mouse outside and put it out of its misery? It has been struggling for so long."

"I don't want to—but I will."

"Let's see, I've got the brandy. Now where's my purse?"

"Your purse?"

"Of course. Don't you know a woman can't go anywhere without her purse?"

"Clara. Are you joking? Or raving?"

"Probably both—but I need my purse. I have a back-up in there. Just in case."

FROM DEEP WATER PASSAGE: A SPIRITUAL JOURNEY AT MIDLIFE

(1995)

Ann Linnea

ON JUNE 15, 1992, Ann Linnea, (1950-), and her colleague Paul Treuer embarked from Duluth, Minnesota, in their kayaks to circumnavigate Lake Superior. When Linnea returned to Duluth at the end of a summer's paddling her *Grace*, she discovered that she had been changed irrevocably by her experience. "My sense of hearing had become so keen that we had to have the phone ringer set to mute for weeks. My sense of smell was so acute that I couldn't walk down the street without smelling neighbors' back-yard garbage cans. . . I had gotten as close to becoming a woman of primitive culture as a white, North American, middle-class woman could become in the twentieth century."

-→══◎═╬-◄-

She-Who-Finishes-Grieving

PUKASKWA PROVINCIAL PARK campground is at the end of a dead-end road a long way from any population center in Ontario. As far as I could tell, every site had a vehicle. Those that didn't actually have a truck or car parked there had a plethora of equipment, ranging from Coleman lanterns on picnic tables to huge, blue plastic rain tarps strung between pine trees, all of which clearly could not have fit in a kayak. We were probably the only ones who had paddled to the park.

•   •   •

Cars were driving in and out of the park, stopping to pay the entrance fee or to look for maps to their newly acquired campsites. I knew I would have to strain to hear anything from that outdoor phone, but I really needed to talk with someone. And once again, I was calling her the day after a traumatic experience. In Grand Marais I had totally fallen apart. I reassured myself that would not happen again, that I was only looking for helpful articulation from someone with outside perspective. I dialed her number, then recited the well-memorized digits of my credit card to an operator. The phone started ringing in another country, six hundred miles away. The ringing stopped. I heard a click and expected Christina's answering machine, but a friendly "Hello" spoke to me.

"Hi," I said, trying to sound casual. "Am I interrupting anything?"

"Annie, where are you calling from this time?"

"Pukaskwa Provincial Park. It's in Canada, over on the far shore of the lake."

"What's all the background noise?"

"Well, I'm calling from a phone booth on the outside wall of park headquarters. Cars are driving back and forth."

"Cars, phone booth. I keep imagining you on some remote wilderness shore and then you call me from a phone booth!"

I realized, again, what different worlds we were living in this summer. That even people following our progress by map had no idea of the conditions we lived in, on land or sea, or the impact of the relentless weather. "Well, mostly it is wild country and we don't see anybody for days." I tried to steady my voice. "When we come to a spot of civilization, I really look forward to mail or to talking to someone."

"I am writing. Did you get my package there?" she asked.

"No, I haven't gotten any mail in Canada."

"Shit. I mailed it by Express five days ago. Didn't you get my letter in Rossport, either?"

"No." I wanted to keep my voice calm. "What are you up to today?"

"Trying not to drive myself nuts," she said, and laughed. "I'm having a hard summer, too, in my own way. Something very basic is changing. I'm at the end of a cycle, and I can't see my way through."

"Like fog . . . ," I said. "We've been paddling blind a lot of days this summer." I held my breath, waiting to see if the city woman and the wilderness paddler could find a way to connect.

"Yes," she responded. "I feel a lot like I'm in a fog. Not a real one, like you are, but I can't see my way ahead. It scares me, makes me uncomfortable in my own skin. My life feels like a cold, soaked wet suit. But for me that's just a metaphor, for you it's reality. . . . How are you?"

Though she admitted to her own troubles, her voice sounded calmer and more steady than my own. I remained determined not to break down, but I felt tears rising in my throat. I guess I was quiet for a long time. The voice that came out of the black plastic phone hanging from the metal cord said, "I'm so sorry you haven't received mail. I want you to know that I'm listening as hard as I can as you share your trip in letters to me. You say things like 'four- to seven-foot seas' and 'small craft advisory,' and I, who have kayaked only a few times in relatively calm water, can't begin to comprehend what you're going through."

Her willingness to reach out, to have compassion and honesty, melted my resolve to remain She-Who-Stands-Strong-Alone.

"Well, I'm not doing very well," I said, and again burst into tears. "The weather is still gruesome, cold and stormy most of the time. The physical challenges haven't relented."

"Are you staying safe?" she asked in concern.

I laughed—an odd, checked chortle, considering I was crying at the same time. "There's no way to do this and stay safe. But we are being careful—and I am still alive. Yesterday we paddled thirty-nine miles."

"That sounds like a lot," she said. "Is it?"

"Almost unheard of."

"Why didn't you stop?"

"There was either no place to stop because of the fog, the dangerous shoreline, or the waves, or when we did stop it was all rocks and dense brush—no place to pitch tents. Christina, I don't know if I can take this anymore."

A car crunched over the gravel on the road next to the phone, reminding me that my level of vulnerability was public. I started openly sobbing on the phone.

"I'm so sorry that we're this deeply separated," she said. "Can you tell me what's wearing you down? Is it the exertion, the exhaustion?"

"I'm still in this internal battle between my absolute determination to take this life journey and the reality of what actually paddling and living in these conditions is doing to my body. I'm just physically battering myself. Hour after hour, I push on and keep asking, Why am I doing this? What am I doing?"

Now she paused before answering, "Do you get any answers?"

"All my life I've trusted my body. You learn through your mind—but I learn through doing things with my body, by moving until I have insight."

I heard concern in Christina's voice. "Well, that's fine, as long as it doesn't kill you."

"I don't know how to do it any other way. . . . This is my only chance. I've carved out this stretch of time and created this experience, and if I give up, if I just go home . . . I'll lose something important. And I don't even know what that something is because I haven't gotten it yet."

"Then you have to keep going," she said. "My first impulse was to tell you it's okay to quit—and it is okay, Annie. Your survival must come first. If you quit, you will live to make another time, to find another way. My second impulse is to tell you that your job is to find your wisdom."

In my mind's eye I could see the way she leans forward when she's earnest, almost felt her hand on my shoulder, trusted her to know the words my heart needed to hear.

"You are in some kind of race with time, with unbelievably harsh daily circumstances," she continued. "You must paddle with the questions that will most help you awaken into the next phase of your life. Your pilgrimage is to find the stamina to endure these questions, in addition to everything else you're enduring."

I knew this challenge was what I needed to hear, to be reassured that someone else understood what was driving me. The Longest Day had stripped me down to my lowest point of confidence and energy. I needed help remembering why I was on the trip, why all the pain might be worth it. I sobbed into the phone, "Please keep talking."

"You have left the shore of what you think you know about yourself, your life, your relationships, your direction, your purpose. You must ask God more deeply than you have ever asked: 'Who do you say that I am? What do you want me to do?'"

Though she couldn't see me, I nodded in agreement.

A man had gotten out of his car and was waiting behind me to use the phone. The lawn on the median strip of grass surrounding the entrance booth was a lush green. It was midday, July 9, and the sun was not yet warm enough for me to take off my wool jacket. Everything around me was common and ordinary and unchallenging, and I was still crying so hard I could barely talk.

◆　◆　◆

That night, as per our pre-trip schedule, a friend arrived from Duluth bearing letters, packages, and our next food resupply. Some of the packages held candy bars. There was a loaf of homemade bread for each of us from our dear friend Fran. Paul's wife, Mary, had sent the neighborhood butcher's best beef jerky. Clearly, word had gotten out that we were losing weight. I was especially excited to receive letters from Dave and the kids. I tried to remember what gift Brian and Sally would be opening tonight. Each of the six times we were resupplied they got to open presents I had wrapped before the trip with certain dates on them. Was July 9th a jump rope and a new baseball? or spending money for a trip to the movies? I honestly couldn't remember, my old life seemed so far away.

Sally had drawn me several pictures, and in her perfect handwriting had written a short note saying she loved and missed me. I studied the pictures carefully. One was of a lake with a rainbow and two tiny boats. The other was a mottled blue-and-green ball with these words written in crayon around it: "The World Is Our Home, We Only Have One of Them." She had just finished third grade, just learned cursive, and here she was, perfectly penning the few short messages she knew were important to me. I pulled out my sacred pouch, which held the children's photos. Tears started rolling down my cheeks when I looked at my beautiful, smiling daughter.

Brian's letter was the quickly scrawled note of a sixth-grader waiting to enter junior high. My solid boy, my buddy, the child with whom I'd had deep spiritual conversations since he was a toddler, smiled out at me from the wallet photo. Letters were not his medium of expression. We needed to be physically present with each other. I ached to see him.

Dave's letter was written in the neat half printing, half writing style that he uses to outline course notes on the university's blackboard. It was written on one side of a six-by-nine-inch sheet of white tablet paper. There was an acknowledgment of the fact that they were having cold weather, too; a brief reporting of kid activities; a wish for my good health.

As good as it was to get this one and only packet of written communication from my family, it was also hard. They were so far away, had so little idea of my reality, were simply doing the best they could to cope. I didn't detect joy or enthusiasm from their letters, so guilt settled over my sadness. All the words of people skeptical of the trip trumpeted into my ears: "How can you go away and leave a third-grader and a sixth-grader for the summer?" I had hoped that Dave and the kids would create their own adventure out of this time, but my heart now told me this was not true, that they, too, were having their own endurance test. Like the phone conversation with Christina, the words of my family brought only temporary sunshine into the fog of my increasing despair.

That night in my tent I held the little blue cylindrical flashlight in my teeth and wrote in my journal:

> They don't understand. My family writes me letters like I'm off on vacation. Our friend delivers our resupply of food and letters from home, watches us react like kids on Christmas morning, and she thinks yesterday's grueling ordeal is little more than some athletic contest finished and won. Christina is the one person who seems to understand the urgency I feel about not giving up my quest, but I can't really convey to her the unbelievable strain of what I'm doing to my body. No one understands how desperate I feel. I don't know how to communicate what is happening to me.

• • •

We stopped paddling at the Pukaskwa River. We had come fifty miles in three days. A faster pace than we had set out to do, but nevertheless, reasonably relaxing. Over a driftwood fire on a small spit of sand formed where the river ran into the lake, Paul and I cooked our favorite of the dehydrated dinners: pizza. It was a meal we could only cook with the coals of a wood fire on a night when we were not rushed. While the Bisquick crust was browning slowly in the well-greased iron skillet, we silently watched the pink-and-orange sunset. I liked how easy silence was between us.

Paul's words broke the tranquillity. "I've been thinking about paddling out to Michipicoten Island."

I stared at him in disbelief and said, "You've got to be kidding!"

"I've been studying the map. It's eight miles out and back, forty miles around the island."

Once again I felt like we were not on the same journey. I was savoring the first nice weather, the leisure of a slow-cooking meal, the quiet of the sunset, muscles that didn't hurt for the first time on the entire trip. And he wanted to keep pushing, to add an extra fifty-six miles! My whole life had been about pushing. Pushing to get good grades, a good job, a good home, good children. I couldn't push anymore. I just had to stay still, to keep up with nobody but myself.

"Are you excited about going?" I asked.

"Yeah, I am. Everybody says it's magical, partly because the fog makes it treacherous to get there. It's got an inland lake, steep cliffs, and few people." He looked at me. Our eyes remained locked. Lake Superior-blue eyes reflecting the soft orange sunset.

This time I was the one to break the silence. "It's okay with me if you go, but I don't have any interest in joining you. This is the only stretch of the trip where we scheduled ourselves shorter days. I really need to rest. Let's see what the weather is going to be up to over the next few days," I said, rising to get my radio.

Ten minutes later I was back from my twenty-foot walk. "Paul, my radio is missing! I must have left it at our last stop."

Virtually every piece of our equipment was indispensable. We constantly checked and rechecked the ground around us after lunch breaks and in the morning. But this time a black, hand-size radio set on a black rock had remained camouflaged. I would have to backtrack and find it.

The next morning Paul and I were on the water early: he to continue down the shore, to watch the weather, and to decide about venturing out to Michipicoten Island; I to circle back to Richardson's Point to find my radio. I would stay another day at the Pukaskwa River before moving camp. Paul would leave rock cairns at Redsucker Point: "One if by land, two if by sea." If there were two cairns, I would know he'd gone out to the big island and I wouldn't see him until I got to the Michipicoten River. If there was one, I would look for him in the vicinity of Cairn Point the next day. It was the first time we had split spontaneously for solo time, had openly honored the differences in our journeys.

I was determined to paddle my nearly empty boat as fast as I could to retrieve the radio, and then enjoy a day to wash clothes, swim in the river, read, and write. I paddled as if I were swimming laps in a pool—an athletic endeavor with little concern about my surroundings. The radio was exactly where I had left it on the rocks near the Pukaskwa Pit we had stopped to explore. We had met a ranger in a patrol boat near Otter's Cove who had told us about the ancient site. "One of the most distinctive of these structures anywhere around the lake: a circular depression three feet deep, five feet in diameter, with a three-foot-high wall around it," he had said.

We had read about the Pukaskwa Pits before beginning our trip. Once we reached the park we consciously began making rest stops on shores that seemed to hold potential for finding them. The areas are generally three to ten feet across and two to four feet deep and seldom have walls like the one at Richardson's Point. Archaeologists are just beginning to understand them, and speculate that they were used for ceremonies, rituals, rites of passage, or lookouts by native people just prior to the modern-day Ojibway. I kept looking for them, hoping to recapture some of the feelings I'd had at the stone altar and deepen my connection to indigenous wisdom on the lake. I had sat for a long time in the one at Richardson's Point, imagining myself a young woman off on a moon-time solo. Retrieving the radio, I paused to look again at the structure, scrambled down the boulder field, and hopped expertly back into *Grace*.

The water was flat calm. The air was cool and beginning to warm. There was no sight of fog lurking anywhere. I felt strong and confident. Stroke, pull. Stroke, pull. Stroke, pull. I was a yellow dolphin cutting a path through the smooth waters of its own sea.

After a short time, I detected a movement out of the corner of my eye. Turning my head slightly, I saw a caribou standing on the shore of the island I was paddling by! The rack on his head was at least four feet across, a complex maze of bends and curves. Wrapped in brown-black fur atop the six-foot-high island, he towered over me like an ancient king. I stopped paddling and stared in disbelief. He returned the stare with complete disdain, walked down off his rock island into the water, and began swimming toward the mainland. Slowly, I pulled my camera and telephoto lens out of their stuff sack and paddled behind him at what felt like a nonintrusive distance. I started snapping pictures as he got to the shore of the mainland and walked out. He turned, looked at me, shook his great antlers free of water, and ambled into the forest.

"Holy shit," I whispered to myself, "I don't believe it." I had been looking for caribou ever since we left Rossport. And here, when I was not looking, was racing along paying no attention to anything, what do I see but the caribou I've been straining to find at the edge of every fog bank. I sat in my boat with the paddle across my lap, staring at the section of brush where this most magnificent of northern creatures had disappeared. "We are so far north," I said aloud to the still water, "that caribou still roam and ancient sites have scarcely been studied."

I resumed paddling. Slower now. Reminded once again that every moment holds the potential for magic. That those of too directed purpose can often pass by greater purpose.

•   •   •

On the map Redsucker Point is a distinctive landmark. When I paddled up to it in the morning sun, my heart dropped. The point was marked by a house-size granite rock. I realized that Paul would not have been able to land his kayak and make a cairn. I'd been expecting to see his signal easily, one pile of a half-dozen or so rocks stacked atop one another or two piles of stacked rocks. Now what was I supposed to do? There was no civilization between here and the Michipicoten River. Did I keep paddling until I reached the campground there, not knowing for three days where or how my friend was? I paddled around the point, looking for some other spot he might have been able to leave me a sign.

There! A single pile of rocks was carefully placed on a low-lying boulder next to the lake. He had not gone out to the island! "Thank God," I said aloud to a guardian seagull.

Paul was waiting for me at noon at Cairn Point, as happy to see me as I was to see him. We didn't paddle much farther, so we could take our time making camp, studying maps, exploring the land. It was a luxury to think about doing some hiking. A luxury we could afford, having come off a schedule of ten- to twelve-hour paddling days. To climb the hill behind our campsite we had to pull ourselves up and over tree roots, work our way around areas of cliffs, but finally we reached a hilltop several hundred feet above the lake's surface. Michipicoten Island was visible to the south. The entire eastern half of the sky was purple-black and dotted with intermittent lightning flashes. Paul pulled out his weather-band radio. "An area of extensive and severe thunderstorms preceding several days of thick cloud cover and rain due to hit the Pukaskwa Provincial Park area this evening."

For the next two days we paddled in dense, unrelenting fog, more three- to five-foot waves, and occasional rain. The physical challenge of the lake returned and so did my doubt. On July 16, I made this entry in my journal by flashlight:

University River or Dog River, depending on whether you believe the navigation chart or the sign at the mouth of this river. Nine P.M. This is a lovely spot to camp, like so many places we make camp. But what do we see of them? We arrive late and leave early. And why *am* I doing this? Day after day of physical exertion that hurts. I hope I "come through to the other side," come to see this as more than just the most difficult, grand adventure I've ever attempted. But tonight, dear God, I'm not sure. I'm just exhausted.

The fog had again driven out my determination, returned my doubt. Where was the steady courage I needed? I had abandoned it, like the radio, at the sunny sand spit at the river mouth. There was no easy way to circle back and reclaim a mood. How could I get to a place of simply accepting what was and not wishing for something different? I turned off the flashlight in my little tent on yet another sandbar at the mouth of yet another river, and let the sound of rapids meeting surf pound the doubt out of my brain and make way for dawn and a return to determination.

However, the real transformation, the real movement out of doubt and into courage, happened on July 18. We were paddling out of the mouth of the Michipicoten River. It was warm and sunny. Our weather-bands, now tuned to Canadian stations, promised a whole day of sunshine and temperatures in the fifteen- to twenty-degree centigrade range (Fahrenheit translation: the sixties!). It was to be our first full day of summer paddling.

"Now this is the kind of day I signed up for!" I said to Paul.

He grinned. "Yeah, we might even be able to take off our long underwear today!"

Paul was to spend the night with a friend at Old Woman's Bay in Lake Superior Provincial Park. The bay was named for the silhouette created by the headlands. I requested solo time on an island where I could view this impressive cliff face. By 1 P.M. we spotted the Old Woman—an immense, continuous wall of rock whose top edge held the silhouette of forehead, large nose, lips, and chin. We were paddling by a group of small islands. I wished Paul well and said I'd choose one of the islands and wait at my campsite for him the next morning. We were both so excited to be heading into our respective adventures that we didn't stop to think how difficult it would be for Paul to find my campsite if the fog rolled in. This time, though, the lake was kind to us. This *was* the kind of day we had signed up for.

"I don't know if anyone has a right to be this happy," I wrote in a letter to Christina that afternoon. I was alone on a cobblestone beach, totally naked on a huge white, body-size granite boulder smoothed by the waves. My freshly done wash was scattered on boulders all over the beach, beautiful in its wild array of colors. My tent was perched thirty feet up on the top of a small cliff, surrounded by ripe blueberries. The sky was cloudless. There was a light breeze. The waves were gently lapping against the shore. There were no bugs. I was neither too hot nor too cool. I was in heaven.

When the sun sank below the horizon, I put on my clothes, lit a fire for supper, and set out a candle, my children's pictures, and a feather on top of a boulder. I started to read aloud Martha Courtot's wonderful essay "Tribes," the last chapter of a book published in 1977 by the same title:

> We tell you this: we are doing the impossible. We are teaching ourselves to be human. When we are finished, the strands which connect us will be unbreakable; already we are stronger than we have ever been. The fibers which we weave on our insides will be so tight that nothing will be able to pass through them.

The water in the trusty old black pot over the campfire was boiling. It was time for me to drop the rice in. I couldn't. I just started crying. I bent over at the waist and wailed. I was finally safe enough for the terror, the fear, the agony, the confusion to pour out of me. I was a lone woman on a lone island, howling to Old Woman. This journey to teach me my humanness was the loneliest journey of my life. But then I remembered another lonely night, the night Betty had died.

I had made many journeys from Minnesota to her Utah bedside during her five-month bout with cancer. When the call came that she had gone into a final coma, my friend Marge had said, "This time you're not going alone. I'm coming with you." We traveled by Greyhound bus. It took us forty-eight hours to get there, heading by stops and starts across the frozen plains of the Dakotas and Wyoming. In that time, three of her sisters flew in from New York and Betty was taken by ambulance from a Salt Lake City hospital to the Logan hospital, so she could die in her own town.

Her eldest sister greeted us in the hospital lobby. "Ann, we have been telling her you're coming. The doctor never believed she'd last this long. You know Betty; she's probably been cussing you out for being so slow. None of us has any idea what will happen once you go into the room, so we'd each like to take a moment with her first if that's okay." I nodded as Betty's three sisters and our mutual friend Rosalie filed one by one into the room with the closed door.

The door to the private room was huge and heavy. When it was my turn to go in, I struggled to push it open. There she was, the woman I had hiked with in the Zion National Park not two weeks earlier. The woman who had recovered enough after being carried down from the mountain to hike several other short trails. Now she was a skeleton with sunken, glazed eyes and yellow skin. A sheet with a head, loudly inhaling and exhaling. A body clinging desperately to the cliff-edge of life. "Dear God, help me," I whispered.

When I reached Betty, I felt under the covers to find her hand and bent to kiss her cheek. Touch. Yes, touch. She is real. She is the same woman I love. I laid my cheek on hers. Rested in the security of our togetherness. And then the words came. "Hello, my friend, I'm here. I know you can hear me." I stood up and rubbed her hand and arm as I spoke.

"Betty, you are the best friend I've ever had. It is you that has made me alive, who has opened my heart and brought me amazing companionship.

"There are so many good memories between us. We have lived together so passionately. Climbed, skied, backpacked, kayaked, run marathons. We have explored mountaintops and deserts, lakes and forests. You have helped me change diapers, build Lego cars, mop up spilled Jell-O, and take toddlers camping. All of these things, at a time when I was far more interested in being a mom than being a good friend. You have taught me so much about love, loyalty, and devotion.

"I am going to try as hard as I can to be worthy of that honor, to love more deeply, to live more deeply. But I am going to miss you so much."

Betty's memory was bringing me out of loneliness, into companionship. I straightened up, resettled myself on the granite boulder, pulled on her jacket for warmth, and went deeper into the memory of that moment two and a half years earlier.

"I know how much you like to sing. I want to sing you the prayer I always sing to the children:

> *Mother we thank Thee for the night*
> *and for the blessed morning light,*
> *for health and food and loving care*
> *and all that makes the day so fair.*
> *Help us to do the things we should,*
> *to be to others kind and good.*
> *In all we do in work and play*
> *to be more loving day by day.*

"Betty, I've come to give you Brian and Dave's love." And then I paused and leaned down to touch my cheek to hers, and said, "And that of your daughter, Sally, for she is your daughter, you know. She bonded to you first.

"You have battled this awful disease so valiantly. You lived your life with great courage and you have shown us all how to die with great courage. Betty, those of us here will try to take care of one another. I cannot hold your hand any longer. God has it. It will be peaceful, Betty. It's okay to let go. You deserve peace so much."

Suddenly I became conscious of the hospital room, of Betty's labored breathing. It felt as if I'd been far away. I again became aware of my own thought processes. And the first thought I had was, "A person could be in a coma for weeks. I am just going to sit here and hold her hand until she dies." I pulled up a chair and sat down.

Almost instantly, her breathing was no longer labored. It was quiet and peace-

ful. I heard the door open behind me and felt hands on my shoulders. "Ann," Marge's voice said, "the doctor would like to talk with you."

"I'm not leaving. She's letting go." The hands left my shoulders and I heard the door close.

The door opened again and the doctor appeared at the other side of the bed. He took her pulse. He looked at me and nodded. The door opened and closed behind me again. Rosalie, Marge, and Betty's sisters all filed in around her bed. Betty heaved a huge sigh, and it was over. I let out a terrible wail, the same lonely wail I had let out into the darkness on the unnamed island where I was camped.

I had felt so alone that night, had never really recovered from the loss of my beloved friend until right now. I was still alone, but somehow I wasn't lonely anymore. I was glad to be here in only my own company. I looked around at my fire and tent and boat, and felt proud about how I did things. Confident about who I was. I reached over to the pouch holding Betty's ashes and sprinkled a few of them on the flames.

"I'm going to do this, my friend. I'm going to make it all the way around this lake. And I am going to come back so different, so changed that the fibers on my insides won't ever again allow doubt to come in and dissolve my ability to live life as fully as I can."

NO-KO-MIS

(1992)

Joanne Hart

But, sitting here, I know that this is
Grandma, old and gnarled.
                              —Barton Sutter

I

In the North Shore Hospital
the old ones cannot navigate
the long night voyage without machines
to tow them through the troughs of pain.

No-ko-mis, faithful widow,
ninety-three, crochets acrylic
shawls and waits. Carefully
she lies back on the bed, murmurs,

admonishes herself, whispers
to the black-braided girl she was,
waiting dockside at Pete's Island,
watching the ship *America's*

hold unloaded, learning omens.
Her steady whispered hiss unravels
old webs of lists, lies, fears, against
the shuttle pacemaker threading

fidelity through fitful sleeps,
through birthwails blowing down the hall,
wind at cedar boughs, storm cries
in rigging of the ship she waits.

II

Poets and artists see a woman's trunk,
hip jutting against storms, arms raised, root-feet
gripping the rock crevices, a girl
grown old in an unlikely place. The way
a woman comes back from the birthing bed,
the cedar yields, retreats, then returns

misshapen, somehow stronger, powerful,
willing each survival. Hazel points
a portrait of her standing self, her arms
uplifting her son's daughter overhead.
She paints the woman's triumph as a tree,
the power bearing fruit beyond her time.

III

Spirit Cedar. Witch Tree on Hat Point,
wind dancer, wild with hair of thunderbirds,
bowsprit breasting seas, grain weathered
all shades of grey, girl young long ago,
who stood the storms of waiting for her love,
old woman, grandmother, No-ko-mis,
wise wealth of years, strong bones, survivor, source.

On the North Shore of Lake Superior stands an aged cedar tree, *ManidoGeezhigance*, "Spirit Little Cedar," sacred to Native culture. For hundreds of years it has clung to the rock face at the edge of lake, stunted and twisted by wind and waves. To the Anishinabeg it represents rock, wind, water, and fire, the four elements of life bestowed by the Great Spirit. It is, like the land, "Nokomis," or Grandmother. "No-ko-mis" is from *Witch Tree: A Collaboration* by Joanne Hart and Hazel Belvo.

ACKNOWLEDGMENTS

My greatest thanks go to the members of the Association for Great Lakes Maritime History, an organization of historians and directors of Great Lakes maritime museums, who have patiently listened to my presentations at annual conferences over the years, and then, once the conferences were over, remembered to take time from their over-scheduled days to send me clippings and notes that they had found and knew would interest me. For their friendship, knowledge of Great Lakes history, and support I wish to thank especially Fred Stonehouse, Patrick Folkes, David T. Glick, Hawk Tolson, Dorris Akers, Joyce Hayward, Pat Labadie of the Canal Park Maritime Museum, Joanie Kloster of the Wisconsin Maritime Museum, Bob Graham of the Institute for Great Lakes Research, John Polascek of the Dossin Great Lakes Museum, Maurice Smith of the Museum of the Great Lakes at Kingston, and John Cary of the Marine Heritage Group, Save Ontario Shipwrecks.

I have also received generous grant support from several agencies: the National Endowment for the Humanities, the Canadian Embassy, and especially from John Gracki, Vice-President for Academic Affairs at Grand Valley State University. GVSU also paid the salary of two research assistants, Barbara Stradley and Jeanne Arends, whose help was invaluable.

As always, I could not have completed this book without the dedicated and cheerful help of librarians. Especial thanks go to Evelyn Leasher of the Clarke Historical Library at Central Michigan University, Nancy Bartlett of the Bentley Historical Library at the University of Michigan, Eric Norberg of the Michigan Technological University Archives, the librarians of the United Church Archives in Toronto and Montreal, the Robarts Library at the University of Toronto, the Royal Ontario Museum, the Toronto Public Library, the National Archives of the United States, the Archives of Ontario, the Minneapolis Public Library, the Guelph Public Library, and the Sarnia Public Library.

Volunteers and historians at historic sites have also provided help for this book. Phil Porter at Mackinac Historic Parks and the volunteers at the Michigan City Lighthouse Museum were especially helpful.

BIBLIOGRAPHY

Anderson, Miss Soaphy. "The Journey of the First White Settlement Across the Georgian Bay." *Mer Douce 1* (September-October 1921): 8-12.

Atwood, Margaret. "Marsh, Hawk." In *Two-Headed Poems*. New York: Simon & Schuster, 1978.

————. "Marsh Languages." In *Morning in The Burned House*. Boston: Houghton Mifflin, 1995.

Baird, Elizabeth Thérèse. *Reminiscences of Early Days on Mackinac Island*. *Wisconsin Historical Collections* 14 (1898): 17-63.

Battenfeld, Esther Rice. "In Grandpa's Wake." *Inland Seas* 9 (Fall, 1953): 195-199.

Baylis, Emma. *Journal*. Toronto: United Church Archives.

Bird, Isabella Lucy. *The Englishwoman in America*. London: John Murray, 1856. Reprint. Madison: University of Wisconsin Press, 1966.

Christian, Sarah Barr. *A Narrative of Life on Isle Royale During the Years 1874 and 1875*. [n.p.]: [n.p.], 1932.

Cleveland Plain Dealer. October 30, 1922.

Colfax, Harriet. Logs: Michigan City Lighthouse, Michigan City, Indiana. U. S. Light House Service Records. Record Group 26, National Archives and Record Administration, Washington, DC.

Curwood, James Oliver. "The Girl Diver of the Great Lakes." *Woman's Home Companion* 32 (June, 1905): 17-20.

Davison, Ann. *In The Wake of The Gemini*. Boston: Little, Brown, and Company, 1962.

Detroit News. October 11, 1934.

Doner, Mary Frances. *Not By Bread Alone*. New York: Doubleday-Doran, 1941.

English, Mrs. Mary. "My Love Has Departed." Song. In *Chippewa Music,* by Frances Densmore. 1910. Reprint. Minneapolis: Ross & Haines, 1973.

Fuller, Iola. *The Loon Feather*. New York: Harcourt, Brace & World, 1940.

Hart, Joanne, and Hazel Belvo. "No-ko-mis." In *Witch Tree: A Collaboration,* Duluth: Holy Cow! Press, 1992.

Hurlbut, Frances B. "The Fall of the Lighthouse." "Going After Strawberries." In *Grandmother's Stories*. Cambridge: Privately Printed at the Riverside Press, 1889.

Jameson, Anna. *Winter Studies and Summer Rambles in Canada*. 3 vols. London: Saunders and Otley, 1838.

Jamison, Bev. *Widow of the Waves*. Superior, Wisconsin: Savage Press, 1994.

Jiles, Paulette. "Mackinac Island." In *Celestial Navigation: Poems*. Toronto: McClelland & Stewart. 1985.

Johnson, E. Pauline. "Red Girl's Reasoning." In *The Moccasin Maker*. Toronto: William Briggs, 1913. Reprint. Tucson: University of Arizona Press, 1987.

Kelly, Sylvia. "Ozymandias." Unpublished Manuscript.

Kinzie, Mrs. John H. *Wau-Bun: The Early Day in the Northwest*, 1856. Reprint. Portage, Wisconsin: The National Society of Colonial Dames of Wisconsin, 1948, 1968, 1975.

Lee, Mary Per. "To Michigan By Water-1844." *Inland Seas* 10:1 (Spring 1954): 51-53.

LeRoy, Uldene Rudd. *Six on an Island: Childhood Memories From Lake Huron*. Exposition Press, 1956.

Linnea, Ann. *Deep Water Passage: A Spiritual Journey at Midlife*. New York: Little Brown, 1995.

Mansfield, John B., ed. and comp. *History of the Great Lakes*. 2 vols. Chicago: J. H. Beers and Co., 1899. Reprint. Cleveland: Freshwater Press, 1972.

Maskwawanahkwatok. "How A Menomini Woman Earns Money." In *Menomini Texts* by Leonard Bloomfield. Publications of the American Ethnological Society, ed. Franz Boas. New York: G. E. Stechert & Co., 1928.

Mayberry, Rosalind Srb. "Sleeping Bear." Unpublished Manuscript.

Minty, Judith. "Palmistry for Blind Mariners." In *In the Presence of Mothers*. Pittsburgh: University of Pittsburgh Press, 1981.

Niedecker, Lorine. "Lake Superior." In *North Central*. London: Fulcrum Press, 1968.

Nodinens. "Narrative." In *Chippewa Customs* by Frances Densmore. Smithsonian Institution Bureau of American Ethnology Bulletin 86. Washington, D. C.: Government Printing Office, 1929. Reprint. St. Paul: Minnesota Historical Society, 1979.

Powell, Ann. "Letters From Miss Ann Powell Combined in a Journal During a Tour to Niagara and Detroit, 1789." *The Essex Institute Historical Collections* 86 (1950): 331-349.

Power, Susan. "Lake of Dreams." *The Utne Reader* 79 (January-February 1997): 82-84, 111.

Ritzenthaler, Robert. "The Underwater Lion." In *Wisconsin Chippewa Myths and Tales and Their Relation to Chippewa Life* by Victor Barnouw. Madison: University of Wisconsin Press, 1977.

Schoolcraft, Jane Johnston. "Mishosha, or the Magician and His Daughter." "Moowis." In *The Literary Voyager or Muzzeniegun 5* (January 1827). ed. Philip Mason. East Lansing: Michigan State University Press, 1962.

Skelton, Joan. *The Survivor of the Edmund Fitzgerald*. Moonbeam, Ontario: Penumbra Press, 1985.

Stafford, Ida. "The Life of a Lake Superior Fisherman Family" ed. Lillian Stafford. *Michigan Alumnus 100* (March/April 1994): 40-45.

Stuart-Wortley, Victoria. *A Young Traveller's Journal of a Tour in North and South America During the Year 1850*. London: T. Bosworth, 1855.

"The Buffalo Whore." Song. Ivan H. Walton Papers, Michigan Historical Collections, Bentley Historical Library, Ann Arbor, Michigan.

The Daily Inter Ocean. Chicago, Illinois. 1875-1883.

Toledo Blade, June 18, 1906.

U. S. Life-Saving Service Records (Coast Guard). Record Group 26, National Archives and Record Administration, Washington, DC.

U. S. Light House Service Records. Record Group 26, National Archives and Record Administration, Washington, DC.

Williams, Elizabeth Whitney. *A Child of the Sea; and Life Among the Mormons*. [n.d.]. Reprint. St. James, Michigan: Henry Allen, 1905.

Williamson, Ethel. *A Light on The Seaway*. St. Catharines, Ontario: Cyril E. Williamson, 1972.

Wilson, Grace Margaret. "A Husbandless Vacation." *Water Way Tales: The Magazine of the Great Lakes*. Detroit: Detroit & Cleveland Navigation Company, 1915: 3-15.

Woolson, Constance Fenimore. "St. Clair Flats." In *Castle Nowhere: Lake Country Sketches*. New York: Harper, 1875. Reprint. New York: AMS Press, 1971.

Young, Anna G. *Off Watch: Yesterday and Today on the Great Lakes*. Toronto: The Ryerson Press, 1957.

We gratefully acknowledge permission to reprint materials from the following sources:

"Marsh, Hawk" by Magaret Atwood. From *Two-Headed Poems*, ©1978 by Margaret Atwood and reprinted by permission of Simon & Schuster, Inc.

"Marsh Languages" by Margaret Atwood. From *Morning in The Burned House*, ©1995 by Margaret Atwood and reprinted by permission of Houghton Mifflin Company. All rights reserved.

"Lakes" by Ann Davison. From *In The Wake of The Gemini*, ©1962 by Ann Davison (Little, Brown, and Company). Reprinted by permission.

"The Best Laid Plans" by Bev Jamison. From *Widow of the Waves*, ©1994 by Bev Jamison and reprinted by permission of Savage Press (Superior, Wisconsin).

"Mackinac Island" by Paulette Jiles. From *Celestial Navigation: Poems*, ©1985 by Paulette Jiles (McClelland & Stewart). Reprinted by permission.

"The Caretaker's Daughter" by Uldene Rudd LeRoy. From *Six on an Island: Childhood Memories from Lake Huron*, ©1956 (Exposition Press). Reprinted by permission of the author.

"She-Who-Finishes-Grieving" by Ann Linnea. From *Deep Water Passage: Spiritual Journey at Midlife*, ©1995 by Ann Linnea. By permission of Little, Brown, and Company.

"Palmistry for Blind Mariners" by Judith Minty. From *In the Presence of Mothers*, ©1981 by Judith Minty (University of Pittsburgh Press). Reprinted by permission of the author.

"Lake of Dreams" by Susan Power, ©1997 by Susan Power. Reprinted by permission of Henry Dunow Literary Agency.

"The Underwater Lion"—A Chippewa Tale collected by Robert Ritzenthaler (1942) from *Wisconsin Chippewa Myths and Tales and Their Relation to Chippewa Life* by Victor Barnow, ©1977 (University of Wiscosin Press). Reprinted by permission.

Excerpts from "The Survivor of the *Edmund Fitzgerald*" by Joan Skelton, ©1985 by Joan Skelton (Penumbra Press: Moonbeam, Ontario). Reprinted by permission of the author.

"The Life of a Lake Superior Fisherman Family" by Ida Stafford (edited by Lillian Stafford). ©1994 in *Michigan Alumnus*. Reprinted by permission of Ida Stafford.

"We Begin Life at the Port Weller Light" by Ethel Willaimson, ©1972. From *A Light on the Seaway* (Cyril E. Williamson: St. Caterines, Ontario). Reprinted by permission of Ethel Williamson.

VICTORIA BREHM is a professor of American literature who writes about Great Lakes literature and history. Her work includes *Sweetwater, Storms, and Spirits: Stories of the Great Lakes* and *"A Fully Accredited Ocean:" Essays on the Great Lakes* (The University of Michigan Press). She holds a Coast Guard mariner's license to 100 tons for the Great Lakes and Inland Waters. She lives in Tustin, Michigan.